The
Construction
of Gothic
Cathedrals

THE
CONSTRUCTION
OF GOTHIC
CATHEDRALS

A Study of
Medieval Vault Erection

BY

JOHN FITCHEN

THE UNIVERSITY OF CHICAGO PRESS
CHICAGO AND LONDON

TO
LEIGH
WHO WANTED TO KNOW
FROM THE START

The University of Chicago Press, Chicago 60637
The University of Chicago Press, Ltd., London

03   6 5

ISBN: 0–226–25203–5 (paperback)

FOREWORD

EVERY YEAR, UNTOLD THOUSANDS OF TOURISTS—FROM EUROPE, from America, from all over the world, in fact—travel to northern France, drawn there in part to see the great cathedrals of the Gothic era. And most of these travellers wonder how in the world they were put together. This book is the first one, in any language, that attempts to give a systematic and reasonable account of how they were erected. It deals comprehensively and expansively with a subject that is certainly of interest not only to the professional architect and engineer but also to the intelligent traveller, to the art historian, and to the student of Europe's cultural heritage.

Architects can find in this book a revealing account of how the medieval building operations implemented the designer's vision. Engineers can be impressed by the empirical rationale of the Gothic builders and their economy of means in disposing of exceptional difficulties of equipment and procedure. And the layman —students and travellers alike—can learn from both the pictures and the text something of the innumerable problems encountered and the way these problems were met and overcome.

Although the book includes a great deal of related and supporting material, much of it is refreshingly original. Not least with respect to originality is the very fact that a book on this subject has at long last been written.

Professor Fitchen has uncovered and evaluated a quantity of material in various languages that deals with early constructional practices and building operations. His clear drawings illuminate and complement a text that is reasonable, informing, persuasive, and impressively original. He has written and illustrated an important book. More than that, he has given us a unique book.

JOHN NOBLE RICHARDS, F.A.I.A.
President
The American Institute of Architects
Washington, D.C.

AT A TIME WHEN WE SEEM TO BE SURFEITED WITH THE OBLIQUE, the esoteric, hollow profundities, self-conscious pontifications and the exploitation of egos, it is most refreshing to come upon a good straightforward scholarly report on this truly fascinating subject.

FOREWORD

There are few who have looked with perception at the great monuments of this great functional period who have not wondered how man, with the then limited means at his disposal, was able to construct edifices which, even if reproduced today, would call for the ingenuity of the builder and the manifold aids and utensils of current construction. Mr. Fitchen explains the mysteries, not of the sacred edifices themselves, but of their accomplishment. He writes not from the religious or political point of view but rather from a pure down-to-earth practical point of view. Despite the somewhat technical title, *The Construction of Gothic Cathedrals*, one enjoys the combination of good learning and good writing, and one does not necessarily have to be an architect to add to one's knowledge from this attractive book.

It is particularly gratifying that an American architect in this day has interested himself so thoroughly in the subject as to have produced a study of profound interest and has reminded us again that man's ingenuity and devotion scarcely reached a higher peak than it did in the days when the great cathedrals of France were built. He reminds us, too, that in the course of our striving to make functionalism attractive, our forebears of some six or seven centuries ago succeeded in an achievement to which we are again aspiring.

We are grateful to Mr. Fitchen.

EDMUND R. PURVES, F.A.I.A.
Executive Director
The American Institute of Architects
Washington, D.C.

PREFACE

IN OUR TIME, MORE AND MORE OF THE GREAT BUILDINGS OF THE
past are being repaired or reconstructed with modern materials—steel and
reinforced concrete—as the real structure. Reims Cathedral, the Chateau of
Chambord, and many other famous buildings have had their timber-work roofs
replaced by time-defying and maintenance-reducing assemblages of reinforced
concrete; reinforced members have been inserted above the vaults of Soissons
Cathedral to tie together the clerestory walls and prevent deformation of the
vaults; and even as long ago as the mid-nineteenth century the vaults of the
Chapter House at Westminster Abbey were laced into supporting girders con-
cealed above these vaults. These and many other instances—the numbers have
sharply risen as a result of the repairs and reconstructions necessitated by the
catastrophes of two World Wars—suggest the urgency of investigating, before
it is too late, the entirety of the building operations in the outstanding structures
of medieval times while the evidence, such as it is, of the original construction is
still extant, or at least before the introduction of materials and methods foreign
to those of the original erection have come to be employed.

The present study does not attempt an exhaustive investigation of single buildings: this would seem to be the privilege and the opportunity of qualified investigators intimately studying each important monument individually on the spot.
Rather, it undertakes to re-create the operational procedures and sequences that
are likely to have been practised, together with the equipment utilized, in the
creation of the great Gothic churches as a class, particularly in France.

The reader should perhaps be advised of the technique of explanation that is
followed in much of this book. There are so many considerations and interrelationships involved in the matter of high vault centering, for instance, that it is
confusing to try to handle them all together, and equally perplexing to attempt
to cover each one, in turn, with finality. The device followed here is somewhat
analogous to the procedure adopted by the modern civil engineer in working out
the computations in a formula involving a number of unknowns. Briefly, this is
what takes place. On the basis of his experience, he starts by assuming certain
reasonable or likely values for all but one unknown, and proceeds to solve for it;
then, solving for the others in turn (using the values he has computed, each time,

in place of the original assumptions), he eventually goes back and recomputes each of the unknowns on the basis of the corrections or adjustments he has had to make along the way.

The subject of this book is a very complex one. There are many unknowns, which are interrelated in that they limit or otherwise affect each other. What would seem to be reasonable assumptions, at the start, are the statements that have been made by previous writers. These must be studied and evaluated one by one, as far as they can be taken as individual considerations, at the time. But then, in the light of the effect upon them of other considerations, they must be revised or modified subsequently.

Obviously, this procedure sometimes means that statements are made, ostensibly of fact, that are later rescinded or at least revised. The consequence of this method inevitably results in a text of somewhat broken continuity. Like a mystery story, preliminary assumptions sometimes lead to dead ends and have to be abandoned; what appear at first sight as promising tips or clear-cut actions or even as seemingly irreconcilable misunderstandings need to be patiently sifted for their degree of dependability and pertinence; the incomplete clues and the partial theories along the way do not fall into place in their proper relationships to the whole until the final denouement (assuming a denouement is possible).

A further reason for adopting this sometimes back-tracking, sometimes incremental mode of procedure is that the subject concerns a dynamic, developing series of building techniques, in the historical perspective of which the variables seem to outnumber the constants. What may have served for the low, thick-walled, small-windowed, simply-vaulted Romanesque of the eleventh century was largely useless in the lofty, skeletal, large-windowed, rib-vaulted Gothic of the thirteenth century. And yet the erectional practices of the latter, no less than the building forms themselves, evolved from the former through many intermediate and partially resolved steps: the Gothic could not have happened if the Romanesque had not preceded it.

All but a few of the drawings have been prepared especially for this work. They, like the text, seek to present the basic or general schemes that may have been adopted by the French medieval builders, rather than specific installations in this or that particular structure: they attempt to be illuminating and clarifying, not precise in respect to a given instance in an actual location.

This clarification, however, has had to involve a considerable amount of simplification through the elimination of those features and elements not immediately under discussion. For example (52), when the method of laying up web courses on light lagging is shown, the centering that supports the lagging is omitted from the drawing. Again (69), when the erection of stone-coursing by means of stone-weighted ropes is shown, the clerestory walls and the masons' trestles are left out of the drawing. Without such fragmentation of representation, the resulting drawings would often be quite incomprehensible from their maze of overlapping or mutually obscuring features.

Part of this difficulty is due to our modern techniques of pictorially representing three-dimensional subjects more or less realistically on a flat sheet of paper. But an even more serious confusion, in the case of falsework structures for vaulting, results from the modern practice of representing them in orthographic projection, as two-dimensional plans, elevations, and sections. *This* kind of fragmentation of the component parts of an assemblage of members is not only impossible for the layman to read, but is often dangerously misleading to the expert designer himself. For, in adopting this practice, he has no sure check upon the clearances, the mutual interferences, and the sequences of assembling and disassembling that would occur or have to be followed in the actual construction of the work.

The medieval builders, however, were not caught in this modern dilemma. Apparently they knew nothing of that branch of descriptive geometry that is involved with revolutions of solids and with the development of surfaces. Perspective representations were never made; and even straight orthographic projection seems to have been employed but rarely, and then only in special instances and for special purposes. Their methods were eminently practical, pragmatic, and direct. At least in the case of important falsework structures, the actual work was invariably laid out at full size, after the problems were all solved via accurate models. In fact, the design of every aspect and detail seems unquestionably to have been worked out almost exclusively in terms of three-dimensional models of all sorts, both for details and for ensembles.

This procedure reveals a habit of mind that is quite alien to us, with our present-day reliance on and preoccupation with formulae, stress diagrams, and all the paraphernalia of modern scientific computation. In place of the speed of our mathematical abstractions, the medieval builders were able to employ a slower but foolproof procedure growing out of direct practical experience and constant on-the-job supervision. This was a not inefficient situation because of the fact that the 'architect' and the 'contractor' were one and the same individual. (In major works, some medieval contracts even required the master builder to agree to take no other job while he was under contract for the building in question.) In medieval times there was neither the specialization nor the separation of functions that is reflected in our design and operational personnel today: the architect, the

ix

structural engineer, the various mechanical engineers, and the general contractor together with his team of sub-contractors. The medieval master builder was really a master of all phases of the work, familiar with each operation and constantly in immediate touch with it. Hence he was an imaginative and creative designer on the one hand, who had to be comprehensively and intimately familiar, at the same time, with the means by which his design could be brought to realization in actual stone and mortar.

This essential familiarity with the techniques of erection (through his experience of on-the-job training), along with the master's familiarity with the design itself (through his authorship of it), accounts for his ability to work out the minimum and most effective falsework structures. What he did, almost instinctively and certainly on the basis of thorough first-hand experience, was apparently to have in the back of his mind the means of execution of his project at the very time when he was being most freely creative in its design. Not that he knew every detail of the erectional operation in advance. Rather, he was familiar enough with all phases of the erectional process, and at the same time resourceful and inventive enough, so that he could be confident of his ability to modify and apply these generally understood erectional procedures to the specific requirements encountered in the building he was designing, when the time came for them to be put into operation. This he did, as we have noted, by working through the assured and familiar tradition, not of elevation drawings, but of models.

Although the present writer made few models, he did make a great many sketches out of which the drawings for this work were evolved. If there are errors in them—and there doubtless are—they may prove to be the result of the very difficulty that has just been discussed; namely, that the modern graphic systems employed to project complicated three-dimensional structures into two-dimensional representations in accordance with certain mechanical hypotheses, may overlook significant details or essential adjustments that can be caught only in intricate and carefully constructed three-dimensional models that reveal not only *what* takes place in the erectional process but *how* and in what sequence.

The reader should be warned that the omissions mentioned above (as opposed to any errors of commission in the drawings) may inadvertently be agents of misinterpretation on his part. For until he has made the effort to study the whole procedure as presented throughout the pages of this book, he may well suppose that some of the more complicated illustrations in it are quite complete. In the case of the more comprehensive-looking drawings, they are not complete and cannot be, for the reasons stated above. But it is hoped that their incompleteness (which is presumably not inconsistent with the completeness they seek to explain in the aggregate) will none the less prove to be instructive and clarifying to the serious student of this complex subject.

A few remarks about the bibliography.

Scholars will note that a few quite unscholarly books have been included. This is not because of their text, but because popular travel books and the like occasionally include photographic views of buildings taken at a time when scaffolding was in place or when some other unusual and transient feature came to be recorded.

It will also be observed that, in addition to the works of recent modern writers, a considerable number of old titles are listed, some from the first half of the nineteenth century, and even before. There are two reasons for going back to early publications.

One reason is that many of the old practices are now often quite obsolete, and one can learn about them only from books written before they became obsolete. For example, timber framing without metal, cranes and lifting devices powered by men or by animals, lashed pole scaffolding, and structural stonework have now been almost universally superseded, respectively, by steel or reinforced concrete framing, by steam or gasoline or electrically powered motors, by tubular steel scaffolding, and by structural concrete with a mere veneer of stone hung upon it. Books that tell about the former of these methods and materials at the time when they were vigorous, current, and of immediate concern, are apt to have a quite different coverage from today's historical or antiquarian accounts of the same matters, written in the light of subsequent technological advances.

The other reason for referring to early books is that sometimes one is hard put to it to find even very slight coverage of a given subject in the publications of our own day. For example, the thirty-volume 1949 edition of the *Americana* encyclopedia gives only a one-sentence definition of 'Centring or Centering', and omits any mention whatsoever of the arch 'Groin' as a separate article. However, in Rees's *Cyclopaedia* of 1810–24 (41 text vols. plus 6 vols. of plates), there are two large double-columned pages of text, in fine print, on carpentry 'Centers' together with at least 13 plate illustrations; and there are over seven pages of fine-print text, plus plate illustrations, on 'Groin'. This is sometimes the situation even when, as in the case of centering, the need for these falsework structures is fully as essential nowadays for reinforced concrete construction as it was for stone construction in the past; yet, as indicated in Appendix A, there is an unaccountable lack of published data on this subject today. Hence one must search for whatever information is to be found wherever and in whatsoever incomplete form it can be come upon; and this is sometimes in books that are not only long since out of print but also frequently obscure and not generally included in even extensive libraries.

The glossary has been especially prepared for this book. In the case of terms that have more than one meaning or application, definitions are given that pertain to the matters covered in this study. Hence the glossary is not a general dictionary of architectural terms but an explanatory and interpretative vocabulary designed to clarify those technical words and expressions that apply to the subject under consideration.

Since the subject of this book is both a complicated one, and one about which there has been only scattered and incomplete information in the publications to date, this present study is an attempt to combine, in effect, two books in one. The first is represented by the illustrated text proper, designed substantially as an entity by itself. It is directed to that segment of the general public, including teachers and their pupils, who wish to get some basic understanding of the probable medieval techniques and practices of vault erection, including their relationship to the dynamic structural innovations and developments that evolved during the Middle Ages. The second intention has been that of providing the scholar with fairly thorough exploration, analysis, and documentation (via the Notes and Comments, the Appendixes, and the Bibliography) of the material found in the text. This dual intention accounts for the disproportionately large amount of space devoted to the Notes and Comments. They, and the Appendixes, provide a substantial supplement rather than a mere footnoting of the text.

The matters covered in this study are little known and incompletely understood except by a very few highly skilled practitioners and a handful of unusually well-informed professional men. Perhaps the basic reason why so little has been written on it is that although the subject of falsework requirements and practices is of concern to both architect and engineer, no clear-cut or exclusive responsibility for it attaches to either one of these parties. The contractor, who *is* responsible for it in practice, is invariably too busily occupied with the multiple demands encountered in the actual erection of the building to have time or even the inclination to write about the problems and solutions to his falsework requirements. His records of these problems are graphic solutions, not literary analyses. And with their immediate function fulfilled upon completion of the building, even these drawings are invariably destroyed. Consequently, even today the subject remains esoteric and removed from the public, locked up in the competent and experienced heads of a relatively small number of professional men.

Furthermore, the whole question is complicated by the fact that the writings of the engineers and the architects have traditionally been kept in separate categories, isolated from each other, and that very few if any architectural historians, so far, are equipped by either training or interest to bridge the gap between the two. It is the hope of this writer that his book will make a significant contribution towards narrowing such a dichotomy.

As a result of this situation, documentation cannot be the usual apparatus of abbreviated references and occasional short quotations, as inconspicuous footnotes on the same page with the text they refer to. The separation of text and documentation, with the latter removed to another portion of the book, certainly makes for less distraction and therefore easier, more uninterrupted continuity of reading on the part of the general public. As for the scholar, he is accustomed to digging out information, to co-ordinating text and reference. If two books *can* be successfully combined into one—if both the general public and the scholar can be addressed at the same time—then it is the latter who suffers some inconvenience. It is hoped that his inconvenience in turning pages back and forth will be compensated by his finding that the material not incorporated in the text is worth his while to turn to.

Although the analyses and interpretations as well as the proposed solutions and conclusions presented in this book are very largely my own, I am deeply conscious of my debt of gratitude to the many authors quoted throughout this work: to so many who have made distinctive contributions over such a long period of time and in such varied categories of specialized investigation, observation, and knowledge. Whatever merit the present study may have in furthering an understanding of medieval constructional practices has built upon the varied but collective base previously established by a kaleidoscope of writings by others. To them, known or unknown, named or anonymous, my appreciation and admiration for their shared experience, their diligence, their speculations, and their insights.

My thanks go to Dr. Richard M. Strauss, formerly of Vienna, for his generous interest and help in translations from the German; and to the staff of the Clarendon Press for their care, patience, and skill in converting the manuscript into the book's finished form. It is a pleasure to acknowledge here the delight and the rich benefit I have had, over the years, from many wide-ranging talks on architecture with my friend and former student, Arthur Meggett, architect. My son Allen took the photographs that appear as Figs. 5 and 11, during a trip whose memories remain the brighter because of his pictorial record of it. To my wife I

PREFACE

owe the incalculable example of good humour and intelligence, of versatile industry and domestic equilibrium that formed the day in, day out environment in which this work was produced.

Finally, my special gratitude goes to the Board of Directors of the American Institute of Architects for granting a large subvention from the Henry Adams Fund of the Institute, which made it financially possible to publish this book.

JOHN FITCHEN

Colgate University
Hamilton, New York
24 February 1960

CONTENTS

LIST OF FIGURES   *page* xvii

1. SOURCES OF INFORMATION   1
    The structural aspects of medieval building, and the contemporary sources of
    possible information about its execution.

2. CONSTRUCTIONAL MEANS   9
    The multiple nature and scope of the falsework requirements—scaffolding,
    shoring, formwork, and centering—with some provisionally assumed solutions.

3. MEDIEVAL TYPES OF VAULTING   42
    An analysis of the chief structural developments in medieval times: problems,
    innovations, and solutions.

4. GOTHIC FORMWORK   86
    The significance of the rib. An assessment of what others have written on the
    nature and extent of the formwork used in Gothic vaulting, together with a
    possible solution of the formwork problem.

5. GOTHIC CENTERING   123
    An analysis of the centering problem in Gothic vaulting, along with the types
    of falsework employed as support for the centering.

6. ERECTION OF RIB VAULTING WITHOUT FORMWORK   175
    Systems of construction that dispense with falsework. The Gothic system of vault
    erection without formwork. Summary review of the erectional sequence and
    procedures in French Gothic rib-vaulted churches.

NOTES AND COMMENTS   197

APPENDIXES
    A. *An Annotated Bibliography of Falsework Literature*   241
    B. *The Occurrence of Putlog Holes and the Location and Extent of the Scaffold-
       ing They Reveal*   248
    C. *Passageways in Lincoln Cathedral*   253

CONTENTS

APPENDIXES (*cont.*)

D. *A Tower Vault of the Eleventh Century* page 254
E. *Medieval Vault Thicknesses* 256
F. *Surfaces of Double Curvature in Gothic Vaults* 260
G. *The Slow Setting Time of Medieval Mortars and Its Consequences* 262
H. *Oblique or Skew Vaults of Masonry* 266
I. *Pole Scaffolding* 271
J. *Arch and Vault Ties in Medieval Construction* 275
K. *Medieval Falsework Practices in England* 280
L. *Abbot Suger on the New Work at St-Denis: A Reinterpretation* 289
M. *Strutting Systems Used in Centering Frames* 296
N. *An Instance of Vault Centering that Survives from the Gothic Era* 299
O. *Intersecting Centering Frames, and the Use of Models to Solve the Difficulties Encountered* 301
P. *Medieval Lifting Devices and Procedures* 303

GLOSSARY 307

BIBLIOGRAPHY 317

INDEXES

1. Author 337
2. Subject 340
3. Places and Buildings 342

LIST OF FIGURES

1. Medieval Manuscript Illumination of Masons Replacing a Column Drum   *facing p.* 6
2. Details of Conjectural Falsework for the Pont du Gard   *page* 10
3. Conjectural Falsework and Decentering Procedure for the Pont du Gard   12
4. Masons' Scaffolding Platform of Hurdles   16
5. Photograph of Modern Scaffolding at Notre-Dame-de-Mantes (13 April 1953)   *facing p.* 16
6. Scheme of Scaffolding for Clerestory Piers   18
7. Schematic Diagram of Circulation System: Vices and Passageways   22
8. Viollet-le-Duc's Drawing of False Bearing   24
9. The Erection of the Nave Roof (Reims Cathedral)   27
10. Concentric Orders of Arches   29
11. Photograph of Vault Erection at Anacapri, Island of Capri, Italy (March 1953)   *facing p.* 30
12. Saw-Cut Method of Striking Centering Frames   33
13. Rolling Scaffolding for Banded Barrel Vault   35
14. Semicircular Arch and Semicylindrical Vault   43
15. Abutment of Simple Barrel Vault   44
16. Diagrammatic Scheme of High Barrel Vault's Abutment   45
17. Diagram of Small Banded Barrel Vault in Cut Stone   46
18. Continuous Bays of Simple Groin Vaulting in Cut Stone   48
19. Three Bays of Simple Groin Vaulting in Cut Stone, with Boundary Arches   49
20. Systems of Groin Vault Centering where the Formwork is Continuous for the Longitudinal Vault   52
21. Possible Types of Barrel Vault Formwork and Centering   54
22. The Shape of the Groin Voussoirs in a Simple Groin Vault over a Square Bay   56
23. Consequences of the Semicircular Diagonal Arc in the Domed Groin Vault   57
24. Herringbone Pattern of Web Coursing in the Domed Groin Vault   60
25. Stone Coursing and its Formwork in the Domed Groin Vault   61
26. The Occurrence of Rib Stems in French Gothic Vaulting   70
27. Schematic Layout of a Sexpartite Vaulting Bay   72
28. Schematic Layout of a Quadripartite Vaulting Bay   74

LIST OF FIGURES

29. Viollet-le-Duc's Drawing of the Tas-de-Charge   *page* 76

30. Stilting and Its Consequences in the Quadripartite System   79

31. The Catenary Curve and the Gothic Pointed Arch   81

32. Viollet-le-Duc's Drawing of the Fill in the Lower Portion of the Vaulting Conoid   82

33. Pol Abraham's Drawing of Typical Fissures in Gothic Vaults   84

34. Disparity in the Beds of Courses at the Groin, in Rectangular Bays of Rib
    Vaulting   90

35. Rectangular Bay of Cut Stone Vaulting, with Unstilted Semicircular Boundaries   91

36. Rectangular Bay of Cut Stone Vaulting, Horizontally Projected, with Level
    Crowns   92

37. Rectangular Bay of Cut Stone Vaulting with Level Crowns and Groins Straight
    in Plan   93

38. Trapezoidal Ambulatory Bays   94

39. Early Vault Forms over Three-Aisled Churches   95

40. Viollet-le-Duc's Cerce Device as Support for Each Web Course during the
    Erection of the Vault   101

41. Viollet-le-Duc's Scheme of Interlocking Voussoirs along the Groin   110

42. Construction Details near the Crown of a Diagonal Rib, in a Square Bay of
    Ribbed Vaulting: Viewed from Below   114

43. Construction Details near the Crown of a Diagonal Rib, in a Square Bay of
    Ribbed Vaulting: Viewed from Above   114

44. Stone-Coursing in Lateral Compartments of Quadripartite Vaulting   116

45. Vault Formwork of Planks   117

46. Possible Development of Individual Lagging Units   119

47. Flying Buttress Centering   127

48. The Parallel-Beam Scheme of Stiffening, Claimed by Viollet-le-Duc to Have
    Served the Medieval Builders in Lieu of the Truss   131

49. Centering Frames for the Intersecting Ribs of a Trapezoidal Bay of Gothic
    Vaulting   136

50. Convergence of the Rib Frames at the Top of the Tas-de-Charge   137

51. The Raising of Large Keystones   139

52. Erection of the Vault Web, One Course at a Time   140

53. Cross Lagging under the Crown of Gothic Vaults   141

54. Assemblage of the Diagonal Centering Frames at Their Common Crown: Scheme
    with X-Shaped Insert Unit   142

55. Assemblage of the Diagonal Centering Frames at Their Common Crown: Scheme
    with Hexagonal Insert Block   144

LIST OF FIGURES

56. Detail of Double Centering Frame — *page* 146

57. The Seating of Lagging Units — 149

58. Required Shaping of the Groin End of the Web Courses' Lagging Units — 150

59. Detail of Falsework Assemblage along the Groin, Using Lift Blocks — 152

60. Detail of Falsework Assemblage along the Groin, Omitting Cleats — 154

61. Method of Securing the Groin Ends of the Web Courses' Lagging Units — 155

62. Schematic Section and Reflected Plan Views of Centering Conditions under the Transverse, Diagonal, and Wall Ribs — 156

63. Four Diagrammatic Schemes of Framing and Undergirding the Half-Frames of Gothic Ribbed Vault Centering — 160

64. Diagrammatic Schemes of Framing and Undergirding the Half-Frames of Rib Centering: Minimum Units — 162

65. Assemblage and Keying of Four Diagonal Half-Frames of Rib Centering at Their Common Crowns: Scheme with Rectangular Insert Block — 164

66. Location of Decentering Wedges in a Quadripartite Vaulting Bay: Provisional Conjectures — 167

67. Gantry Schemes for Supporting the Working Platforms in High-Level Vaulting — 172

68. High-Level Hung Scaffolding: Pier-Girdling Gantry Scheme — 174

69. Stone-Weighted Rope Device for Building Web Courses without Lagging or Other Formwork — 182

70. Lightest Scheme of Rib Centering for French Gothic Ribbed Vaulting — 191

71. Assemblage of the Diagonal Centering Frames at Their Common Crown: Scheme with Single Frames — 192

72. Assemblage of the Double Poles Tying Together the Feet of a Pair of Centering Half-Frames — 193

73. McMaster's Drawing of Cross-Lagging Scheme in Tunnel Falsework, for Masonry Construction in Brickwork — 232

I

THE PRIMARY STRUCTURAL PROBLEM IN BUILDING IS THAT OF
spanning space. Basically, there are not very many systems of doing this: the
post and lintel, the arch with its vault and dome derivatives, the truss, the metal
skeleton, the suspension cable, and, largely in the twentieth century, the thin
shell, typically of double curvature.

In the medieval period, in western Europe, it was the vault that was almost
exclusively the system for spanning space in masonry. But the medieval vault
system underwent remarkable diversity of shape, and developed the most effective, the most daring and expressive forms by the time the Gothic era was in full
flower.

Parallel with the development of the structural system as such, there was unquestionably a corresponding development in the techniques and procedures of
its execution. It is here proposed to consider these latter, with particular reference
to French achievements.

If we study the equipment and the methods available to the medieval builders,
if we investigate the innovations they adopted along with the structural problems
they faced, perhaps some insight can be gained into the ways in which their buildings came to be constructed. The attempt will be made to discover something of
the building procedures they evolved, something of the technical problems of
erection they overcame in the actual operation of achieving the great thirteenth-
century cathedrals, in so far as it is possible to do so at this time, some seven
centuries after these fabulous structures were built.

It should be stated at the outset that unquestionably the motivating force in
Gothic church architecture, as in all Gothic art, was a spirit, an affirmation.
What caused the Gothic churches to be built at all, what accounted for the

1

dissemination of Gothic design everywhere throughout Europe, what stimulated the daring achievements of astounding height and glass-walled wonder was a religion-generated compulsion, an urgent and compelling spiritual vision.

It has been said, however, that the Gothic builders undertook self-imposed structural problems which they proceeded to solve, as though building were a kind of exhibitionist game in which the aim was to set up unprecedented and 'impossible' problems whose unprecedented and 'impossible' solutions astounded all by their unbelievable cleverness. There is certainly no doubt about the un-precedented nature of both the structural problems and their solution as the medieval period advanced, but the reason for both is to be found in the search for an expressive *form* that was new and unprecedented. It is both ignorant and absurd to look upon the Gothic achievement merely in terms of a pretentious contest of engineering extravagances.

This is not to deny the stupendous structural complexities, however. The very measure of their achievement in creating a new architectural form of such pro-found expressiveness is a key to the difficulties the medieval builders encountered. Their erectional and structural problems, confronted in the process of implement-ing the Gothic dream, were indeed legion. Yet their solutions came to be so skilful, so resourceful and masterful, that the engineering means were entirely integrated and subordinated to the aesthetic aim, and the ensemble effect remains one of man's greatest achievements, an overwhelming expressiveness.[1]

This spiritual expressiveness was the goal of the builders, to be sure, but obviously such a goal was not achieved automatically. The structural innovations and adjustments and modifications had to be numerous and continuous over a considerable period of time in order to bring into material being the desired spiritual aim; many fumblings and hesitations mark the builders' progress in achieving that aim. Some of the steps in the gradual development that led up to the mature Gothic form in church architecture can be traced, and a prodigious amount of the most careful, scholarly effort has gone into accurately dating indi-vidual buildings, classifying schools and sub-schools of architectural develop-ment, and assessing the influence of one area—occasionally even one building—on others sometimes very distant from it. Out of these general and preliminary lines of investigation have grown, from time to time, studies that seek to penetrate and cast light upon the basis of the distinctive character of medieval building. For a long time, for instance, the pointed arch was very widely accepted as the key to the nature of Gothic architecture, and this viewpoint has in late years been revived by a number of writers. Similarly, the buttress was at one time singled out as the most crucial feature to differentiate Gothic architecture from that of all

2

other periods.[2] On the other hand, a whole series of writers has advanced an esoteric geometry as the basis for Gothic proportion, crediting visual effects entirely to abstract mechanical ratios, without thought for the exigencies of practical construction. In contrast to this view, many scholars have seen in the ribbed vault the primary governing feature of Gothic architecture, and the clue to its original and distinctive character. However, out of the assertions of this latter group arose a counter-claim, based ostensibly on mathematical computations, which denies all structural function to the ribs.

Not long ago, aeroplane designers were quoted as saying that, aerodynamically, the bumble-bee should be unable to fly. This statement merely served to show the incompleteness or insufficiency of contemporary scientific knowledge of aerodynamics; and the denial of all structural function in the ribs and flying buttresses of the Gothic system is perhaps a similar indication of the limitations of recent engineering knowledge with respect to the complex and interacting stresses to which Gothic buildings have been subjected over the centuries. They, like the airborne bumble-bee, exist; and it is more than a little absurd to deny either, by scientific 'proof' of their non-existence. Actually, the empirical knowledge of the Gothic builders may well have been superior to our present-day scientific computations as applied to their buildings, for this reason: our scientific formulae (which are after all based upon empirical observation of natural forces, and which undergo revision from time to time as those observations become more exact and comprehensive) are concerned primarily with materials such as steel and reinforced concrete which resist both tensile and compressive stresses; whereas the medieval builders had to solve all their major structural engineering problems in terms of one material, stone, which is trustworthy only in its resistance to compression. Hence the medieval builders came to have the most thoroughgoing and explicit first-hand experience in all aspects of a material that is seldom employed structurally today. Their achievement in solving their structural problems in this material has never been surpassed, or indeed even closely approached, in any other period of the world's history, the present included.

There is ample evidence for this superlative statement. For example, except for the substitution of mechanical for manual operation in the case of a few tools, the tools themselves and the operation of hewing blocks of stone and carving stone ornaments have not changed since medieval times. Actually, the hand-craftsmanship is infinitely superior to the machine-operated process, since the skilled mason can note the quality and cleavages of the stone at every stroke, and accommodate his work to whatever variations or imperfections he may encounter

3

in it. Again, when churches 'in the Gothic style' are built today, their stone-work is almost invariably a thin veneer, hung at all vital points on steel or reinforced concrete, the real structure. In this situation the stonework is reduced to a mere surface treatment in which only appearance is the governing require-ment: there need no longer be a reconciliation and integration of both structure and appearance, as in the Middle Ages.

The superiority of the Gothic achievement in stone over the justly great achievements in stone of the Egyptians, the Greeks, and all other eras of the past is due to the twin aims of Gothic church architecture: maximum height and maximum light. The former demanded the utmost in vertical extension, in spite of the latter's demand for less and less material support, imposed by the over-riding urge for expansive window-openings.

The fabulous achievement of these twin aims of the medieval builders, par-ticularly in France, fills one today with amazement and awe at their daring, their creative imagination, and their driving persistence in following through to the eventual realization of the aspiring Gothic vision.

Countless writers have sung of the visual glories of the great thirteenth-century churches, and much has been written on the spirit that animated their erection. Scholars have dealt with the economics and the politics of financing these build-ings.[3] Particularly in England, a considerable number of documents survive, giving in minute itemized detail the contemporary expenses of the building's construction, upkeep, and enlargement.[4] The building trades have undergone studies that have disclosed their guild organization and practices;[5] and the some-times distant travels of outstanding individual architects, to fulfil commissions or to act in a consulting capacity, have been patiently plotted.[6] Developments in the plan arrangements and the changing spatial requirements of Christian worship have been traced through many steps, going all the way back to earliest Christian times.[7] Scholars have analysed the geometrical layout of medieval buildings, both in plan and elevation, thereby seeking to uncover the 'secret' of their design.[8] The types and varieties of vaulting have been differentiated and classified with respect to their appearance;[9] and the techniques of laying out the origin and intersection of vault ribs graphically, in order to proceed with their erection, have been recon-structed.[10] The Gothic structural system itself has undergone investigation and analysis at the hands of distinguished architects and engineers;[11] and models have been constructed to test or demonstrate the theories of the engineers, and to investigate the equilibrium of the forces at work in the buildings.[12] Even the effects of war bombardment,[13] and methods of repairing damaged medieval buildings,[14] have been dealt with. Almost the only aspect of these great

4

Gothic churches that has not been subjected to penetrating and thorough investigation is the actual technique of their erection, the operational machinery and procedures followed by the medieval builders during the course of construction.[15]

This present-day failure of coverage is no mere oversight, nor does it stem from a total lack of interest in the subject. Rather, the total lack is that of either first-hand or documentary evidence upon which such a study would need to be based if it were to attempt a definitive account.[16] Certainly no accurate or detailed descriptions have survived into modern times; nor is it likely that any were ever written until a late date, since those who undertook to chronicle events and activities at the time seem universally not to have been interested in describing building operations except in the most general terms. Actually, it is highly doubtful if any but the master masons could have been competent to write a factual account of the specific procedures followed in erecting a building. However, not only were these men much too busy to write; above all, they were at once practitioners and custodians of the 'mystery' of their professions, and in both capacities they had a vital interest in *not* disseminating the close and jealously guarded trade secrets, thorough knowledge of which was held only by these men of superior ability and experience, the masters themselves.[17]

By now, when so much active scholarship has combed the fabric rolls, the inventories, the wills of architects, and all such likely documents, it seems highly improbable that any significant detailed account of actual erectional procedures will yet turn up. Gervais's account of the rebuilding of Canterbury after the disastrous fire of 1174,[18] and Abbot Suger's account of the building of St-Denis,[19] chronicle very little technical information, and that only in the most general, layman-like terms. For these men were not master masons, not architects familiar with technical building problems and experienced in the step-by-step constructional operations of building erection: the one was a monk, the other an important and accomplished man of affairs, tremendously interested in building, to be sure; but not trained in its mysteries.

It seems, then, that the total lack of written documentation on both the engineering structure and the erectional procedures must be accepted.

Along with such accounts, if they ever existed at all, the architects' models, too, have generally perished. There is a good deal of scattered evidence that scale models—the 'portraits' of buildings—were constructed for study and for instruction. Apparently the only medieval example of a model, from northern France, that has survived to our time is that of the late Gothic church of St-Maclou at

Rouen.[20] Most of them were destroyed when the Renaissance, with its 'enlightened' attitude that condemned the Gothic period and all its works as uncouth, barbarian, and degraded, came into vogue.

For contemporary illustrative material, then, one is reduced to searching through the illuminations in medieval manuscripts, and to examining the panels in stained glass windows. The occurrence of architectural subjects in course of erection is not frequent in the case of either of these sources. Furthermore, those that do occur almost invariably date from the fifteenth or sixteenth century; there are few indeed from the fourteenth or the late thirteenth century.

The chief difficulty in gaining information from these contemporary pictorial sources, however, is a consequence not so much of their late date as of the character and intention of the pictures themselves. This is even true in the case of the skilful drawings in the sketchbook of Villard de Honnecourt. Villard was a well-trained, extensively travelled and successful 'architect' of the thirteenth century, and the drawings—with his own comments and explanations—in his unique sketchbook are of major importance and interest.[21] But it is difficult for us to understand, at times, what his careful drawings represent, even when they are compared to existing buildings which they delineate. Thus he shows no flying buttresses on the exterior of Reims' nave, although these are known to have existed from the beginning. It may perhaps be argued that he omitted them because their representation would have got in the way of what else he wished to show. The fact, however, that he omitted these essential features (and included non-existent ones such as blind arcades below the side-aisle windows, within) indicates with what caution any medieval drawings should be viewed. As Andrews says:[22] 'A very curious feature about Villard's sketches was that he did not draw everything just as he saw it, but rather as he would have executed the work had he done it himself, and so much so, that in some instances it would be hard to recognize the work he portrayed were not the identifications made sure by his careful annotations.'

There are, to be sure, some precisely laid out, full-sized working drawings that have survived from the Middle Ages, such as those incised on the lead or stone surface of side-aisle roofs, or on the flat surfaces of vault springers.[23] These authentic contemporary delineations of architectural details are extremely interesting and valuable indications of how accurately portions of buildings were designed and drawn at full size. But they reveal nothing of the techniques of erection, the order of procedure followed in the work, or of the equipment utilized in its construction.

6

1. *Medieval Manuscript Illumination of Masons Replacing a Column Drum*

A square, a trowel, and a mason's hammer, together with two column drums, lie on the floor, while a helper mixes mortar in a trough, to the right. The mason behind the column appears at first glance to be supporting it, although actually he is holding some sort of cylindrical block in his left hand and tapping it with a hammer held in his right hand. The nearer workman seems either to be aligning the two drums under this cylindrical block or about to remove them. Of course, none of these operations is possible without adequate falsework support for the upper half of the column and the masonry superstructure it carries. But no falsework whatsoever is shown.

As for the illuminations in manuscripts,[24] these were done by painters, with no practical training in or knowledge of the structure of buildings. Their interest was pictorial, not scientific or technical, and their purpose did not include that of giving accurate practical information. The miniaturists and illuminators were ready enough to show specific items, such as masons' or carpenters' tools, and the characteristic actions or attitudes of the men using these tools; and they sometimes became fascinated with the striking silhouette or the pictorial effect of such features as a crane or a ladder.[25] But where there was no understanding or knowledge, there was lack of interest in accuracy, at best, if not downright misinformation.

Furthermore, like a great many painters of more recent times, the medieval illuminators resorted to (1) distortion (e.g. people drawn large in relation to the size of a building), (2) the elimination of what was not to their purpose (e.g. the flying buttresses in Villard's Reims), and (3) the inclusion of what *was* to their purpose (e.g. angels in the 'Tower of Babel' scenes).[26] In this respect it may be seen that the *intention* of the medieval delineators was served, not through photographic realism or accurately projected representation, but in the imaginative portrayal of a scene, a visual interpretation of some activity or event. Thus the large, disembodied hand (of God?) in Villard's drawing of one of the towers of Laon,[27] or the structurally ludicrous but glittering and splendid towers and canopies enframing some scene of sacred liturgy or holy sacrament in many an illuminated manuscript.

Perhaps one of the clearest instances of how incomplete, and hence how untrustworthy, the illuminations of the period were in furnishing accurate illustrations of building processes is the picture of masons replacing a column drum[28] (1). Here there is no underpinning or shoring shown, nothing to support the vaulted superstructure or to relieve the weight upon the upper part of the column. In an actual situation of this sort, the replacing of the column drum would unquestionably necessitate strong shoring of the part of the vault bearing upon the column, and the cradling of the column itself.[29] But to have included the *temporary* timber-work of the shoring would have been to obscure the *permanent* features of the building, and perhaps the activities of the workmen and the master who directs their work; so, the pictorial artist omitted from his representation the required shoring without which this building operation could not have been performed.

And so we return to the buildings themselves for information and enlightenment on the problems of construction.[30]

Even here, however, the picture is tantalizingly clouded and obscure. For, in the finished state of these structures, the information they disclose of the ordering and sequence of the work, of the operational techniques employed, and of the auxiliary structures which accompanied their erection, is neither abundant nor self-evident. What there is of it needs careful seeking out, in the first place, and then as careful interpretation. Much of the full account must necessarily be pieced together by deduction, interpreting the rare and scarcely noticeable points of evidence with an experienced eye and informed common sense.

We will probably never know the true account of the erectional processes of the medieval period, either in its completeness or with unassailable documentation. But we can review and clarify what is definitely known; we can perhaps differentiate the areas of speculation from those of substantiation; we can assess the assumptions of previous writers, noting how far and on what premises they reasoned, at what point they were content to leave off both investigation and theorizing, and wherein they substituted supposed theory for the trade practices they either did not know about or, being informed of, misunderstood. And we can also, perhaps, suggest to future scholars certain directions for carrying on investigation and original research that appear likely to prove fruitful.

2

'We cannot ask What? *in presence of any architectural feature or general effect without also asking* Why? *... If we ask the reason why, we are brought at once to the study of constructional facts.'*

MRS. SCHUYLER VAN RENSSELAER*

IT IS THE FINISHED BUILDINGS—OR TO BE MORE PRECISE, THE buildings that have been completed save for the final removal of certain features employed in their erection—that are the rare and welcome illuminators of some of the constructional secrets of the past. In this respect, the unfinished Greek temple at Segesta in Sicily is many times more informing than the Parthenon. Correspondingly, the Pont du Gard in southern France is one of the very few Roman buildings, out of the hundreds of monumental works constructed throughout the whole empire, to disclose clearly some of the erectional procedures that were followed by the Roman builders.

It is worth noting the kind and extent of the information that can be learned from an analysis of certain unusual features of the latter structure, for the Pont du Gard exists today substantially as the Romans left it, being a ruin only at its extreme ends, at the top. This enormous structure, built throughout with huge blocks without mortar, has been admired by travellers of all sorts and by professional masons alike, throughout the ages. One of its most striking erectional features is the inward projection of certain voussoirs, in pairs or in threes. As a consequence of this revealing feature, various writers beginning with Choisy have been able to call attention to the way in which the Romans conserved centering in each of the great masonry arches of the first and second tiers, noting that the voussoirs of the lower part of the arch ring were laid up like ordinary wall blocks, without centering, from the springing to the angle of friction; that just below this point, double or triple voussoirs were used which projected inward beyond the line of the intrados; that the ends of a relatively thin timber-framed centering, one stone thick and of segmental shape in elevation, were poised upon the horizontally cut tops of the inward-shelving voussoirs at the angle of friction; that the

* *Handbook of English Cathedrals*, New York, The Century Company, 1893, pp. x, 25.

9

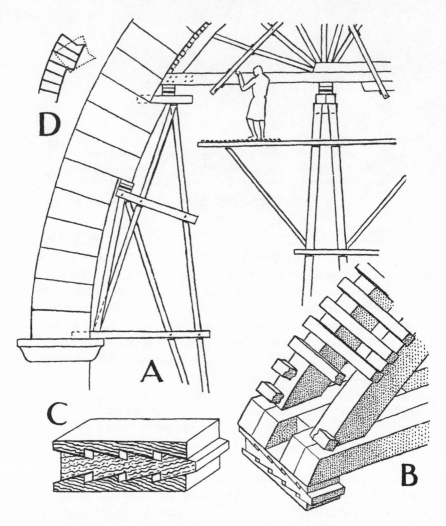

2. *Details of Conjectural Falsework for the Pont du Gard*

At A, one end of the centering frame is shown resting on the top member of a shoring complex that involves wedges under the lowest of the projecting voussoirs as well as decentering wedges at the top, under the frame's end. Photographs of the soffit of the Pont du Gard's central span reveal a series of square putlog holes just above the impost and also at the level of the horizontal shelf provided by the uppermost of the inward-projecting voussoirs. The use to which these holes may have been put is here indicated. The human figure is standing on a staging from which the decentering wedges could have been retracted by hand with heavy mallets. B is a detail of the end of a double centering frame together with some of its heavy cleats and the compound wedge it rests upon (shown more clearly in C). D shows the pivoting action that would have taken place in the block of inward-projecting voussoirs when they became weighted by the centering frame, had it not been for the shoring of these voussoirs in some such fashion as that indicated at A.

CONSTRUCTIONAL MEANS

outer ring of arch stones having been completed above this centering, the centering itself was shoved sideways to a position midway between the upstream and
the downstream faces of the structure, to act as support for the middle arch ring;
that it was shoved sideways once more to furnish support for the third arch ring,
thus completing by successive thirds the full thickness of the structure. So much
is clear enough from the inward-projecting voussoirs, which the Romans did not
bother to hew off subsequently, and from the unbroken circumferential joints
between the arch rings,[31] around the soffit of the arches. Today we are justifiably
amazed at this rationalization of erectional techniques by which the permanent
stone structure was utilized for the support of part of the temporary centering,
whose timber-work, in turn, was further reduced to only a third of the thickness
one might expect to find employed for each of the great arches of the aqueduct.

But however clearly this procedure may be indicated from a careful assessment
of the existing evidence, certain essential details are far from being apparent. For
instance (2 D), when the timber-framed centering was first placed in position,
its weight would have tilted the projecting blocks of the voussoir shelves inward
and downward if adequately strong provision had not been made to prevent this
from happening; namely, sturdy timber props wedged between the under surface
of the lowest of the inward-projecting voussoirs and the projecting impost mouldings, or propped up from the roadway level below, or both (2 A). The existing
evidence does not advertise this necessary erectional feature, although the procedures outlined above would not have been possible without it.

Again, and much less clearly deducible: what kind of device was employed for
freeing the centering? Any centering, whether Roman, Gothic, or modern, and
whether for stone or for brick or for concrete, must be provided with some device
for freeing it from the under surface of the arch or vault it has been supporting—
retracting it from the soffit and from the points of springing of the completed
permanent structure—so that it may be removed and eventually dismantled without damage to the arch structure itself or to any of the work below it. How this
critical operation was managed, in the case of the Pont du Gard, is not disclosed
from a study, no matter how minute or painstaking, of the structure itself. But it
is important to speculate on the problem, for, as stated, it is a universally recurrent
one wherever arch or vault construction occurs.

3 A shows an assumed schematic layout of the timber falsework which might
have been employed for the 80-foot central span, although this scheme is of
course purely conjectural. In any case there would unquestionably have had to be
at least the number of intermediate supports shown in the drawing, for an arch of
this size.

11

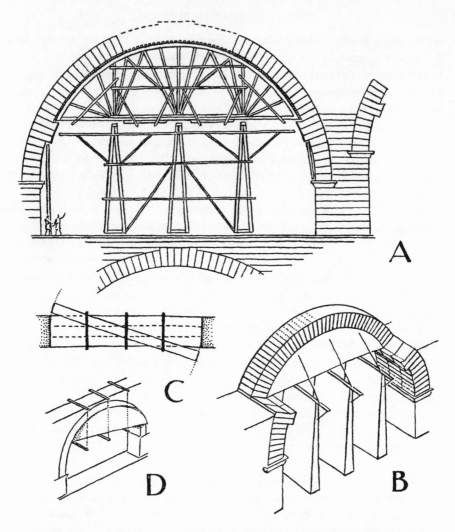

3. *Conjectural Falsework and Decentering Procedure for the Pont du Gard*

The centering frame for the 80-foot central span of the Roman Pont du Gard would have needed to have at least three intermediate points of support in addition to those provided by the inward-projecting voussoirs at either end, and these voussoirs themselves would have needed to be shored from below by one or both of the devices indicated to the right and the left in A. The schematic drawing at B shows the first arch ring completed above the centering frame that would next have been moved to the middle position, then to the near third, of the structure's thickness, for erecting the remaining two arch rings. With these completed, the centering frame may have been pivoted from the middle position, as shown in the plan view at C, so as to clear the inward-projecting voussoirs at its ends. D shows slings, suspended at the quarter points from heavy transverse beams above, which would permit the falsework below to have been dismantled and removed so that the centering frame could be lowered to the pavement via these rope-supported slings.

The dismantling process, in the case of the centering falsework for the Pont du Gard, could have been as follows. After the last of the three arch rings had been completed and the masonry superstructure had been raised to a level platform above them, the centering would then have been moved back to a position under the middle arch ring, the levelling wedges retracted and removed so as to free the timber frames from the arch as much as possible, and the whole assemblage pivoted on its mid-span support so that its ends would project beyond the faces of the structure, one on the upstream the other on the downstream side (3 C). Heavy transverse beams, resting on the upper platform level and projecting out beyond its edges on both sides at about the quarter points of the timber frame's span, would have supported cables, to the lower ends of which would be hung thick horizontal beams at a level just below the horizontal bottom members of the timber frame (3 D). With these cables tightened, the two falsework towers at the quarter points could have been removed and dismantled, then the tower at mid-span, and the whole centering frame gradually lowered on the cable-supported slings to the road-level platform.

These operations would have required no additional scaffolding during the process of removing the falsework structures, and would have allowed the work of dismantling to proceed in orderly and manageable stages, one after the other.[32] This is not, however, a procedure that could have been followed in medieval vault construction, where the depth of each bay of vaulting is far greater than the three arch rings of the Pont du Gard, and the bays are not open-faced at either end but continuous with their adjoining bays. It is none the less evident from this conjectural account that some provision for decentering is one of the most critical considerations in the operation of building an arch or vault. And it needs no special emphasis to realize that where centerings are to be re-used, as in successive bays of medieval vaulting, the problem is intensified by the requirement of working out effective means for placing, retracting, and moving the centering in a repeated sequence of operations.

The whole subject of temporary structures essential for the construction or the reconstruction of permanent buildings may be broken down into three general categories: (1) *Scaffolding*, which consists of temporary elevated platforms, either rigidly and independently supported from the ground or suspended from the building itself, from which the workmen are in a convenient position for doing their jobs; (2) *Shoring*, which consists of heavy sloping timber struts or timber grillages that maintain the superstructure or part of an existing building in its proper upright position while its permanent supports are being readied or strengthened or rebuilt or replaced with some other construction; and (3) *Centering*, which consists of timber frames or cradles making up a sufficiently strong and rigid falsework whose upper surface is built to conform to the desired shape of the soffit of the permanent arch it has to support during the course of erection.

Actually, a centering—at least for an arch of more than minimum size—consists of a number of parts. Starting at the top, there is (1) the planking or lagging: the stout wooden cleats or joists, usually set horizontally around the curve of the arch, on which the voussoirs (the wedge-shaped arch stones) are laid. This lagging, in turn, is given the proper contour by (2) curving timber segments attached in a continuous series making up the profile of the arch shape. (In simple arches these timber segments, together with their cleat-like lagging, are often called cradles.) To give support and provide stiffness throughout to the continuity of these curving segments, there must be (3) a framework of struts and braces; that is, an assemblage of stout timbers that, along with the segments of the cradle, make the whole into a rigid frame. In simple arches of modest span these frames —which nowadays are assembled as true trusses—usually span from one abutment to the other as single rigid ensembles.

The rigidity of the centering—the indeformability of its curve—is a consideration of major importance. One of the principal reasons for failure and collapse of an arch structure during the course of erection is that the centering has not been properly designed to resist deformation as the loads of the finished structure start to be applied. Obviously, the voussoirs are normally built up around the curve of the arch or vault from either side; hence the haunches of the supporting centering become heavily weighted at a time when the higher middle portion of the arch is as yet unloaded; and this condition tends strongly to depress the haunches and to cause the crown to rise in compensation.[33] It is doubtless with this ever-present danger in mind that Choisy, the engineer, makes such a point of the function of salient arches and, later, the Gothic ribs, together with their centerings, throughout his discussions of medieval erectional practices. Thus, in speaking of the underlying arches of the banded barrel vault system, he says:

Obviously these arch bands were reinforcements to stiffen the thin vaults. But it is especially during the construction of these vaults that they were useful. In the centering of a simple barrel vault, what is to be feared is not the collapse of the timber frames but their deformation; and the presence of the transverse arches allows these frames to be made indeformable, so to speak. The transverse arches were executed first; they gave to the timber-work of the centering an extreme rigidity, and it is on the timber frames thus stiffened that the body of the barrel vault was raised.[34]

14

It is nothing short of amazing, if not incomprehensible, that this·subject of falsework, involving as it does in one way or another indispensable operations in practically every structure of importance that has ever been erected, anywhere and at any time throughout the centuries, should be almost completely devoid of literature. Even today, when the most highly technical subjects have their voluminous handbooks and specialist treatises and trade journals, the problems and the design of falsework structures are almost completely ignored in the literature of technical subjects.[35] Yet what Viollet-le-Duc wrote a hundred years ago in regard to one phase of this subject—scaffolding—is quite as true today as it was in his own day. It is therefore worth quoting him at some length on the subject of the design of scaffolding.

A well-made scaffolding [he says[36]] is a feature of the builder's art which engages his best intelligence and his thorough supervision, for the real skill of the builder can be judged from the manner in which he places his scaffold. Well-designed scaffolding saves time for the workmen, gives them confidence, and obligates them to regularity, method, and care. If the scaffoldings are massive, if they employ wood in profusion, the workmen are well aware of it: they judge the chief's degree of practical knowledge from this provisional work, and they recognize any inclination of his from this abuse of means. On the other hand, if the masons are called to work on a daring scaffolding whose solidity, in spite of its apparent lightness, is convincingly proved and quickly recognized after a few days, they very readily appreciate these qualities and understand that what is required of them is care and precision in their work: 'almost' will not be good enough. In restorations of old buildings the scaffoldings require of the architect a great variety and inventiveness of combinations. His attention cannot be too strongly directed to this study, because economy, the sequence of the work, and above all the very lives of the workmen depend on it.

Elsewhere in the same article Viollet-le-Duc has a number of things to say about the fact that the medieval builders went to considerable pains to reduce their scaffolding requirements. Materials rather than workmanship, he says, were the predominant factors in the cost, and this has continued to be true, in Europe, to the present day. The buildings rose as a result of scaffolding usually attached to and supported by (instead of independent of) the permanent masonry, and this scaffolding was placed during the course of construction as the building rose. Materials of large size were never raised on the platforms, or 'bridges' of the scaffolding, but on the walls themselves by means of cranes or derricks sometimes located on the ground but more often on the construction itself. Besides, almost always the materials were raised from the interior,[37] loaded on a hand barrow on the walls, placed in position and later pointed by the workmen circulating on the

15

walls themselves or on the scaffoldings, whose 'hurdles' provided the platform from which the masons worked, analogous to the planking employed nowadays (4). Thus the scaffolding of a medieval building rose along with the building, fre-

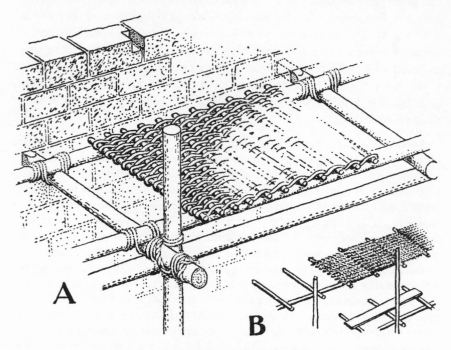

4. *Masons' Scaffolding Platform of Hurdles*

For working platforms on which no heavy materials needed to be placed, the medieval builders customarily stood upon hurdles instead of planks. These hurdles were composed of straight rods interwoven with withes. If they were set so as to span the 3 feet or so of the platform width, they would have rested on an inner as well as an outer ledger, both supported on the putlogs, as shown at A. When planking came to supersede the hurdles only a single ledger, lashed to the standards, was needed, and the putlogs rested on this at their outer ends. Hurdles could have been used with this scheme, too, their rods spanning longitudinally (as in the case of planks), as at B. In either case, cords (not shown in the drawing) could have quickly and easily secured the hurdles against shifting their position or sliding off the horizontal scaffold members.

quently in leap-frog fashion as explained and illustrated by Viollet-le-Duc,[38] with the minimum of outlay for materials and the minimum of expense.

Except for the scaffolding used in the erection of the upper part of lofty stone towers and their stone spires, however, the ingenious scaffoldings described by Viollet-le-Duc are largely limited to structures that have continuous wall surfaces

5. *Photograph of Modern Scaffolding at Notre-Dame-de-Mantes.* (13 April, 1953)

The standards of this pole scaffolding are double on the outside, single on the inside, between the buttresses. Both the inner and outer ledgers, and the outer guard rails, are securely lashed to these standards. However, planks are used instead of round poles to support the platforms proper, and these platforms in turn are of planks rather than of hurdles, as in medieval times. The photograph does not reveal whether the scaffolding is tied to the building at any point, although this is likely in such a tall structure.

with few if any window openings. Consequently, he does not specifically describe or illustrate the types of scaffoldings that would have been used on the great cathedrals of the developed Gothic period, where masonry walls as such are largely replaced by window openings, and where the tall slender piers of the nave arcade and the clerestory offered scant attachment for the customary putlog type of scaffolding.

Yet, undoubtedly, attachment by means of putlogs inserted into holes that were left in the masonry may well have been the customary technique followed in the erection of these isolated, deeply splayed and often moulded members. The occurrence of square blocks here that may have been inserted subsequently, to plug these holes flush with the surface of the finished masonry, is rarely noticed, and it is very seldom mentioned in any accounts.[39] That this was at least one of the techniques followed in their erection, however, seems likely. Up to the spring of the arcades each nave pier was undoubtedly built independently from an ordinary pole scaffolding—the sort pictured in other locations in some of the medieval manuscripts,[40] and the type often still employed in Europe[41]—which rises from the ground (5). Higher up, each of the clerestory piers, in turn, could have been erected from a similarly independent, tiered staging resting on a masonry ledge, or supported from the clerestory window sills before their ridged topmost stones were set in place, using only one or two putlogs not as main supports but as anchors tying the falsework to the masonry[42] (6). Even the arched heads of the great clerestory windows appear to have been constructed without wooden centering frames, making use of the permanent though seemingly fragile support of the stone tracery.[43] The glazing would certainly have been filled in subsequently,[44] perhaps even from stagings lowered from above on ropes, after the masonry had been carried up to the clerestory wall tops.[45]

Viollet-le-Duc's comments on the distribution and arrangement of falsework in the main body of Gothic cathedrals are of a general nature, possibly because he did not think that the scaffolding required to erect these portions of the building had involved the medieval builders with difficulties commensurate with those they encountered elsewhere (for example, in such operations as spire building, which he describes and illustrates in careful and thorough detail, based on the traces of their fastenings that still exist in the buildings themselves). He does state, however, that as occasion demanded, the carpenters of the Middle Ages made scaffoldings of timber-work that were independent of the masonry construction. But he warns that it is inconceivable to think that, in the case of some of the lofty Gothic buildings, these structures were erected all the way to the top by means of scaffoldings built up from the ground. Instead, 'they raised the lower

17

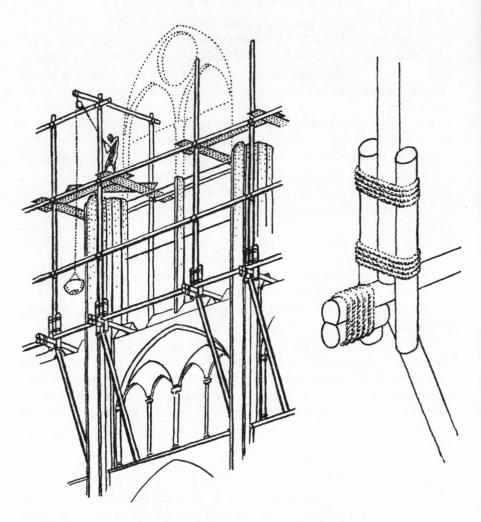

6. Scheme of Scaffolding for Clerestory Piers

Above the height at which pole scaffolding on standards rising from the floor would be either feasible or desirable, hung scaffolding would have been used. In the scheme illustrated, raking struts slant out from the triforium passageway level, their slope held in check by horizontal ties passing through window openings to secure attachment on the outside. Stones of the window sill's coping are here omitted in order to provide some stable bearing, directly on the masonry, for these horizontal ties; but alternatively the latter could pass through the window opening above this level, permitting all the sill blocks to be laid at once. From the top of the raking struts, vertical pole standards have been erected, the alignment and bearing of their feet secured as indicated in the detail at the right, possibly with some additional lashing.

18

portions from scaffoldings set on stilts and putlogs; they profited by carefully arranged off-sets in order to take new points of support at upper levels; then, having arrived at the height of platforms or galleries, they unscaffolded the lower parts in order to raise up and re-use the timber-work necessary to construct the higher portions'.[46] The bays of towers, particularly, were of great help in placing solid scaffolding and securing it against the violence of the wind and all the causes of damage which multiply as the height above ground is increased.

Viollet-le-Duc goes on to say that, above a certain height, the evidence of the scaffold holes testifies that the scaffoldings were suspended; that is, not hung by ropes, but attached to and supported by the immediately adjacent masonry under construction, instead of supported from the ground. He speaks of the evidence of 'dispositions still existing on the exterior of the great buildings of the Middle Ages' as proving the widespread utilization of these suspended scaffoldings.[47] Certainly he had intimate knowledge of a great number of medieval buildings, from repairs, reconstructions, and additions he made to them. It is most unfortunate, therefore, in the case of the great cathedrals, that he appears to have recorded no comprehensive, systematic drawings of the occurrence and spacing of putlog holes in specific church buildings. He does show the pattern of these holes in the case of the donjon at Coucy, but nothing comparable to this is designated for the much more complex cathedral structures.

Nevertheless, it seems fair to conjecture that both the openness and the galleried stages of each of the faces of these great ecclesiastical buildings provided abundant means for supporting and bracing small, independent scaffoldings, at successive levels, that could be shifted and repositioned without great difficulty as the work advanced.

In this connexion, the so-called service passageways of the medieval churches, and particularly the great cathedrals of the Gothic era, deserve more attention and analysis than they have received heretofore. Again, it is Viollet-le-Duc who has discussed the function and arrangement of these galleries and service passageways as thoroughly as anyone.[48] He notes that they are to be found at different levels both on the inside and the outside of Gothic churches, where they contribute conspicuously to the design and decoration of the building.[49] Fundamentally, they serve as communication from one place to another, as circulation at different stages of the building's height. Viollet-le-Duc cites by way of example the high façades of the northern cathedrals, where the many stages of galleries permitted communication from interior to exterior, the maintenance of the masonry facing, the repair and replacement of the glass of the rose windows, and the special decoration of the façades, on the occasion of great ceremonies, by means of hangings and festoons of various sorts.

Although much of his article deals with the description and analysis of specific cathedral façades, he also comments at some length on the occurrence of galleries and passages elsewhere, especially on the interior of these buildings, where their functions are similarly multiple. These interior locations regularly include the triforium passageway;[50] in Burgundy, particularly, it is usual to find a higher service gallery, above the triforium, which passes behind the formerets of the vault; and in both Champagne and Burgundy service galleries are placed in the side aisles and chapels above the arcades of the ground story, near the window sills. Invariably, in the great Gothic churches, there is an exterior walk, guarded by a parapet, at the gutter level of the nave roof, with another exterior walk at either the base or the top of the side-aisle roofs.[51] Certain buildings have additional, exceptionally placed passageways.[52] Viollet-le-Duc sums up the importance of these service passageways as follows:

> The galleries are always useful. In their great buildings, the medieval architects established the means of easy circulation at different levels in order to be able to provide surveillance of and maintenance to the building's fabric, to the roof coverings and the stained glass, without being obliged, as we are nowadays, to erect expensive and harmful scaffoldings, harmful by reason of the damage they cause to the carving and the delicate portions of the architecture.[53]

If, from this, it is evident that the service galleries provided a built-in scaffolding, as it were, from which constant inspection and ready repair could be made almost everywhere throughout the building, at many levels both without and within, then it is equally evident that these passages of circulation were also of primary utility during the course of erection.[54] In fact, it is quite possible that their usefulness was absolutely indispensable at the time the building was under construction, when the saving in the amount of scaffolding they were able to bring about must have been a matter of considerable significance in the building's cost. For the stable platforms they provided were immensely useful in furnishing support for the timber-work of various kinds of falsework at the higher levels, as the work of erection proceeded. In addition, their contribution would have been the more welcome because, by largely eliminating all but small localized units of scaffolding hung aloft on the structure as the higher portions of the building rose, the ground level would have been freed of the encumbrance that is always inevitable with the employment of pole scaffolding supported at the ground level. Since portions of the church came to be used for worship as soon as space for the services could be made available, the earliest freeing of the ground story was a pressing consideration.[55]

The whole development of medieval churches with respect to their incorporation of service passageways seems to bear out the fact that these passageways had a major role in progressively reducing the amount and extent of the temporary staging needed during erection. The early Romanesque churches had no service passages whatsoever.[56] On the exterior, façades were essentially flat and in any case invariably unrelieved by galleries. There were no eaves gutters and hence no possibility of exterior walkways at either the nave or side-aisle roof levels. On the interior, the only stages above the ground story were those in towers, if such existed, and, when occasion and resources permitted, the triforium galleries or tribunes. These double-storied side aisles which were favoured in the tenth and eleventh centuries occur at Montier-en-Der, Issoire, Jumieges, Saint-Étienne at Nevers, Notre-Dame-du-Port, Saint-Remi at Reims, Saint-Sernin at Toulouse, and elsewhere, but none of these churches is provided with service passageways as such. Although these and many other churches display considerable variety and numerous innovations in vaulting practices, it is not until the Gothic system is foreshadowed that service passageways begin to be incorporated systematically. The first occurrence of built-in galleries of circulation, apparently, is that of clerestory passageways such as those of Boscherville, Saint-Étienne at Caen, and Saint-Germer. But unquestionably, the deliberate planning and the multiplication of these service passageways are uniquely Gothic developments.

Incorporated along with the service passageways and keeping pace with their development were spiral stairs, called 'vices',[57] which intercommunicated with them at various points to make the system of circulation complete, both vertically and horizontally, throughout the building.

These vices were most ingeniously fitted into buttresses or corners of the building, some of them off-setting from their ground-floor place of origin in order to accommodate themselves to the contraction in the building's area as it rose above the side-aisle vault level. Unlike many of the later English examples, those of the French throughout the entire Gothic era were rarely featured in the design of the building visually.[58] Instead, they were as far as possible contained within the customary size of normal features of the structure, so that today their presence is not suspected by the layman, either without or within the church, and even the doors of entry to them are obscure and remain all but unnoticed. This may be evidence, of a sort, that they were thought of from the beginning as of a purely service function, not open to the public,[59] and contributing nothing visually to the

7. *Schematic Diagram of Circulation System: Vices and Passageways*

Here is shown in cut-away view, for much of the eastern portion of a generalized Gothic cathedral, the minimum that is typical of its circulation system above the floor level. On the exterior, a gutter passageway is found at the eaves of both the side-aisle and the high roof, together with a passage at the top of the former's slope where it meets the clerestory wall. On the inside, there is of course a passageway at the triforium level; and, within the dark tunnels of both side-aisle and high central roof, there are plank walk-ways laid across the tie-beams above the vaults. Often, as the text recalls, there are passageways at other levels, both within and without, not to mention the special and seemingly redundant conditions of the western façade with its many gallery levels. All of these horizontal passageway levels are interconnected by spiral stairs: often a pair at each transept end (as here), as well as those in the bell-towers of the western façade and perhaps others that terminate just above the side-aisle roof, as at Beauvais.

vertical design of the building. These vices were, however, essential features in the circulation system of churches and cathedrals alike, above the ground level, giving access to and linking together the various horizontal galleries at higher levels, inside and out, that have previously been described[60] (7). They, as much as any factor, made possible the freeing of the ground floor as the building rose during erection; for they incorporated stable and enclosed means of access, without temporary ladders or stagings, to the higher portions of the work where alone the localized scaffolding occurred. Except for materials raised by cranes, not only the workmen themselves, but the hods or cut blocks a man might carry, could go or be brought aloft from the mason's yard up to the point at which work was progressing, without interfering with whatever might be taking place on the ground-floor area of the building.

Furthermore, there was another erectional advantage in these built-in 'ladders', the spiral stairs. The very nature of their masonry construction came to obviate the use of any external scaffolding whatsoever during their erection: from an erectional standpoint the spiral stairs together with their shell of enclosing masonry were completely independent and self-contained, inasmuch as the ascending treads of the stair acted as successive platforms from which the mason worked conveniently on small trestles in laying both the next higher steps and the encasing masonry alike.

These vices, then, are further convincing evidence of how the Gothic builders came to dispense with all but the scantiest amount of scaffolding, since they required none at all for their own erection, and provided convenient, relatively easy access to successive levels of service galleries as the building rose.

The second general category of temporary structures used in connexion with building operations is that of *shoring*.[61] Although of much more frequent occurrence in reconstructions or in the alteration of finished buildings, shoring nevertheless may have played a role in certain portions of Gothic churches at the time of their erection. In general, shoring was probably employed to stay or brace lofty elements of the building against lateral swaying or deflexion during the course of erection, until higher elements could be brought into play to stabilize or brace them integrally and permanently. Thus both Choisy and Viollet-le-Duc indicate that the isolated, relatively slender clerestory piers of the great Gothic churches may have been held true and erect by shoring until the wall arches at their tops were built across from pier to pier and the clerestory wall-top thus became a continuous strip of masonry, later to be weighted and stabilized transversely by the great timber roof.[62]

23

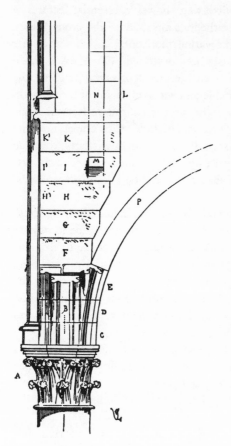

Actually, the need for some sort of shoring here was not only precautionary but necessary in the case of many of the great Gothic churches. For, as analysed and clearly demonstrated by Viollet-le-Duc and others, the piers that supported the high vault often had a considerable amount of false bearing near or just below the triforium level,[63] deliberately introduced in order to develop counteraction in resisting the primary vault pressures, in order to stiffen the clerestory supports by splitting them and pairing the two parts in a transverse direction, and in order thus to prevent a flame-like warping or deflexion in these vertical members (8). Thus the portions of the clerestory piers that corbelled out above the side aisle from just below the triforium level,[64] and in addition the inner face of the buttresses whenever they encroached on the void above the side aisles,[65] doubtless had to be shored temporarily in order to keep these two towering masses of masonry erect as they rose above the triforium

8. *Viollet-le-Duc's Drawing of False Bearing*

This is one of the numerous drawings in connexion with Viollet-le-Duc's thorough and detailed analysis of the dispositions and adjustments adopted by the medieval builders in order to assure equilibrium in the skeletonized structure of the church of Notre-Dame at Dijon. Above the capital, A, of a nave pier, stones G, H, and I are seen to corbel well out over the side-aisle vaulting, P, in order to provide depth for O, a pier cluster of the triforium arcade; the triforium passageway between O and N; a buttress, L; and the wall of the triforium, N, supported on an arch sprung from

the skewback projection on stone I, at M. In his long account of this church (see especially *Dictionnaire*, iv, pp. 136–46, figs. 78–82C (Huss, pp. 182–94)), the stiffening advantage of splitting the supports for the superstructure at the triforium level (which necessitates this corbelling, with its false bearing) is amply and convincingly demonstrated.

For another instance of false bearing, see 32, a reproduction of Viollet-le-Duc's sectional view through a pier and buttresses at one side of the choir at Amiens.

level, and to prevent them from leaning towards each other due to the offsetting of their centers of gravity.

It should be noted that timber shoring was always of a definitely temporary nature—that its life-expectancy, so to speak, was not likely to exceed a number of months, perhaps a year or two at the most. This was due to the rate of deterioration not so much in the unprotected timbers as in the lashings of the shoring assemblages; for in practically every instance of shoring it is inevitable that the timber-work is exposed to all the hazards and vicissitudes of the weather. None the less there were often very long delays and hiatuses of many years' duration in the course of constructing the great majority of medieval buildings: it was most exceptional for the work to have been continuous from its start to its completion.[66] Hence the perishable nature of the lashings of timber shoring (and, to a lesser extent, of the other falsework structures of wood)[67] came to have a direct bearing not only on the sequence of the work but sometimes, much more fundamentally, on the very structural system itself.

Before commenting on this last remark it should be recalled that a prolonged and thorough study of medieval architecture appears to corroborate the claim that the Gothic structure, as finally perfected in the French quadripartite system, is completely integrated throughout, and that therefore each element or feature has its distinct and essential contribution to make in the ensemble. This is what the greatest Gothic churches have revealed to the serious student of their antecedents, their development, and their finished actuality. But there is also another aspect of their integration, which stems from the fact that they did not burst upon the scene, Athena-like, complete and fully achieved in one sudden, definitive convulsion of creativity. On the contrary, each building had to be *built*: stone by stone, patiently, painstakingly, expediently. And this step-by-step process, this gradual bringing-into-being, demanded certain structural interrelationships of elements of the building *as the work progressed*: it necessitated that integration be achieved not only in the final ensemble but *at intervals during the course of construction*, without reliance on projected features that would come into existence only at a later phase of the work.

Thus, although the action of some of the structural features of the developed Gothic system did not become fully operative until the high vault—normally the last masonry feature to be constructed—had been built and freed of its supporting centering, nevertheless these features sometimes had to be installed well before they were called upon to fulfil their major purpose, in order to meet secondary, or even provisional, requirements.

A striking instance of this may be seen in the situation just alluded to. The *permanent* strutting of clerestory wall and buttress tower (to prevent their side-aisle-encroaching masses from tilting towards each other) was provided by flying buttresses, whose ultimate function would become operative only after the nave vaults were built. Thus any *temporary* shoring that may have been used in this situation was needed only while the clerestory wall and the buttress towers were being carried up from the triforium level to the level of the flying buttress arch. From that point on, as we shall see, the flying buttress *centerings* took over and fulfilled the temporary function of strutting between the clerestory piers and the buttresses proper, until the erection of the nave roof was consumated. It was the nave roof, bridging across from one clerestory wall top to the other, that permanently consolidated, along with the flying buttresses themselves, the entire superstructure.[68]

In connexion with the temporary shoring of the piers of the clerestory walls, this might be an appropriate place to comment on the erection of the Gothic roof. Throughout the Romanesque period, the roof over the nave of churches had steadily increased in pitch from a rather slight slope to 45° or so by about the middle of the twelfth century. The structural developments of the Gothic system, however, were accompanied by a marked increase in the pitch of the roof slopes, which now were made to be generally between 54° and 57°, with some examples as much as 60° and even 65°. At least in northern France, the Gothic roofs were invariably completely independent of the vault.[69] The latter constituted the masonry ceiling of the interior; the former constituted the timber structure of the roof proper; and there was sometimes as much as 5 or 6 feet—almost 10 feet at Reims—of clearance between the crowns of the stone vault and the great tie-beams, the lowest members of the timber roof structure.

Some writers have noted that the Gothic builders apparently thought of these tie-beams as compression members, whereas to the modern engineer the principal function of a tie in this location is recognized as that of a tension member, resisting the tendency of the two roof slopes to spread apart at their bases. However, the medieval builders were interested in making sure that the triangular prism of the roof would always act as a rigid entity under variable conditions of live as well as dead loading; and this could be assured, when the wind blew against one slope, only by having a beam of large enough cross-section to transmit such a load from the windward base of the triangle to the lee base by compression. Furthermore, these great tie-beams were called upon to transmit and therefore neutralize the inward pressure of a pair of upper-tier flying buttresses by a strutting action, as Fitchen has demonstrated.[70]

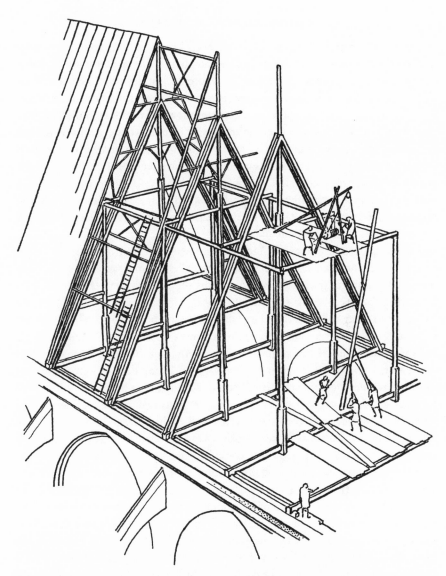

9. *The Erection of the Nave Roof (Reims Cathedral)*

The simplified progress drawing given here does not necessarily indicate the exact order in which the various members of this massive timber structure were assembled. Actually, not even all the elements of the ensemble are designated. What can be shown in a single drawing is, rather, the general impression of the procedure, together with the use of the gin as a lifting device. It should be recalled

that the shaping, notching, and test-assembling of the units took place on the ground, so that the subsequent erection, up aloft, could proceed in fairly rapid and orderly fashion, without the need for correction or further adaptation.

See Viollet-le-Duc's *Dictionnaire* article 'Charpente', vol. iii, p. 19, fig. 14, for elevation drawings of this roof.

27

In addition, moreover, there may have been important erectional reasons for making these tie-beams much the heaviest members of the timber-work complex, even before the uses of the completed structure, as just described, became operative. It has been noted that the vaults were normally the last features of the building's permanent fabric to be constructed, after the great roof was in place. Consequently, the timber ties were the first transverse elements to be put into position, the first units to tie together the nave's lofty wall-tops, whose somewhat precarious lateral stability was until then dependent, as we have seen, on some form of temporary strutting from without. Undoubtedly these heavy beams provided the support for a temporary staging or platform of planks, stretching across from one tie-beam to the next, some 8 or 10 feet away, from which the whole superstructure of the roof was erected without additional or independent scaffolding. For in most timber roofs over large naves there were one, two, or even three points in the length of these tie-beams at which vertical members of timber arose to act as intermediate supports for the higher portions of the roof.[71] These timber columns were in bearing on the tie-beams and therefore created loads which, at least during the course of erection, required that the tie-beams should be heavy members resistant to bending from the weight imposed on them[72] (9). Finally, in addition to the platform which the tie-beams furnished in facilitating the erection of the entire roof construction, there is evidence that powerful lifting devices were sometimes installed within the roof structure,[73] sustained on the tie-beam-supported platform, by which heavy loads such as bells, timbers destined for the roof assemblage itself or for subsequently projected spires, and perhaps large key-stones carved into complicated bosses with rib stems to accommodate the crown-converging diagonals of the future ribbed vault, could be lifted and set in place.

All these functions would require a heavy tie-*beam* of timber rather than a slender tie-*rod* of metal. Its employment demonstrates once again that the medieval builders were interested in economy of erection, that one feature of their construction often fulfilled multiple aims, and that the operational procedures they adopted in erecting a building were thoroughly foreseen, if not from the ground-breaking start, at least in time enough so that the various interrelated steps in the sequence of the work could be co-ordinated without the necessity for duplication of effort or interference, one step with another.

Of all the categories of falsework, the most difficult and complicated, and that about which there are the least definite clues, the minimum of direct information in the buildings themselves, is *centering*. The problems and difficulties encountered in the use of centering increase greatly in proportion as the span of even a simple arch is increased. These problems and difficulties are very much intensified when it is a vault, rather than a simple arch, that is to be erected. And when the vault to be built is a large one, set high above the ground, the difficulties of its erection, even today, are formidable.

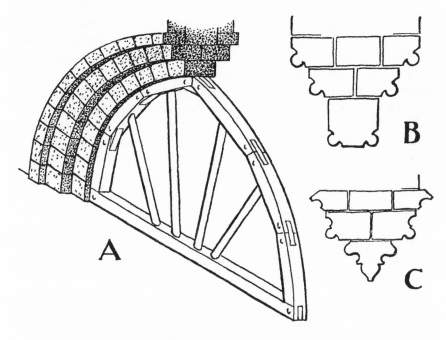

10. *Concentric Orders of Arches*

Here is a device, at once decorative and constructional, for building door or window or nave arcade arches. At A is shown a slender centering frame, narrower than the thickness of the first arch ring it supports. This first arch ring, in turn, becomes the permanent centering for a second double ring of voussoirs which corbel out on either side from the faces of the innermost arch ring. The total thickness of the wall may require three or more such concentric rings, corbelling out in successive steps. For the sake of simplicity, no mouldings are indicated in A, but B (from Tours) and C (from Paris) show the moulded profiles, in section, of actual examples.

Centering was certainly the most demanding erectional problem encountered by the medieval builders. When its inherent difficulties are considered along with the builders' evident determination to rationalize and reduce the amount of material used for the falsework structure, it is inescapably clear that the design and technique of placing centerings became a major preoccupation of the architects, exacting from them the utmost in resourcefulness, ingenuity, and practical experience.

So central is this problem of the centering of arches and vaults that various writers have not hesitated to acknowledge that its devices and practices have had a major role in determining the finished form and appearance of various aspects of medieval buildings. Thus the concentric, offset rings of voussoirs above a Romanesque window or doorway have been explained as a technique that was at least originally dictated by its erectional economy: temporary wooden centering was required only for the first ring of voussoirs; thereafter this first ring acted as permanent centering for the next order of the arch, whose faces were corbelled out beyond the inner and outer faces of the first ring; and so on for as many successive rings as were necessary to arrive at the full thickness of the wall[74] (10). Again, some writers have asserted that the adoption and widespread use of ribs in medieval vaulting were primarily due to the opportunity these ribs provided to permit a major reduction in the cost of centering.[75] In any case, some comment needs to be made at this point on the general nature of the centering problem, together with examples to illustrate the practices that have been employed in a representative number of cases.

Perhaps the most ancient method of providing support and the proper shape for vaults was the practice of filling the room to be vaulted with earth, as its walls rose, and then mounding up additional earth as formwork for the vault itself. This method had been extensively used in ancient Egypt, not only for vaults but also for flat-ceilinged hypostyle halls, and as the exterior falsework for all types of masonry structures including pyramids, pylon towers, and monolithic obelisks.[76] Its advantages were that the operation of positioning and setting each stone of the structure, from floor to roof, always took place at the 'ground' level; and that, as the earth or sand was removed afterwards, its retreating levels provided the most convenient 'scaffolding', as it were, for working the delicate finish—carving and painting—of ceiling and walls alike, from the top down. Among its numerous disadvantages was the outward pressure exerted by the earth or sand fill against the walls as they rose. In consequence, this practice was confined (on those occasions where it was used at all in the Middle Ages) to the construction of crypts or to basement stories whose walls had to be thick and massive because of the successive floors and the heavy superstructure these walls were destined to support. Thus the ground stories of many early bell-towers were undoubtedly built on an earth embankment filled in solidly all the way up from the floor, at the real ground level, to the under side of the vault. In the thirteenth-century Merveille at Mont-Saint-Michel, the ground-story Almonry and Cellar have neither transverse nor diagonal ribs, which fact would appear to corroborate the

11. *Photograph of Vault Erection at Anacapri, Island of Capri, Italy.*
(2 March, 1953)

Continuous planking has been erected in five planes—half a decagon in elevation—on a false-work of poles. At the forward end of each of these structures a narrow semicircular band has been fashioned out of small stones and mortar whose surface will determine the curving soffit of the subsequent, permanent arch. Behind these carefully shaped bands or strips of masonry form-work the workman has begun to build up the form for the vault, using rough stones well up the haunch, and packed dirt higher up. (The stones needed to be used in the lower portions since packed dirt could not be counted on to maintain the desired contour, where the curve was so steep.) As the building up of stones and dirt continues, the carefully executed strip of mortar will act as a template to assure an even and regular curve throughout the body of the vault's soffit. When this smooth cylindrical form has been completed, flush with the contour of the narrow masonry band, the permanent vault proper will be laid upon it in rubble masonry.

likelihood that they were built, even at this advanced date, on forms of mounded earth.

This practice, however, could not possibly have been employed, outright, in the case of vaulted naves, particularly as the medieval churches became loftier, with walls that came to have increasingly large voids. Instead, a variant on this practice was sometimes adopted in certain churches of Romanesque times, whereby the earth fill was used only close under the vault, supported on a platform that was shored up on poles from the floor.[77] In order to reduce the amount of labour involved, and more especially to reduce the amount and hence the weight of earth needed to give the vault its shape, the platform came to be made in three or more planes instead of a single horizontal plane established near the level of the springing. This method is still practised in some parts of Europe, particularly where the vaults to be constructed are of relatively simple design and of small span, as shown in the illustration, 11.

Although there were serious limitations and disadvantages in this practice, it had, and still has, distinct advantages. It required only materials that were cheap and plentiful, and the workmanship did not demand a high degree of skill in any phase of the operation. Its most important advantage, however, lay in the flexible means it provided for forming vaults that were other than cylindrical in shape. The domed groin vault, for example,[78] where the crowns were strongly bowed instead of horizontal, would have been almost impossible to form with continuous wooden centering: every board would have had to be warped to a curve, not only, but tapered from narrow to wide to narrow, like barrel staves, in addition. The cutting and the fitting of these boards would have taken an inordinate number of man-hours of skilled carpentry-work; and it is even very doubtful whether the amount of practical geometry in general use at the time would have been equal to such an assignment. All this was obviated in the case of small units of vaulting by the practice of using tamped earth to give the vault its shape. And so this method was used, with variations; and it continued to be used, particularly by local builders, for structures where neither funds nor materials nor skilled labour were in abundant supply.

It was a disadvantage, however, to have to have the entire interior of the building obstructed during the course of erection. And the operation of dismantling this extensive earth-on-wood centering was messy and hazardous, both to the workmen and to the already completed portions of the building itself.

This latter disadvantage raises the whole question of *decentering*: the technique of removing the formwork. One begins to be aware of the magnitude of the problem and the multiple difficulties of vault erection when it is realized that there are many steps that have to be foreseen and accounted for. Chief among these are: (1) the design of the formwork and centerings themselves so that their shape cannot deform under conditions of partial loading during the placing of the masonry; (2) the provisions for supporting the centerings; (3) the means for erecting this falsework and accurately setting it in place; and (4) (what is seldom considered by the layman or even by the architectural historian) the technique of freeing the centering from the finished vault and either lowering or otherwise dismantling it. In addition there are such attendant problems as synchronizing the sequence of numerous related operations so that all necessary phases of the work can proceed without mutual interference; lateral bracing in the case of thin centerings; the materials and their mode of attachment, especially in the case of timber frames or cradles; and provision for moving and resetting the centerings without damaging existing work, where re-use of the same centerings is indicated. Finally, there is the concomitant requirement of subsequently providing a scaffolding under the vault, after its erection, from which the workmen could plaster the vault and paint regular but false stone joints on this smooth finish, as was customary in medieval times.

After all the voussoirs making up an arch have been set in place, making the arch complete and self-sufficient, there are really two phases in the operation of removing the centering. One is that of freeing it from the load of arch stones it has been supporting; the other is that of removing it and placing it in a new position, or lowering it to the ground where it may be dismantled and disposed of.

Where a centering is supported exclusively on poles from the floor or ground, one time-honoured method of decentering is to have the poles set in sand-filled drums or kegs: at the time of decentering, holes around the base of each drum are unplugged, and this allows the sand to run out, thus gradually permitting the poles and their falsework superstructure to sink a few inches as the feet of the poles settle to the bottom of the drums. The fact that dry sand is practically noncompressible makes this a useful technique of decentering where obstruction of the ground by poles is not a serious inconvenience. However, this is a method that can normally be used only once for a given centering; so, where it is planned to re-use the centering in one or more subsequent locations, some other method is likely to be used.

In general, pairs of wedges, the two wedges of each pair pointing in opposite directions, are the simplest and commonest devices for solving the decentering problem. For they can be applied in a great variety of situations, they can be located either high up or at the ground level, and they may be re-used again and again. In addition, at the start of operations, they provide a means for ·adjusting and levelling the centerings at the proper height with the greatest precision and accuracy. To be sure, there has to be some scheme for forcing the wedges apart at the time of decentering, but various mechanical means for doing so were not beyond the abilities or the practical skill of the medieval builders, judging by some of the devices illustrated in Honnecourt's *Album* and elsewhere. Various

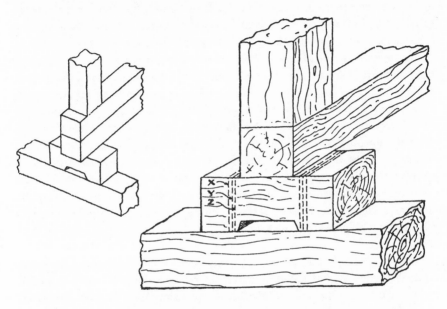

12. *Saw-Cut Method of Striking Centering Frames*

This exacting and dangerous method of freeing the centering frames from their masonry burden, upon completion of the arch structure, makes use of a series of hardwood blocks that have had a void cut out of them, below, at the time they were placed in position under each of the supporting stantions of the falsework. The process consists of making pairs of saw cuts successively closer to the void (as at X, then Y, then Z) until the remaining wood at either side of the voided portion crushes with the superimposed weight, and the falsework structure thus subsides an inch or so.

forms of jacks, windlasses, and rams, for example, were known and used, at least on works of major importance; and if wedges are seldom illustrated in the manuscript drawings, there is no reason to suppose that so fundamental and essentially simple a device was not extensively employed.

A variant on pairs of wedges as a means of closely controlled decentering is that of three long, notched sleeper-beams or sills, as indicated in 3 C. Oftentimes, a considerable portion of the falsework can be retracted all at once by this arrangement, with the automatic assurance that the lowering operation will take place evenly throughout, and that the falsework superstructure will maintain an exactly horizontal position whatever the degree of gradual lowering may be.[79]

Sometimes, when a structure takes an unusually long time to build, and the natural fluctuations of dryness and dampness, of heat and freezing weather affect the wooden wedges to such an extent that their lubricants become stiff and more glue-like than slippery, it may become almost impossible to retract these wedges. Such conditions, if foreseen before the falsework is assembled, can be circumvented by another type of decentering scheme: that of sawing, as indicated in 12. Here successive pairs of saw cuts, each closer to the voided portion of the support block, permit its wood to crush with the weight of the centering superstructure, so that the framework may subside slightly.[80] For the decentering operation, this scheme requires many men (two at each support) sawing at the same rate and at exactly identical intervals from the void in the support blocks. Although the scheme described here, or some variation of it, has been occasionally used with success in heavy constructions, it does not permit of such precise control as do the other schemes mentioned. Whether some such device was ever used by the medieval builders is not known, of course. Probably the simpler scheme of wedges was the usual practice they followed.

Great cumbersome towers of wood, many stories high, were built by besieging armies in medieval as well as in Roman times, and these were mounted on wheels and trundled up to the walls of fortified towns whose lofty defences they overtopped.[81] If these engines of war could be manœuvred successfully, under fire, upon the makeshift uneven ground of a hastily filled moat, then it is clear that mobile stagings, mounted on wheels, could be employed by the medieval builders to support their centerings and to move them from bay to bay as the work proceeded.[82]

This device of rolling centering must certainly have been used in erecting the banded barrel vaults of important early Romanesque churches, where the successive bays of vaulting were numerous and uniform, or approximately so. And as vaulting practices improved, so too this falsework device would have been modified and improved. For example, the builders would perhaps have found it more convenient to have the assemblage in two parts: one from the floor to the spring-line, approximately, with a platform or at least an arrangement of planking at the top; the other part, the centering proper, starting from a little above the spring-line and provided with a series of wedges or jacks at the platform level

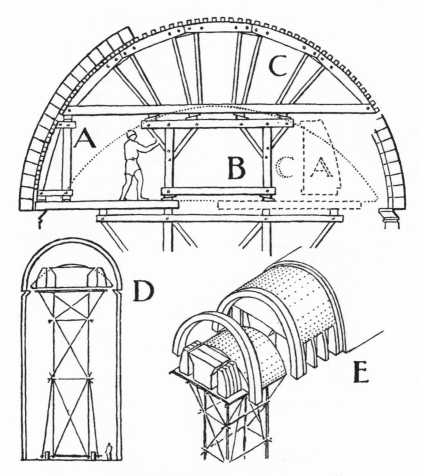

13. *Rolling Scaffolding for Banded Barrel Vault*

A high, wide-spanning banded barrel vault (such as that for St-Sernin at Toulouse) may have been built with the rolling scaffolding indicated here. In assembled position a pair of A units, one on each side, provided end supports for unit C and furnished the proper contour for the lagging units from the arch springs up to the angle of friction. Main support for the segmental centering frame C was given by the central bracketed structure B. All three of these units were adjusted to the proper level on wedges, as shown; and doubtless a horizontal strut was inserted between A and B, on both sides just above the workman's head, to prevent unit A from tilting inward.

To move this assemblage to the next bay; both unit A and the beam on which the workman is standing were moved inward from a bearing on the string course at the two springs of the vault; C was temporarily supported while B and the pair of A's were moved out from under C; and C was then lowered.

The isometric drawing at E explains this more fully. Here, in the nearest bay defined by a pair of floating arcs, unit C is shown lowered to the platform level, with a thick pair of B's and four thin pairs of A temporarily stacked out in front on the shelving projection of the platform. In the second bay, C is in the raised position with the other units in place supporting it. (The loose, short-length lagging supported by the A units up to the start of C is not shown.) D indicates the clearance of the formwork in its contracted and lowered position during the operation of moving the high staging from one bay to the next.

35

where there would be head-room clearance for the convenience of the workmen in driving in and subsequently retracting the wedges.

The rolling staging could have been made a foot or two narrower than the minimum clear distance between opposite piers across the nave, so that when this staging was moved from bay to bay there would be no danger of its scraping against or damaging the existing masonry. Furthermore, the centering would have been made less than a full semicircle in elevation (somewhat the proportions of the Pont du Gard centerings, in fact), so that it could be lowered to the floor of the platform when the staging was rolled from one bay to the next, and thus clear the crown of the inward-projecting transverse arches separating the bays of the vaulting. If the chord length of the centerings were thus sufficiently shorter than the diameter which constituted the span of the vault, the centering could also clear the inward projection of the transverse arch at either side, when lowered to the platform level and moved to the next bay. As in the Pont du Gard, moreover, this abbreviated length of centering might sometimes involve the building up of the arch ring from the springers at either end without support from the centering, until the encroachment was sufficient to be taken care of by the centering.[83] However, if this meant too much of the vault to have to raise above the springing without either guidance or support from centering, it would have been feasible to provide curving guides or portions of centerings at either side, under the main centering, supported like out-riggers on beams laid across from the platform to the impost at the spring of the vault (13). Particularly in the earlier Romanesque vaulting, this impost provided a wide shelf, not only due to the projection of the mouldings there, but also because the vault at its spring was usually in considerable retreat from the face of the wall below it.

Some writers appear to believe that these shelves may have provided the only support for the centering, which then would have spanned all the way across the nave as a single rigid unit.[84] If the medieval churches had been only a single bay long,[85] and if there had been no problem of the removal, let alone the re-use, of centering, then this might have been the general practice. But it has been pointed out that the centering problem is multiple and complex, involving a good deal more than simply the location at which the two ends of a centering were seated. Many of the assertions about centering have been made by writers unfamiliar with the problems and the practical difficulties involved in falsework, including provision from the start for decentering and removal without damage to the building. Obviously, it is important to study the problem in all its phases, practical and operational as well as economic. As has been stated repeatedly, economic considerations have a major influence upon the practical and operational procedures;

but these latter nevertheless set the requirements of the actual work to be done, and must be fully understood by the builders before economies in their accomplishment can be worked out. By the same token, it is well for the student of medieval vaulting to try to re-create *all* the steps of the erectional process if he wishes to understand *what* took place and *how*, always keeping in mind the builders' preoccupation with economy of means.

One of the reasons why it is so difficult to reconstruct the erectional procedures of the Romanesque period is that that era of creative ferment was so experimental and diversified in its building practices. This is true not only of its vault forms but also of its decorations and of the very shapes and plan arrangements of its buildings as a whole. With so much experiment and variety in the vault forms themselves, it is only natural that there should have been similar wide-ranging experimentation in the erectional means of constructing them. Thus there are obscure and usually early instances of inward-projecting voussoirs similar to those of the Pont du Gard;[86] of massive and sometimes unfinished capitals intended for later carving, that may have provided the end seating for the vault centerings; of unfilled voids, like putlog holes, above the springing of domes and of barrel vaults.

But except for a few existing clues such as these, there is little direct evidence of erectional practices in the buildings themselves. This lack of evidence is particularly noteworthy in the larger and more prepossessing buildings—even early ones—where in spite of certain unresolved and awkwardly handled problems there is the stamp of superior building skill and intelligence. Such buildings rarely if ever disclose any of their erectional secrets. So, one is tempted to rely exclusively on those material clues mentioned above which occur in rare and scattered instances in the churches of small and out-of-the-way places.

Yet this is a questionable practice, more likely to be misleading than illuminating, for all its seeming authenticity in citing certain actual details instead of speculating on what *may* have been. A moment's reflection will suggest why it is that, in regard to erectional practices, probably much less can be learned from the smaller buildings located in rural or sparsely settled communities than has been credited to their study. To be significant, the analysis of erectional procedures must be directed to those buildings which were major works for their time and their locality. For in every era, including our own, there has been a marked and fundamental distinction between the limited number of outstanding major undertakings and the multitudinous average or minor ones. It is the former that make use of the most thoroughgoing organizational set-up, the most accomplished skills, the most advanced techniques, machines, and procedures that the era can command. The latter are at most but a dim and tardy echo, a modest paraphrasing, of the supreme effort involved in the former.

Actually, the two are separate and practically independent developments in all ages; so that even an exhaustive study of the techniques of minor works can reveal almost nothing about those of the major buildings. One category is essentially local, revealing at most the traditional predilections, preferences, and skills of that locality; the other transcends the immediate locality and represents the creative imagination, the inspired realization, not of a single region but of a whole era.

Many examples bear witness to the extra-nationalism of the great buildings of any age. Charlemagne sought the best craftsmen of Italy for his church at Aix-la-Chapelle; Tamberlaine selected the most skilled artisans from the peoples he conquered, to build and decorate the Mosque of Gour-Émir in Samarkand;[87] Milan Cathedral was designed largely by an imported German architect; Hungary sent for and employed the French architect Villard de Honnecourt. Experts, often from far distant places, were called in for advice or were commissioned to undertake the design and supervision of important buildings, because of their fame.[88]

Moreover, it was not merely a question of single architects and the skilled cadre of men they took along with them on their commissions in a foreign land. For along with the coming and going of masters and journeymen—helping to make their professional travels safe and widespread, in fact—there came to be a sort of internationalism of working conditions (including the recognized training of apprentices, the immunities and privileges as well as the obligations of the workers, their legal status, &c.) that established a favourable environment for these important building operations throughout all of Europe. Harvey rightly insists that the great medieval constructions presuppose a high degree of organization as prerequisite to their achievement: with respect to finance, transportation, the several building trades, and other related categories.[89] Just as today there are great contracting firms, in America for instance, that undertake to build a dam in Asia, a bridge in Africa, a hydro-electric generating plant in South America, so in times past there have had to be companies of some sort whose organization, resources, equipment, experience, and knowledgeable personnel could make possible the most important building operations of the times. The Pont du Gard for Roman times, and the great thirteenth-century French cathedrals for Gothic times, are superlative examples of this fact, in the past. It is not just the larger works, however, that have commanded the most consummate skills and the most enlightened practices of the period. For example, the relatively small church of Saint-Urbain at Troyes is one of the most perfect structures of the entire Gothic era. It gives evidence throughout, in every aspect and detail of its construction, of the most creative and knowledgeable design, the most finished and assured craftsmanship.

Such enlightened and progressive examples as these, whether large or small, represent the 'growing edge' of a developing, advancing architecture. Compared to them, the small and unpretentious works, often then as now located in obscure and remote places, were pale reflections indeed of the major works. Usually the builders of these minor works no more attempted to emulate the exceptional structures, with the inferior means and insufficient technical knowledge at their command, than does the farmer of today, in building his barn, attempt to copy the great market halls or the exhibition arenas of the metropolis. Thus, even where the early dates of small and unpretentious works are definitely established, they seldom if ever can tell us how the important buildings were constructed.[90]

It should be recognized and freely acknowledged that the minor buildings that are native to any locality or region truly reflect the character and the predilections of the people of that region, and are valuable manifestations of the local milieu. However, here we are concerned with the engineering and constructional practices, not the visual, spatial, or expressive character that differentiates regional schools of architecture, or that gives to that architecture an indigenous 'sense of place'. We are concerned primarily with the erectional means rather than with the visual actuality of finished buildings. And in this concern it is of course the major products of extra-regional architectural *teams* that were the agencies that commanded the superior skills and the means by which the exceptional structures were achieved.

Yet, paradoxical as it may seem, it was out of the architectural soil prepared and fostered by the unpretentious native buildings that the great thirteenth-century structures blossomed. As folk-lore and folk-song provide the matrix from which a richer literature and a more inspiring music developed, so these folk-buildings, growing everywhere in response to actual need, created the indispensable environment for the aspiring structures of the Gothic culmination. A study of the minor buildings is valuable from many points of view, but it does not appear to be essential for discovering how the great cathedrals were actually erected. For, the native builders of some obscure parish church achieved clumsily and often inconsistently with makeshift equipment and less than fully informed skill; while the supra-national builders of the exceptional works achieved consistently and designedly with the best equipment and the best skill the times could provide.

As the monasteries of the Romanesque era gradually gave way in architectural importance to the cathedrals of the Gothic era, it would have been in the new centers of creative ferment and activity, the cathedral cities themselves, that this development would have been most energetic. It was there that wealth, resources, and power to command the best in materials and craftsmanship were concentrated; it was there that the pride of rivalry would have acted as a powerful goad. This fierce local pride, along with the actual need for providing greater buildings for accommodating an increasing population in and near these centers, again and again caused the deliberate razing of existing church structures and their replacement by ever larger, more daring, and more up-to-date buildings.[91] Hence the really significant developments, the most progressive innovations,[92] were likely to have occurred in those very centers where the increasing size as well as independence of the populace, the desire to surpass all other previous works, and the technical ability to achieve these daring realizations of a soaring, all-encompassing expression of man's religious aspirations, led to destruction and rebuilding from the ground up. This helps to account for the almost total lack of extant intermediate developments in the Île-de-France region, for example: the very locale in which the new Gothic spirit in architecture seems to have been most keenly pursued, most creatively undertaken. In the light of subsequent achievements, the earlier buildings were recognized as being unworthy of man's finest efforts, as representing something less than his fullest capacities, his supreme potential.

How, then, should the problem be approached of inquiring into the erectional procedures of the Middle Ages? Certainly not, in view of what has just been discussed, by studying and comparing hundreds of individual examples in a chronological sequence of dated monuments, big and little, clumsily or skilfully built. Inasmuch as there is practically no direct evidence in the buildings themselves that would give a clue to the type and extent of the centerings used, and to the practices followed in placing and dismantling it, it would seem to be necessary to proceed deductively. However, deductions can fruitfully be drawn from the buildings themselves, if at all, only by examining the multiple structural problem as specifically as possible in the light of the changes and improvements that came to be adopted. It will therefore be necessary to review the significant steps in the development of medieval vaulting, in order to try to determine what gains were made at each step: what advantages followed from each innovation, what clumsinesses or hesitations were overcome, what practical conveniences were discovered.

In the ensuing review it will be noted that only those significant innovations that constitute a sort of ideal stream of medieval development are considered. Thus the progression from one step to the next, as here presented, is by no means strictly chronological for a given region of France, but is offered as the most logical sequence of development for the overall medieval progression, in retrospect.

In such a review it will be well to keep in mind the major intentions or aims of the builders, chiefly their compelling desire for maximum soaring height and maximum natural light within their churches. But this investigation will be directed primarily towards an assessment of the effect or influence these developments were likely to have had, concurrently, on the requirements and the techniques of centering. For with each new adaptation or innovation in vaulting practices there must then have been, as there is in the case of structural advances today, a corresponding development in the means and the practices of their execution. Perhaps, then, if a careful enough analysis of these vaulting *developments* can be made, some light may be shed upon the *practices* by which they came to be executed.

3

'Not infrequently men have hit upon new methods of construction in endeavoring to meet utilitarian necessities, and these new methods have stimulated new artistic expressions.'

H. W. DESMOND *

THE SIMPLEST TYPE OF TRUE VAULT, AND THE EASIEST TO BUILD, is the semi-cylindrical *barrel vault*. In early medieval times it came to be used in churches in place of the prevalent wooden constructions employed from time immemorial in western, eastern, and Scandinavian Europe.[93] At a time when Christianity was militantly expanding at the expense of the paganism of the northern tribes, and later when the plundering incursions of water-borne Danes sought out the transportable wealth of altar-plate and other church fittings, a small-windowed church of masonry was not subject to incendiarism, and it could be successfully defended by force of arms. A church of stone, too, was more permanent and more monumental than one of wood, and therefore seemed more worthy of being the House of God.

But there were signal disadvantages in the barrel vault system itself, irrespective of how its execution may have varied in different examples, from rude to relatively skilful. The most serious of its disadvantages, in the light of the subsequent developments in medieval vaulting, have to do with the twin visual aims of church builders throughout the entire Middle Ages: maximum height and maximum light. In initiating the practice of covering their churches with a stone vault of the simplest possible shape to construct, the early medieval builders had to put up with the barest minimum of both natural light and height. The series of drawings in 14, 15, and 16 shows why.

First, as there is a downward and outward thrust exerted by the simple semicircular arch (indicated by arrows to right and to left), so there will be a plane of thrust on either side when the vault is thought of as being a semicircular arch projected horizontally in a direction at right angles to its span. In the simple arch,

* 'The Alphabet of Architecture', *The Architectural Record*, 1893, vol. iii, p. 45.

the thrust (represented by these sloping lines of pressure) is grounded, and the disruptive force of the voussoir action is counteracted, by building out the supports at either end of the arch, extending them laterally in the vertical plane of the arch, thus forming buttresses. When this scheme of abutment is projected horizontally, as explained above, it may be seen that what was only a buttress for

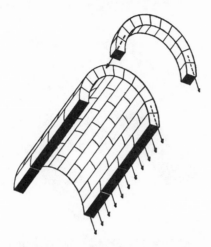

14. *Semicircular Arch and Semicylindrical Vault*

The diagonal thrusts, downward and outward from the crown, are indicated in shorthand fashion in the simple arch. These become 'planes' of thrust in the barrel vault, which may be thought of as a simple arch projected horizontally at right angles to its span.

the simple arch becomes a thick continuous wall for the barrel vault. As the buttress is essential for the stability of the arch, so the thick wall is essential for the stability of the vault: it is dangerous for it to be pierced with large openings for windows.

Actually, the line of pressure in an arch is not a straight line (as indicated in short-hand fashion by the arrows in 14) but is a curve whose direction at any given point is the resultant, in magnitude as well as direction, of the horizontal and vertical pressures at that point. The horizontal pressures are due to the cumulative wedge action of the voussoirs; the vertical pressures are due to the weight of masonry or of any other superimposed loads that bear down from above upon the area in which the lateral thrust of the arch is acting.

The general rule for stability, for the arch ring as well as for the supports on either side, is that the curve of pressure must remain within the middle third (or, at most, the middle half) of the thickness of the structure. Thus if the line of pressure passes too close to the intrados of the arch at its haunch, the arch will crack and burst outward there. Again, if the buttress is of too shallow a projection at the ground level, so that the line of pressure passes close to the outside face at this point, the buttress is in danger of overturning by failing to prevent the arch

15. *Abutment of Simple Barrel Vault*

The continuous planes of thrust exercised by the
barrel vault are usually met and grounded by continuous walls of considerable thickness, in order
to prevent the arch action from pushing the
supports apart.

from spreading at the springing. This explains why buttresses are frequently offset on their outer faces: the downward-curving line of pressure is thus maintained within the middle third of its projection at all levels without the undue amount of masonry that would be involved if the total horizontal area needed at the base were carried all the way up without any diminishment.

When the situation explained above for the simple arch is applied to the barrel vault, it is apparent why neither maximum height nor maximum light could be secured with the adoption of this system of vaulting. As the height of the vault above the ground was increased, the thickness of the supporting walls had to be increased proportionately. Yet obviously it would have been absurd to wind up with walls on either side that were as thick at the ground level as the width of the space the vault spanned. Furthermore, but little of these walls could safely be sacrificed for window openings, which thus tended to become mere tunnel-like

44

slits in the lower portions of the walls and quite ineffective as a means of illuminating the interior. From a structural standpoint, only the ends of a barrel vault can be used for ample window openings. But even here, the early medieval builders did not take full advantage of the possibility of large window openings, being fearful of the consequences of leaving large voids *anywhere* in their un-

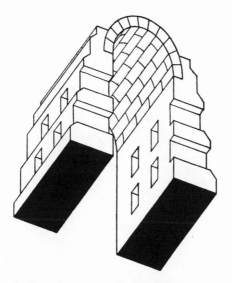

16. *Diagrammatic Scheme of High Barrel Vault's Abutment*

The higher the vault is raised above the ground, the more the thickness of its supporting walls must be increased, in order for them to take care of the horizontal component of the vault's lateral thrusts. The required thickness of these walls at the ground level does not have to be carried all the way up to the spring of the vault, but the line of pressure must remain within the middle third (or at least the middle half) of this thickness at all levels in order to assure stability.

accustomed medium of masonry construction. Actually, with the strong Western preference for long naves, the possibility of leaving barrel vaults open-ended for illumination by natural means would scarcely have helped the lighting problem except near the two ends of the church; and from an early period liturgical requirements came to dominate the structural arrangements at the altar end of the church, necessitating other schemes of providing natural light there.

What was probably the most difficult feature to reconcile, and hence the most stringent influence upon the vaulting practices throughout the Middle Ages, was the adoption of the three-aisled plan as the standard for all but the very smallest churches, and a few of the very largest, which were five-aisled. With a single-aisled church it was not too difficult, structurally, to vault the central space between the two side walls, and to abut or thicken these walls in order to furnish

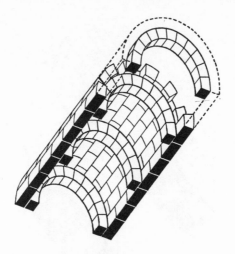

17. Diagram of Small Banded Barrel Vault in Cut Stone

The spaced arches of the banded barrel vault were built first, then the continuous vault proper, one bay at a time. The transverse bands or arches acted as cover-joints that permitted this constructional procedure of building the vault in successive bay-length increments. They also stiffened the vault effectively; and this made it possible to build vault shells that were much thinner than those of simple barrel vaults of similar span. Moreover, this marked reduction in thickness resulted in much lighter vaults that had less powerful thrusts, and hence required less massive abutments.

stable supports for the vault. To be sure, the lighting problem was inadequately handled, at first; but in the disordered state of the times this lack of large window openings was not a serious matter in the early medieval period because of the need to defend the church against hostile attack. However, a three-aisled church necessitated opening up the interior so that there might be no more than a minimum of obstruction between nave and side aisles. The lower part of the nave walls thus became the nave arcades, of fairly wide-spaced piers or columns separating the arch openings; and consequently the provision for taking care of the nave vault's thrust had to be transferred to the outside walls of the side aisles. Thus the means for stabilizing and grounding the thrusts that operated against the nave walls had to be removed from these walls by the width of the side aisles. Because of the abutment problem, moreover, the three-aisled division of the ground plan immeasurably complicated the lighting problem as well. For the height at which the nave vault needed abutment precluded the insertion of windows by which the nave could receive adequate light directly, instead of by borrowing it across the side aisles.

The satisfactory solution to these many difficulties was beyond the capacity of the early medieval builders to solve all at once. For a long time it was the stability of the nave vault that chiefly preoccupied the builders, once they were bold enough to undertake the construction of these central vaults in the first place. In this search for stability, one of the most typical means of abutment for the continuous thrust of the nave's barrel vault came to be provided by continuous half-barrel vaults ramping from the thick outer walls of the side aisles, up to about the spring-line of the nave vault. In this situation, light for the nave could only be borrowed across the side aisles from windows in their outer walls.

Erectionally, the barrel vault was built on a centering that had to stretch continuously from one end of the church to the other.

From this unimpressive beginning, the first forward step in the long development of medieval vaulting was dictated primarily, not by an attempt to achieve better natural illumination within the body of the church, but by the desire to reduce and rationalize the centering requirements. This first step was the adoption of the *banded barrel vault* (17), about whose centering procedures some mention has already been made.

The banded barrel vault was a distinct forward step in four respects. One (the most important, probably, at the time) was the *erectional advantage*, as a technique by which the vault could be constructed one bay at a time. The second contribution of the banded barrel vault was that the bands or underlying arches *stiffened the vault* at intervals, thereby helping to maintain its semicylindrical shape throughout.[94] The other two contributions were aesthetic, as follows. First, by dividing up and compartmentalizing what had previously been a smooth semicylindrical ceiling of stone, the salient transverse arches *gave more scale* to the stone vault, and brought it into an appearance of closer size relationship with the subdivided lower portions of the interior. Second, the adoption of the transverse arches was the first step in the direction of a structural design that was organic.

47

If what is meant by *organic design* is an organization of the various elements of a structure wherein each part is related in size, position, and function to every other part as well as to the whole, then this innovation of the banded barrel vault

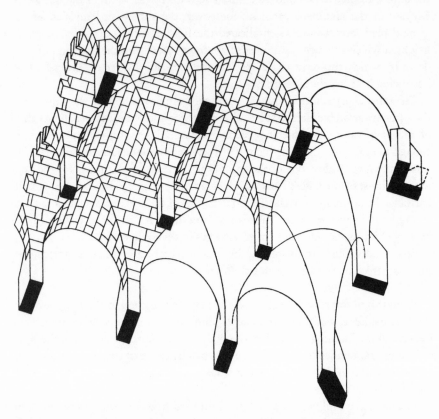

18. *Continuous Bays of Simple Groin Vaulting in Cut Stone*

Here the space-wise advantage of the groin vault is evident: compared to the necessarily continuous supports of the barrel vault, the groin vault's system of discontinuous or isolated supports opens up the area to be covered to the full width of each of its cylindrical vault components, in the direction of both co-ordinate axes. Salient abutment is required at bay-length intervals only along the outer boundaries of the vaulted area.

was the first essay in a progressive development that was carried on deliberately and continuously throughout the entire medieval period. Whereas before, in the simple barrel vault, there was no feature of the stone ceiling that related it to what went on below, design-wise, now this was no longer true in the case of the banded barrel vault. With its adoption, the transverse arches divided the vault into bays corresponding to the bays defined by the arches and piers of the nave arcade down below. These piers, in turn, came to be of compound form instead of a single square or cylindrical shape, with an engaged member carrying up to the spring of the transverse arch. Thus the bands—the transverse arches—of the

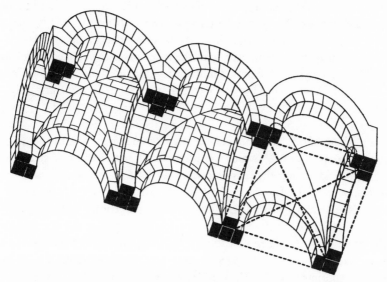

19. *Three Bays of Simple Groin Vaulting in Cut Stone, with Boundary Arches*

Whereas the entire vaulted area shown in 18 would need to be constructed all at once, here each bay could be built independently, thanks to the transverse arches underlying the vault proper from pier to pier. These transverse arches are similar in function to those shown in the banded barrel vault of 17.

banded barrel vault, in receiving visual support from one of the pier members, were related to what went on in the design lower down; and, in addition to this, the two sides of the nave were visually connected by the continuity of their engaged columns with the arch above.

It is worth reiterating, however, that the primary motivation for these transverse arches of the banded barrel vault was to permit the vault to be erected in successive bays one after another, instead of all at once from end to end of the church. Here was a true case of where the arches, built independently before the vault proper was constructed,[95] acted as cover joints, permitting the vault to be built in short sections as funds or the weather allowed. Thus the erection of the vault could be stopped or postponed indefinitely, as occasion demanded, at any one of these junctures. As the work on the vault progressed from bay to bay, preceding bays became freed of all falsework encumbrance, so that the more delicate work of carving or decorating or furnishing the nave could proceed, and the freed portion of the church could be put to use for religious services as soon as possible.

Particularly in the quantity of materials required for the erectional falsework, as well as in the labour of setting it up and subsequently dismantling it, there was a very considerable saving in the case of the banded barrel vault compared to the continuous barrel vault. Moreover, with the adoption of the banded barrel vault, the principle was established of building one bay at a time; and this procedure continued to be followed, with but few exceptions, throughout the entire medieval period.

The next significant step in medieval vault development was the adoption of the *simple groin vault* (18), which was usually built with transverse arches corresponding to and having the same functions as those of the banded barrel vault (19). The two major advantages of the simple groin vault were its emancipation from the barrel vault's continuous planes of thrust and, consequently, its provision for direct lighting of the nave.

The groin vault in its simplest form results from the right-angle intersection of two semicylindrical barrel vaults of equal span. In series, units of these groin vaults gave continuity of span throughout the length of the nave; but at the same time their cross vaults, up to the level of their horizontal crowns, freed the side walls for window openings. Each cross vault defined a bay of the vaulting, which was supported at the four corners and therefore needed abutment only at these intermediate points. The construction of these intermediate points, the piers, was thick and heavy, and yet the builders almost never dared to leave as window opening the full area of the semicircular lunettes at the cross-vault ends. Because of the thick masses of supporting masonry, however, their stability was sufficient to allow the side-aisle vaulting, which partially braced them, to be set some distance below the level of the nave vault's spring, so that one or more windows could be pierced through the lunettes above the side-aisle roof where its slope abutted the nave wall.

Under this wooden lean-to roof, nevertheless, it was early recognized that there had to be some bracing of transverse masonry above the level of the side-aisle vaulting. Sometimes this was accomplished by a diaphragm wall from pier to outer wall, supported by the transverse arch of the side aisle, and filling the whole space from the latter to the underside of the roof.[96] In this scheme, the side-aisle roof was supported on horizontal beams (the purlins) spanning longitudinally from diaphragm wall to diaphragm wall; and hence the timbers of the roof neither leaned against the nave wall nor transmitted to the outside wall any of its tendency to tilt outward due to the vault pressure. Later, other schemes used a heavy half-arch of abutment in place of the diaphragm wall, which allowed passage from one bay to the next at the triforium level, above the side-aisle vaulting. As long as these arches were located under the shelter of the side-aisle roof, they had to be set too low to permit adequate-sized window openings above this roof, but at least the simple groin vault system they helped to stabilize did permit some direct illumination of the nave.

Although countless examples of this type of vaulting exist in side aisles, it was actually only in Burgundy that large naves were sometimes vaulted with simple groin vaults.[97] In retrospect, however, this scheme was unquestionably the next important step in medieval vaulting after the banded barrel vault, for the reasons cited above.

Most writers, if they mention the matter at all, seem to feel that no great difficulties were encountered in the erection of groin vaults over side aisles, partly because of the relatively low height of these vaults but mainly because of their modest spans. But speculation on the nature of the falsework for the high nave vault, which was usually at least twice as wide as the side-aisle vaulting, has been much more limited. Choisy seems to assume that the centering was of planking supported on timber frames, although he has very little to say on the subject.[98] Bond is probably the most explicit of the English writers in this respect. In connexion with his long chapter on medieval vaulting,[99] he has reproduced many details and line illustrations, notably those of Viollet-le-Duc, from other publications. Among his illustrations are a number of sketches copied from Ungewitter's *Lehrbuch*,[100] one of which shows a planking arrangement for the centering of continuous bays of groin vaulting. Bond's description of the procedure illustrated is erroneous, for it is a scheme for a series of groin vaults *without* transverse arches, not with them as he says. However, it is difficult to see how this scheme could be used even if there were provision for lowering the staging slightly to disengage the planking from a finished portion of the vault. For in the longitudinal vault there is no cover-joint or reveal at any point where the work could stop while decentering and relocation of the planking might take place.

Even though the shortcomings of this scheme of Ungewitter are incompletely accounted for, it is possible that certain features of it, such as some sort of separate planking for the transverse portions of the vaulting, may have been made use of in one fashion or another.[101] But in any case, where transverse arches allowed bays of groin vaulting to be built one at a time, the situation required more rationaliza-

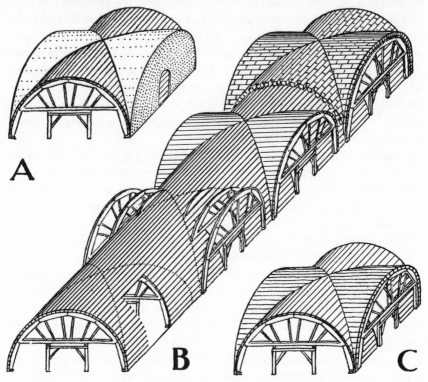

A

B

C

20. *Systems of Groin Vault Centering where the Formwork is Continuous for the Longitudinal Vault*

A shows mounded earth formwork for the transverse vault compartments. The upper part of the nave walls, though not shown here, would have been in place by the time this falsework had been erected, necessitating a boarded-up opening through which the earth could subsequently be removed, previous to dismantling the longitudinal formwork. B indicates a sequence of four steps in a system that uses centering frames in the cross vaults. The nearest bay shows the continuous planking of the longitudinal vault voided between two of its successive frames in order to get at the transverse vault's frames when they are to be dismantled and removed. The second bay shows these frames in position, the third with their planking installed, and the fourth with the masonry vault laid over the plank formwork. C is similar to the system in B except that there are no intermediate frames for the cross vault: the heavy lagging spans from the outside lateral frames to a bearing on the longitudinal planking without intervening supports.

tion and subdivision of the falsework than could be accomplished via the rolling formwork we have envisaged with respect to the banded barrel vault. For now the cross-vault formwork, as pictured in Ungewitter's scheme, would have got in the way and utterly prevented a bay of groin vault formwork from being moved from its first location to an adjacent bay. Obviously, in order to be shifted, a bay of groin vault falsework would have had to consist, not of one massive ensemble, but of many separate portions or members, if it were to be re-used in successive bays. This necessity would suggest either a multiplicity of secondary frames in the transverse vault cells, or separate heavy lagging units that could span across the space between the continuous formwork of the longitudinal vault and the outer or end frames of the cross vault (20).

It would seem that, at best, very massive timber-work would have been involved for vaults of the size needed to span the naves of major churches; and in this respect, as we will see, the employment of ribs under the groins doubtless reduced to a quite considerable extent the amount (and the weight) of the timber-work required in building high vaults of wide span.

Architectural historians seem generally to treat the falsework, and particularly the actual formwork of vaulting—if they discuss or illustrate it at all—as though it were a finished and permanent structure, like a roof. They seem to forget that it is highly temporary, and that it can be freed from the vaulting proper, dismantled, or shifted to a new position *only from below* the finished vault. This is a stringent condition, for it exercises an absolute control over every aspect of the design and erection of vault centerings.

Too often, for example, writers have thought in terms of centerings made up of timber frames that spanned all the way across the nave from one vault impost to the other in a single rigid unit.[102] These would have been relatively heavy, cumbersome, and hard to place; and from a practical standpoint they could not have been eased directly from one bay to the next, past the narrower point at which a transverse arch momentarily reduced the nave span. It would certainly have been much more convenient, and it was unquestionably a practical necessity, for the timber frames to have been built in two or three units, as diagrammed in 21.

We have already seen how the Romans reduced the length and size of their simple but huge falsework frames in the Pont du Gard. Undoubtedly they did this not so much merely to limit the amount of material used but to reduce the weight and cumbersomeness, so that the difficulties of handling the massive timber structures of the falsework would be lessened. These temporary timber structures would have been hard enough to manœuvre into place, to shift laterally, and to remove without dislocation or damage to the masonry structure, as it was. And yet it is obvious that, in constructing the enormous Pont du Gard, the

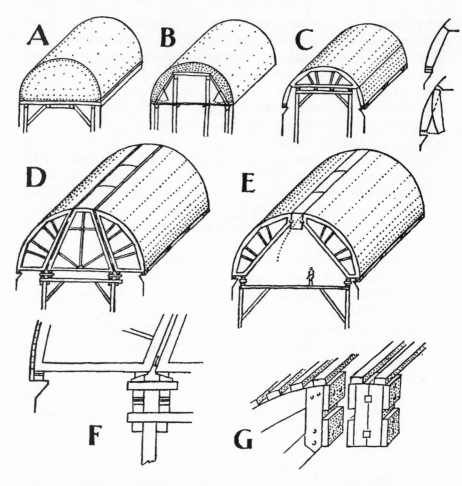

21. Possible Types of Barrel Vault Formwork and Centering

A shows a strong platform at the level of the vault spring, on which earth has been mounded up in a semicylindrical shape. B shows another earth-mounded form, but involving much less material (and therefore less weight). Ports are shown through the sloping boarding, beneath, from which the earth may be removed in order to de-center the finished vault. C is a formwork of continuous boarding in three parts: the details to the right show how the lower portions, up to the angle of friction, may be removed when their own wedges are retracted, thus allowing the main center portion to clear the projecting impost mouldings when it, in turn, is taken down. (Note

that this kind of scheme would be feasible in the case of early half-barrel vaults above side aisles.) D is a boarded formwork in three major sections, in which the middle section is decentered first. E uses much less wood (and is therefore cheaper and lighter than D). It employs a pair of quadrant forms with a spacer-block at the crown. This spacer-block, secured against vertical slipping by square pins driven in from the sides (detail at G), is first to be removed during the decentering operation, allowing the two frames (temporarily held in place with a few light shores) to pivot downward and inward, one at a time, as their wedges are retracted.

Romans had much more powerful engines and a much larger complement of workmen than even the most well-equipped of the medieval builders could ever have counted on. So the latter must surely have resorted to every technique of simplification they could possibly devise for rationalizing and limiting their erectional difficulties, chiefly those that were the result of heavy and cumbersome assemblages of centering.

Much of this simplification could have resulted from the use of units of centering that were less in size than those that could span the entire width of the nave, especially if these units were placed and shifted about from a high-level platform. For, working on such a staging, no outside cranes would have been needed to handle the units of centering: they could have been erected and manœuvred by jacks and by windlasses stationed on the platform itself. And with these partial arcs of centerings, instead of full-span ones, there would have been room for the workmen to handle the various portions of the falsework structure conveniently and directly at the exact locations where they were needed.[103]

As far as the masonry of the vault itself is concerned, the principal problem encountered was that of the difficulty of laying out the shapes of the groin voussoirs.[104] The dihedral angle formed along the groin by the beds of the intersecting courses of the two vaults is different at each level: it diminishes from an angle of 180° at the spring-line to 90° at the crown (wherever a joint instead of a keystone occurs there). Because a given groin voussoir must accommodate itself to the conditions of both vaults, its outline, seen from above, is V-shaped; but the upper and lower surfaces are non-parallel, on the one hand, and broken rather than being in the same plane, on the other. In addition, every groin voussoir has two intradoses, one for each of the intersecting vault surfaces, and these intradoses of course are curving. Each groin voussoir is therefore a ten-sided stone, no two surfaces of which are parallel, and four of which are curving. None of these curves or angles or surfaces is arbitrary, but must fit and agree with the requirements of the stone's position in the vault, which makes it different in shape from all its fellows from spring to crown.

If this abbreviated description appears to be complicated and cryptic, it at least indicates in some measure the difficulty of making a comprehensive drawing of a groin voussoir, and, much more, of hewing one out, on the part of the medieval stone mason[105] (22).

The next significant step in medieval vault development involved an innovation that had the most far-reaching consequences. This was the *domed groin*

55

vault. An account of how it came about will help to explain its importance to all subsequent vaulting developments.

When two semicylindrical barrel vaults of equal span intersect at right angles, the resulting bay of simple groin vaulting is a square, in plan, whose diagonals

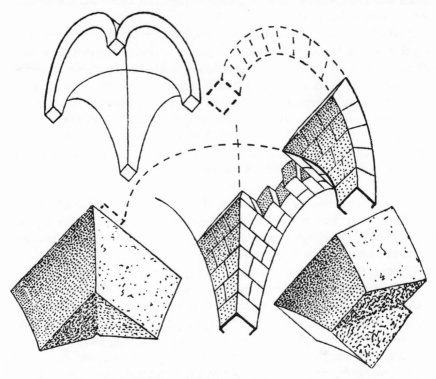

22. *The Shape of the Groin Voussoirs in a Simple Groin Vault over a Square Bay*

It is evident from this series of drawings that, although the ordinary voussoirs may be identical throughout a groin vault, each of those along the groin from spring to spring is unique in its shape and different from all others. The two blocks that are individually detailed at larger size occur in the middle drawing at the level of the fourth course up from the springing. In the interest of clarity, all the blocks here are shown as being accurately cut. In most medieval vaulting this was not the practice; instead, the voussoirs were roughly hewn to shape and their irregularity of surface compensated for by thick mortar joints.

are the groins (the solid angles of intersection). These groins are the weakest areas of the groin vault on three accounts: (1) being diagonals, they constitute the longest spans of the bay; (2) being the lines of intersection of the two vaults, they receive vault pressures from two directions; and (3) being formed by the horizontal projection of points around the semicircle of the boundary arcs, their contour in a vertical plane is semi-elliptical, not semicircular.[106]

In the attempt to strengthen the critical area along the groins, nothing could be done, directly, about (1) or (2). It was only the third consideration—the contour of the groin arc—that could be changed or corrected in any way. This the builders did by arbitrarily changing the shape of the groin arc from that of a semi-ellipse, with its longer axis horizontal, to a semicircle.[107] The semi-elliptical arch

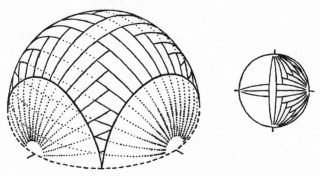

23. *Consequences of the Semicircular Diagonal Arc in the Domed Groin Vault*

In a square bay, if the diagonals as well as the four boundary arches are semicircular, the resulting vault surface will normally be spherical. This drawing shows what the shape of the stone courses would be—going from narrow to wide to narrow —were they to be determined by great-circle arcs radiating from the longitudinal and transverse axes of the bay. Although the intersecting courses meet each other above the diagonals of the bay, they do so in the 'plane' of the spherical surface, and hence produce no groin saliency. This results in no difficult stereotomy above the diagonals, as inevitably occurred in the simple groin vault because its voussoirs along the groin partook of the contour of *both* vault surfaces. In the domed groin vault illustrated here, however, each voussoir is a unit in the *single* spherical surface even where the intersection of courses occurs. But because of the variation in width of the courses, this scheme of stone coursing was seldom if ever used in actual vaulting practice.

is weaker than the semicircular because it is flatter; and it has the further disadvantage of producing a stronger thrust, requiring deeper abutments and thereby limiting the height at which it is safe, or at least economical, to raise it. Hence the deliberate adoption of the semicircular groins strengthened the vault in the areas of its greatest vulnerability.

Because of the use of semicircles along the groins as well as at the lateral boundaries of the bay, the two crowns of the domed groin vault over a square bay are arcs of great circles, whose diameter is the diagonal of the square. Geometrically, the entire surface of the vault becomes that of a sphere, and hence the groins, as solid saliences, disappear altogether: it is only the serrated stone-jointing of the web courses' intersections that recall the true groins of the previous non-domed form of groin vault. Thus the bed joints of *all* the courses, as they depart from a semicircular boundary arc at each side of the bay, are arcs of great circles that lie in planes revolved through one or the other of the horizontal co-ordinate axes of the square bay (23).

By eliminating salient groins, the uniform geometry of this spherical shape resulted in much more than making the contour above each diagonal of the square less weak. For one thing, the now non-existent groins were no weaker than any other portion of the vaulting. For another, the stone-jointing above the diagonals of the square was no different from the stone-jointing elsewhere throughout the vault: there was no problem of complicated stereotomy such as that encountered along the groin of a simple groin vault. The intersecting courses now met each other in the same spherical 'plane', and thus all the courses intersected in the same fashion. Finally, with web courses that sliced the dome up in this pattern, the arch stresses tended to press against the boundary arches quite as much as against the 'groins' (that is, those portions of the vault that lay above the diagonals of the square bay). These boundary arches therefore had to be thick and wide in order to absorb and ground their share of the thrusts, which thus were brought down to the piers indirectly instead of via the groins, as in the true groin vault.

However, some modifications with respect to the strict theoretical conformation of the vault shape either came about naturally or came to be imposed, in actual practice. For, instead of geometrically arrived at surfaces and edges, it was solid masonry of far from negligible thickness that was the real concern of the builders. For instance, in most domed groin vaults, apparently, the builders did not adopt great-circle lines in radial planes as the bed joints of the courses, according to which these courses had to taper considerably, from wide near the crown to very narrow slices at the outer boundary arches. (Incidentally, this would have involved tilted centering frames of variable slope.) From a practical standpoint the builders seem to have preferred to make the courses more nearly the same width throughout, which could be accomplished, geometrically, by semicircular (or less than semicircular) cradles which represented vertical slices, at intervals, parallel to the co-ordinate axes of the bay. Although this procedure, too, maintained the spherical surface, it could, by varying the stone-jointing and direction of the courses in the lower portions of the vault, result in some slight saliency at the groins. (To be sure, this saliency was frequently rather negligible, with none at all towards the crown of the vault; and it is thus shown as dying out in some of the pictorial drawings of this vault form.)

However, the chief and most frequent way by which, in actual practice, a definite saliency was achieved along the groin was by fashioning the cradles of the formwork in arcs of less radius than those produced geometrically by slicing up the spherical surface. In other words, the four units of the vaulted bay, each triangular in plan, were made more or less strongly cambered. Thus the axial section along the crown, both through the longitudinal and through the transverse vault, was not a single unbroken arc spanning between opposite boundaries of the bay, but two arcs that met in a downward point above the middle of the square bay. (It is thus shown in many sectional drawings, not only of domed groin vaults but of ribbed vaults as well, far into Gothic times.) This common practice, of strongly cambering not only the crown but the stone courses generally, automatically produced salient groins throughout, and thereby created a vault that was definitely not spherical, either with respect to the contour of its surfaces or to the stone-coursing of its structure.[108]

Although small units of this vaulting erected at relatively low levels, such as those over bays of the side aisles and in the ground story of towers, were doubtless formed on mounded earth, it is very unlikely that the high, wide-spanning bays of the nave vaulting would have been given their contour by earth mounded up in this fashion. We will have much to say, subsequently, about planking and lagging formwork in the case of Gothic ribbed vaults. Here it will suffice to indicate one or two methods that could have been followed for supporting and giving the desired shape to the masonry of a large bay of domed groin vaulting.

Whereas the timber frames or cradles of the *barrel* vault were set *across* the vault, at right angles to its axis and with longitudinal planking, the secondary frames or cradles for the *domed groin* vault were probably set *parallel* to its co-ordinates. In the case of geometrically arrived at shapes, the two crown cradles would of course have been shaped to great-circle arcs. All the other shorter cradles would then have been laid out as less than great-circle arcs, set vertically rather than radially, and resting at either end on powerful timber frames of semicircular shape above the sides and the diagonals of the square bay. Next, the parallel spaces between these separate cradles would doubtless have been spanned by short cleats, to form a continuous but open-work surface on which the stones of the vault could be laid. Since the soffit of the vault was destined to be a spherical surface, continuous boarding (as in the case of the barrel vault) would not have been practicable, or probably even possible. Bridging across each truncated gore—the superficial area defined by adjacent parallel cradles—individually by means of a series of short-length cleats, however, would sufficiently approximate the spherical surface that was aimed at; and this continuity of the formwork's slotted surface would even have permitted non-continuous courses, split or divided courses, or herring-bone patterns of the stonework of the web (24).

Principal centering frames were required not only at the sides of the bay but along the diagonals as well, and these would all have had to be shaped as arcs of circles. Consequently, the cradles for the formwork proper could have spanned

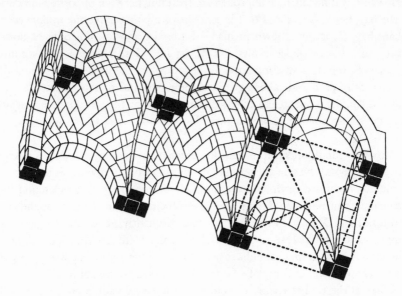

24. *Herringbone Pattern of Web Coursing in the Domed Groin Vault*

The strongly bowed-up crowns of the domed groin vault sometimes led the builders to adopt types of web coursing other than that in which the courses went through from one boundary arch to its mate opposite. Here one of these alternative schemes is shown, in cut stone, by means of which the excessive widening and narrowing of such through

courses was circumvented. In order to achieve salient groins, the surfaces of the vault (which are spherical and therefore groin-less in examples that are laid out in strict geometrical fashion) are here shown constructed with strongly concave courses in each vault cell, which was often the way they were built.

between these supporting frames in a direction either (1) parallel to the co-ordinates, i.e. from side frame to diagonal (25 A), or (2) at right angles to the co-ordinates, i.e. from diagonal to diagonal (25 B). The former scheme would have involved shorter cradles of less rise in their bowed tops than the latter, and would seem to have been the easier, more direct and practical method to be followed in actual construction.

In the light of subsequent vault developments, the first of these methods appears to have been unquestionably the scheme that was generally adopted, at least in most French examples. For out of this scheme grew the possibility of

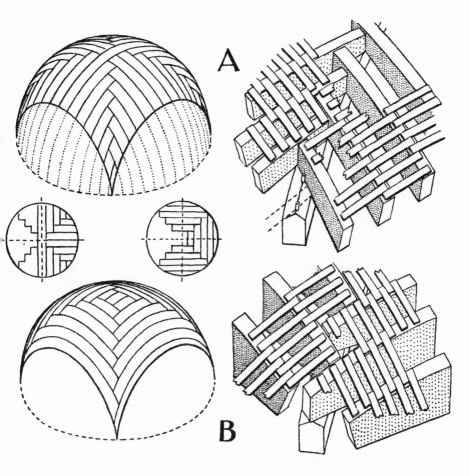

A

B

25. *Stone Coursing and its Formwork in the Domed Groin Vault*

Assuming that the builders maintained, throughout, the strictly spherical surface of the vault produced by making the diagonal arcs semicircular, the drawings to the left of A and B indicate actual schemes of stone coursing in a square bay bounded by semicircular arches. Of these schemes, that at A was the more common, at least in western Europe. It was the more natural, in view of the vaulting practices that preceded the domed groin vault, and it involved much simpler falsework. For here, with centering frames at each side of the bay as well as along its diagonals, lagging units that were not excessively bowed could be fashioned to support the stone courses, instead of the almost semicircular ones that would have been needed close to the sides of the bay, in scheme B. In addition, the lagging units in scheme A would have

found a less complicated and more stable seating upon the diagonal centering frames than in B. As for the cleating (if, indeed, cleats were used at all), they could have been set across each pair of lagging units in the staggered arrangement illustrated by the large-scale details to the right of A and B, and secured by small nails. Cleats would seem to have been essential, however, only perhaps in the case of a herringbone pattern of web stones (as indicated in 24). In any case, the accurate spacing, alignment, and prevention against displacement of the lagging units along the diagonal centering frames may well have been provided for in advance by inserting projecting dowels in the extrados of the centering frames, as shown in A.

61

introducing boundary arches that were other than semicircular ones. Thus, when pointed arches came almost immediately to be employed in order to achieve more nearly level crowns, this direction of the cradles made possible the construction of pointed vaults that intersected in semicircular groins. With cradles set at right angles to the co-ordinate axes of the bay, the geometry of their varying contours would have been complicated and quite beyond the capacity of the designer-builder to figure out, in terms of cradles, by any of the methods he had utilized up to that time. But with cradles set parallel to the bay's axes, the variable conformation of the vault surfaces came about naturally and inevitably, without any intricate geometrical computations.

In order to dismantle the formwork sufficiently for it to be moved and set up in an adjacent bay, the cleats would have had to be knocked free of their supporting cradles. With the formwork lowered a few inches at the time of decentering, the cleats (either nailed or pegged to the cradles) could be hammered loose from below, freeing the cradles from each other so that they could be dislodged and taken down individually, to be re-erected subsequently in an adjacent bay. Without such a comprehensive procedure of dismantling, there would have been no way of shifting the centering of a bay of domed groin vaulting for re-use in a sequence of locations along the nave.

In the case of smaller units of this vaulting system, many of the difficulties were appreciably lessened by the nature of the formwork that could be employed. Arched centers, usually semicircular, were placed not only at the four boundaries but also above the diagonals of the square bay; and, with these as guides, earth was mounded up in a series of shallow wood-supported embankments to produce the desired shape of the vault.[109] Thus the earth provided a continuous and easily fashioned mound which circumvented the need for any of the complicated laying out, shaping, or cutting on the part of skilled carpenters that a formwork of continuous boarding would have required.

Inevitably, the bowing up of the stone courses that resulted from the form of the domed groin vault created a widening and narrowing of these courses. Consequently, the courses had to accommodate themselves to this condition either by becoming wider and narrower themselves, or by breaking into two courses in the wider portions, or by being set more or less irregularly in mortar joints of variable thickness.

Two of the chief disadvantages of the domed groin vault were its undesirable effect in series, and its need for thick and powerful abutment. The latter has been noted in connexion with the oblique downward pressure impinging against the sides of the bay's boundary arches as a consequence of the domical or near-domical form of the vault. With respect to the former point, the bowed-up crowns of the vault bays created an unpleasantly jumpy effect in their longitudinal progression along the nave; and this condition was undesirable, further, because the center of the vault, being higher than its windowed transverse sides, emphasized the busy discontinuity of effect by the unevenness of the light that shone from these lateral windows onto the bowed surfaces of the vault.

As for the outstanding contribution made by the domed groin vault, it was this: that *the conformation of the vault surfaces was now determined by the shape of the boundary arcs, including the diagonals.*

Heretofore, the shape of practically every vault had been determined by the horizontal projection of points along the curve of a given arch, whether semi-circular, elliptical, or pointed. Roman barrel vaults, Roman groin vaults, and even Roman domes had been so shaped. The early Romanesque vaults—semi-cylindrical or pointed barrel vaults, the ramping half-barrel vaults above side aisles, cloister vaults under towers, and of course the simple groin vaults of count-less side aisles—had all taken their shape from the projection of some generating arch. The adoption of the domed groin vault, however, released the centuries-long stranglehold of this method of arriving at the shape of vaults.

In its purest geometrical form, to be sure, the domed groin vault was not as great a break with the previous schemes of projected points as would at first appear. But by modifying the strict geometrical shape in the interest of practical expediency along the lines indicated above, the way was opened to freedom of experimentation and innovation in the development of unprecedented vault forms. For the builders could not help but have learned, through practical ex-perience with this domed groin system, that different shapes could be given to the side and the diagonal arches, and that within the boundaries they provided, the curvature of the vault web could be modified to a significant extent.

Hence, this innovation was an essential prerequisite to the ensuing progress of vault development in the Middle Ages. In fact, this emancipation from the arch-generated projection of vault shapes was probably the most influential factor in forcing the invention of the ribbed vault, upon whose universal adoption the Gothic structural system was based.

It has been stated above that the accurate shaping of the groin voussoirs was a very difficult job for the stone-cutter, requiring exceptional skill and experience, since the science of stereotomy here was empirical rather than based upon geo-metrically projected drawings. Yet, as we have seen, the lines of the groins were the most critical areas in the whole vault, and it was therefore essential that their workmanship should be first class. Hence, in order to assure strength along the groins, and at the same time to circumvent the difficulties of stereotomy in the groin voussoirs, the Romanesque builders eventually resorted to the practice of starting their construction of bays of intersecting vaulting by first erecting masonry arches at the groins. The fact that these were at first embedded, either completely or to a variable extent, within the rubble masonry of the vault shell, indicates that in the beginning the builders were intent on merely *correcting* the short-comings and constructional difficulties of the system: the portions of the vault proper merely fitted against or partially surrounded the solid armature provided by the groin arches; and the stone-cutting where the vault panels met these arches was less complicated than it had been before these arches came to be employed. Hence the heavy, wide groin arches of early examples, whose soffits are those of their diagonality, conforming to neither of the vault surfaces whose intersection they marked.[110]

However, it was soon recognized that both economy and greater ease of con-struction could be achieved by building the groin arches, not as a more or less integral part of the vault, but as independent ribs established below the surface of the subsequently erected vault proper. It was usual in the earlier ribbed vaults, once this system was well established, for the entire cross-sectional area of the ribs to lie below the surface of the vault. Where this was the case, the meeting edges of adjacent vault panels could be cut without much skill or care, their somewhat irregular joint along the groin being filled out with mortar. For the underlying rib acted as a cover-joint, permanently hiding the irregularity from view. The panels of the vaulting abutted each other above the backs of the ribs; and by the time the mortar had thoroughly set, not only along the groin but throughout the masonry, the vault became practically monolithic.

This cohesion in the vault webs has been noted by various writers in many kinds of vaulted structures throughout the centuries,[111] but with some uncertainty and confusion, so that extravagant claims have been made for it (e.g. that there is no thrust at all in the dome of the Roman Pantheon on account of the homogeneity of its concrete mass).[112] Much of the misunderstanding stems from the fact that there are really two different kinds of situation involved in the matter of vault cohesion. The one which many architectural historians have noted is that in which thick masses of rubble concrete, of small span in relation to their thickness, and in many cases overlain with additional concrete in order to form a floor above the vault, come to act as solid masses through sheer bulk. Vaults of this sort, once their mortar or concrete has had time to become thoroughly consolidated, are some-what analogous to a natural cave, in which the cohesion of the rock mass above the void acts integrally with the immovable massiveness of the rock arching up from either side.

Obviously, since there is no voussoir action in operation, stability depends on the complete rigidity of the whole and the necessity for it to act throughout as a single unit. This condition is seldom encountered in actual buildings, where parts of the structure are pierced and therefore weakened by openings for doors or windows, where settlements in the foundations are apt to occur unevenly, where temperature variations may produce sufficient expansion and contraction in dif-ferent parts of the mass to cause serious cracks to develop, and where, over the years, there may be dislocations due to earthquakes, &c. Sheer inert mass cannot be counted on in a climate subject to frost and the disintegration caused by the freezing of infiltrating water. Where this kind of construction has been noted in medieval work, it has almost invariably been in early vaults of very thick section, constructed either in crypts below ground (where the ground itself acted as abut-ment both during and after construction) or in the lower stages of towers where the superincumbent masonry provided more than adequate stability.[113]

Very different is the case of cohesion in a thin-shelled vault. Here it is the curva-ture, rather than the thickness, that accounts for the rigidity. Actually, more than minimum thickness is a detriment rather than an assurance of any additional margin of safety in thin-shelled constructions. It is this situation that has been little understood by the architectural historians; indeed, until recently the en-gineers themselves have been little concerned with the structural possibilities of, and the strength inherent in, thin shells whose curvature is the source of their stiffness.[114] Consequently, nothing has so far been written regarding the applica-tion of the thin-shell theory to the webs of Gothic ribbed vault construction. What has been written on the Gothic structural system in the past two decades or so ignores this modern knowledge and continues to speculate on the nature and characteristics of Gothic vaulting as though its action were solely and exclusively a voussoir action throughout.[115] Viewed from the standpoint of curving shells, however, the crease at the groin where the panels abut each other above the backs of the ribs is seen to have provided very powerful stiffening—like the folds of accordian-pleated paper—which was by no means dependent upon additional support from the ribs.

Under these circumstances the entire vault was somewhat like a stiff crust with creases at the groins and the crowns, in which the curvature of the surfaces accounted for the web's rigidity and stability of shape. Whether intentional or not, the camber of the vault surfaces in combination with their normal, primary curvature created a remarkable degree of rigidity throughout the vault by reason of the double curvature alone.

This system is worth noting and investigating, for it is only on the basis of its structural contribution, particularly in the remarkably accomplished vaults of some of the great thirteenth-century cathedrals, that certain vault conditions and phenomena of stability under injury can be explained or accounted for.

One of the very early applications of this system was that used by the Romans as one of the steps in the erection of their concrete vaults. The construction of a typical Roman barrel vault of wide span began with the erection of transverse frames of heavy timber-work. The distance that these were set apart was such that the thick planking or lagging they carried (for forming the vault) would not sag appreciably from the weight of a few workmen and the materials that they themselves could carry. The planks were not tongue-and-grooved as is the wooden formwork of many concrete structures today, for the Romans had no power machinery for producing matched lumber. Actually, the planks were set fairly widely apart instead of being lined up tightly along their sides, because the first operation of building the vault proper was the laying of large Roman bricks (approximately 2 feet by 2 feet by $1\frac{1}{2}$ inches) flat-wise around the curve of the vault. A second layer, of either the large or smaller-sized bricks, was laid flat-wise on top of these in a thick bed of mortar so as to break joints with the first layer.[116]

When the mortar in these joints had set, two important things had been accomplished. First, the flat layers created an impervious dam which prevented the liquid ingredients of the subsequently placed concrete from leaking out. Thus the function of holding the liquid concrete in place until it had set was taken over by an element of the finished vault, rather than by the planking of the falsework. Second, the brickwork laminations created a stiff shell which augmented, or perhaps in some cases even substituted for, the supporting function of the planking.

The Romans did not exploit this system, for they were interested in massiveness, not lightness of construction. And so they used it only as a technique of erection, a built-in adjunct by which the temporary falsework could be reduced and simplified.

It was not until the latter part of the nineteenth century that this system was studied and developed into a means of spanning space in its own right. This was done by the Spanish architect, Guastavino, who built 'timbrel arches' and 'timbrel vaults' in what he called the 'Cohesive System', though it later came to be named after him, the 'Guastavino System'.[117]

This system made use of thin tiles, usually with corrugated faces, set flat-wise in relatively thick mortar beds, the tiles of successive layers breaking joints. By this means a very thin vault shell of slight rise could be built which, when properly anchored, was stiff and rigid out of all proportion to its weight. Structurally the system was completely different from a normal vault, which produces a thrust due to the wedge action of its voussoirs. The Guastavino System, on the other hand, develops the frictional resistance between laminations (the flat sides of the tiles, as in the Roman vault construction described above) to support itself. For if the arc of the structure is maintained throughout, so that there is no distortion of the curve in cross-section, the structure is stiff enough to span a considerable distance and strong enough to support a considerable distributed load. In the Roman example cited above, the timber-frame-supported planking maintained the integrity of the vault curve throughout. In Guastavino's own structures, sometimes the fill to provide a level floor above, sometimes tie-rods or filler pieces of one sort or another, accomplished this essential function.

A more recent development of a thin-shelled type of structure is that originally called the 'ZD System' of reinforced concrete construction (named after the inventors, Zeiss and Dywidag, in the mid 1920's) but known more generally as the Concrete Shell Dome or Shell Vault System.[118] This is more nearly analogous to what takes place to some extent in thin Gothic vaults; for, unlike both the Roman practice and the Guastavino System, it does not exploit the frictional resistance between laminations but, instead, makes thorough use of the strength to be derived in thin shells from their three-dimensional shape alone. In this respect it is comparable to such structures in Nature as the egg shell, the rose petal, the clam shell, and the morning-glory blossom.[119]

What the ZD System does have in common with the man-made systems described above, however, is the requirement of maintaining the integrity of the curve in cross-section. Where there is simple curvature, as in a segmental barrel vault, diaphragm filler pieces of reinforced concrete, poured integrally with the vault shell, are sometimes used to assure constancy in the cross-sectional shape throughout. But where there is double curvature, the curvature itself creates the stiffness.

ZD structures of amazing span and phenomenal lightness have been built, including concrete domes 200 feet in clear span that vary in thickness from $6\frac{1}{2}$ to $2\frac{5}{8}$ inches! In the case of shell *vaults* the spans are not as great as those that can be achieved in shell domes (because of the double curvature of the latter), but both the spans and particularly their thicknesses are remarkable.

What is so radically different in the appearance of these shell vaults is that although their shapes may be those of barrel vaults—usually segmental rather than semicircular in cross-section—they are without any support along the sides, at the very locations where true barrel vaults must have supports to take care of both the weight of the vault and the thrusts it generates. This omission is due to the completely different nature of the shell-vault structure. It is a longitudinal beam, not a transverse vault, and its resistance to deflexion is due to the arc of its cross-section; the thinness of its shell becomes resistant to longitudinal bending by reason of the rise of its arc in the transverse section.

This is perhaps sufficient explanation of the simplest applications of this system to indicate that certain thin-shelled structures act as rigid units on account of their curvature, provided only that they have sufficient cohesion to remain intact. In the modern Shell Vault System this cohesion is assured by the layers of its embedded steel reinforcement. In the webs of thin Gothic vaults there is no positive tensile reinforcement; but the cohesion of the mortar, when it has achieved its final set,[120] is often such that large areas of the vault web have been observed, particularly in war-damaged cases,[121] to act as single rigid pieces without voussoir action.

It is not known definitely, and it probably cannot be known, to what extent the Gothic vault acts in this way, as large connected curving triangles of rigid shells without arch action. If the vaults (once their mortar joints had become thoroughly set) were not subject to settlement or dislocation from such causes as expansion and contraction due to temperature variation, or movement due to high winds, or vibration due to the ringing of bells, &c., it may be that the cohesion of the mortar would sufficiently serve as the supporting principle in place of normal vault action. As it is, however, these and other stresses and disturbances have occurred, and still do occur from time to time, in Gothic churches; so that, lacking any positive reinforcement within the vault webs, the shell system could never have been counted on as the primary structural system. And yet, this system unquestionably is operative to a greater or lesser extent in every intact Gothic vault.

The error of architectural historians has been consistently (1) to ignore this actuality of construction for which there is such abundant evidence; and, in spite of the obvious tenacity of most medieval mortar after it has set, (2) to persist in assuming that the individual blocks of stone that make up the vault constitute free units, as though they acted exclusively as individual voussoirs. The shell action, at the very least, is an adjunct or supplement to the normal vault action, providing a generous factor of safety to withstand any abnormal or special stresses the vault might undergo. And it is clear, from the evidence of ribbed vaults which still stand after their ribs have been torn away or have fallen from one cause or another, that at times this shell action may be the predominant condition of stability that is operative in Gothic vaults. In this connexion, the presence of camber in the vault compartments adds appreciably to the rigidity of these compartments by providing shells of double curvature,[122] as explained above.

As the ribs of the Gothic system came to be made more slender and enriched with various combinations of mouldings, the masons sometimes cut them so that the webs of adjacent vault panels no longer abutted each other above the rib, but fitted upon narrow shelves rebated along either side of the rib, near its extrados. Thus the stem of the rib in cross-section projected up into, or even through, the thickness of the vault web, which gave the rib increased depth and hence increased strength as a rigid arc.[123]

This scheme of cutting the ribs with rebated shelves to receive the ends of the web courses was common in England where it appeared fairly early and continued throughout most of the medieval period.[124] Its use in the nave vaults of French Gothic churches, however, was probably confined to the transverse ribs alone. Here, where the French did sometimes adopt it, it was a logical and effective development. For it maintained the vault curvature with augmented rigidity at the junction between adjacent bays, midway between the stiffening boundaries provided by the diagonal groins. In these transverse ribs, the vault-penetrating stem of the deeper rib section finally superseded the broader and heavier section of the earlier transverse arches in fulfilling the function of maintaining the cross-sectional integrity of the web's primary curvature.[125]

However, it seems most unlikely that French Gothic *diagonal* ribs, in high nave vaults of either sexpartite or quadripartite form, were ever cut with stems projecting up into the web. This assumption would need to be checked against the actual condition in existing buildings, of course;[126] but there are at least two good reasons for doubting the existence of rib stems here. One is that there would not be room for such a stem, at least in the lower half or two-thirds of the vault compartment, unless the web on the cross vault's side (together with this web's mortar joint) were as little as 2 inches thick: a patently unsafe and unstructural condition (26). The other reason to doubt the existence of rib stems in the diagonals of French Gothic vaulting is that they are not needed to stiffen the vault so as to keep its curvature from deforming. The two webs, longitudinal and transverse, that converge upon the back of the diagonal rib form a stiffening crease in the vaulting, and this creates far more rigidity than any stem could possibly produce.

This latter consideration conclusively demonstrates the reason for a situation that has baffled and confused many art historians; namely, how to account for the fact that the longer and apparently more heavily stressed diagonal ribs were customarily made narrower and smaller in section than the transverse ribs. Even with their vault-penetrating stems and/or their usually greater width, these transverse

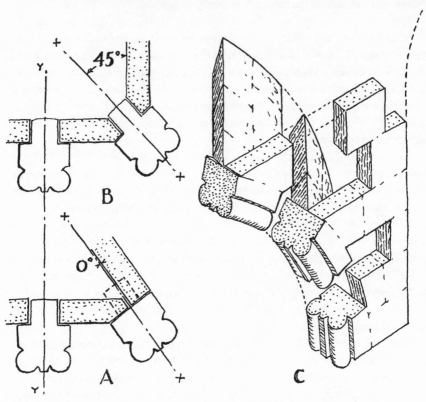

26. *The Occurrence of Rib Stems in French Gothic Vaulting*

This series of drawings indicates why there can be no vault-penetrating rib stem in the case of the diagonal rib in a rectangular bay of Gothic quadripartite vaulting. The transverse ribs (on the axis Y–Y) are a straightforward case of rib stems used to add to the depth, and therefore the stiffness, of these ribs. The rib stem is even possible, though certainly not as necessary, in the diagonals of a *square* bay of vaulting, as shown at B. But the stone courses in the lower portions of the transverse compartments of Gothic *rectangular* bays meet the diagonal ribs in the plane of these ribs (as shown at A and C); consequently there is no room for a stem.

ribs were more often subject to fracture and disruption than were the more slender diagonal ribs, for the reason that the creased junction of the vault webs themselves did the job in the latter case, while the transverse ribs alone had to stiffen the thin vault and maintain its shape, in the former case.

This situation also explains one of the chief reasons for the conflicting statements about the structural or supporting function of the ribs in Gothic vaulting, wherein both those who maintain the structural theory and those who deny it base their arguments on the incontrovertible 'proof' of existing evidence in the case of damaged or partially dilapidated buildings. As previously explained, where the vault is continuous above the ribs, shell action can and frequently does take over if the ribs are completely destroyed. On the other hand, where Gothic ribs are heavy and deep in section compared to the vault thickness, the ribs are so much stronger than the webs that if anything causes the webs to perish (such as disintegration from a persistently leaking or non-existent roof), the ribs will continue to remain in place indefinitely by themselves.[127]

Once the salient ribs were systematically adopted at the groins, the Gothic ribbed vault system had become a structural reality whose influence spread and affected many other parts of the building. The progress of refining the structure—of relating and unifying its component parts—developed rapidly. One final step, before the typical mature Gothic vault was achieved, needs to be considered. This is the *sexpartite vault*. It made a most significant structural contribution, as will be seen, although it was probably derived originally from aesthetic and perhaps erectional considerations.

We have seen that, from the time the simple groin vault was used to span space, the builders were unable to vault any but square or nearly square bays except in the smallest compartments. And, because it was almost invariably their custom to make the nave approximately twice the width of the side aisle, this meant that there had to be two square bays in each side aisle corresponding to one square bay in the nave. The piers which supported the corners of the nave bays of vaulting received a quarter of the load of each high vault bay as well as their share of the side-aisle vaults. But the intermediate pier received only the latter load: there was nothing in the high vault for it to support at this point. The logic of the builders therefore led them to make this intermediate pier smaller than those at the corners of the high bay, in order to make visually apparent what was structurally true. Hence the so-called 'Alternate System' in the nave arcade, in which the piers separating nave from side aisles were alternately large and small.

But there was still no structural connexion between the high vault and the intermediate pier, which the builders' interest in an organic design led them to desire. Structural continuity and some degree of organic relationship between the high vault and the dispositions at the nave arcade level were achieved by the adoption of the sexpartite vault. In this scheme an extra transverse rib was introduced,

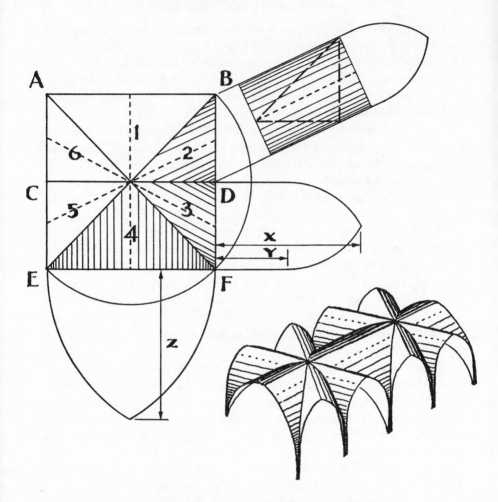

27. Schematic Layout of a Sexpartite Vaulting Bay

Each of the six compartments or severies is numbered in the plan view, where AB and EF represent the normal transverse ribs, CD the additional transverse rib, AF and BE the two semicircular diagonal ribs. The vault crowns are designated by broken lines, the two transverse ones crossing obliquely and intersecting each other in a common point at the center of the square bay. Z shows the rise of the longitudinal vault, and X is made equal to Z by means of the stilt, Y, of the transverse vault panel

no. 3 where it meets the clerestory wall DF. To the right of B is a plan view of a length of pointed barrel vault within which a triangular-shaped compartment similar to no. 2 is indicated. It should be noted that these representations are nothing more than diagrammatic simplifications of the general scheme, since they ignore such things as vault and rib thicknesses, pier diameters, and the inevitable warping of the vault surfaces of the lateral cells as they approach the springings.

spanning across the nave from above one intermediate pier to its mate opposite.

This addition created a profound change in the vault itself. For in order to bring the intermediate transverse rib into play as a functioning member of the vault, there now had to be not one but two cross vaults for each of the large square bays of the nave. Moreover, their directions were not at right angles to the longitudinal vault but criss-cross as indicated in the diagrams, 27. Furthermore, the ends of these criss-crossing vaults, where they met the walls of the nave, were much narrower than the span of the nave vault; in fact, they were only about half the width of the longitudinal vault which spanned the full width of the nave. So, in order to make the crowns of these cross vaults attain the level of the longitudinal vault's crown, the cross vaults were strongly stilted; that is, the pointed arch of their intersection with the wall did not begin its curve at the common impost level but only at a considerable distance above it. Thus the compartments of the longitudinal vault were well launched on their curve across the void they spanned before there came to be any vault curvature near the wall in the lateral compartments. This condition inevitably produced warping in the lower portions of the vaulting conoid, the first such intentional warping in medieval vaulting.

In the longitudinal compartments it is evident that the normal practice of the French masons was to make their vault webs with horizontal courses parallel to the crown of the vault. This could not be done, however, in the lower portions of the cross vaults because of the warping of their surfaces. The courses of stone usually went from wall to diagonal rib directly enough; but the angle, in plan, of successive courses in the lower portions was a shifting one until well above the spring of the cross vaults where they abutted the wall. Moore has demonstrated that this warping, far from being a clumsy makeshift which the builders had to put up with, was of the very essence of the Gothic structural system: a system in which the stresses were channellized and delimited, where the leanness was the result of the convergence, not the divergence, of forces.[128]

Much of the foregoing review of significant steps in the development of medieval vaulting may be considered from the standpoint of progression towards a structural system which focuses forces instead of dispersing them. The Roman hemispherical dome is an example of the latter, for in it the stresses radiate downward and outward in a full 360° circle. It is significant that, except for a limited area in the center of the country, the Romanesque builders of France did not make use of the dome, and that the Gothic builders never did. The early medieval masons started with the barrel vault, but from its broadly distributed planes of

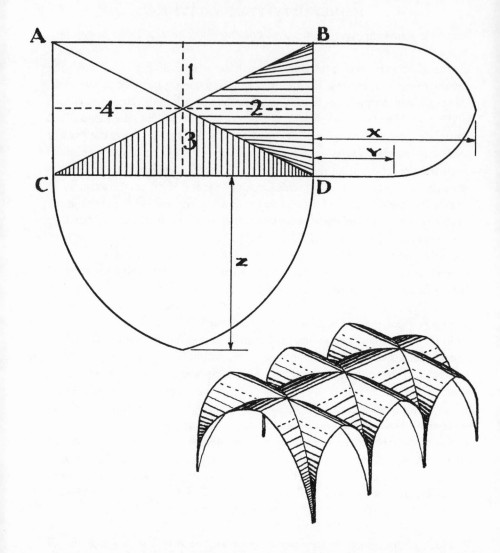

28. *Schematic Layout of a Quadripartite Vaulting Bay*

The four cells or compartments of the strongly rectangular bay are numbered. The broken lines indicate the level crowns of the longitudinal and transverse vaults, which intersect at right angles. Z designates the rise of the longitudinal vault. By means of the stilt, Y, of the transverse vault, X is made equal to Z, even though the profile of the lateral vault as it meets the clerestory wall BD is similar to the longitudinal arch CD. Although there is some indication of the warping of the vault surfaces in cell no. 2, the representations given here are purely schematic, since no thickness is designated for either the ribs or the vaulting itself, and no pier diameters are indicated at the corners of the bay.

thrust they came more and more to reduce the area in which the vault thrusts operated, until they evolved a unique system of masonry construction in which convergence of forces was the dominant principle, and these forces were confined within the narrowest limits and taken care of with the greatest economy of means throughout.[129]

All these interdependent conditions and partial solutions were finally reconciled and resolved in the mature Gothic system with the achievement of the typical *quadripartite vault*[130] (28). Here at last the structural system was completely rationalized, the aesthetic appearance unified, and the organic design integrated throughout. In the quadripartite system a single bay of the high vault corresponds to but one bay of the side aisles. This is accomplished by making the nave bays strongly rectangular, their transverse span about twice that of their longitudinal span. Now there was complete unity between the high vault and the dispositions at the triforium and the nave arcade levels below it; and the Alternate System was superseded by uniformity and regularity in the piers. Here was a system that could meet the demand for flexibility of design, largeness of openings, harmonious unity of effect, and lightness of weight. Here was a system in stone by which the twin aims that had fired the builders for so long could at last be realized: now they were able to build churches that were flooded with light and that soared to the skies.

It is upon the Gothic ribbed vault system in general, and particularly on the mature realization of this system as represented in the quadripartite vault, that the greatest skill, rationality of means, and economy of execution were focused. Two features of this system have yet to be noted: the tas-de-charge and the flying buttress.

In the persistent development towards leanness of construction to permit the maximum amount of wall area to be devoted to window openings, the individual ribs in each cluster that came down to the high vault's points of springing were brought so close together that many of their mouldings were mutually absorbed, and there was no room for each rib to be a separate block of stone. So, the stone courses in the lower portion of the vaulting conoid—the solid defined by each rib cluster—were fashioned out of single blocks up to the point at which the ribs diverged sufficiently for each to acquire its full cross-sectional shape. Furthermore, these single blocks, one on top of another for five or sometimes seven or more courses, had level beds and hence no thrust: it was only at the top of the highest block that joints normal to the curve began[131] (29).

This feature, known as the *tas-de-charge*, accomplished a number of desirable and effective ends. It allowed the clerestory wall, now reduced mainly to a pier separating the window openings, to continue upward without weakness at this

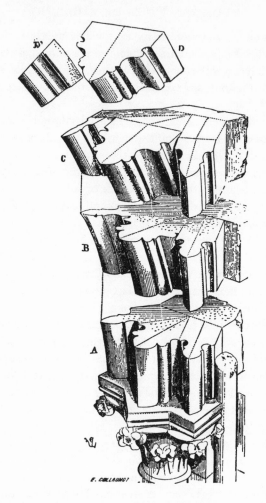

29. *Viollet-le-Duc's Drawing of the Tas-de-Charge*

This is an exploded view of a tas-de-charge of but three courses, A, B, and C, with normal voussoirs for the transverse and a diagonal rib shown at D and D' respectively. The beds of the tas-de-charge blocks are horizontal; only the top of the highest block has the rib portions finished in planes which slope at an angle normal to the curve of each rib. In the lower right is the stump of a column shaft that would normally continue upward to the spring of the wall arch, some distance above the capital that marks the spring of the transverse and diago-

nal ribs. It may be seen that the lateral face of the tas-de-charge blocks continues back to the clerestory wall in the plane of the diagonal rib's side (as indicated more fully in 26 C), thus allowing the vaulting shaft of the wall rib to continue upward in a vertical direction. In the lower blocks, A and B, the mutual absorption of the lateral mouldings of the ribs is evident; only at the top, in D and D', have the rib profiles become completely free and disentangled from each other.

point, so that its stability was assured in supporting the superstructure of masonry spandrels together with the lofty timber roof. It also provided a solid and unified base from which the various members of the vault, both ribs and curving triangles of the infilling, might spring. It reduced the span of the vault appreciably, due to the corbelling of its successive courses; and it probably thereby reduced somewhat the thrust of the vault. Finally, it implemented the principle of convergence by assuring that the vault stresses would be focused only on a narrow area at which one of the slender flying buttresses could receive these stresses.

The *flying buttress* was the final solution to the problem of abutting the high vault in such a way as to allow for windows of full bay width and maximum height above the side-aisle roof, to light the nave directly. It has previously been explained that the side aisle constituted a gap between the point at which the high vault thrusts were concentrated, on the one hand, and the point outside the building, on the other hand, where these thrusts could be met and grounded. Deeply salient buttresses were the massive anchors of this system, by which the vault thrusts were resisted and grounded. These buttresses rose high above the side-aisle eaves in the form of solid rectangular towers, their long axes set at right angles to the church's enclosing wall and hence in the vertical plane of the resultant of the vault thrust at each pier. The *flying* buttress was the strut that received the collected pressures at these pier intervals and transmitted them across the void above the side aisle, to the lofty buttress proper. Of course, in shrines and chapels and other one-aisled structures—such as the Sainte-Chapelle in Paris—there was no side-aisle gap to bridge; and so the vault thrusts here are met and grounded by the buttresses directly, and there are no flying buttresses because there are no side aisles for them to leap across.

In many of the larger churches, as well as in practically all of the great cathedrals of the thirteenth century in France, there are two or even three tiers of flying buttresses, one tier superimposed above the other. Elsewhere it has been demonstrated that the upper tier normally receives no vault thrusts but is required for stability against the force of wind acting on the clerestory wall and more particularly on the steeply pitched roof.[132]

Since these towering nave roofs were invariably built before the vault proper was begun,[133] it is apparent that the upper tier of flying buttresses, which were elements in the stability of the superstructure, *could* have been constructed before the lower, thrust-transmitting ones would have had to be brought into play. This sequence might have taken place (though it probably didn't) in the case of Saint-Denis, Soissons, Bourges, Paris, Narbonne, Reims, the nave of Amiens, Beauvais, and many other great churches where the half-arches of the two tiers are not connected with screen-like open panelling and are therefore independent of each other. But it could not have happened in the case of the choir of Amiens, the great collegiate church at Eu, the cathedrals of Bayonne, Bordeaux, and Limoges, the churches of Saint-Jacques at Dieppe, Saint-Maclou at Rouen, Saint-Antoine at Compiegne, the fifteenth-century nave of the cathedral of Troyes, or the early sixteenth-century Abbey Church of Saint-Vulfran at Abbeville. For in these latter instances the upper flying buttress is a sloping, jointed bar of masonry blocks which, because they are set in a straight line, would not be able to maintain their position were it not for the support they receive, via the open panelling, from the arch of the lower flying buttress.

The reason for the development of this later scheme, with its open-work panelling connecting the upper and lower struts, was not primarily decorative but structural. In the first place, material and labour for centering the flying buttress arches needed to be expended for only one arch, the lower one. Furthermore, both arcs of the earlier flying buttresses, being portions of true arches, had a crown thrust which pressed inward against the clerestory wall; and this inward pressure was augmented by reason of the fact that these half-arches were usually charged with a considerable amount of masonry piled up on their backs in order to form straight slopes along their tops. Once the vaults were built, however, the inward pressure from this source, in the case of the lower arch, was not too serious a matter because it helped somewhat to counteract the outward pressure of the collected vault thrusts. But in the case of the upper arch in a two-tier arrangement of flying buttresses there was normally no outward pressure to meet the inward-acting crown thrust of this arch. Hence it was advantageous to have the upper strut a straight bar of stonework, which consequently created no inward pressure, on the one hand, and which weighted and further stabilized the lower arch that supported it, on the other hand.

In the past, much has been made of the contribution of the *pointed arch* to Gothic structure. As previously mentioned, some of the earliest writers of the nineteenth century, and even before, saw in its adoption the basis of distinction between Romanesque and Gothic architecture, if not, indeed, the pervading structural characteristic of the latter era. By now, however, it has long since been recognized that there were many occasions on which the Gothic builders retained the semicircular arch: that they were free agents, in fact, in choosing either the broken or the semicircular arch as it suited their purposes. It is certainly true that, aesthetically, the pointed arch everywhere appears to be the predominant shape in spanning space, whether in window arch and doorway or in the vaults themselves. But actually there are innumerable instances of the Gothic use of semicircular shapes. For example, in the great majority of diagonal ribs,[134] whose intersecting arcs produce the *effect* of pointed arches although their semicircular *actuality* made them somewhat easier to lay out and construct at the size they attained over

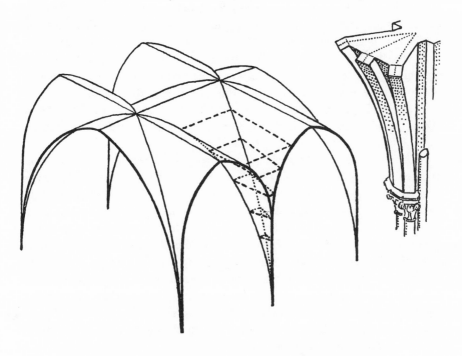

30. *Stilting and its Consequences in the Quadripartite System*

This simplified sketch of the vault surfaces in two rectangular bays shows by broken lines in one of the vaulting conoids the varying shape of this conoid. The broken lines designate the contours of the conoid at successive levels when horizontal planes are passed through it. It may be seen that, because of the stilt of the wall arches, these outlines progress from triangular shapes through trapezoids to rectangles high up near the crowns. The schematic detail to the right indicates the triangular shape of the lower part of a vaulting conoid as defined by a rib cluster.

naves,[135] and doubtless made them less likely to rise at their common crowns. Again, the ends of the cross vaults at Chartres, together with the window-heads they enframe, were made semicircular, without doubt so that more void might be provided for glazed window area than would have been the case if pointed shapes had been used.

The outstanding structural advantage of the pointed arch, as employed by the

Gothic builders, is of course that it has less thrust than the semicircular arch; that is, for a given span there is a smaller horizontal component of arch pressure with the pointed shape than with the semicircular shape, and the former consequently requires less in the way of abutment. The fact, however, that some of the outstanding cathedrals of the Gothic era—Rouen, for instance, and the choir of Le Mans—had vaults that were but very slightly pointed, would appear to indicate that the medieval builders did not seek at all costs to reduce vault thrusts by these means. Undoubtedly the visual effect of pointedness, which could be achieved by departing only slightly from the semicircular contour, was a more compelling motivation than the reduction of thrust, which the builders had other means of handling. Even a slightly pointed arch or vault advertises itself as such, and produces an effect of upwardness which, in the long vista of a nave vault, is emphasized by the crease at its crown.

Many writers have said that the pointed arch was adopted in order that arches of different span might all achieve the same height at their crowns. In a rectangular as opposed to a square bay this was impossible to achieve with semicircular arches (see 35), because their rise is automatically half their span. But the ability of pointed arches to have crowns at various higher levels than the distance of half their spans was not the major consideration of the builders in adopting pointed arches for the lateral boundaries of their vaulting bays, at least in France. For it will be noted that, whatever the profile of the wall rib in France (and sometimes it is semicircular, as at Chartres), it is invariably stilted; that is, its curve begins at a much higher level than do those of the transverse and diagonal ribs. What is of major significance in French Gothic vaulting, therefore, is the *stilting* of the wall rib, not the contour of its arc (30).

There were two chief reasons for the stilt. It permitted the maximum of void between the clerestory piers, so that the area of the clerestory windows could be as large as possible. (See the two curves in the right-hand detail, 37.) And structurally, the stilting brought about that narrow concentration of vault thrusts—so characteristic of the Gothic system—that made it possible for a slender flying buttress to receive and transmit these thrusts across the side-aisle interval, to the stable buttress towers.

As the Gothic era progressed, however, a large number of vaults came to be strongly pointed, and this created some trouble, structurally. In a free arch system such as a vault which carries no surcharge and therefore supports only itself, the line of pressure is an inverted catenary curve. If one envisages a chain or cable suspended loosely from two points that are at the same level but separated by much less distance than the length of the chain, each link then constitutes an identical unit of weight along the curving loop of the chain and is in tension with its neighbours. Together, these links form a curving line whose axis is the line of stress—in this case, the line of tension—in the freely suspended chain. If this loop of chain were considered as being rigidly fixed so that its curve would not deform, and if it were then inverted, each link or unit would now be in compression with its neighbours, and the axis of the curving line of units would be the line of pressure. This

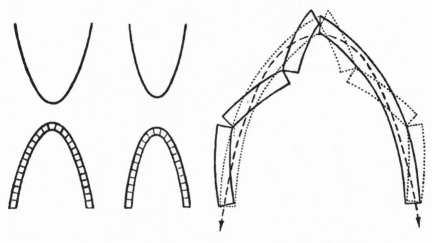

31. *The Catenary Curve and the Gothic Pointed Arch*

Above, to the left, are catenary curves designated by single lines of tension, below which are inverted catenaries in the form of arches whose units are in compression. The larger figure, to the right, indicates the consequences which follow when the inverted catenary line of pressure (the broken line, with arrows) comes too close to the extrados or the intrados of a pointed arch of masonry, or even passes outside of this arch, as under the crown: (1) the springs of the arch tend either to spread apart or to open their joints at the intrados, (2) the arch tends to burst outward at the haunches, (3) the joints of the intrados near the crown tend to open, and (4) the crown tends to rise.

is what happens in an arch, where the voussoirs constitute the 'links' of the inverted catenary curve (31).

We have previously seen that, in order to secure stability, the line of pressure should remain within the middle third—at most, the middle half—of the structure; and it is this nature-imposed condition that tends to cause trouble in vaults that are strongly pointed.

Obviously, no catenary curve, normal or inverted, can ever be pointed.[136] So it is almost inevitable that the line of pressure in a sharply pointed vault should pass outside (below) the masonry of the vault at its crown, and perhaps also pass

81

E. CHENNOT.

32. *Viollet-le-Duc's Drawing of the Fill in the Lower Portion of the*
Vaulting Conoid

This is a section through a pier and buttresses at one side of the choir of Amiens Cathedral. In the upper left-hand portion of the drawing, on the extrados of the nave's transverse arch, is the indication of the very thin vault. The fill behind the haunch of this arch attains a level considerably more than three-quarters of the arch rise. Other features to be noted are (1) the open-work panelling of the flying buttress, linking the vault-resisting arch proper with the straight sloping strut of its channelled top, (2) the large through-wall block of the highest unit of the tas-de-charge, and (3) the multiple-coursed corbelling above the pier of the nave arcade, out over the side aisle.

82

beyond (above) its extrados high up along the haunches. In such a situation the vault would tend to rise at its crown, a condition that can be observed in certain medieval vaults today.

But the medieval builders resorted to certain schemes and practices to prevent this from happening, even when their vaults were strongly pointed. One scheme was to fill the concave funnel of the vaulting conoid, from above, to a considerable height—perhaps as much as three-fifths or more of the total vault rise—with light-weight rubble of one sort or another, so as to maintain its shape intact against any possibility of deformation[137] (32). This would conclusively prevent any dangerously disruptive cracks, as well as any pressure-imposed dislocations, from forming at the haunch, for as high up as the conoid was filled in. It was not so much that the vault was surcharged in its lower portions by this relatively light and fairly loosely concreted fill (although this, too, was a consideration); rather, it was that the fill maintained the shape of this portion of the vaulting conoid intact.

Actually, except for Picardy and the Ile-de-France, the Gothic vaults in France were rarely of uniformly cut voussoirs until a very late date. Instead, they were made up of only roughly squared blocks in courses that were frequently not parallel to each other, especially in the lower portions, and which were drowned, as the French say, in mortar. These thick mortar beds were the means of producing thin, more or less homogeneous shells which frequently acted as single units over large areas of the vault panels. Sometimes, indeed, even whole panels appear to act in this way; at other times, judging by the cracks that have formed in certain vaults, large areas of the vault shell appear to act as units which span from one rib-accented boundary to another, or even right around the pointed curve of the vault in a short length of lateral vaulting[138] (33). The fairly high filling of the vaulting conoid was a means of limiting the unfixed amount of the vault shell to its central area—from the top of this fill to the crown of the vault—and therefore reducing very much the area in which dislocations would normally occur.

At least in part, it was probably with the idea of making these upper portions of the vault more rigid that the builders (particularly in England) sometimes overlaid the web of the vault with a layer of concrete almost as thick again as the vault proper.[139] This was a very questionable practice, to say the least, for it undoubtedly created more trouble than it ameliorated (because of the unyielding rigidity it imposed, its additional weight, its relative amount of shrinkage, and its different coefficient of thermal expansion, as compared to these factors in the vault proper). It is significant that in many cases this additional layer was often subsequently removed; and that in the later vaults, which were in most cases remarkably thin,[140]

33. Pol Abraham's Drawing of Typical Fissures in Gothic Vaults

Three types of fissures are identified here: (1) tensile fissures in which the joints of the transverse and diagonal ribs (and sometimes those of the vault itself) open up near their crowns (see 31 for clarification); (2) fissures that indicate the pulling away of the heads of the transverse vaults from the clerestory wall they abut; and (3) 'fissures of Sabouret', which are cracks that develop, parallel to those at (2) but some distance inward from them, at the junction of the portion of the transverse vault that springs from the solid tas-de-charge and the portion that springs from the diagonal ribs—that is, the central portion of the cross vault.

84

their thickness was sometimes further reduced by chipping away a good deal of the upper surface of the blocks of the cells themselves, after the vault was built.[141]

A much safer and more effective practice than that of an overlay of concrete was introduced late in the Gothic era. (It had been adopted at a fairly early period in England, though for quite different reasons.) This was the large and heavy keystone at the apex of the transverse arches but particularly at the intersection of the groin ribs, which was carved into a figured or floral or shield-emblazoned composition, sometimes with pendants, and invariably with the stems of the moulded ribs cut so as to receive these members as they converged upon this block.[142] The purpose of the great keystone was not so much decorative (although the sculptors came to make full use of this opportunity once it was presented) but rather, structural: it weighted the pointed ribs with a large heavy block at their crowns and thus corrected their tendency to rise, as indicated in 31.

Thus far, we have considered the main stream of structural development in the Middle Ages, from the low and heavy barrel vault to the high and thin-shelled rib vault. By the time the Gothic quadripartite vault was adopted, all the major structural problems had been recognized, and one or more solutions evolved to meet them. What is next to be done is to try to assess the ways by which this Gothic structure could have been *con*structed: how the vaults as we see them today in their impressive finished state might have come to be erected.

4

*'In writings of a miscellaneous kind we often find precious scraps of
information which explain at once circumstances that have, without
them, elicited the vain conjectures of a succession of modern writers.'*
THOMAS WRIGHT*

THE FOREGOING PERSPECTIVE VIEW OF SIGNIFICANT ARCHITEC-
tural developments reveals many points at which our knowledge is incomplete.
It does emphasize, however, certain general attributes of the medieval building
programme.

One circumstance it corroborates is the multiplicity and *complexity of the
building programme*, especially by the time the great Gothic churches were being
designed and constructed. Considerations of aesthetics, of structure, and of practical operation in the process of erection had to be decided upon, worked out, and
reconciled. The builders aimed at nothing less than maximum natural lighting
and maximum height. They insisted on achieving a thoroughly integrated organic
design throughout, that was expressive of their most creative imagination, their
noblest vision. This brief survey has touched on only certain features of this complexity, and not in great detail, either. It has covered little else than the typical
vault systems. Actually, there was a good deal more to compound the complexity:
the construction of slender, sky-piercing spires, the security of foundations, and,
in regard to the vaulting itself, the special conditions and problems of curving
ambulatory and high-windowed apse. Each of these latter warrants separate and
independent study. However, enough has been revealed of innovations, modifications, and procedures, in the characteristic systems here discussed, to impress us
with the bewildering scope of the difficulties and complexities that the medieval
builders faced.

Another circumstance that is apparent from this survey is the *plurality of functions* in a given feature: the multiple reasons for its adoption. Many instances have
been implied rather than specifically noted. But certain ones have been pointed

* 'Notes relating to Architecture and Building from Medieval Manuscripts', *British Archaeological Journal*, 1848, vol. iii, p. 99.

out and discussed; for example, service galleries and vices, the great tie-beams of the high roof, stilting of arches, the tas-de-charge device, and of course the ribs.

This account has also called attention throughout to still another attribute of the medieval building programme; namely, the *economy of means* which was constantly sought after by the builders. Not only was this effected by making one device or feature of the structure serve various ends, as indicated above. In addition the builders sought constantly, by various means and ingenious schemes, to economize on direct costs.[143] Thus blocks were roughly shaped to their finished size at the quarry, in order to reduce their weight and bulk so that transportation costs would be lessened.[144] Sometimes, indeed, such carved features as capitals and the moulded sections of rib voussoirs were completely finished at the quarry before shipping to the building site.[145] We have seen something of the ways by which scaffolding requirements were economized or even, in certain situations such as the erection of vices, eliminated entirely. Furthermore, considerable attention has been given to pre-Gothic practices by which the amount and extent of centering for vaults could have been lessened. The Gothic ribbed vault itself was certainly a major contribution in making the process of vault erection easier as well as less prodigal of materials, both directly in the stone vault itself and indirectly in reducing the bulk of massive masonry that had been needed to support and abut the earlier types of vault.[146] Not that the builders shied away from fabulous expense where it enriched the fabric, as in the stained glass windows of Chartres and Bourges; nor that they hesitated to glorify the House of God everywhere with carvings and figure sculptures resplendent in colour. But the whole trend of architectural development in the medieval period was towards greater lightness, towards an elimination of the superfluous, with a corresponding economy both in material structure and in execution.

One of the most striking revelations that an historical review of erectional practices brings out is the *role of the rib* in the operation of building a medieval vault. It was the medieval practice, as opposed to that of the Romans, to erect arches *under* the vault instead of within its mass. This innovation originated early in the medieval period with the employment of the banded barrel vault. Both at this time and in subsequent early vaulting systems these heavy, independently erected arches were sometimes dispensed with.[147] But in the historical perspective they are seen to have made one of the most significant and influential contributions to the development of medieval vaulting. Enhanced and lightened in effect by deeply profiled mouldings, they came to be the dominant decorative elements of the vaulted ceiling. But let it never be forgotten that the ribs were there to begin with, for erectional reasons: the vast Roman vaults, which were the grandiose inspiration for some of the earliest medieval vaults, provide overwhelming evidence that, whether salient or not, the ribs were not originated for decorative purposes. Their primary and indispensable role was constructional. This role, which they had from the start, became augmented as the medieval builders came to appreciate the usefulness of the rib, and to comprehend its advantages in the erection of vaults of larger span, higher up, and of relatively thinner, lighter shells.

To understand this augmented constructional role of the rib as it had come to be employed by the time Gothic vaulting was arrived at, it is necessary to recall how the shape and nature of these vaults had come about. It has been stated above that the far-reaching consequence of the domed groin vault was that it at last opened the way to the vaulting of areas other than those that were square in plan, by demonstrating that individual vault compartments could take their shape from that of their boundaries. As boundary shapes, not only semicircular arches but half ellipses, with their longer axes set either vertically or horizontally, and a variety of pointed arches were tried. The shape that came to be used predominantly on the shorter sides of rectangular bays—that is to say, for the wall rib or formeret next to the clerestory wall—was a not too sharply pointed arch that was highly stilted. The stilting, by which the crown of this arch could attain the level of the other ribs' crowns, produced a strongly warped surface (the 'ploughshare twist') in the transverse vault compartments, because the wall-rib boundary of this compartment didn't start to curve until the curve of the groin-rib boundary was well launched across the void of the nave.

Constructionally, then, the rib was used first of all to reduce the amount of centering required, by compartmentalizing the vault.

It should be noted, however, that the *diagonal* rib had a very special role, or series of roles, to play. For instance, it would have been impossible to arrive at such forms of vaults as the sexpartite and the strongly rectangular quadripartite vaults of Gothic times if it had not been for the adoption of these independently built groin ribs. What was significant about the Gothic use of the rib—what differentiated the Gothic vaulting system, in fact, from that of former rib-employing vaults—was the presence of the rib under the groin. The *transverse* rib's functions in Gothic times were no different from those of the banded barrel vault of Romanesque times. But the Gothic *diagonal* rib was the generating feature of an entirely new system of construction. For now, as we have seen, it was pre-eminently the groin ribs that determined the conformation of the vault webs, even to the extent of producing the characteristically warped surfaces that made possible the lightening of the vault webs and helped to channelize the vault pressures.

It has been noted above that the shell action of thin Gothic vaults made the diagonal rib, if not largely superfluous, at least of diminished importance in its purely structural role (as opposed to its erectional, aesthetic, and practical roles).

At the same time, however, the diagonal rib, no matter how slender it may have been, was able to reinforce and perhaps even for a time to *carry* its share of the vault, due to the fact that it was kept from deforming by the deep crease of the intersecting vaults—by the rigid conformation of the very load it carried, in fact. In this respect the roles of the diagonal and transverse ribs were somewhat reversed in Gothic vaults. Thus the transverse rib, far from supporting the vault, was there to maintain the contour of the vault and thereby to prevent the vault from collapsing or deforming. The diagonal rib, on the other hand, may well have been called upon at times (e.g. after the centerings were removed and before the mortar joints had achieved their months-long final set) to help support the vault along the very intersection whose crease maintained the rib's contour intact.

Since the diagonal rib served to cover up the awkwardly jointed salient meeting-line along the groins, where the stone coursing of two adjacent compartments came together, the uniform continuity of its arch ring furnished positive reinforcement there. This reinforcing function was particularly desirable early in the independent life of the vault, after the centerings had been removed. For it gave the thick mortar in the web joints, subsequent to the original set, a chance to harden completely—and hence to shrink as much as it was going to—until the vault web had thoroughly consolidated throughout to the point where the cambered compartments came to approximate monolithic shells.

In connexion with the cover-joint function of the diagonal ribs there is a further reason for their existence that has apparently not been noted by any writers heretofore. It is a contributing reason for the long delay on the part of the medieval builders in arriving at the ability to construct stone vaults that were other than square or nearly square in plan. Obviously, in a rectangular as opposed to a square bay of vaulting, there are fewer stone courses making up the web of the transverse vault than there are in the longitudinal vault: the latter span is a longer contour than the former. Hence the stereotomy of the groin voussoirs, which is difficult enough in any event, is made practically impossible in the case of rectangular bays of ribless vaulting by the necessity for accommodating this discrepancy in the number of the longitudinal and transverse web courses when they come together along the groin. If the courses of each of the intersecting vaults are of

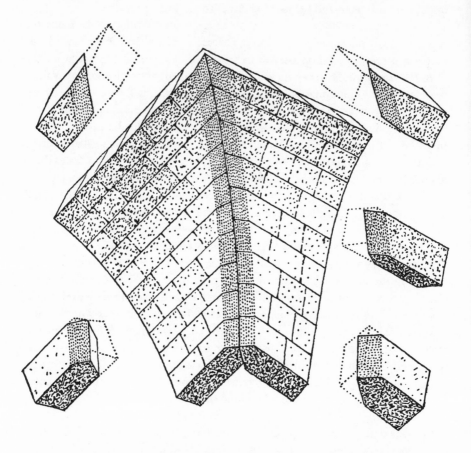

34. *Disparity in the Beds of Courses at the Groin, in Rectangular Bays of Rib Vaulting*

A portion of adjacent panels of vaulting, from about the top of the tas-de-charge to somewhat below the crown, is shown here. In an actual vault, the shaded portion along the groin, together with its continuous joint, would be hidden by the groin rib. But the absence of the groin rib reveals the discrepancy in alignment of the web coursing coming in from right and left, due to the different spans of the transverse and longitudinal vault compartments respectively, which prevents these courses from interlocking above the diagonal rib.

approximately the same width (as was the common practice), the intersections of their beds seldom if ever coincide, since there are more courses in the longitudinal than in the transverse vault (34). If, on the other hand, the number of the courses in each of the intersecting but unequal vaults is made the same, there will be a marked and variable difference in the width of these web courses; and those in the transverse vault will have to taper as they go towards the clerestory wall from the diagonal rib. Either of these alternatives would be extremely difficult, expensive, and slow in execution: quite in contrast to the ease and directness, the relative inexpensiveness, and the speed of construction that the ribbed vault system made possible. For this reason, then, the cover-joint function of the groin rib in Gothic quadripartite vaults, as well as in sexpartite vaults, was a compelling practical necessity.

This circumstance, moreover, discloses the impossibility of the vaulting diagrams given by some writers.[148] And it is emphatically demonstrated in the theoretically arrived at drawings of ashlar vaults, strongly rectangular in plan, and without ribs, that are illustrated in 35, 36, and 37. It is reasonably certain that no vaults were ever stone-jointed in this fashion at any time during the Middle Ages,

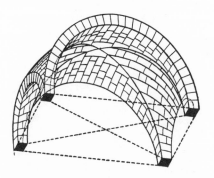

35. *Rectangular Bay of Cut Stone Vaulting with Unstilted Semicircular Boundaries*

Not only the arcs above the short and long sides of the rectangle, but the groins as well, are full semicircles. These conditions produce a highly domed form of vault that would require outside abutment around the curve of the smaller arches, especially at their crowns, because of the steep outward slope of the vault there. The stone courses which go from one short side to the other are shown as widening and narrowing, of necessity, throughout their strongly bowed arcs. Thus all the web voussoirs are of different size, and the groin voussoirs are of very special shape. If such a vault were to cover only the rectangle defined by the inner angles of each pier, its theoretical surface would be spherical and hence without salient groins. However, carrying the vault out to the outer boundaries of the square piers prevents the surfaces from being spherical, and results in the inward-projecting groins (even though these largely die out at their common crown).

where rubble vaults with thick mortar joints were so generally the rule.[149] But these drawings serve none the less to point up the difficulties that would have been encountered, particularly in the voussoirs along the groin, in the case of rubble vaults as well as in those of ashlar.

In any case, it was absolutely essential, visually as well as erectionally, to establish the boundaries of each vaulting compartment. This is evident enough, constructionally, from the medieval builders' growing insistence on securing approximately level crowns throughout, in a bay that was strongly rectangular. For where the rib arches and the vaults were thus of quite unequal spans, the vault surfaces were, in places, vigorously warped. In this situation the ribs—particularly the diagonal ones—served important aesthetic functions. They drew attention away from the twisting, unequal, and at times confusing vault surfaces, by focusing visual interest upon the chief structural lines of the vaulting. Thus they visually simplified and made clearly evident the main elements of the vaulted construction. Furthermore, they revealed by their own slenderness the lightness of the whole vaulted canopy. And they expressed, in their own tensely bowed arcs, the fastidious economy and discriminating precision of design to be found throughout the entire structural system.

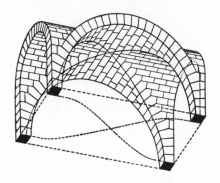

36. *Rectangular Bay of Cut Stone Vaulting, Horizontally Projected, with Level Crowns*

Here the groins result from the intersection of lines projected horizontally from points around the boundary arches. With the smaller of these arches strongly stilted so as to raise their crowns to the level of the other arches' crowns, there is no curvature in the former until the latter are well launched out across the void. This produces serpentine and therefore highly unstructural groins, as may be seen in their projection on plan. It is evident, too, that because of the discrepancy in the two spans there are fewer stone courses around the arches on the short sides of the rectangle than there are around those of the long sides, in spite of the narrower width of the formers' courses. The adjustment of these differences creates specially shaped blocks along the groins.

All these aestheic or visual reasons for the Gothic vaulting ribs are unquestionably valid. But from the practical standpoint the overwhelming reasons for the ribs were erectional ones. As they were the first elements of the Gothic vaulting to be constructed, being erected on their own independent centerings, they determined the curve of the boundaries and hence the subsequent shape of the infilling, or vault surfaces proper, of each compartment.[150]

This is nowhere more clearly demonstrated than in the Gothic trapezoidal bays of the ambulatory where typically the lines of the groins, in plan, do not run straight through as diagonals but break their direction so that they usually intersect above the center of the bay (38 A). There had always been difficulty in vaulting these ambulatory bays because basically they were not even rectangular, let alone square. A certain heavy clumsiness of effect had been inevitable here as long as the vault forms were generated by the projection of semicircular arcs.[151] For in these circumstances the intersection of the groins could be made to occur at the center of the bay only at the expense of having S-shaped and therefore highly unstructural groins (38 B). Although the medieval builders tried a number of different solutions to this problem,[152] none of them was satisfactory until the Gothic

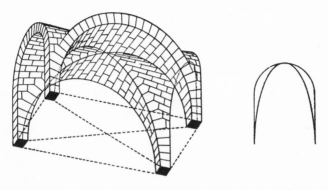

37. Rectangular Bay of Cut Stone Vaulting with Level Crowns and Groins Straight in Plan

This is a structurally sound vault, although one that is demanding of exceptional skill on the part of the stone cutters. Here the boundary arches and the groin arcs are all semicircular, and of these the two pairs of side arches are stilted, the larger only slightly, the smaller considerably. Because the groins are *not* the result of the horizontal projection of points around the curves of the outer arches, neither of the intersecting vaults is cylindrical. The elevation of the curves (looking along the longer axis of the rectangle) is that indicated in the figure to the right, which shows the intrados of the highly stilted semicircular boundary arch within which is the semi-elliptical curve, viewed from this direction, of the groin arcs. On this account, the stone courses in the narrower cells must taper down as they go towards the center of the vault. The horizontal section through the legs of the vault is neither square nor rectangular at any point between the spring and the crown; it is a trapezium.

ribbed vault system was introduced. Only then were these odd-shaped bays brought into correspondence with the lightness of effect and the structural stability and directness that was to be found elsewhere throughout the Gothic vaulting system.

Fundamentally, then, the utilitarian function of the ribs in Gothic vaults was to provide a permanent constructional armature to which the various compartments of the vault proper accommodated themselves. Once built, the ribs thereupon constituted an open framework, each member of which became a boundary for one side of a vaulting compartment whose subsequently erected shape conformed to the curve of these boundary arcs.

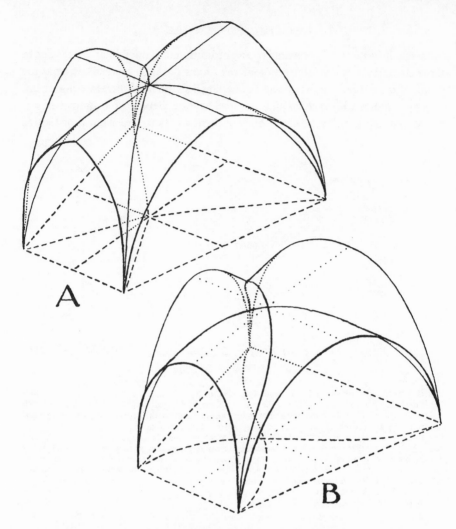

38. *Trapezoidal Ambulatory Bays*

B shows the groin curves and the vault surfaces that are arrived at by the projection of points; i.e. *the geometry of the vault surfaces determines the contour of the groins.* Here the bay is bounded by three equal semicircles and one much smaller, stilted semicircle. The sinuous groins result from the intersection of an approximately semicylindrical surface (from upper left to lower right) with a semi-conical surface (whose axis is tilted in order to produce a level crown from upper right to lower left). Since the groins do not lie in a vertical plane, they are very weak and unsafe.

A shows what is possible with Gothic ribbed vaulting (for clarity, the ribs are not indicated), where *the boundary ribs, including the diagonals, determine the conformation of the vault surfaces.* Here the bay's boundaries are pointed arches, as desired, and each of the half-arches of the diagonals, although breaking direction at their common crown, lies in a vertical plane. The result is a stable and structurally sound vault in which the critical areas along the groins are straight rather than serpentine in plan view.

94

It may be well, at this point, to emphasize again the structural distinction between the function of the groin rib—that essentially Gothic innovation that has just been analysed in the preceding pages—and the transverse rib, whose direct line of antecedents traces back to the banded barrel vault.

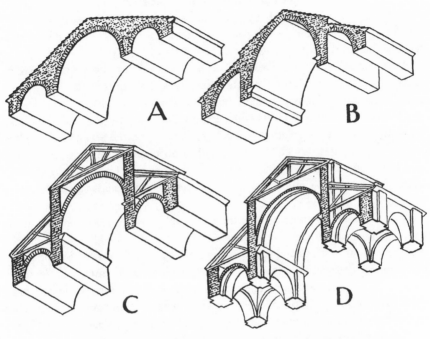

39. Early Vault Forms over Three-Aisled Churches

A and B are rubble vaults whose masonry is solid between the vault intrados and the roof surfaces. A has two small barrel vaults flanking a larger central one, and the roof slopes are unbroken. The pointed barrel vault in B is flanked by ramping half-barrel vaults; here there is less material and hence less weight at the crown of the vault, whose thrusts are abutted more directly by the side-aisle vaults. In C and D vaults and roofs are separated. The latter have now become timber-work structures, completely independent of the vaulting. But the action of the gutter walls and the nave roof assemblage is that of weighting the high vault at its springs, thus helping to stabilize the vault by bending its thrusts in a more downward direction. C is a simple barrel vault with smaller ones flanking it. D shows a banded barrel vault, its shell able to be much thinner than the continuous cylindrical one in C. In D, too, the side-aisle bays corresponding to the intervals between the nave vault's stiffening arches, are covered with groin vaults.

We have seen that both types of rib were indispensable, erectionally, in order to provide boundaries for each vaulting compartment whereby its curvature and conformation were determined. Furthermore, as cover-joints, both types of rib were essential, too, in the interests of erectional economy, in allowing the vault to

95

be built one bay at a time. But the transverse ribs alone, as mentioned above, also had to perform the function of maintaining the cross-sectional contour of the vault. This was a function from which the diagonal ribs, as ribs, were exempt, because the problem was most effectively taken care of along the groin by the deep creases created there by the intersection of the vault webs.

A quick review of some of the significant steps by which the vault shape had previously been maintained will reveal the nature of the problem and its importance in medieval vaulting systems from the start.

At first, in early Romanesque times, the problem was often by-passed by making sheer massiveness absorb this and other difficulties. As long as walls could be very thick and almost windowless, there was no compelling need for understanding much about the nature of vault action, and no sharp incentive for working out an economical and nicely adjusted rationality of means, on the part of the builders. Thus the early masonry churches had either no break at all, or a very slight one, separating the low-sloping planes of the nave's roof from those of the side aisles (39, A and B). Ceiling and roof together were one massive concretion of rubble.

With the desire to give a sense of monumental grandeur to the interior of the church, the nave came to be increased considerably in height. However, the designer did not want to add to the encumbrance at the floor level by increasing the diameter of the nave arcade's piers, although he was tempted to do so on account of the increased height and weight of the superstructure. So now he built great barrel vaults—simple tunnels, but independent, at any rate, of the timber roof above them—in order to lessen the weight (39 C). Irrespective of the tradition of massiveness inherited from the previous ceiling-and-roof-in-one-piece scheme, the chief reason why these simple tunnel vaults had to be very thick was that the builders wanted to make sure that the vault's shape would not deform from that of a semicircle in cross-section to any one of various unsightly, weaker, or even unsafe shapes.

It was next found that the entire vault did not need to be of such massive thickness throughout. Thus the stiffening rings of underlying arches, often in not one but two concentric courses of voussoirs, brought about the banded barrel vault, with its great potential saving in material and hence in both the thrust and the superincumbent weight of the vault (39 D). These single or double-thickness arches of the banded barrel vault maintained the cross-sectional contour of the vault proper, and prevented its semicylindrical or sometimes slightly pointed shape from deforming in any radical degree. The wide spacing of the underlying arches in most of the earliest banded barrel vaults, together with the wide but shallow

96

depth of the bands themselves, presupposes the great thickness of these vaults, and hence the builders' hesitancy in coming to rely upon the bands for maintaining the vault contour as fully as they did later.

With the introduction of groin vaults (doubtless brought about primarily, as we have seen, more for reasons of gaining light directly into the nave), the cross vaults themselves effected an integral stiffening of the contour at regular intervals, on account of their intersection with the longitudinal vault at each bay.

Of much greater significance in the matter of stiffening the vault curvature, however, was the adoption of the domed groin vault. This system was much the most thoroughgoing innovation with respect to assuring the rigidity of the vault shape. For, as we have seen, surfaces of double curvature are in themselves the agents of indeformability. It was doubtless because of their demonstrated trustworthiness in this respect that domed groin vaults were the first vault forms to be used systematically over naves of major span. And the continuing widespread employment of exaggeratedly domed vaults, even into the Gothic-influenced thin-shelled systems of Poitiers Cathedral and of many Angevin churches, gives convincing evidence of the builders' awareness of the rigidity inherent in shapes of double curvature.

However, we have already noted previously that the medieval designers tended to disapprove of the jumpy effect and the irregularly lighted vista of domed groin vaults in series up the nave. Consequently, the twelfth-century designers sought other means than that of doming in order to secure transverse stiffness in their nave vaults.

With sexpartite vaulting, the longitudinal crowns in many instances were made to be nearly horizontal—at least, they appear so as seen from below—from one end of the nave to the other. In spanning the nave, the pseudo-sexpartite vault made use of an extra transverse rib with a thin diaphragm wall on its back reaching up to the level of the cross vault's crown. These spandrel walls above the cross arch gave it a rigid, non-deformable shape, thereby providing stiffness transversely across the nave midway in each bay.

The true sexpartite vault extended this lateral stiffness of the high vault over a larger area than could be done by a simple diaphragm wall above the intermediate transverse rib, as in the pseudo-sexpartite system. For now the two criss-crossing transverse vaults spread their stiffening action throughout much of the upper part of the vault; while the lower portions were kept from deforming (1) by the masonry fill in the funnel of the vaulting conoids, at the corners of each bay, and (2) by the diaphragm wall carried on the back of the intermediate transverse rib up to the level at which the curve of the cross vaults began. In both types of sexpartite vaulting the main transverse rib, located at the junction of successive bays, was usually kept heavy and deep to assure rigidity in that area.[153]

The final mature development of the Gothic system, wherein the bays were strongly rectangular, integrated all the components of the vaulting problem, including that of assuring adequate rigidity transversely in the high, wide-spanning nave vaults, in spite of their sometimes excessively thin webs. This was accomplished partly by the stiffening creases of the vault intersections along the groins, partly by the twisting or cambered contours of the webs (especially in the lower portions of the vault), partly by the light masonry fill in the funnel of the vaulting conoids, and partly by the emphatic stability of relatively heavy transverse arches spanning across the nave at the junction of each successive pair of bays.[154]

These deeply salient transverse arches, then, are seen to be essential in maintaining the cross-sectional contour of the great Gothic nave vaults at a point midway between the groins of successive bays. No such stiffening arches, comparable to these transverse ribs of the longitudinal vault, are needed in the cross vaults, of course. For one thing, these latter are of much smaller span. But above all, no transverse stiffeners are needed in the cross vaults because they are rigidly tied together in series from one end of the nave to the other, along the clerestory wall tops, by the continuous masonry of the spandrels and the gutter walls above them. Obviously it would be almost impossible for longitudinal movement of any consequence to occur here, weighted as these wall-tops are by the great roof, anchored as they are at either end by towers or by the piled-up bracing of the chevet complex, and linked as they are, lower down, by the nave arcade and triforium spandrels, as well as by the clerestory spandrels and their masonry superstructure, at the top. It is only in the great *longitudinal* vault of Gothic naves that no commensurate positiveness of rigidity throughout is automatically provided; and in this respect the transverse ribs have a major function to fulfil, to whatever extent they can.

Wherever they occur, in medieval vaults of any sort, the ribs were of course the first members to be constructed. In Gothic vaults their erection was a much less cumbersome operation than in the case of typical Romanesque vaults. For they could be constructed independently, one bay at a time, over centerings that were thin and relatively easy to handle, that could be used again and again in subsequent bays. The simplification they effected, moreover, applied not only directly with respect to their own erection, but also indirectly with respect to their influence on the ensuing erection of the vault webs. For the edges of these webs, as has been noted above, rested upon the ribs and conformed throughout, of necessity, to the arcs of the ribs. The web of each compartment, therefore, departed from a normal arc-generated curvature by being more or less warped, as dictated by its conformity with the boundary edges.

In addition, the Gothic vaults were almost invariably cambered;[155] that is to say, the surfaces of the web compartments were made to bow out slightly, and the crowns of the vault somewhat arched, instead of running through straight from one boundary rib to another. The variable surfaces of these warped and cambered webs would have been almost impossible for the Gothic designer to lay out graphically; and even if he had been able to make accurate projection drawings of these irregular surfaces, none of the workmen could have translated them into actual stone and mortar. As it was, each vaulting compartment was an independent and isolated job from the standpoint of the mason who undertook to build it. Actually, with the fixed boundaries furnished by the ribs to guide him and to limit his difficulties,[156] the mason could proceed in the confident assurance that the warped and cambered contour of the vault web would result naturally—one might almost say inevitably—out of the erectional techniques he was by then accustomed to employ.

Just what these customary techniques were, however, is far from clear at this distant date. There is more than a little uncertainty and ignorance with regard to the precise nature of the Gothic practices employed in erecting the web. Nevertheless, in his famous *Dictionnaire*,[157] Viollet-le-Duc postulates the use of the *cerce* with such a confident air that this device and his explanation of its operation have received very widespread acceptance.

But there are a number of difficulties about the use of the cerce as a means of building the webs of ribbed vaults, and these difficulties his account either ignores or skims over without adequate clarification.

For example, it is hard to believe that the two slotted boards of his cerce, at their maximum extension, would be able to support a course of even quite thin stonework across a span of at least 20 feet; that is, half the span of a 40-foot-wide nave.[158] Yet a gap of this extent would have occurred in the transverse compartments of almost all the great Gothic churches near the vault crowns, the very location where the coursing of the web was most dependent for support, from this or any other type of formwork. In this situation the cerce device would have been most extended, and therefore weakest in resisting both bending and lateral deflexion, at the very time it was called upon to support its greatest load. For obviously the load was greatest at the courses closest to the crown, both because of the length of these courses and hence the amount of stone they had to carry, and also because of the near-verticality of their bed joints.[159] It seems difficult to believe, then, that a cerce light enough in weight to be manipulated from one finished course to the one next to be constructed above it would be strong enough to do the job it was called upon to do in such an extended position.

At the very least, the marked variation in the length of the web courses from spring to crown would have required a *set* of cerces in graduated sizes, so that each might accommodate safely and effectively a small number of successive courses as the construction of the web advanced.

Another difficulty that is insufficiently accounted for involves the hanging of the cerce. Viollet-le-Duc insists that the two boards forming the cerce must be held in a vertical position, on edge. His illustration shows a metal strap which terminates in a horizontally projecting flange or lip at the top of the board, one at each end.[160] Viollet-le-Duc says that these flanges 'are fixed upon the extradoses of the arches'—the top surfaces of the stone ribs—'by pins or by a handful of plaster'.[161] The difficulty here is that the lip of the cerce's end would be resting on the top of the rib just where the end stones of the web course would have to bear. This would make an awkward enough situation even if the ribs, instead of being curved, ran horizontally. But the fact is that the ribs curve from a near vertical to a near horizontal slope as they approach the crown of the vault. Hence, in order to maintain the boards of the cerce in a vertical plane, the flanges would have to be cocked at a variable but considerable angle with the extrados of the rib. This would produce a condition in which an end stone of each web course would be held away from the top of the rib (which was destined to be its permanent support) by the temporary interference of a cocked flange.

Obviously the cerce could not be removed until the cambered course of stonework it temporarily supported went all the way across from rib to rib, with the course's end stones resting on the backs of the ribs. Yet as long as the cerce was in position, its cocked flanges would hold these end stones an appreciable distance from their intended support on the rib extrados at each end. Even close to the vault crown, where the curve of the ribs becomes more nearly horizontal, the end stones would be held free of their proper support by something more than the thickness of the cerce's metal flanges. And it is clear that the weight and pressure of the end stones must not confine these flanges so closely or tightly that there would be danger of dislocating the stone course that had just been completed, when the cerce was retracted and its flanges pulled free.

In any case, it is hard to see how both temporary cerce and permanent web course alike could be supported from the same points. Where the vaulting rib was rebated, the shelf for receiving the edge of the web panel was normally not over

2 inches wide. This provided little enough bearing either for the end stone of a course or for the metal flange of the cerce. To expect both to be independently accommodated—especially when the stone courses of the web were as narrow as the masons usually made them—seems patently improbable, if not impossible.

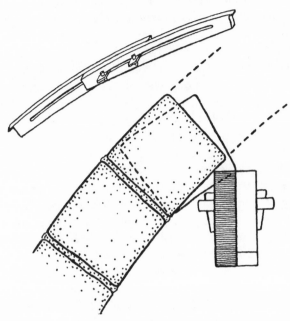

40. *Viollet-le-Duc's Cerce Device as Support for Each Web Course During the Erection of the Vault*

The smaller-scale drawing shows a cerce, based on Viollet-le-Duc's representation and description. Its extended position clearly indicates how one slotted board laps the other. Hung vertically as support for the stones of a web course, it is seen (in the detailed section) that the stones of any given course cannot line up throughout: those that lean against the far board (shown in outline) tilt much more than those that lean against the near board (shown hatched). As no such break does occur in the alignment of the web stone-coursing, it is obvious that the cerce device was not used in this fashion, in spite of Viollet-le-Duc's assertion that it was.

A further difficulty occurs in connexion with Viollet-le-Duc's insistence that the boards of the cerce be kept in a vertical plane. The cerce device, as clearly illustrated in the *Dictionnaire*, consists of two cambered and slotted boards which are held side by side with wedges through their curved slots. Except only in the position of maximum contraction, each board stretches somewhat less than the overall length of the cerce. In fact, the evident advantage of its employment would be that

101

the cerce's length is subject to controlled variation within fairly wide limits. As it becomes extended, more and more of its length at either end is seen to consist of a single board; thus only in a varying amount of length at mid-span do the two boards remain lapped. Consequently, the upper vault-side edge of the cerce does not continue through from one end of the cerce to the other in a single cambered line; instead, it breaks back at the point where the near board ends its lap past the far board. Thus, with the upper vault-side edge of the inner board set in position to support the stones of a web course, a break in the line of that stone course would inevitably occur where this first board ended, for here the stones of the course would have to lean farther out to get their support from the other, outer board (40). The fact that no such break does occur in the surface of the web courses is conclusive evidence that Viollet-le-Duc's explanation is incomplete, at the very least, on this point.

There is a very serious difficulty in connexion with lateral pressure against the ribs during the course of erection. It seems to be fairly well understood that in any completed vault of stone masonry based on the arch principle, the major lines of pressure follow the direction that a steel ball would take, starting on the extrados at the crown and rolling outward and downward following the shortest, most direct path in response to the effect of gravity. But during the process of erection, one course upon another up the curve of the vault, the courses close to the ridge would receive very little support from the previously completed ones, on account of the steep pitch of their beds.[162] Until the whole shell of a vaulting compartment was completed, therefore, these uppermost courses would derive their chief support not along their lower side but at either end. Hence, for a short while during construction, each of these uppermost courses in turn had to undergo arch action longitudinally, throughout its length from rib to rib.

If some kind of cerce device had actually been employed, it would obviously have been in consideration of this arch action that the French Gothic builders took the precaution of cambering their vault webs. For the length of the uppermost courses near the crown was too great for these rows of small stones to span from transverse or wall rib to diagonal rib in a perfectly horizontal line. Where the vault was not sharply pointed, the camber was necessary in order to develop the arch action of each of these high courses of stone, one after another, during the process of erection. Otherwise, as flat arches, the individually constructed courses would have been in serious danger of collapsing upon removal of the cerce.

Such arch action, however, would have pressed strongly against the ribs at either end of the stone course when the temporary support of the cerce was withdrawn at the completion of each successive course. By themselves, and even with their own falsework supports, the ribs would have been powerless to withstand pressure from this lateral direction. Hence, if the cerce technique was ever employed at all, its use was possible only when the coursing of *all* the compartments of a vaulting bay were carried up at the same rate. Only with such a procedure could there be assurance that the nearly horizontal arch action of individual courses in adjacent compartments was mutually abutted at the rib.

But even if the progressive succession of courses in all the compartments of a vaulting bay were executed at a uniform rate, the lateral pressure against the *transverse* rib near the crown of the vault would be unaccounted for in the direction of the next bay to be vaulted. Although it would have involved additional expense and labour, this deficiency *could* have been provided for by introducing temporary struts or braces outside the bay currently under construction, until the webs in that bay were completed. Upon completion of the bay of vaulting, the lateral action of the upper courses against these transverse ribs (as against all the ribs, in fact) would no longer be a serious consideration, of course. For, in a completed compartment, whatever voussoir action may take place is that of the normal vault action from the crown downward and outward. This normal action, upon completion of the vault, supersedes the individual arch actions of successive web courses, from rib to rib, which would be operative during the course of erection if a cerce were used.

With construction by means of a cerce, moreover, the transverse rib's width and heaviness, which often persisted far into Gothic times, would have been influenced by this rib's temporary role (doubtless with the help of some lateral bracing externally) of abutting the arch action of the upper courses of the vault web at the time of their erection. As far as the primary action of the finished vault itself was concerned, however, these transverse ribs had a negligible function. They were there, as we have seen, principally to help maintain the transverse contour of the vault, and to act as cover-joints so that the bays could be constructed one at a time.

A final difficulty in the employment of the cerce is that of the time needed for the mortar joints to harden. It is likely that the mortar in the joints between successive stones forming a web course would have had to set a longer time than would be suggested by the use of a cerce. For at the time of erection, as previously noted in the case of courses close to the vault crown, these stones would have constituted a flat arch of very slight camber. Hence their mortar joints would have been subject to much higher than normal compressive stresses at the moment of decentering the cerce, when the mortar was still green; otherwise the cerce would have had to be left in place for each course, in turn, for a considerable period of time: for many days if not weeks, in fact.[163]

Apparently the builders were aware of the fact that there should be no haste in removing centerings of any sort, if we can accept in this respect the evidence of some of the manuscript illustrations. For example, a fourteenth-century illumination shows a window-arch centering still in position although the arch ring is complete and the mason is laying a course of stone above it.[164] Again, a fifteenth-century manuscript illustration depicts a doorway-arch centering which remains in place although the masonry construction has proceeded a whole story and a half above it.[165]

It is conceivable that some kind of cerce device might work for dry-wall construction where the stones were carefully cut to fit without mortar (provided the cerce's other shortcomings could be adequately disposed of). But the individual web stones of Gothic vaulting were invariably set in thick beds of mortar. In any case, it seems highly doubtful that the medieval builders would have used the little wooden wedges that are employed today with the accurately cut blocks of monumental stonework as a means for maintaining the proper width of joint against the pressure of the blocks. The stones of medieval vaults were normally much too small to make it feasible to use these little wedges; and furthermore, the blocks to be held apart were fairly roughly shaped and hence had joints of variable width.[166]

The difficulties discussed above appear to be conclusive enough to prevent the full acceptance of Viollet-le-Duc's cerce device as the method employed by the French Gothic builders in erecting their vault webs, at least for vaults of wide span above the naves and choirs of their great churches. It is possible that the cerce *principle* was adapted and made use of in some fashion for the construction of Gothic vaults. Indeed, as we have seen, the whole trend of French medieval vaulting development was in the direction of simplification, rationality, and reduction in the amount of centering required. But if Viollet-le-Duc is correct in postulating a light, adjustable, and easily movable centering, course by course, for the erection of high nave vaults of large span, then some modification of his specific details would seem to be required. Either his *theory* of the cerce's use is inadequately reasoned out, or his description of its operation in *practice* is incomplete and ambiguous in accounting for some of the details of its operation.

In this connexion it will perhaps be of interest to comment on what certain subsequent writers have said on the subject.

One of these writers, Arthur Kingsley Porter, published a thin, photographically illustrated volume which purports to explain the erectional practices followed in early Gothic vaults. Porter's thesis is that the medieval builders came to adopt the ribbed vault because these vaults were 'easier, or less expensive than others to build'.[167] This is a cogent observation, which recognizes the universal principle that economic considerations are always substantial factors in determining of what materials a structure is built and how these materials are used. But Porter says that these economic considerations were the 'sole motive that induced the French builders to adopt the ribbed vault' (p. 2). This is a very exaggerated claim. It would be a sorry day indeed for architecture if its forms were ever determined 'solely on the basis of economy'. Even Porter himself admits that after the completion of such a vault 'the ribs strengthened it, prevented cracks at the groins, and tended to oppose deformation' (pp. 16, 21). But his admission is somewhat perfunctory, without discussion or clarification. Furthermore, Porter's mere assertion that ribbed vaulting was adopted solely for reasons of economy is not very illuminating to us, either in respect to explaining the steps leading up to the development of the ribbed vault system, or the technique of actual erection once this system had come to be adopted. He relies almost entirely on the supposed use of the cerce to substantiate his reiterated assertion that 'ribbed vaults were built practically without centering'.[168]

Porter's uncritical acceptance of the cerce as a panacea for practically all Gothic vaulting difficulties is without specific and detailed explanation of its actual functioning. Not only does he fail to account for the difficulties and contradictions mentioned above, but he unwittingly raises one of his own without resolving it. This has to do with the coursing of the web masonry.

It will be remembered that Viollet-le-Duc insists that the boards of the cerce must be kept in a vertical plane so that each cambered course, as it continues through from one rib to another, may have its individual stones lean against the vault-side top edge of the cerce. Yet Porter says: 'In the vaults the stone courses are seldom perfectly regular. It is not rare to find them as irregularly disposed as in Fig. 9, one stone being cut to fill an odd-shaped opening between two others, courses twisting and dying away, at times frankly broken.'[169] This admission of the occurrence of non-continuity in the examples cited (and illustrated by photographs) denies the technique of erection with a cerce which is explained so confidently by Viollet-le-Duc. For, with twisted or broken continuity, the stones of a single course could not have been supported solely by one upper edge of the cerce, as Viollet-le-Duc claims they should be. Furthermore, the independent arch action of each successive course during erection, which is readily acknowledged by Porter (p. 8), could never have been operative in a situation where the courses are twisted or broken.

Most of the early ribbed vaults Porter cites—and upon which his thesis is based—were those over side aisles, in crypts, or in towers, all of which would normally have been destined to support a horizontal pavement. Not only their small span but also the built-up and surcharged loading of their tops produced vaulting conditions of a quite different nature from those of the relatively thin-shelled vaults of large span built high above the naves of Gothic cathedrals. If it is true, as Porter and others have maintained, that ribbed vaults were first built under towers and in crypts, where the vault was surcharged and there were no abutment difficulties, such vaults had little in common with the structural problems encountered in the high vaults. The rib pattern, springing levels, and shape of arches; the disengaging of the ribs at their springing, and their seating on capitals or other imposts: these and like considerations could all be worked out without serious involvement with the special and complicated problems of equilibrium and the mechanics of vault thrusts that would be encountered in building high vaults. At most, it seems evident that the adoption of ribs under towers and in crypts facilitated the erection of the vaulting there; and in addition the usually massive ribs encountered at these places in the building undoubtedly reinforced the structure locally. But as for any unsubstantiated claim that ribbed vaults could be built 'without centering', these heavy vaults of small span can tell us nothing about the procedures that were followed in constructing ribbed vaults of wide span raised high above the lofty naves of the great cathedrals.

It is quite possible, however, that one of the chief reasons for the adoption of the ribbed vault came to be not so much that it economized on centering, as Porter insists, but that it made possible much thinner vault shells (primarily because of the rigidifying creases along the groin) than were felt to be necessary in barrel or even groin vaults. We have seen (note 146) that Choisy calls attention to the fact that the webs of simple groin vaults must be as thick, throughout, as their intersection along the critical groin required them to be. With the adoption of the diagonal rib under the groin, however, this compulsion was removed, since thereafter it was the ensemble of the uncomplicated mitred seam of the intersecting vaults, together with the cover-joint reinforcement of the rib along the groin crease, that assured adequate strength and stiffness in this critical area of the vaulting. Innumerable examples testify that, almost at once, vault thicknesses were reduced to half, or less, of what they were wont to have been in pre-ribbed types of vaulting. Since this reduced the weight of the vault by approximately half, and correspondingly lessened its thrust, the builders could now fashion a church, similar in size to a former barrel- or groin-vaulted one, with far less material. However, they chose to take advantage of this startling diminishment in the amount of material required by making much loftier, larger, and more light-flooded structures.

It was, therefore, the economy of *means*, via this economy of materials made possible by the adoption of the ribbed vault, that constituted the significant and far-reaching advantage of the ribbed vault system. We will see that, at least in the high nave vaults of early Gothic cathedrals, the falsework requirements were anything but negligible; on the contrary, they would seem to have been complicated and demanding of substantial amounts of both labour and materials. The early economy that was brought about through the agency of the ribbed vault was certainly of the greatest and most pervading significance, not only to the vaulting itself but to the entire structural programme—the very appearance and character, indeed—of subsequently built churches. But at the time the ribbed vault first came to be adopted, this extraordinary economy could hardly be said to have been exclusively, or even primarily, in terms of the reduction or near elimination of erectional falsework, which Porter keeps harping on.

The English writer, Francis Bond, accepts Viollet-le-Duc's cerce device in his earlier book,[170] but in the 105-page chapter on vaulting in his two-volume work, seven years later, nothing is said about a cerce. Instead, he says: 'It is not certain what particular method was employed by the masons for filling up the cells. Probably planks were laid across from rib to rib, and on them was built the web; these would be re-used in all other cells of the same shape and dimensions.'[171] Later (p. 319) he enlarges upon this speculation: 'These webs of ashlar were built up in slightly arched courses, the bottom course starting at the tas-de-charge. To obtain the arched form, a wooden centre for each course would be wanted; a short one at the bottom, and others successively longer as the ridge of the vault was neared. . . .' Although he says that these planks, one for each course, could be re-used in successive vaulting cells of the same dimensions, he does not suggest how these planks would be prevented from deflecting with the weight of stones in one of the long courses—up to 20 feet or more—close to the vault crown. Nor does he say how the ends of these planks were supported.

In regard to the latter problem, most architectural historians, including Bond, follow the explanation given in Viollet-le-Duc's illustration of formwork for the webs of Romanesque vaulting, which involves planks set flatwise, their bevelled ends supported on the downward-tilted outer edge of the rib's extrados.[172]

Actually this technique was probably never used in Romanesque vaulting except perhaps in a few cases where the span was very limited; and certainly, for Gothic vaults, it is a patently improbable if not an impossible scheme. There is nothing here, except for their strongly bowed shapes, to indicate how the planks were kept from deflecting under the weight of the stones they would have had to support; and if the planks were sprung into their bowed position—a most unlikely practice—there would have been no easy way to decenter them. Weighted with the stones of a web course, they would have tended to press the ribs at either end out of alignment. Furthermore, this scheme could work if at all only with highly domed vault panels; and we have seen that the crowns of Gothic vaults are reported to be only slightly cambered. Finally, there is no evidence that the outer edges of the ribs were chamfered, as shown in Viollet-le-Duc's drawing, in order to receive the tapered ends of the planks. Not only Viollet-le-Duc himself but all other writers who have published profiles of actual rib sections fail to show a single instance of this feature. French Gothic rib-sections are invariably shown either with level tops or, in the case of the later rebated type, with ledges that are right-angled in cross-section.

The simple explanation, which seems to have escaped all the writers to date, of how the web formwork—whatever it may have been—was supported at the ribs, is that *it rested not on the extrados of the stone rib itself but on one of the top edges of the rib centering.*

We have previously emphasized the fact that the centerings for the ribs would have had to remain in place for a considerable length of time while the mortar in their joints set. It is clear, moreover, that the presence of these rib centerings was absolutely indispensable while the webs were under construction, in order to prevent any distortions or deformations in the curves of the ribs due to the gradual increment of their loading, up the curve from either side, as each web course came to be added. So, as they had to be there in any event, what could be more efficient and economical than to make use of the top edges of these timber-work centerings, rather than the top of the stone ribs, to support the web's formwork? With a technique of this sort, the improbable situation would have been eliminated in which both the web course and its plank or cerce formwork would have been bearing on the same narrow ledge, during erection. Instead, the temporary formwork would have been supported on the temporary centerings, and the permanent web courses would have received their support from the back or rebate of the permanent stone rib: what was to be permanent and what was to be temporary would not have interfered with each other. If planking of some sort was used for the formwork of the web, this technique would even have aided in the decentering operation. For in this case, whatever scheme was used for freeing the rib centering would have automatically freed the web formwork along with the temporary falsework on which the ribs had been erected and to which the web formwork was attached.[173]

Ten years or so before his *Dictionnaire* came to be published, Viollet-le-Duc himself wrote a number of chapters 'On the Construction of Religious Monuments in France' that were published in serial form in the French archaeological periodical *Annales archéologiques*. It is interesting to note that in these articles he has nothing to say about the cerce device, although he does deal specifically, in his chapter v,[174] with a technique of erecting the vault web. This consists of planks set *on edge*; but instead of their hanging vertically, as he subsequently insists the cerce must do, these planks are set *radially*; that is, normal to the curve of the vault and in line with the bed joints of the web (his fig. 15, p. 197). He shows the upper edge of these planks very strongly cambered (fig. 13); and indicates that they were supported, not on the backs or extradoses of the stone ribs, but on a rounded moulding at the side of the ribs (fig. 14).

This latter point of support would have provided a most unlikely lodging for the planking on which web courses of any length might be constructed. For here the bearing is very slight and precarious, being rounded instead of flat. Such a bearing would cause the plank, as it became loaded, either to break off the salient moulding it rested against, or at least to press the whole rib block out of alignment by wedge action against it. Furthermore, each plank of this formwork would be at an acute and dangerous angle with the diagonal rib that supported one end of it, not at right angles as implied by the drawing. And again, there is no provision indicated for decentering the planking.

It is highly unlikely, therefore, that any but the very smallest vault webs were ever built with the lagging supported by grooves in the moulded ribs, in the fashion indicated. But it is worth noting that Viollet-le-Duc originally conceived of the web course lagging as consisting of planks set both on edge and in a radial position, rather than as continuous formwork with boards set flatwise, or as a single extensible cerce hung vertically.

Incidentally, Viollet-le-Duc's fig. 12 (p. 196) indicates the way in which, he claims, the stone coursing of adjacent panels of the web were interlocked above the groin rib: instead of abutting each other in a straight groin joint above the center-line of the rib, they create a zigzag joint. If this condition actually did obtain above the diagonal ribs of any ribbed vaulting, the two adjacent panels would appear to be knitted together in a seemingly effective fashion. But his drawing is misleading. It looks logical and simple enough in this ostensible plan view. However, it must be remembered that the beds of the intersecting web courses are not in a common plane, nor do they intersect (because of the curve of the vault surfaces) at a constant angle. Consequently, as described here by Viollet-le-Duc, there is a series of partial voids, alternately on either side of the valley that marks the extrados of the groin (41). These voids are created by the alternating projection,

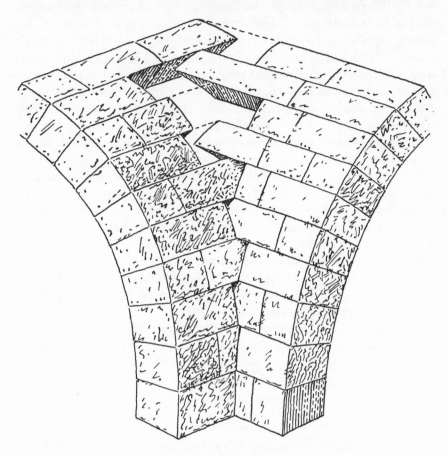

41. *Viollet-le-Duc's Scheme of Interlocking Voussoirs along the Groin*

This scheme looks effective and logical enough in the ostensible plan view and the description given in Viollet-le-Duc's *Annales* account. But the omitted blocks in the upper part of the present drawing show how highly unstructural and even impossible it would be in actual practice. A further conclusive reason why this scheme could not have been adopted in other than square bays is demonstrated in 34, where the web courses of the intersecting vaults are shown to lack mutual conformity.

beyond this valley, of both the backs and the beds of the web blocks of one vault as they continue past the point at which those of the corresponding course of the other vault would normally meet them.[175] These alternating voids could be elimi-

110

nated only if the masons stuffed them with masses of mortar (a very unstructural and even unsafe makeshift) or cut the groin blocks in the complicated, many-faceted shapes demanded in the case of simple groin vaults without ribs.[176]

One of the very reasons for the introduction of groin ribs, however, was to eliminate this costly and difficult operation of stereotomy. As we have seen, the rib's function was not only the erectional one of determining the contour of the vault panels but also the erectionally simplifying aesthetic one of covering the joint along the groin, which was made as simple to build as possible. The zigzag joint of the scheme indicated in Viollet-le-Duc's fig. 12 would certainly not have been the simplest possible one to build. And the alternating voids it would produce (unless the most difficult and complicated stone-cutting were adopted) would have created weakness rather than strength along the groin, the most critical area in any intersecting vault.

Finally, a conclusive reason why this interlocking of the web courses would never have been possible along the groins of a Gothic quadripartite vault is that the number of web courses in the longitudinal and transverse compartments did not agree, as we have seen above; so that the bed joints of the courses in adjacent vault panels almost never occurred at a common level, as implied by Viollet-le-Duc's fig. 12. The normal and easiest practice—one can almost say, the invariable practice—where there were ribs below the groins, was to have the joints continuous, not zigzag, along the actual seam of the groin. Thus the full cross-sectional thickness of both vault compartments was maintained only to the edge of the rib, on each side; whereupon the cross-sectional area of the rib more than compensated for the bevelled reduction in the web's thickness.

The French writer and editor, Marcel Aubert, does not completely rule out the cerce device. He states that

In the medieval texts the raising and keying of the diagonal ribs, the transverse ribs, and the formerets constituted the first and most important operation in the construction of the vault; the compartments were built of masonry afterwards, and generally without its being a question of new scaffoldings. . . . On this skeleton of stone ribs, while it was still reinforced by the centerings that had served in erecting it, the lagging or the movable cerces were established on which the infillings were built. On the extrados of certain arches one can still observe the longitudinal rebates and the grooves designed to receive the ends of the lagging and [*sic*] of the cerces. . . . In general, the lagging rested directly on the extrados of the arches, and the interval thus created between the upper ledge of the voussoirs and the intrados of the vault had to be stuffed with mortar and hidden beneath a plaster coating. . . . Light scaffoldings, disposed from one centering to another, could relieve the laggings when the surface to be covered was considerable.[177]

We have dealt in the preceding pages with many of the items in this account, indicating which of them can be accepted and which of them is incomplete or actually misleading. We see with what caution Aubert speaks of the cerce, although at one point he accepts the employment of *both* lagging and cerce in the construction of the web. He doubts whether the erection of the webs required 'new scaffoldings', but later suggests that light intermediate scaffoldings may have been used where the spans of the lagging were considerable.

This is an interesting speculation. It is worth investigating the particulars and the consequences of these suggested intermediate scaffoldings. First of all, it seems highly unlikely, in France as opposed to England, that they would have been laid out as separate arch centerings, as though for additional ribs. For we have seen that the ribs determined the vault surfaces for each of the web panels they defined, with whatever warping or cambering might occur in the intervening surfaces of these panels therefrom. Intermediate centerings or 'scaffoldings', to support the longer spans of the lagging, would have upset the naturalness of these windings and bowings of the web surfaces. And everything we learn from contemporary texts about the medieval knowledge of mathematics would indicate that the practical geometry of the times would not have been sufficient to have guided the designers in laying out these intermediate curves on the drafting table. Certainly the nature of the web's curvature of surface strongly substantiates the fact that it was the contour of the boundary ribs that determined it, for each panel of infilling.

Yet in the case of planking there may well have had to be some reinforcement against deflexion in the formwork which supported the longer stone courses, near the crown of the vault, at the middle of their spans. Perhaps this reinforcement may have been supplied by a sort of light scaffolding or even a few diagonal struts to brace the lagging—if the latter were of planks on edge rather than planking set flatwise—after this had been shaped and placed on its supports (the rib centering at either end of the planking). Such a procedure, with planks on edge, would not be in disagreement with Bond's suggestion of a separate plank for each of the stone courses of the web. In any case, such additional bracing would be needed only in the upper portion of each of the *transverse* vault panels, for the maximum length of the courses in the longitudinal panels of quadripartite vaulting would be only about 10 feet, and this distance could be adequately spanned by simple planks on edge. However, additional support would have been needed in the transverse vaulting panels, both because of the greater length of these high courses in the quadripartite system and because, in this region of the high courses, considerable support would no longer have been provided for each range of stones by the course immediately below it, due to the greater slope of the radial beds there as compared to those of the lower courses.

It would have been quite possible for the medieval carpenters to have fashioned this bracing to conform to the planking *after* it was in place, spanning from rib to rib, so that no difficult geometrical layout would have been involved: the bracing would only have had to accommodate itself to the *planking*, once that was put in place in the normal rib-to-rib fashion. After being scribed to the previously in-stalled lagging, these additional struts in the higher part of the formwork could probably have received their seating diagonally from convenient points in the falsework structure lower down. In any case, the fact that they would have been needed only to brace the actual formwork (that is, the planking) would indicate that these additional struts could be an adjunct to both the formwork and the rib centering, and therefore attached separately, independently, as need arose.

In line with the suggestion that a separate cambered plank served for each stone course of the web, it is probable that *the cerce was no more than an adjustable template.* Placed in position at a given height on the backs of adjacent rib centerings, its extension could be marked and then a single plank cut to the shape of that degree of extension. In this way the cerce would have become, not itself the support for the stone courses, but the adjustable pattern from which each successive plank that was destined to support the stone courses would be fashioned.

This scheme would have taken care of many of the difficulties noted above in regard to the use of the cerce as advanced by Viollet-le-Duc. With a single plank spanning all the way from rib to rib, there would now be no break produced in the surface of the web courses such as would have had to occur in the case of the lapped boards of the cerce. Suggestions have already been offered in regard to how additional support for the longest courses, close to the crown, may have been provided. And we have seen that the lodging of the planking on the rib centerings, instead of on the stone ribs themselves, obviated another of the unworkable features of the cerce device as described. Finally, with plank formwork supported by the rib centerings and remaining in place as long as these centerings did, to be decentered automatically along with the rib centers, the two remaining difficulties were over-come: insufficient drying time for the mortar in the web joints, and lateral pressure against the ribs when the cerce was removed upon completion of each successive web course.

As for the difficulty inadvertently raised by Porter, that some of the web courses twisted or died away, this is a condition that seems to have occurred only in some

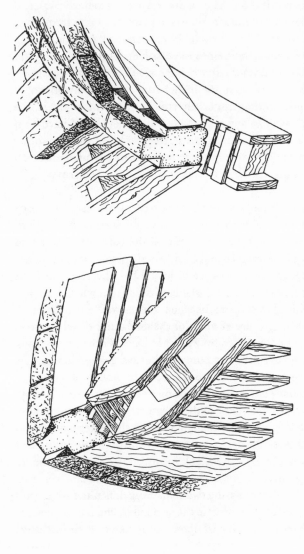

42 and 43. *Construction Details near the Crown of a Diagonal Rib, in a Square Bay of Ribbed Vaulting: Viewed from Below and from Above*

These two drawings show how this portion of a ribbed vault over a square bay might conceivably be erected nowadays. Although this is unquestionably not the kind of formwork used in Gothic times, certain features of it are analogous to the practices that may have been employed by the Gothic builders: for example, (1) a centering frame whose cleated extrados is wider than the stone rib it supports, so that (2) the lagging units can rest upon this frame at either side of the rib; (3) these lagging units being set on edge rather than flatwise, one for each stone course. In the downward view it is worth noting that the crease along the groin, though inappreciable at the crown, becomes deeper at the corner of the bay, until the stone courses of the two intersecting vaults approach each other at right angles just above their springings. This view also demonstrates that the extradoses of the diagonal rib and of each intersecting vault are portions of surfaces that curve in three different directions. As previously noted, rib stems which penetrate the thickness of the vault along the groin could occur in French vaults only over square bays, not over the strongly rectangular bays of quadripartite vaulting.

114

of the earliest rib vaults,[178] where the less proficient and less economical erectional practices of earlier vaulting types were probably still employed. Certainly such broken or twisted courses do not seem to be found in the great vaults of the mature Gothic churches, except in the lowest portions of the vaulting conoid where the spans of the courses are very short and where the beds of these courses are probably far less steeply inclined than the angle of friction.

A further advantage of this scheme would have been the guidance it provided to the masons in determining the direction and width of the web courses so that they might become parallel to the crown in the upper part of the vault. Instead of the snapped chalk-line as guide, each of the planks, installed of necessity in advance of the stone-setting, would indicate the exact number of stone courses intended to complete the infilling, as well as their direction and the taper, if any, of their sides in order to adjust to a slightly different direction as the courses came to be brought into alignment parallel to the ridge.

We have previously noted, in the case of the transverse vault compartments, that the web courses immediately above the tas-de-charge cannot be parallel to the crown, in plan, because of the 'ploughshare twist' warping of the vault surfaces. Moreover, it is conspicuously evident in many Gothic churches that these courses are far from being horizontal; indeed, they are not parallel to the crown either in plan or in elevation, but usually slope downward (in French as opposed to English vaults, where another procedure of web coursing was frequently operative) as they go from diagonal rib towards the clerestory wall.

This probably came about via a practical consideration in the laying out of the web coursing, as follows. Knowing that the courses must be parallel at the crown, so that there would need to be no difficult or unstructural fitting of the stones there, the masons would have started at the crown of the formeret and at the crown of the diagonal rib in laying out the spacing of the web courses. But the length of the diagonal rib's half-arch was so much longer than that of the formeret that there would have been some of the diagonal rib left unaccounted for (working down from the crown) by the time the wall arch, including its stilting, had been marked off all the way down to the tas-de-charge. Hence, in the subsequently built masonry, the vault courses immediately above the tas-de-charge would have had to be constructed in strongly sloped directions, to compensate for this discrepancy of rib length, gradually becoming more level as the higher courses approaching the vault crown came to be built[179] (44).

To the objection that planks on edge instead of flatwise would seem to require an inordinate number of boards for the formwork, it can be pointed out that, on

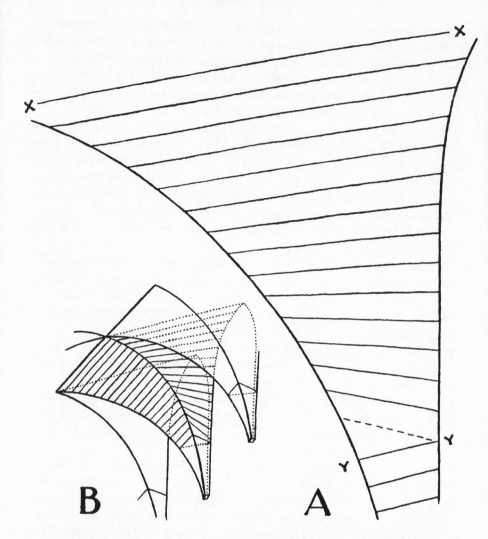

44. *Stone-Coursing in Lateral Compartments of Quadripartite Vaulting*

The diagram at A represents the development of one of the lateral surfaces of the vaulting conoid, in a strongly rectangular bay, and demonstrates the successive tilting of the web courses as laid out from the crown downward (though erected, of course, from the bottom up). A triangular or trapezoidally shaped block results, by way of transition, immediately above the horizontal beds of the tas-de-charge. The crown line, x–x, is approximately *horizontal*, as is y–y, the top of the tas-de-charge. As demonstrated in the schematic detail drawing at B, however, these bed joints are *not parallel* in the vault itself, due to the ploughshare twisting of the vault surfaces in the lateral compartments.

the contrary, less wood was needed. To be sure, A in 45 indicates a slight increase in the depth of the planks (in combination) over their width when they are set flatwise (as at B) to provide a continuous surface. But the latter would necessitate a large amount of intermediate timber-work support to prevent the planks from sagging under the weight of the stone coursing: in fact, possibly at intervals as

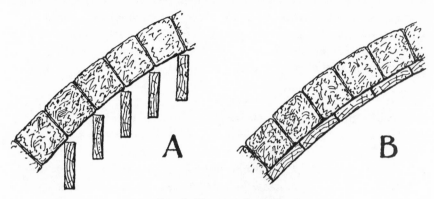

45. *Vault Formwork of Planks*

The section through a portion of the vault, at B, shows planking set flatwise; that at A, planks set edgewise in a vertical position, one for each stone course. For the warped and cambered surfaces of Gothic ribbed vaulting, it is highly doubtful that the planking could have been fashioned, or adequately supported, in accordance with the flatwise scheme.

close as 5 feet as the crown of the vault is approached. On the other hand, planks set on edge as at A would be able to resist vertical deflexion by themselves, because of their depth, except for the highest (and hence longest) courses near the crown of the transverse vault compartments, where a single additional bracing at their mid-span would have sufficed.

With respect to labour, A is far less expensive than B. The edge-wise planks at A needed to be shaped along only one edge, their upper surface; while the flat planks at B would have had to have both of their narrow edges shaped, because of the vault's camber. Furthermore, the situation at A is very simple to dismantle and shift, one board at a time, to a new position in a subsequent bay; whereas the continuous formwork at B would probably have had to be removed, somehow or other, in a single large unit instead of plank by plank, and then manœuvred and shifted bodily to a new position under a subsequent bay.[180]

Finally, a conclusive reason why a formwork of flatwise planking could not have been used for the construction of Gothic quadripartite vaulting is that too much of each plank would have had to be bevelled and sliced away (as we will see)

117

in order to provide a seating for its groin end at the side of the diagonal ribs, especially in the transverse vaulting compartments.

We have seen that the ribs automatically determined the conformation of the web surfaces. It is now equally evident that these plank centers or laggings for the individual web courses automatically determined their width and direction. Hence no special skill was required on the part of the masons in laying out their work, and there was little chance that costly or dangerous errors might occur by the time the actual masonry-work came to be started, since the layout and conduct of the work was by then definitely and visibly determined.

Actually, all that has just been said about formwork planks on edge (rather than a continuous formwork surface of planks set flatwise) is logical enough, but it was probably not quite the way it was done in medieval times.

Today we are so used to power-sawn boards and planks that we take them for granted; and we also accept as both obvious and axiomatic that a plank set on edge is many times stiffer in resistance to bending than one set flatwise. But in the Middle Ages the situation was quite otherwise. Planks were usually riven. Whether riven or sawn, however, it was invariably the flat side that was utilized: two or three of them side by side fashioned into doors or solid shutters, or as carved or painted panels in wainscoting and ceilings, or even occasionally as workmen's platforms on scaffoldings and stagings. Apparently it never occurred to the medieval builder to set them on edge in such fashion as to take advantage of their depth in resistance to bending. Timbers were adzed into approximately square cross-sections (this was normal for floor beams and joists), while rafters developed from (1) round poles, to (2) poles with their upper surfaces made flat so as to form a better, more even seating for the roof laths, to (3) poles split longitudinally and adzed to roughly rectangular shape, where the greater dimension in cross-section was horizontal rather than normal to the slope. In other words, in their structural members the medieval carpenters habitually utilized the full diameter of the tree, of whatever size they deemed sufficient for the work each member was called upon to do.

However, this circumstance does not mean that we have to discard the effective scheme of formwork planking that has just been described above. There is no need to think in terms of a clumsy and heavy assemblage of roughly squared poles or timbers whose camber would be difficult if not impossible to manage. Instead, we can assume with considerable confidence a modification of the above scheme that is lighter and even more efficient than planking on edge.

118

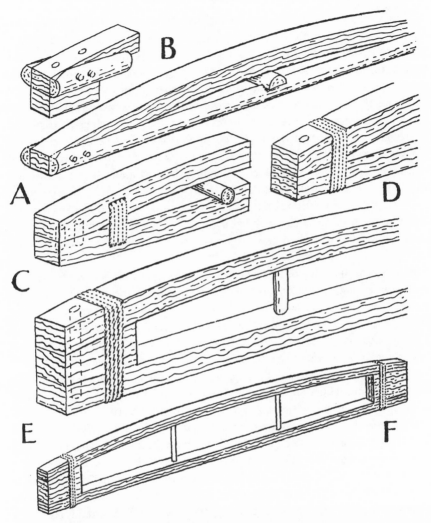

46. *Possible Development of Individual Lagging Units*

A shows a lagging unit in which the squared curving member is dowelled at both ends to the two halves of a split pole, its camber maintained by a wooden piece inserted transversely at mid-span. B is the same scheme with a dowelled lift block secured under the end of the unit. C and D show different lashing schemes by which the superimposed members of the lagging unit are prevented from springing apart at the ends due to their bowed shape. E is a detail, and F a complete view, of a lagging unit of the sort that may well have been used by the Gothic builders. It is light but strong, it permits any amount of camber, it makes use of techniques and materials of the sort and in the form of those customarily then in use, and it permits rigid assemblages over any of the spans the Gothic builders would have encountered for web courses.

This scheme involves, not a single plank for each lagging course, but an assemblage of two poles, probably squared, that are mortised or pinned or lashed together at or near their extremities in one of the fashions illustrated in 46, so as to prevent the upper member from slipping along the lower in the action known as shear. The insertion of a strutting block at mid-span, or of two such at the third points for the long courses near the crown of the vault, would so far stiffen the bowed assemblage that it is quite certain that no additional external bracing or strutting, such as Aubert has suggested, would have been needed even in the longest units. For, with a given curvature in the top element, the longer the unit of this lagging the more resistance to bending there would be as the web stones were set in place upon it, on account of the rise of the arc. Thus the problem of sufficient strength and stiffness against bending would have been adequately taken care of in the lagging itself, for any of the spans normally encountered in Gothic vaulting, without having to have recourse to separate and additional falsework between the centering frames of the ribs.[181]

Moreover, one of the most practical advantages of this device was that it permitted cambering, to whatever extent might be desired in the vault webs, to come about in the easiest and most natural fashion. When the domed groin vault was first adopted, as we have seen, its bowed and expanding courses may well have involved erection by means of tamped earth mounded up on supporting platforms. It is unthinkable, however, that the later highly cambered vaults of some Gothic churches—such finished vaults, for example, as those of the nave and choir of Paris Cathedral, which are strongly bowed—should have been formed in this clumsy, heavy, and messy fashion. Yet none of the formwork techniques heretofore proposed has been able to account adequately and realistically for the erectional methods that resulted in vaults of this form. Not even planking on edge could have produced the contours of the nave vaults of Paris, since their camber is so marked that the longest planks near the crown would have had to be a number of feet deep at their mid-span. The conclusive fact militating against their employment, certainly in any falsework capacity, is that such planks would have been prohibitively expensive if not impossible to secure in one piece of the requisite length and width.

The scheme just described, on the other hand, would have been formed of more or less squared poles of whatever length was needed, with what would have been, for the medieval carpenters, the minimum amount of cost and effort in both materials and workmanship, and the minimum difficulty of handling because of the relatively light weight of each unit of lagging. Furthermore, by using the more flexible and lighter kinds of wood, the degree of camber could be made to whatever reasonable curvature the builders desired it to be: they were not limited by the availability of wide planks from which to cut the segment-shaped lagging.

Actually, the diminishment in the camber of the crowns and the bowing of the vault surfaces generally, as the Gothic period advanced, may have come about partly in consequence of the carpenters' increasing skill in assembling and handling these units of lagging, so that the masons, too, became more assured in their reliance on them. Where the vaults—at least at the crown—appear to lack any camber, this would have been managed by the perhaps at first fortuitous employment of these lagging units upside down: that is, with the stones of the web courses resting against the straight side of the lagging unit, whose bowed opposite edge hung away from the vault surface. Set in this fashion, the lagging would suspend itself quite naturally from the rib frames that supported it at either end.

Thus light but strong units of lagging were provided, one for each web course, so as to guide and simplify the masons' work. These simple frames were economical both in material and in workmanship. For they made use of quickly squared poles instead of laboriously fashioned planks; they were readily pinned or mortised at either end with types of all-wood fastenings or with lashings that were habitual to the medieval carpenter; and their relative lightness required less massive materials, less difficult and time-consuming labour, in the supporting falsework.

The ends of each unit of lagging in the transverse vaults rested upon the diagonal ribs' cradles at varying angles. But being independent and separated from its neighbours, each could be tentatively set in place, scribed, and cut to conform to the particular seating condition its position demanded.

When it came time to decenter, all the lagging units could be removed intact, one by one, for re-use in a subsequent bay, by sliding the groin end of each unit higher up along its support on the diagonal cradle.[182] Because of the divergence of the rib cradles (those of the transverse and diagonal ribs for the longitudinal vault compartments, of the formerets and diagonals for the lateral vault compartments), this higher displacement of the lagging units made too long a span for them to reach across, and thus they could be freed from the cradles so as to be removed one at a time.

Before we go on to consider the most likely assemblages and arrangements of the centering frames and their falsework substructures, it is perhaps worth recapitulating what we have deduced about the scheme of lagging that might have been followed in the erection of Gothic ribbed vaults. Through specific and detailed analysis of the multiple problem of how Gothic ribbed vaults could have had their masonry both *supported*, during the course of erection, and *decentered*, subsequently, we have visualized individual lagging frames, one for each web course, spanning from rib cradle to rib cradle.

These lagging frames were lighter in weight than any other formwork scheme anyone has so far proposed, and therefore easy to handle.

Nevertheless, they were of adequate strength in resistance to bending under the load of web stones they supported during the construction of the vault, requiring no additional support at mid-span even in the highest (longest) courses near the vault crown.

They were highly economical in both material and workmanship, making use of adzed poles instead of sawn or riven planks and boards.

This technique of lagging permitted any amount of camber to be given to the vault courses, with no need for either complicated geometry or heavy and messy mounding up of tamped earth on boarded platforms.

Each of the lagging frames, spaced at intervals with a void between, automatically determined the direction and the width of each web course, so that the masons' work was laid out and visibly indicated before any of the web stonework was started.

With the lagging units resting on the backs of the rib cradles instead of on the backs of the stone ribs themselves, the entire falsework of timber frames and lagging for the vault was integrated so that it could be decentered evenly and gradually, all together.

The lagging frames were completely salvageable; that is, they could be taken down one by one and re-erected subsequently in the next bay without taking them apart and rebuilding them.

These substantial advantages of the lagging frames appear to meet and solve the practical difficulties of formwork in the case of the great Gothic nave vaults with their twisting and cambered webs, their need for re-usable, light-weight falsework, and their provision for economy in erection throughout.

5

Theoretical views, even when only partly true, or even when false,
may serve to exhibit clearly and pointedly relations which would
otherwise seem vague and obscure; and, with proper warning, they
need not pervert our view of facts.'

WILLIAM WHEWELL*

MOST WRITERS WHO TOUCH UPON THE STRUCTURAL ASPECTS OF
the architecture of the Middle Ages get their information second-hand, from
knowledgeable investigators like Willis in England or Viollet-le-Duc and Choisy
in France. This accounts in part for a certain number of conflicting statements
among different writers, and undoubtedly explains some of the misquotations of
the above writers that are found in subsequent books.[183] But there are also serious
lacunae in the information given by the most significant writers themselves. Even
Viollet-le-Duc and Choisy, both distinguished practitioners, the one primarily an
architect, the other an engineer, whose monumental writings, like their first-hand
experience and their practical knowledge of building, are impressively comprehensive and encyclopedic, are silent on some of the consequences of their statements or are incomplete in their analyses of building operations from the practical
standpoint of their erectional procedures.

This discrepancy of analysis has already been demonstrated in the case of
Viollet-le-Duc's description of the cerce device. Choisy's account of the sequence
of constructional operations in the case of high Gothic vaults raises some unex-
plained difficulties, too.

After giving his interpretation of a drawing of Reims Cathedral in the *Album*
de Villard de Honnecourt,[184] Choisy goes on to say that:

From this authentic document it turns out that the sequence of construction was as
follows: they raised the piers of the high vaults; they erected the roof; and it is under
its protection that they built the high vaults. The flying buttresses were built at the same
time as the vaults, and the tie-rods resisted the consequent thrusts while awaiting the

* *Architectural Notes on German Churches*, 3rd edn. 1842, p. xii.

123

completion of the final decisive abutment. The roof itself, during this period of the work, was a valuable feature of consolidation. Not only did it add to the stability of the piers by its own weight, but its ties above the vault added a role equivalent to that fulfilled by the tie-rods at the springing. . . .[185]

The need for a tie-rod at the springing of the high vault is not clear, at the stage of the work that is illustrated in Choisy's fig. 17. If anything were needed here it would be a strut, a compression member,[186] rather than a tie-rod in tension. For in Choisy's drawing the lofty superstructure of the high-pitched roof and the towering clerestory piers are as yet unstayed by the permanent bracing of the buttress, whose mass is to be linked to the future vault action by the flying buttress. This superstructure of the roof, poised on its high clerestory stilts, would be precarious enough in any event; but with a strong wind blowing it would have to be powerfully stayed against swaying and collapse. Bracing from without could have been furnished, as we have noted above, by some sort of temporary strutting which would prevent the two clerestories, one on either side of the nave, from swaying towards the exterior or from bursting outward. A tie-rod, however, would help not at all to prevent these clerestories from bursting *inward*; and any temporary shores that might have been employed would have increased the danger of inward collapse by leaning against the clerestory piers from without.

Choisy himself seems not very convinced by his own explanation, for elsewhere (p. 316), after noting that the Romanesque builders made frequent use of the tie-rod as a means of counteracting the thrust, he says that 'In the Gothic era it is employed especially to prevent disorders that occur upon removal of the centering during the period when the masonry is settling. The flying buttress makes the help of the tie-rods superfluous as permanent tension members; their role is limited to the period when the masonry is shrinking.'

Choisy's evidence that the tie-rods were used at the springing of the high vaults is apparently based upon (1) his interpretation of some rather obscure marks at approximately this location in Villard's drawing, and (2) the actual cut-off remains of these members, not in the nave vault but in the smaller and lower side-aisle vaults. He says (p. 316): 'The vaults of the side aisles at Amiens and at Reims preserve the marks of their tie-rod links: each of the transverse arches was undergirt by a stringer of wood engaged at one end into the masonry of the pier, at the other end in that of the wall. The metal attachments of tie-rods that were probably of iron are to be seen at Beauvais.'[187]

As for the direct evidence of the actual remains themselves, Viollet-le-Duc has much more to say about them than Choisy does.[188] He cites only one case of their occurrence at the spring of the high vaults; namely, in the late eleventh-century abbey church of Vézelay. This church was originally built without flying buttresses; hence the spreading action of its early ribbed vaults was not abutted from the exterior. But even here Viollet-le-Duc thinks that the tie-rods would have remained in place only 'until the clerestory walls were charged, or until the mortar of the vaults had acquired its final set, that is to say, until the decentering'.[189]

Whether temporary ties were customarily used for the high vaults or not, they were certainly used in the side aisles of mature Gothic churches such as Amiens and Reims. There was more need for them here than in the high vaults, for two reasons. One was the inward pressure of the side-aisle vault against the nave pier; the other was the false bearing of the wall at the back of the triforium passage; a wall which, together with its superimposed columns of long stones set on edge outside the clerestory piers, was part of the stiffening armature of the mature Gothic structural system.[190] Against these double inward pressures there could be no abutment, on the nave side, comparable to the reverse situation at the level of the high vault, where the *outward* thrust of the vault was received and transmitted to the buttress by the flying buttress.

It is clear, then, that there was a very real need for these temporary tension members during the course of erection in the case of the side aisles. Viollet-le-Duc cites many examples of these ties of wood, about $4\frac{3}{4}$ inches square, which have long since been sawn off close to the surface of the plaster or rough-cast with which the stonework was originally coated.[191] He says:

They were placed during the course of erection between the double centerings on which the archivolts and the transverse arches were built, and were left in place until the building was completed; that is to say, until the moment when the interior piers were charged to the point where the builders no longer needed to fear any buckling produced by the thrust of the side-aisle vaults.[192]

Viollet-le-Duc goes on to say (p. 402) that, before these temporary tie-rods of the side-aisle vaults came to be generally adopted,

many interior piers of churches built at the end of the twelfth century had tilted out of the vertical,[193] provoked by the thrust of the side-aisle vaults before completion of the structure; for, in order to interrupt the services of worship as short a time as possible, the builders closed in the vaults as soon as the side aisles were raised, they decentered these vaults, they established a ceiling over the central nave at the height of the triforium, and they were able to move into the church.

The purpose of this 'ceiling over the nave at the triforium level' is neither explained nor substantiated. Elsewhere, as we have seen, it is established that the masonry materials—those out of which the clerestory piers and their superincumbent strip of spandrel wall on either side of the nave were built—were raised from the interior. This would have been true, also, of the timber-work of the great roof.[194] We have just noted that the side-aisle tie-rods were not cut off until the masonry above the nave arcade piers was carried all the way up to the eaves of the great roof. Hence there seems to be no ready explanation for the necessity of ceiling-in the full width of the nave at the *triforium* level.[195] It is possible that the kind of ceiling Viollet-le-Duc speaks about may have been a workmen's platform or staging at about the level of the high vault springing. The masons' helpers would perhaps have kept trays of mortar on this staging; and it may have furnished a convenient upper landing on which a small but constantly replenished supply of stones would be kept for ready use as the vaulting proceeded.

In this connexion, the photographs published by Gilman, of Soissons Cathedral after the World War I bombardment, are most revealing.[196] His fig. 2 is taken looking up into the roof from below, which is possible because the vaults have collapsed; fig. 18 is a horizontal view of the same, at a level just below where the crowns of the vaults had been before their destruction. Except that there is no scaffolding, these views present what must have been approximately the appearance of the structure at the time the original builders were ready to construct the high vaults. The fact that all but one pair of the upper and lower flying buttresses are intact, in spite of the absence of the high vaults, shows how little they press actively against the clerestory walls.[197] In fact, it looks as though they could safely have been built before the vaults were begun. The crown thrust of their supporting arches was certainly a great deal less strong than the thrust of the side-aisles' transverse and diagonal ribs (together with their share of vaulting) against the nave arcade piers lower down. And here at Soissons, as elsewhere, the crowns of the flying buttress arches abut in a vertical joint against column-supported blocks projecting from the clerestory wall in such fashion, as Viollet-le-Duc has demonstrated,[198] that the top of each arch is reasonably free to settle independently from the clerestory masonry.

This situation allows us to corroborate and elaborate our previous assumptions on how the clerestory piers and superstructure may have been braced or shored, both during the course of erecting them and while the roof was being constructed, until the high vaults were turned. Clearly, it would have been quite feasible for the flying buttress centerings themselves to have acted in this stabilizing capacity. Centerings, as we have noted, must be made strong and rigid in order to prevent any deformation in the arches they support, due to their incremental loading at the

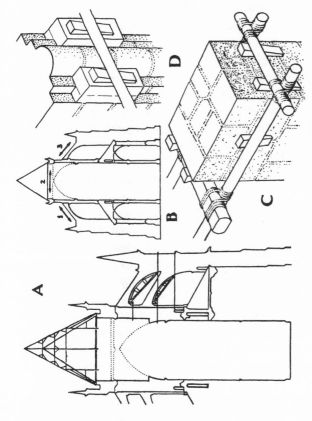

47. Flying Buttress Centering

At A, with the vault yet to be built, is shown in transverse section the upper portion of Reims Cathedral, with centering frames in place for its two tiers of flying buttresses. The upper and lower ends of the frames are supported respectively by pier-girdling and buttress-girdling assemblages of poles, securely attached to the masonry by wedges in some such fashion as that indicated in the details at C and D. At the far side of C, instead of a horizontal pole there is a wider member that

acts as a sill on which the decentering wedges can be lodged. These horizontal pole assemblages not only support the centering frames but also act, with them, as temporary compression struts, holding the masonry of pier and buttress in alignment against their tendency to tilt towards each other because of their corbelled encroachment above the void of the side aisle.

The schematic section at B shows the strutting system of a typical Gothic superstructure previous

to the erection of the vault. Here the towering, deeply salient buttresses act as the massive anchors at either side, between which the flying-buttress arches, 1 and 3, together with the rigid triangle of the roof complex, 2 (and especially its great tie-beams), afford an adequately stable bracing for the high and vulnerably exposed central portion of the church.

127

time of erection. They can therefore be counted on, when properly seated and fixed at either end, to resist a considerable amount of stress longitudinally, both in tension and in compression. Hence the flying arch centering itself, which has no lateral thrust of its own, could have acted as a strut from buttress proper to clerestory wall; and this rigid unit of timber-work could have resisted any bursting tendency of the clerestory wall, both inward and outward, by tying it to the stable buttress (47 A). Furthermore, as long as these centers remained in place during the setting period while the mortar consolidated, there could be no inward pressure on the part of the flying buttress arches, since any arch action they might create could develop only after decentering took place.

This, then, could be sufficient reason why the evidence of tie-rods has not been encountered at the spring of the high vaults in the great Gothic churches: the tying would have been adequately accomplished on the outside of the building by making use of the flying buttress centerings. These timber centers, or some equivalent,[199] had to be employed for the erection of the flying buttress arches in any case; and merely by attaching them securely to the masonry at each of their ends they could act as rigid stays anchoring the clerestory wall to the solid buttress. No other shoring would have been required, from the time the clerestory walls had been raised high enough for these centerings to be placed in position, until the great nave roof was in place. Thus was the interior freed of the necessity for tie-rods spanning across the nave at the spring of the high vaults, where they would have got in the way and would have hampered the manœuvring of the centerings for these vaults, together with their decentering and shifting to the next bay to be built.[200]

In most instances, moreover, the flying buttress centerings were probably dispensed with entirely, once they had fulfilled their immediate function of supporting the voussoirs of these arches during their erection, and once the roof had been raised. For we have seen that the sequence of building operations was in all probability that of raising both the clerestory walls and the solid buttresses together (with the flying buttress centering employed, in lieu of other shoring, as bracing or strutting between these two elements), until the huge and heavy Gothic roof came to be poised on top of the clerestory walls, weighting them and bridging across the nave from one to another.

At least in England, some great churches, in fact, were never carried beyond this point, structurally; that is, they never did receive their stone vaults for which so much of the rest was preparation, but were furnished with a wooden ceiling instead. And yet it is clear from their survival that such vaultless buildings are none the less stable. This stability comes about largely from the great weight of the roof structure, which is ponderous enough to load the relatively slender piers of the clerestory wall with sufficient force to prevent the crown thrusts of the flying buttresses, together with any wind action against the clerestory walls and the roof itself, from pushing these walls inward, out of alignment. Thanks to the strutting function of the roof's heavy tie-beams, the flying buttresses no more push the clerestory walls *in*, with their crown thrusts, than they push the buttresses *out*, with the thrust action at their springings.

Thus (47 B), in a non-vaulted church, there are three spans of compression members, transversely, from one outer buttress to its mate on the other side: (1) a flying buttress (from buttress to clerestory wall), (2) the roof with its rigid timbering (from clerestory wall to clerestory wall), and (3) the reverse of (1), on the other side. Once the timber roof was in place, it locked together this series of three struts, both by its weight and by its rigid structure. Thereupon the flying buttress centerings could be struck, since the building achieved stability either with or without the subsequent addition of the high vaults within.[201]

Unquestionably the most difficult constructional problem of all was that of the centering for the high vaults, whose wide spans were sprung as much as a hundred feet above the pavement of the nave.[202] This problem was multiple. We have already discussed the kind of lagging or formwork that may have been used in erecting the web of the vault. But what of the timber-work centering frames? How were they fashioned and erected; what supports were they seated on; how were they decentered; by what means were they shifted to the next bay; how were they subsequently dismantled and lowered to the ground without damaging any of the work below? And along with these major erectional problems of the building's structure, what of the scaffolding that would have had to be provided subsequently, both for those workmen who plastered the under surface of the vault upon its completion, and for those who later painted lines or patterns on this plaster coat? [203]

These were indeed complicated and interrelated problems, which required solutions to be worked out in advance so that there might not be duplication of effort or interference of operation in the sequence of the work. For instance, although lifting devices located on the tie-beams within the roof might have been used to raise the rib centerings up from the ground, it seems obvious enough that these could have been of little use in shifting the centerings to the next bay, or in lowering them to the ground on completion of the work, because the vaults would by then have come to interpose themselves between the roof and the centerings. The latter, therefore, may have been raised into position originally from above, but they would thereafter have had to be shifted about and relocated, then finally dismantled and lowered to the ground level, from *below* the vault.[204]

In attempting to re-create the erectional procedures and practices followed in high Gothic vaults, we encounter the two major areas of complete obscurity: the form and arrangement of the rib centering proper, and the method of supporting this centering from below. Here the contemporary evidence is either entirely non-existent or so fragmentary and ambiguous as to be virtually useless. We can therefore do no more than to speculate on various ways in which this double problem *might* have been handled, keeping in mind both the complex *conditions* in all their ramifications and interrelationships, and the *schemes*, previously discussed, that manifest the earlier builders' equipment, their approach to their version of the problem, and their rationalization of the techniques evolved in the case of the lower nave vaults of Romanesque times.

What appears to be incontrovertible, however, on the basis of all available hints in the contemporary accounts as well as both the economics and the logic of the situation, is that there must have been a working platform or staging established about the level of the high vault springing, on which the rib centers were supported, manœuvred into position, and later decentered and shifted to a new bay.[205] After the lengthy period during which the mortar joints of the ribs and webs alike became hardened and received their final set, these frames could have been decentered and moved to the next bay, freeing the staging for light and easily assembled trestle scaffoldings from which the plasterers and painters could coat and colour the vault surfaces that had just been decentered.

There are two circumstances that make it particularly difficult for us today to re-create the nature and the details of medieval falsework structures. One is that the builders of that era made very little if any use of metal,[206] which, in the form of nails, bolts, pins, straps, fish-plates, gusset plates, ring connectors, &c., are so much a part of any wooden structure we build today as to seem universal if not downright old-fashioned. The other is that they apparently did not understand or make use of the now universally adopted truss,[207] which is a complex of members, some in tension some in compression, assembled in such fashion as to span a wide space rigidly by making use of the principle of the non-deformability of triangles.

In fig. 16 of his dictionary article 'Flèche', Viollet-le-Duc explains and illustrates one of the carpentry devices used by the medieval builders in lieu of the timberwork truss principle. This is the scheme of doubling members, with cross ties at intervals, so as to furnish very powerful resistance to deformation.[208] The example he illustrates is the pairing of the principal posts that constitute the slightly tilted

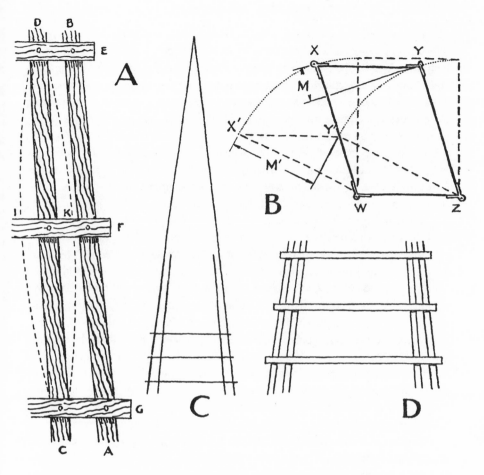

48. *The Parallel-Beam Scheme of Stiffening, Claimed by Viollet-le-Duc to Have Served the Medieval Builders in Lieu of the Truss*

If a parallelogram, as WXYZ at B, is hinged at the corners, it can deform either to the shape of a rectangle or to any more acutely angled shape such as WX'Y'Z. When it does this, however, the position of Y relative to the side XW varies. Thus a perpendicular through Y to the side XW is M distance from X; but a perpendicular through Y' to the same side (now X'W) is M' distance from the same corner (now X'). The tendency of Y to become displaced in its position relative to an opposite side is an instance of the force known as shear.

In Viollet-le-Duc's scheme (A is copied from his diagram, where the principle is applied to the framing of a spire), this shift in one corner's position relative to an opposite side is chiefly prevented from occurring by maintaining strict horizontality in the horizontal members. Their horizontality is assured partly by the duplication of the condition (as in D, where the right side is matched by the left), and partly by the occurrence of one or more triangles somewhere in the timber-work complex, as shown at C. In addition, the presence of spacer blocks between the members AB and CD, at intervals, prevents these members from coming closer to each other.

131

main upright members of a wooden spire (48 A, C, and D). He winds up the analysis of his drawing with the statement that 'hence the quadrilateral *ABCD*, bound by the braces *EFG*, is not susceptible to deformation'. This is not true of his quadrilateral: unlike a triangle, no quadrilateral is, by itself, indeformable. But it *is* true of the assemblage of which this quadrilateral is a part, because the ensemble of the timber-work assemblage involves various triangles; for example, the pyramid of the spire itself, and the multiple complex of diagonal and criss-crossing braces.[209]

There are two general methods by which a quadrilateral such as Viollet-le-Duc's *ABCD* can attain the remarkably powerful resistance to deformation he claims for it. One, as just stated, is via one or more additional members that form a triangle. The other is by furnishing resistance to shear.

If the four angles of a parallelogram are considered as hinged, the parallelogram can collapse laterally to a more and more acutely angled figure in which it is obvious that, as the opposite sides come closer together, opposite points on either side shift their position relative to each other. Thus, in the parallelogram $WXYZ$ (48 B), a perpendicular to XW through Y is displaced from X by the interval M. But in $WX'Y'Z$ (the more slanted position of the hinged parallelogram), a perpendicular to $X'W$ through Y' has become much more displaced from X', by the interval M'. This shift of relative position is an instance of shear. It can be resisted by properly secured blocks, which not only maintain the original interval by which the two sides of the parallelogram were separated but, with respect to shear, prevent any additional interval, as that at M', from occurring relative to points along opposite sides of the parallelogram.

We have already seen (near the end of Chapter 4, 46) how this principle of resistance to shear may have been applied in the case of the lagging frames for Gothic ribbed vaulting.

In medieval practice, the normal means of securing the connexions between the wooden members of *falsework* structures (as opposed to the *permanent* timbering of roof or lantern) was sometimes by the use of oak pins and occasionally by the neat mortise-and-tenon joints shown in many of Viollet-le-Duc's drawings, but much more generally by lashing them together with ropes or withies that were further tightened by long narrow wedges driven between the rope and the wood members.[210]

In Europe today there are few enough examples of this method of attachment to be seen any more, except perhaps for the light pole scaffoldings of masons' platforms. Heavy shoring, and the supporting timber-work for centerings, &c., are no longer assembled in this fashion.[211] What is comparable, today, to the medieval practices of falsework assemblages is not what may be found in Europe or America but rather in Africa and Asia, wherever industrialization has not as yet completely superseded the traditional methods of handicraftsmanship with native materials, in building construction.

In this respect, some of the photographs of native structures—permanent as well as temporary—that are published from time to time in *The National Geographic Magazine* are pertinent and informing. For example, in the issue of March 1955,[212] there are East Pakistani pictures (1) of the heavy lashings uniting the vertical and horizontal timbers of a large and strong trap-door to a wild elephant corral (p. 405); (2) of the stockade itself, both inside and outside, the latter showing the multiple diagonal bracing thickly set about into the ground to resist the impact of the elephants' charges against the palisades of the corral (p. 422); and (3) of the multitudinous lashings of walls, eaves, and rafters, seen from the interior, of a house consisting exclusively of native materials (p. 416). There are neither boards nor planks in (1) and (2), but stout, more-or-less round, hardwood timbers that have not only been debarked but also roughly adzed down to the heartwood, free of the softer and less decay-resistant sapwood.[213] It is interesting to note, too, in the relatively light construction of the house, that the same faceted hardwood is used for the principal members (corner posts, wall plates, and roof hips), while all the rest of the structure is of bamboo of various diameters. All these structures are lashed together, the temporary but very strongly built corrals with native rope, the lighter but permanent house with what appears to be pliable plant fibres such as sennit.

It would be well if these native methods of non-metallic fastening were systematically studied and recorded before they die out, superseded by western techniques. In a few cases they have already been examined and published, but only in scattered instances rather than with systematic completeness.[214] Apparently there is no serious, comprehensive treatise that covers native methods of attaching poles together wherever this is done throughout the world, comparable to Schmidt's treatment applied to pole scaffolding in Germany. If such a study were made, it would doubtless show many analogies with the practices employed in the Middle Ages in Europe for heavy shoring and the falsework substructures of high, widespanning centering.

As for the timber centering frames used for the erection of Gothic vaults, the known lack of true trusses plus the near non-existence of metal fastenings make the reconstruction of the probable forms employed for high nave vaults something of a puzzle. In this connexion, however, it is revealing to study the distribution of the centering *members* that are found in modern frames: not only those earlier ones so carefully represented in Rondelet (even though these are as often as not for domes rather than for ribbed vaults) but especially the countless examples that are given, sometimes in photographs but much more often in schematic linear diagrams, throughout the pages of Séjourné's six large tomes. An attentive examination of these centerings reveals many whose memberings of struts and braces (1) do not consist of a complex of triangles and thus do not constitute true trusses, and (2) are disposed in such fashion that they could well dispense with metal connectors on account of the separation and relative simplicity of their articulations.[215]

However, it is worth noting that, without exception in Séjourné's work, each timber frame for the support of the vault is a distinct entity—an ensemble of timber members in a single plane—no matter how many of these parallel planes (and hence separate frames) there may be that make up the falsework structure. In quadripartite vaulting, on the other hand, only the transverse and the wall ribs could have been supported by single, complete frames; the diagonal ribs, because of their intersection, had to have some sort of break or articulation at mid-span in at least one of the two criss-crossing frames. This discontinuity of one of the timber frames could be accomplished stably enough today (although its scheme of juncture is almost never illustrated in books) by the use of metal plates bolting the two discontinuous halves together across the continuous top and bottom chords of the other complete frame.[216] But in view of the well-established fact that metal was virtually not used at all during the Middle Ages in wooden structures, whether permanent or temporary, the technique of securing the divided portions of one of the big diagonal frames is just one more detail requiring resourcefulness on the part of the medieval carpenters, and ingenuity on the part of any engineer-historian who would seek to re-create their methods.

Probably the sole direct evidence available to us today, in our attempt to re-create the Gothic forms of centering frames, is that of the late medieval Swedish church of Lärbro, Gotland, photographed by Roosval and reproduced as fig. 171 in Forsyth. This illustration is of the original centering, still existing in the church tower, and shows clearly the radiating poles fanning up from their seatings in the assemblage of heavy beams that make up the frames' horizontal bottom members.[217]

But this still extant centering is for an octagonal vault of about 27-foot span instead of for the quadripartite vaults spanning 40 feet or more that are usually found in the great Gothic churches of northern France. Moreover, it is enclosed within very thick and massive walls that are unweakened and uncomplicated by window bays of maximum size. It is a single unit of vaulting rather than one of a continuous series, each opening into the next one to its full width. Here, too, neither the problem of freeing the floor area of falsework encumbrance at the earliest possible moment, nor the difficulty of lodging the supports temporarily on passageway ledges or other masonry offsets, has had to be met: the great wooden beams that undergird the falsework frames span permanently (as it has turned out) from unbroken wall to unbroken wall. And apparently there is no systematic provision for decentering. In fact, judging by what evidence is revealed in the published drawings of this assemblage, one can only suppose that, if decentering *had* taken place, the poles that strut the wooden ribs at groin and crown lines would have had to be sawn off one by one, allowing the planking to fall or be dislodged, and leaving the heavy horizontal beams permanently in place as ties linking together opposite faces of the wall high up within the tower at the vault spring. Consequently, except for the evidence of the use of poles to support the arch cradles, and the fitting of these into sockets in the horizontal beams at the level of the vault spring, there is little enough information at Lärbro that can help us recreate the specific falsework schemes that were employed for the high vaults of the great Gothic cathedrals of northern France: the two situations were too disparate.

The convergence and intersection of centering frames was a medieval falsework problem that was encountered not alone in the diagonals of rib vaulting. A more extreme case of the same problem occurred in the Gothic apse where it was normal to have no less than eight half-frames for as many ribs, all converging on a common key. Actually, the problem is perhaps most clearly pointed up (though the spans involved were much smaller) in the typical Gothic ambulatory bays. For here the lines of the intersecting ribs were broken in plan; so that a pair of ribs, together with their centering frames, could not be set out in a single vertical plane but had to meet each other under the common key at a more or less obtuse angle (49).

All such examples would seem to argue the likelihood that rib centering frames had to be constructed in two halves, each independent of the other and non-continuous from arch spring to arch spring.[218] In other words, just as Gothic pointed arches were made up of two circular arcs of less than a quadrant in extent, so the supporting cradles for these rib arches must have been made up in two separate frames instead of a single pointed or semicircular one.[219] Not only would the centering frames have been discontinuous under the crown, but they would have had to be separated by an interval there because of their mutual interference otherwise, and in order to facilitate the subsequent striking of the frames, as we will see.[220]

135

This break in the centering frames at mid-span had a significant effect on the design of the falsework substructures that supported the centering for the high nave vaults in those instances where powerful and rigid undergirding for these frames had to be provided out in the center of the void, more or less midway between the clerestory walls, as well as near the walls themselves, on either side.

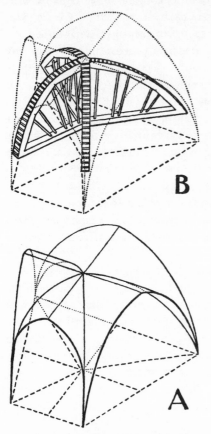

49. *Centering Frames for the Intersecting Ribs of a Trapezoidal Bay of Gothic Vaulting*

The conformation of the surfaces alone (minus ribs) of a Gothic ambulatory bay is given at A. Here the groins, and even more clearly the rib frames in B, show the breaks in the continuity of the diagonals, by which the intersecting groins are made to meet above the center of the bay. In the interest of clarity the centerings are shown here as single rather than double frames. Their lower chords are approximately at the level of the arch stones' angle of friction.

As for the supports for the centering frames near the walls, a condition existed there, in Gothic vaulting, which the tas-de-charge simplified. It will be remembered that one of the reasons for the tas-de-charge in the first place was that, at each corner of a bay, two diagonal ribs and a transverse rib crowded down so close together that most of their mouldings were mutually absorbed, leaving in view only their soffit mouldings and usually not even all of these. By the device of having, at the springing, a single block of stone with horizontal bed for each course of the entire rib complex, one stone above the other, until a height was reached at which the ribs diverged enough to become completely disengaged from each other, the tas-de-charge effectively solved a structural problem that otherwise would have involved weakness through fragmentation at the very point where stability and strength in unity were most essential.

Just as the ribs themselves had no room to come all the way down to the

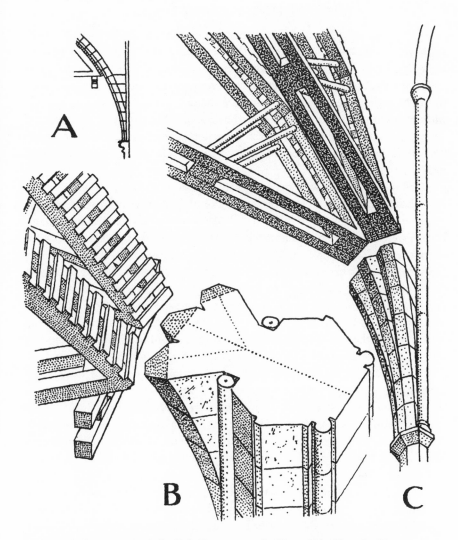

50. *Convergence of the Rib Frames at the Top of the Tas-de-Charge*

The small detail at A shows a tas-de-charge of seven courses, each with horizontal bed. Radial joints begin for the rib voussoirs at the top of this series of corbels, and it is at this level that the centering frames are set. In B and C the ribs are simplified to bevelled instead of moulded profiles. The ends of the centering frames for a diagonal and a transverse rib are seen from above in B, from below in C. The pair of frames has a common end support on a wedged-up sill, in B. This view also shows the large single block—the highest of the tas-de-charge courses—which was sometimes used to transmit the vault's lateral pressures directly to the half arch of the flying buttress.

137

abacus as independent entities, so too their centering frames, cleats and all, could not have found room to curve down to the level of the abacus, nor could they have been supported by it: they would have been completely in each other's way.

The tas-de-charge, then, consisting of monolithic corbelled courses above the spring of the arches, rose to a considerable height above the clerestory capitals without any need for formwork support. By the time the ribs became completely disengaged from each other there was room for the centering frames on which the rib voussoirs were laid to crowd together, side by side, without interfering with each other (50).

Although the cradles were needed for the support of the rib voussoirs, starting from the top of the tas-de-charge and on up around the curve of these arches, the cradles would not have been called upon to support the ends of the web lagging immediately above the tas-de-charge. For here the web courses were short enough, at least in the longitudinal vault compartments, to consist of a single stone laid across from one rib to the next, directly on the rib extradoses. As for the transverse vault compartments, although the horizontal interval here was greater than the one just referred to, the courses immediately above the tas-de-charge needed no support from lagging because of the stilt of the wall arch: the sloping beds of the web courses in the lateral cells did not surpass the angle of friction until higher up.

With the end supports of the centering frames thus removed by an interval of a few feet, horizontally, from the spring of the clerestory pier, there would have been much less danger of damaging the delicate carving of the high capitals (which would probably have been finished on the ground before their placement at the top of the clerestory piers). The amount of clearance here would have been welcome both at the time of erecting and positioning the centering frames, and also when they were struck and eased to a new situation in the next bay.

Although it is self-evident that the ribs were built before the web panels were filled in, it should be noted that the lagging for the web courses would not have been installed until after the ribs were built and keyed. For, in the process of laying up the rib voussoirs from either end of the arch, it would have been easier and more convenient for the masons to work without the web lagging to interfere with their progress. They would have been able to set the rib blocks *from the side*, standing on light and perhaps adjustable trestles, instead of from above, where they would have had to perch on the precarious, narrow, and sloping footing of the cradles. And in the case of heavy keystones, these could have been raised vertically from the level of the nave floor at only a few feet's displacement from their ultimate location[221] (51).

51. The Raising of Large Keystones

The type of roof construction here shown in simplified, cut-away form is that of the nave of Reims (see 9). A great wheel, at the lower right, is supported on the main tie-beams. No platform of poles and/or planks is shown at this level (though it would be essential for the shifting about and positioning of this great wheel) in order not to obscure the rib centerings and their load of voussoirs. At about half the height of the roof complex, where another range of transverse tie-beams occurs, is a double wheel-windlass with hand spikes protruding like spokes, by which four men can operate it. (Only one man is here indicated.) At the midheight level of this particular roof assemblage there is not sufficient headroom underneath the next higher tie for a great wheel to be moved from one carpentry bay to the next; hence, the smaller but still powerful windlass.

It is equally clear that the stones of the web courses, too, would have been set from the side, instead of from above the vault where the masons would have had to work from the courses that had just been built. Certainly by working from the side, facing the courses being laid, there would have been little danger of disturb-

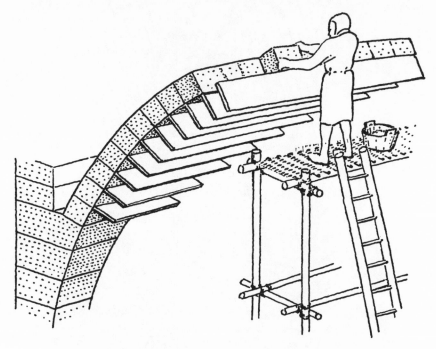

52. *Erection of the Vault Web, One Course at a Time*

This simplified sketch omits the rib centering frames, and shows planks instead of the light, open-framed lagging units the Gothic builders may have used. The mason here stands upon a platform of hurdles supported by a light pole scaffolding; another mason would have been working back to back with him up the opposite curve of the vault, until only the four or so highest courses remained to be done (see 53).

ing the green mortar of the courses just completed. If, as seems undeniable, this scheme of working from the side were actually the one adopted by the Gothic masons, they would have stood on light trestles supported on the platform of the high staging; and one lagging unit at a time would have been placed by the carpenters and then set with web stones by the masons (52).

Obviously, a major shift in formwork technique was involved when the stonework of the vault came to be laid up from the side, having previously been laid

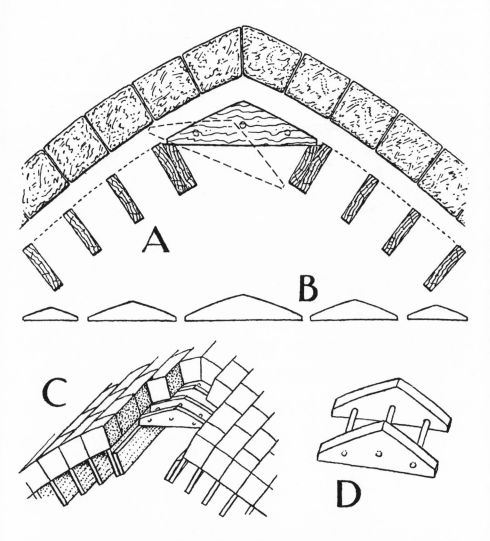

53. *Cross Lagging under the Crown of Gothic Vaults*

C shows units of cross lagging in position as the stones of the four highest web courses are being laid upon them. A is a transverse section through the upper portion of the vault upon completion, at the moment when the centering wedges have been retracted. The broken line connecting the tops of the radial lagging units indicates the soffit of the vault (in relation to the falsework) at the

time of its erection, before the centers were struck. The void created above the falsework by the decentering operation permits the cross-lagging units to be removed, one by one, as shown at the crown. D is one of these units of cross lagging; and B' indicates their graduated sizes, which are a consequence of the normal lagging units being set radially, for a vault with cambered webs.

141

entirely from above, of necessity (as in the earth-mounded formwork of some domed groin vaults, for instance). This significant change doubtless took place when salient diagonal ribs first came to be systematically employed as characteristic features of the masonry vault.

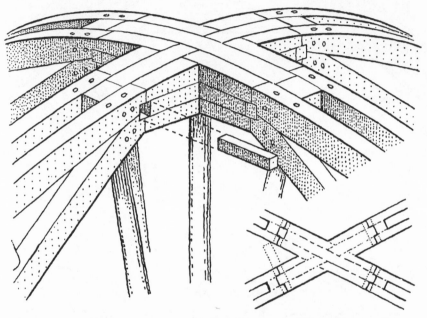

54. *Assemblage of the Diagonal Centering Frames at Their Common Crown: Scheme with X-Shaped Insert Unit*

Here the length of each arm of the X-shaped crown unit is sufficient to permit the square keys that assure alignment and prevent slipping to be driven free without interference from an adjacent arm. This first operation of dismantling, after the folding wedges at the base of the falsework complex have been retracted, is essential in order to disunite the four double half-frames of rib centering that converge on the crown. Only when they have become mutually separated can dismantling proceed under a bay of finished vault-

ing, and the several half-frames be removed to another bay for reassembling there. The insert unit may well have been directly supported by a central post, as shown here; but the square keys were none the less indispensable to prevent tilting of the insert unit, or vertical slipping between it and one or more of the half-arch frames, as they became loaded during the course of erecting the masonry vault above them. In the interest of clarity, cleats are not shown in this detail.

The technique of laying the vault masonry from above was satisfactory enough as long as the vaults were thick in section, fashioned out of coarse rubble, and built up upon continuous formwork. But with progressive refinements in both the vault itself and its falsework, reliance on inert massiveness gave way to a knowledgeable appreciation of the active forces that had to be provided for as economically as possible in both the temporary and the permanent structures. Thus, when vaults of large span came to be built with a total thickness of only some 4 or 5 inches or less, it is highly unlikely that the masons would have thought it either safe or feasible to have laid the stone courses from above, where they would have had precarious enough footing, in the first place, due to the curve of the vault's extrados, and where they would have had to stand upon the courses just completed, whose mortar joints would still have been green. Laying up the stone courses from the side—as in laying up a stone or brick wall, in fact—is the more natural and convenient way of doing it. And this procedure gives the masons more accurate surveillance and control over what they are doing, than in the case of formwork that is fashioned as a continuous surface (as in earth-mounded moulds, or a curving pavement of planking).

When the web courses are laid from the side (as in 52), lagging units are put in place one at a time, one for each web course, in turn. Pairs or teams of masons would have worked up both sides of the vault at an equal pace (so as to load the rib centerings symmetrically), the teams standing with their backs to each other on separate light trestles, each facing the concavity of the vault surface they were erecting, until the highest courses near the crown were reached.

When the space between opposite courses in the ascending webs became only about 18 or 20 inches wide, recourse would have been had to 'cross' or 'keying-in' laggings that were laid upon shelves or rebates in the facing sides of the regular lagging (53 C, D). In this operation, a single mason worked with only his head and shoulders above the vault, facing longitudinally in the direction of one of the arch crowns. With short units of cross lagging he thereupon filled out the masonry of the crown interval, retreating as each unit of the cross lagging was added and its load of stones set in place.[222] The final pocket would have had to be laid from above; but by then the mason would have retreated all the way back along the crown to where he could have set the few remaining stones from the crown of one of the stably undergirt ribs that had been in place for a considerable length of time.

In this procedure of using cross or keying-in laggings, the uppermost of the regular lagging units—those that were longest and received the greatest load of web stones—would have had to be made much stronger than the others. Both to strengthen these topmost units of the regular lagging, and to provide them with the required rebate, they would probably have been made paired or doubled. In this case the additional lagging unit of the pair (the one closer to the crown) would have been assembled 2 inches or so lower along its top edge than the unit it was

143

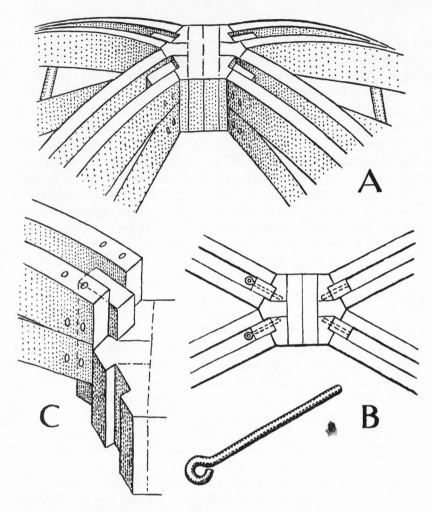

55. *Assemblage of the Diagonal Centering Frames at Their Common Crown:*
Scheme with Hexagonal Insert Block

In this scheme lateral alignment of the four double half-arches of the rib centering frames is secured by constructing each frame so that the end block which separates its parallel assemblages projects into a vertical groove in the crown insert block. Vertical alignment and the prevention of slipping at the crown is secured by metal rods. These must be furnished with an eye or a hook at one end so that, upon completion of a bay of vaulting, they can be drawn out, the insert block removed, and the four half-arch frames disunited. The left-hand side of the plan view at B shows two of these metal rods or pins in place, inserted their full depth except for the eye which makes it possible to withdraw them when the falsework assemblage is to be dismantled. Cleats are not shown. In fact, the detail at C illustrates a possible condition at the crown in the case of a cleatless double frame (such as that shown in 60, where much of the rib-stone's profile in section projects below the level of the centering frame's extrados). This detail is also possible where a keystone at the diagonal ribs' intersection is made to project downward a few inches, below the soffit of any of the rib mouldings that abut it, as sometimes happened in French Gothic vaults.

paired with, thereby providing a continuous shelf for supporting the short pieces of the cross lagging along the line of the crown (53 A).

The thrust towards each other, under loading, of the two frames making up opposite halves of the arch centering could have been taken care of at the middle of the span by filler or separator blocks, secured to the nearest members of the adjacent frames by pegs and/or by wooden keys driven into slots. In fact, the upper separator block could have been framed as a short cradle spanning the gap from one of the half-arch frames to the other, thereby furnishing continuity of support for the rib voussoirs all the way to the crown.

In the case of the diagonal frames, such a separator cradle at the crown could have been an assemblage X-shaped in plan, with one short crown cradle spanning the interval between the opposite halves of one pair of diagonals, and shorter stubs framed into this direct piece to fill out the gaps between it and the opposite halves of the other pair of diagonal half-frames (54). Or, instead of being supported by the converging half-frames, this filler piece may have had its own support independently wedged up from below on a separate post, and pegged or keyed at the top to the four half-frames it abutted (55 shows another quite different scheme).

In any case, it would have been convenient for this separator unit to be the first element of the falsework to be removed at the time of decentering. For this separation of the half-frames by an interval at the crown would have very much aided the process of removing the centering frames after they had been relieved of their arch-supporting function by the retraction of the decentering wedges. By means of the wedges alone, the entire centering falsework could have been lowered and freed from the vault by not more than about 2 inches, at least under the haunches. After decentering, however, the interval between the top of the formwork and the intrados of the vault could have been increased considerably (probably doubled or even tripled, in fact) by dislodging the upper crown cradle and any lower separator unit, and moving the opposite halves of the frames towards each other. This would have freed the haunches by as much as half the interval that had separated each pair of half-frames. And it would have freed the vault near the crown by a larger interval than the retraction of the wedges alone could accomplish, due to the pointed shape of the vaults.

Where the rib mouldings were slender, with sharp crisp arrises, this additional amount of disengagement from them on the part of the formwork meant less risk of damaging them. And from a practical standpoint this double increment of space between falsework and vault allowed room enough to dislodge and remove the lagging units easily and without endangering the alignment of the rib voussoirs,

56. Detail of Double Centering Frame

Because they had to support laggings coming in from both sides, the diagonal centering frames (and doubtless the transverse ones, too) would have needed to be made double. This detail shows pairs of radial struts, the upper ends of whose unsquared poles have been let into the heavy timbers that make up the cradles' arcs. The distance apart of the twin frames, separately made, would prob-ably have been maintained by wooden spacers set horizontally between them at convenient intervals, with ropes or withies linking the pairs of radial struts to prevent their spreading. Thus secured, the cleats would have been laid across the tops of the cradles, to be attached perhaps by wooden dowels (medieval 'tree nails'), perhaps by iron nails.

whose mortar joints may not have achieved their final set when the centering formwork was struck.

In spite of the Lärbro example (which, as we have seen, is not comparable), it would seem to have been essential for the centering frames for the ribs of the great Gothic vaults to be made double, except for the wall rib; that is, two identical frames side by side, with or without cleats set across them around the curve of their tops (56). We have already seen that Viollet-le-Duc assumes a double centering in the special case of the transverse ribs of the side aisles, where there had to be clearance for the wooden tie-beams to pass between parallel frames.[223] Moreover, in order to assure stability of support for the lagging of the web panels,[224] this scheme of double frames was essential, both here and particularly in the high vaults. There was much more weight, of course, from the lagging units and the web courses they supported than there was from the rib voussoirs alone. In the case of the transverse vault compartments of the high vault, for example, courses up to 20 feet in length received their support half from one boundary rib centering, half from the other. This was a weight of masonry imposed upon the rib frames in comparison to which the weight of a single rib voussoir was often quite minor. Hence the location of the supporting frame was of real effectiveness only when it was directly under the ends of the lagging units, where the need for that support was concentrated.

It was particularly with respect to the diagonal ribs—the longest of the rib spans—that double frames were required. For here the lagging came in to rest on the centering at either side of the stone rib from two different directions. Consequently, there needed to be parallel frames that were adjacent but separated by approximately the interval of the stone rib's width, in order that direct support for the lagging and its weight of masonry might be assured, on both sides of the rib. If the cross-section of the cradle were to have been made T-shaped—a single-thickness timber frame scarcely as wide as the rib, with cleats projecting on either side of it—then the unsymmetrical weight on it of lagging and web coursing coming in from either side would have made the loads on the cradle dangerously eccentric. The medieval builders could afford to take no chances in this circumstance: the centering for the high vault was too difficult, precarious, and uncertain in any event, without making the situation needlessly more complicated and hazardous than it already was.[225]

In connexion with these double frames for the ribs, there is the question of whether the lagging units were set radially or vertically (Viollet-le-Duc's *Annales* proposal, or his *Dictionnaire* assertion). This cannot be definitely determined at this date without undertaking very careful and tedious measurements of vaults with cambered surfaces. It is even doubtful whether the data secured from such measurements would be conclusive enough to be worth the trouble of taking them and plotting the curvatures. Stated differently, it may well be that now one scheme now the other was adopted by the medieval builders, in line with their readiness to invent, experiment, and adapt. In lieu of confirmation from existing evidence, however, the radial scheme would seem to have been the more natural and much more direct one, since it did not require bevelling the lower edges of each lagging unit at both ends in accordance with the slope of the rib cradles at that height, and, furthermore, this was an aid to the masons, as we will see.

In this radial scheme the angle at which the lagging units were tilted, around the curve of the rib frames, would be approximately in line with the direction of the loads imposed upon them by the voussoirs of a given web course. In the vertical scheme, on the other hand, the lagging units would be deficient in resisting a lateral deflexion imposed by the vaulting stones leaning against them. In any case, the separator blocks by which the ends of the lagging units may have been spaced and held apart along the tops of the rib cradles would not have been of uniform shape in either scheme, as far as the diagonal cradle was concerned; so there would not have been much choice between the two schemes on this account.

There would, however, have been a slight difference in the simplicity of the cross or keying-in laggings at the crown, depending on whether the regular laggings were set vertically or radially. Here the vertical scheme would have involved identical units and would therefore have required but one measurement and the preparation of the pieces from a single pattern.

It will be remembered that we have assumed that the shelf needed to support the short pieces of the cross lagging was provided by the top of the crown-side unit of a pair of regular laggings, one pair on each side of the crown interval, during construction of the vault webs. If the regular lagging, including these paired topmost units, were to be set vertically, then all the pieces of cross lagging would be of identical contour and size because all their spans would be the same. On the other hand, if the regular lagging were to be set radially, these cross pieces would vary in their spans due to the divergent bowing of the topmost units of regular lagging. Those cross pieces closest to the ribs would be the shortest, and each successive one, moving out along the crown towards the middle of the distance from one boundary rib to another, would slightly increase. In very much exaggerated form, the profile of some of these cross laggings would appear as in 53 B. But as in the case of the regular laggings (which of course were of constantly increasing lengths up the haunches to the crown), the interval could be quickly measured and the short pieces of the cross laggings framed or cut to conform to the particular span at each point. Hence the amount of extra work here due to the radial setting of the regular lagging units, though perhaps worthy of note, was fairly negligible.

The difficulty of seating the lagging ends *along the groin* of a ribbed vault—whether on the backs of the ribs, as postulated by Viollet-le-Duc, or on the backs

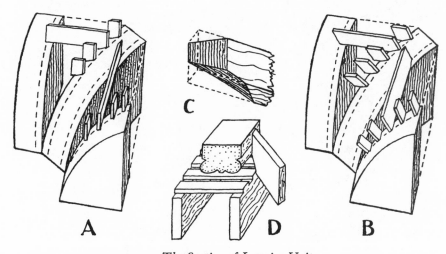

57. *The Seating of Lagging Units*

In exaggerated width, A and B show the different curvature of the extradoses of the transverse, diagonal, and longitudinal centering frames, their dotted lines indicating the width of the stone ribs to be laid upon them. In A the lagging units are set vertically, in B radially. In either case the groin end of a lagging unit climbs up the diagonal frame and must therefore be bevelled below, in order to find as stable a bearing there as possible. This bevelled underside of the lagging unit at its groin end, together with its obliquely cut termination, is indicated in the detail at C; how this shape conforms to the conditions along the groin rib is detailed at D.

of the rib *cradles*, as we have now come to deduce the procedure—is consistently disregarded in the writings of the architectural historians, perhaps because it is almost impossible to make a drawing of this condition that will 'read'.[226] Whatever drawings have been published of the seating of the lagging formwork have presented only the simplest condition, wherein horizontal planks rest flatwise on falsework frames that are at right angles to them. But the *diagonal* rib, which is not at right angles to either the lagging or the other rib frames, poses a very different situation; and this situation involves considerable difficulty not only in the longitudinal vault compartments but particularly in the transverse compartments.

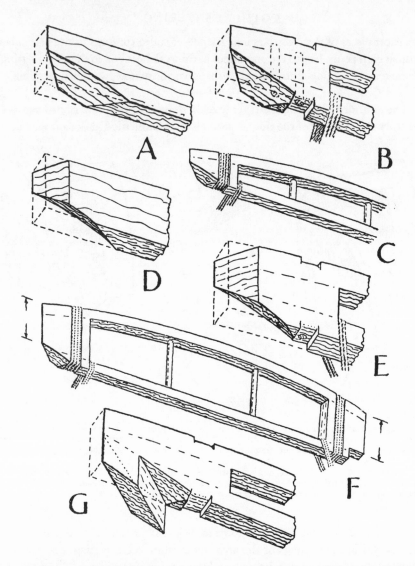

58. *Required Shaping of the Groin End of the Web Courses' Lagging Units*

A and D show two different views—the side towards the crown and the side towards the springing—of a plank end cut to conform to the condition at the groin. B and C show the end of a lagging unit of the sort that may have been used by the medieval builders, cut in a fashion analogous to A; E is one cut as at D. G shows a shaped lift block, attached individually to the groin end of a lagging unit, in order to compensate for the reduction in depth where it abuts the stone rib. F shows a complete lagging unit deep enough, after being cut away at its groin end, to conform to the depth of the stone rib along the groin, the other end being notched beneath to allow it to agree with the transverse or the wall rib's depth.

150

The extrados of each diagonal cradle is everywhere normal to its vertical plane: it is, so to speak, the top surface of a thin slice cut from a continuous vault whose horizontal axis is perpendicular to its span (57). But the longitudinal and transverse vault compartments that make up a bay of Gothic quadripartite vaulting have axes that do not agree with the axis of this thin slice. Their surfaces adjoin its surface in a curving dihedral angle that varies (increases) constantly as the crown of the vault is approached. Thus the groin ends of the lagging units had to be cut to a slightly curving bevel in order to be furnished with stable bearing on the cradle. In addition, they had to be cut off not at right angles but on the bias, so as to gain as much bearing as possible here where their ends came close to abutting the voussoirs of the rib (58).

If this emphasis on the shaping of the groin-rib end of the lagging units seems excessive, it is because the situation there has heretofore been completely ignored. Obviously, lagging units or planking of any sort must be shaped to both an acutely tapered edge and a canted bevel at the end at which they are seated on the diagonal rib frames. Yet this unavoidable condition has been passed over in silence by the architectural historians; in their text as well as their illustrations they have taken into account only the simple rectilinear seating of the formwork, at the transverse and the wall ribs. This has not helped to clarify the problem of Gothic vault centerings. The seating of the groin-rib end of the lagging units *cannot* be rectilinear, either in plan or in end view or in side elevation; and this fact is one of the conditions that made the construction of rib vaulting more difficult and demanding of the medieval carpenters than one would expect from looking at published drawings of the supposed details of Gothic vaulting falsework.

A practical complication which follows from this condition at the groin rib is the discrepancy in the depth of the lagging unit at its two ends: its effective depth at the diagonal rib is less than at either the transverse or the formeret end because, above the groin-rib frame, its seating is not normal to the curve of the cradle there, but at a variable angle. Hence, as we have seen, the lower edge of the lagging unit there must be cut to a bevelled taper, in order to accommodate it to the diagonally climbing curve of the groin-rib's centering frame. Yet in spite of this diminished depth, to fulfil its function as support for a course of web masonry, the lagging unit's depth where it abuts the diagonal rib must be no less than the depth of the stone rib plus a generous mortar joint.

This inevitable situation could have been handled in more than one way. One solution (58 at F) could have been to construct the lagging units of sufficient depth so that the top of their diminished groin end would achieve its necessary level (approximately flush with the rib extrados), and then to notch the under side of

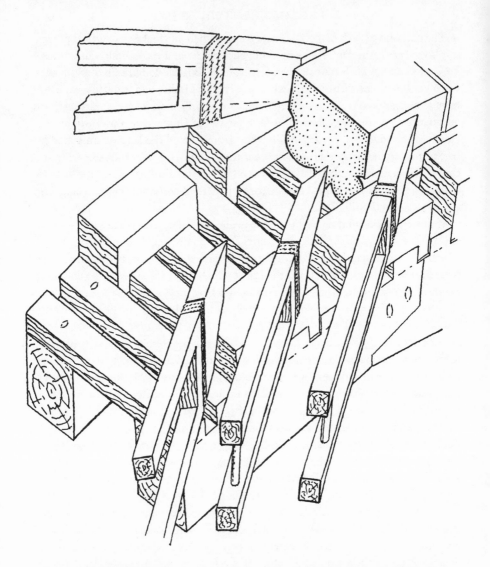

59. *Detail of Falsework Assemblage along the Groin, Using Lift Blocks*

The double centering frames are topped with cleats attached by means of pegs. Because the ends of the lagging units must be bevelled, below, to conform to, the curvature of the centering frame, their depth where they abut the stone rib is less than the depth of the rib. If the depth of the lagging units was not sufficient to allow for this inevitable reduction (see 58 F), wooden lift blocks may have been used to compensate for this diminished depth, although such a scheme would seem to be rather fussy and laborious to have been generally employed.

152

the opposite end so as to lower the top there (to conform to the depth of the transverse or the wall rib). Another scheme (59) would have been to add a row of lift blocks above the cleats of the groin cradle, at either side of the line of rib voussoirs, in order to furnish a sufficiently raised seating for the lagging units as they came in to abut these rib voussoirs. A possible third alternative (58 at G) might have been individual lift blocks, one under the groin end of each lagging unit and secured to it by pins (or even by nails, perhaps) before the unit was set in place.

Of these, only the first seems direct and simple enough to have been generally adopted, granted the type of lagging frame we have envisaged. The effort expended in both the second and third schemes would have been incommensurate with the end to be gained, especially since this end could have been achieved more easily and quickly by some other means. The simplest scheme of all, of course, would have been to construct the lagging frames with one end higher than the other, right from the start. Actually, the medieval carpenters would certainly not have been limited to but one scheme. Each individual case of ribbed vaulting called for individual solution in the design of both the cradles and the seating of the lagging units along the groin frames. The design of these members was influenced primarily by the profile of the rib section. Thus in 60 we see a groin-rib profile that permitted the carpenters to dispense altogether with cleats that linked the top surfaces of the paired centering frames, and that required no lift blocks or additions of any sort for the lagging ends because such a small amount of the depth of the rib rose above their seating.

The necessity to keep the ends of the lagging free of the stone ribs by a safe interval, in order not to dislodge the rib voussoirs at the decentering operation, suggests another reason to substantiate the probability that the centering frames were made double: there needed to be enough room on the extrados of the diagonal rib cradles (in addition to the width of the rib voussoirs) to provide adequate seating for the bevelled and diagonally cut ends of the lagging, plus a generous clearance between these lagging ends and the stone rib. Unless the rib were excessively narrow, this would mean that the cleats of the diagonal cradle would have had to be some 17 inches long (figuring a minimum 9-inch-thick diagonal rib flanked on either side by 1 inch of clearance from a 3-inch bearing for the web lagging). Most cradles would doubtless have been wider than this minimum, wherever the diagonal rib's thickness was greater than 9 inches. The chief reason for double centering frames, however, remains the stability of bearing that they were able to provide for the lagging they supported on each side of the rib.

The whole matter of seating the ends of the lagging on the rib cradles is

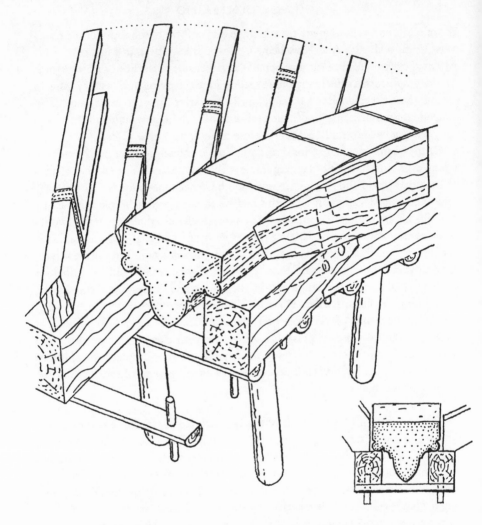

60. *Detail of Falsework Assemblage along the Groin, Omitting Cleats*

Where the cross-sectional shape of the rib permitted it, the scheme illustrated here was much simpler, and involved much less in both materials and labour, than the scheme shown in 59. No lift blocks are necessary, since much of the depth of the stone rib projects down between the cradling timbers of the centering frames: the lagging units can therefore be of normal instead of extra depth.

Positive spacing of the twin centering frames in parallel alignment is achieved by frequent unsquared wooden members that are attached to the under side of the frames' paired upper chords by means of dowels, whose downward projection furnishes attachment for the lashings of the lagging units (see 61).

complicated by the apparently conclusive fact that metal was almost never used in medieval falsework structures. Today we take it for granted that the lagging would be either bolted or spiked to the rib frames, as it is with us. And so it is difficult to envisage nail-less fastenings for medieval falsework, particularly that of the cleats

61. Method of Securing the Groin Ends of the Web Courses' Lagging Units

This schematic detail is simplified by (1) the omission of certain features that would normally be present, such as the adjacent paired frame essential along the groin, and the cleats laid across these twin frames, (2) the impossibly wide spacing of the lagging units, and (3) the variable, too obtuse angle these lagging units make with the centering frame. What the diagram does show, however, are the pegs let into the soffit of the curving sequence of timbers, and the ropes or withies that secure the lagging units to these pegs.

on the extrados of the cradles. Although these may at times have been nailed, particularly in England, they were more probably pegged or dowelled to the curving tops of the timber frames; for, if double frames were used, as seems most likely, these frames would have had to be securely and substantially joined together around the arc of their top members.

Compared to the technique of cleat attachment (perhaps analogous to the way in which the plank flooring of early American houses was pegged at the joists),[227] it is somewhat easier to envisage the manner in which the lagging was secured to the cradles. With the under side of their ends shaped with a hand axe to form a good bearing on the cleats of the cradle, they could have been lashed one by one to pegs inserted in the under surfaces of the cradle timbers (61). (Incidentally, this method of attachment would help to account for the seemingly excessive number

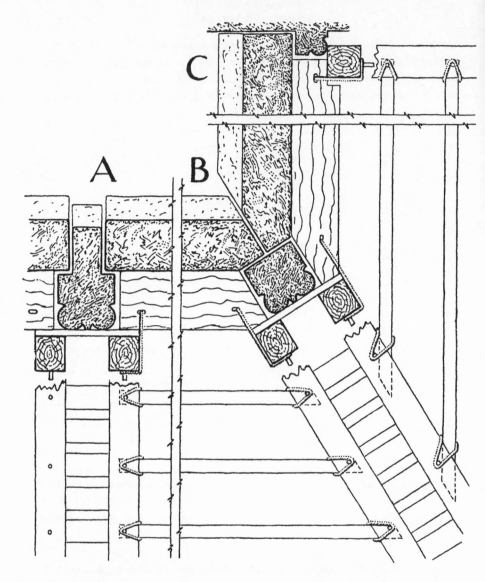

62. *Schematic Section and Reflected Plan Views of Centering Conditions under the Transverse, Diagonal and Wall Ribs*

These combined details show, in diagrammatic form, the cleated double cradles for the transverse and diagonal ribs (A and B) and the single frame, without cleats, for the wall rib (C). The lagging units (indicated here as solid, uncambered planks) are secured to pegs projecting below the top-chord timbers of the centering frames by lashings of rope or withies. Projecting up through the vault is the stem of the transverse rib. The wall rib is smaller than the other ribs, as was normal. The web courses of the longitudinal and transverse web compartments meet above the diagonal rib in a continuous joint lying in the plane of that rib.

of withies mentioned in some of the contemporary English records cited by Salzman.)

The sequence of carpentry operations, once the centering frames were completely assembled in place and the rib voussoirs set, might then have run somewhat as follows. (1) The pegs would have been driven into holes previously prepared for them along the under side of the curving timbers of the cradles, spaced in accordance with the number of stone courses that had been decided on for the web (62). The number and spacing of these would have varied, in the case of the diagonal frames, between those on one side, for the longitudinal vault, and those on the other side, for the transverse vault.[228] (2) The lagging units would be framed (each of an appropriate length in accordance with its position up the curve of the vault) and the groin end of each one shaped to a proper seating on the cleats so as to clear the rib it abutted. (3) The ends of these lagging units would then be secured, one by one, to the rib centering frames between which they stretched, working up from the lowest point on the frames at which they were needed; that is, where the separation between the ribs became greater than what could be spanned by a single web stone.

Unquestionably, the lagging units would not all have been installed before the masons began to set the blocks of the stone vault upon them. Instead, as a lagging unit was raised and lashed into position between its rib-centering supports, the stones of its web course would have been set along it; then another lagging unit secured and the next higher course of masonry laid upon it. In this fashion the masons could work conveniently from the side, as we have previously noted, instead of from above the extrados of the vault.

This procedure of laying up the web courses in the convenient and natural position one would take in building a wall suggests a possible answer to the not yet fully resolved question as to whether the lagging units were suspended vertically or radially. We have seen that the lagging units, one for each web course, were positive insurance that the predetermined number of courses would be followed in laying up the masonry of the vault, and that each of these courses would conform to the width and direction it was supposed to have. In other words, any errors in the building's most difficult and critical feature—the vault—could be caught and corrected at the falsework stage of operations; and the ensuing permanent masonry could thereupon be undertaken with complete confidence that it fulfilled its component requirements without dangerous discrepancies or oversights.

One of these requirements that is basic to any arch construction (including vaults of all sorts) is the necessity for the bed joints to be radial, or at least approximately

GOTHIC CENTERING

so. In this circumstance, it is clear that the lagging units of the falsework structure could serve the function of securing proper execution of the permanent work by themselves being set radially. Thereupon the masons could lay each web course with the upper surface of its stones at the same slope and in the same plane as that of the lagging unit. Particularly in the wide-spanning longitudinal vault compartments of high Gothic naves, where so much depended on regularity and accuracy of workmanship, and no chances could afford to be taken with slipshod practices or careless approximations, this means of guiding the masons in their setting of the stone courses was an assurance of achieving stability in the vault proper.

One further consideration would tend to support the probability that the lagging units were placed radially rather than vertically. This is a consequence of the fact that the bed joint of each web course is itself sloping, as we have just seen. Hence, up to the very crown itself, each stone course above the angle of friction received some of its support, during erection, from the course immediately below it.[229] It tended to slide downward and inward on this masonry surface of the course below it; and hence its pressure against the lagging unit was a diagonal one (of varying slope depending on how high up it was around the curve of the vault) approximately in the direction of its bed. Since the slope of each bed was radial, the temporary support given by the lagging unit obviously needed to be in the same direction. Otherwise, with the lagging unit hung vertically, the pressure of the stones of the web courses would have been diagonally across the lagging unit, tending to warp it out of alignment by loading it from an angle it could furnish less effective resistance to.

As the lowest unit of lagging was set in place and lashed to its pegs by means of withies looped through a slot or passing over part of the frame's assemblage near its ends, spacer blocks, of a width sufficient to separate the lagging units at whatever intervals had been determined for the width of the web courses there, may have been used: if so, they would have been set snugly against the upper side of the lagging unit at its ends. Then, against these spacer blocks (or against wooden pins whose function was analogous to them), the next unit of lagging was laid and similarly secured in place with withies lashed to the pegs underneath; and so on up the curve of the rib frames. If spacer blocks were actually employed, they would have had to be made slightly wedge-shaped, in the case of radially-set lagging, if they were to provide a snug and secure fit between successive ends of the lagging units, one above another up the curve of the rib cradles.

Such an assemblage would have been readily installed, adequately secured against movement or displacement under loading and, what is more, easy to

158

dismantle and reassemble when the time came to move it to the next bay and build another unit of vaulting there. Because of this complete salvageability and opportunity for re-use without waste (which is not true of our nail-attached assemblages of today), the workmanship involved in the preparations and the erectional sequences outlined above was not excessive by medieval standards.

In building operations we are accustomed to think in terms of labour-saving machinery and power-sawn lumber, of speed in erection through the use of nailed or bolted metal fasteners, and we usually think of re-use only in the case of those assemblages that can be lifted and shifted about in large units by a crane. The medieval builders, on the other hand, were accustomed to think in terms of savings in material rather than labour, of a tempo of work that was conditioned and regulated by handicraftsmanship, of the minimum and lightest possible assemblages of falsework. Moreover, when some feature or portion of this falsework was properly made, they were at pains to use and re-use it again and again, for as often and as long as it would serve. What the medieval builders asked of their falsework structures was that they should be as economical of materials as possible; that wherever feasible they should be made up of light members that could be handled and put into position without undue use of mechanical lifting devices; that they should clutter up the area devoted to religious services as little and for as short a time as possible; and that they should be able to be dismantled, shifted, and re-used with the minimum need for replacement due to impairment or unsalvageability of the component parts.

It is in the light of these considerations that the falsework complex described above should be assessed.

There are two additional aspects of the rib centering frames that remain to be clarified: the design of their assemblages, and the location of their decentering wedges.

Without doubt, these centerings were laid out and provisionally framed on a level, smoothly cleared and probably plastered surface on the ground, so that the only drawing that required being made was that of the rib arch, at full size on the plaster surface.[230] Accuracy was essential here in order to cut and fit the timbers of the cradles exactly to the even curve of the future rib's soffit minus the interval of the cleats (if cleats were used). Laying these members out at full size was particularly advantageous because of the fact that the frames, as explained above, were in three units (two approximate halves plus a filler piece at the crown), which necessitated very precise lengths and jointings. The full-size layout eliminated the chance for any errors that would otherwise have shown up only when the centering

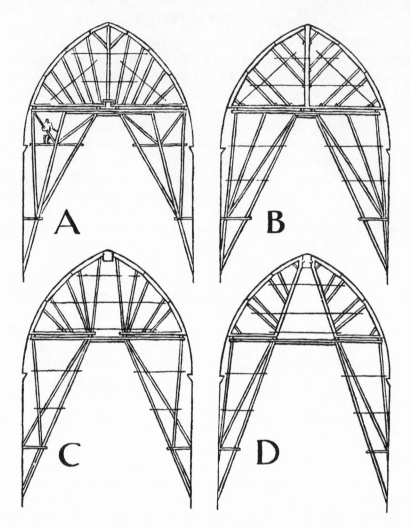

63. *Four Diagrammatic Schemes of Framing and Undergirding the Half-Frames of Gothic Ribbed Vault Centering*

For the falsework assemblage of undergirding gantries, A to D indicate successively less massive timber-work, since support for the rib centerings are needed progressively less close to mid-span, and the major struts lean out over the void at less of an angle with the vertical. These gantries provide a working platform at about the level of the top of the tas-de-charge, on which the centering frames could be manœuvred and wedged up. As explained in the text, the centering frames shown here apply to the intersecting diagonals as well as to the transverse ribs. In A, a large bracketed crown insert is separately wedged up from below. B involves a central tree-like column from which struts incline like branches to all four half-frames. C shows two half-frames of fanning struts, with a single separator block at the crown. D relates centering frames to gantry more rationally by aligning major elements of both portions of the falsework, so that the compressive stresses may be carried down directly to the triforium passageway level. In all four schemes, major timbers and struts are indicated by double lines, secondary ties and braces by single lines.

had been raised aloft and finally set in place. Here on the ground, too, the Master could conveniently indicate the number and direction of the web members or struts which fanned up to the cradle timbers, and could closely supervise all the notching and fitting that was entailed. He could also determine, with respect to the full-size curve of the rib arch and the slope of its radial joints, at what level it was necessary to have the centering frames commence. Finally, he could note what clearances were required in providing for the decentering and removal of the centering frames.

We have seen, from the Lärbro example, that the struts of the frames would doubtless have been of round poles let into the under surface of the cradle timbers, above, and the bottom timbers, below. But because the centering consisted of two symmetrical halves plus a crown insert, it does not necessarily follow that these bottom members were horizontal timbers that spanned from near the top of the tas-de-charge all the way to the middle of the bay. Such an arrangement was one possibility, to be sure. But another possibility is that in which the half-frames were discontinuous both above and below, as in 63 A, where a large bracketed crown-insert is separately wedged up upon the nearly abutting ends, at mid-span, of the half-frames' horizontal bottom timbers. Another possibility, involving quite a different scheme, is that of 63 B. Here, instead of separate half-frames, a central tree-like post is the main element, from which struts branch forth in the vertical planes of the half-arches they are destined to support. This scheme is less efficient, at least by our standards today, than the one just described; for here much of the assemblage would have had to be dismantled, element by element, in the process of moving it to a new bay. One of the disadvantages of both A and B is that the major load of the vault, during erection, would have been concentrated at the center of the span, necessitating a strong tilt in the supporting struts that undergirt the centering assemblage, and resulting in a powerful lateral thrust acting against the structure at their points of origin. C and D illustrate successive schemes that seek to correct this disadvantage. By constructing the centering frames with the horizontal bottom members of one half-frame not only discontinuous with, but widely separated from, the other, much less heavy timber-work was required in the falsework underpinning. Part of this economy comes about as a result of the falsework of the underpinning becoming more effectively related to that of the centering frames, so that the load of the latter carries directly down along the canted members of the former in a more vertical direction, to stable bearing on the ledge of the triforium passageway (as in D).

Any of the schemes illustrated here—and doubtless numerous others—could have been adopted by the medieval builders not only for the transverse ribs of their high vaults but, more significantly, for the considerably more demanding and difficult situation of the intersecting diagonal ribs.

The principal eventuality that had to be guarded against and prevented from

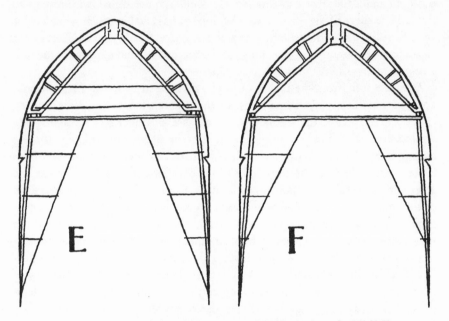

64. *Diagrammatic Scheme of Framing and Undergirding the Half-Frames of Rib Centering: Minimum Units*

Here, as in the previous four schemes of high vault falsework (63 A–D), are shown gantry assemblages and the rib centerings they undergird. The form of the centerings is such that support for them is needed only at either side, close to the curve of the vault. Hence the gantry can be fashioned of quite light membering, since absolute rigidity is required only under the decentering wedges at either side. As before, major timbers of the falsework are indicated by double lines, secondary ties and braces by single lines. The pairs of half-frames are kept from spreading, after they have been raised into position and keyed by a spacer block at the crown, by poles lashed securely to the feet of opposite pairs. Of the two centering schemes, E and F, the latter is the more efficient, since each half-frame rises from but one concentrated point of support, and the deeper spacer block at the crown gives more effective resistance to vertical slippage when the load of voussoirs begins to be applied to these half-frames.

the start in all such centering frames was deformation of the contour of the form as the frames became loaded. This eventuality could be forestalled, in the main, chiefly (1) by securing absolute rigidity in the supporting substructure, (2) by designing an effectively resistant pattern of the strutting members in the rib frames themselves, and (3) by providing secondary transverse ties lashed across the strutting poles of the frames proper, sometimes horizontally, sometimes diagonally. (These latter are designated in 63 A–D by single instead of double lines.)

Once the principle was established of having centering half-frames without continuous or nearly continuous horizontal timbers at the bottom, it would not have been too great a step to progress to half-frames that had the minimum amount of horizontal timber-work at the bottom, as in 64 F. In this scheme the centering frames themselves were reduced to relatively light, easily manœuvrable assemblages. And these, in turn, could be rigidly undergirt with almost vertical underpinning, which thus had practically no lateral thrust to act against the existing permanent masonry construction lower down. Secondary members of horizontal poles lashed to the main members of the underpinning could keep them in alignment at the same time that they secured the light members that would have been sufficient to provide various scaffolding stages up to the main working platform at the level of the top of the tas-de-charge. Above this level other horizontal poles, lashed at opposite ends to a pair of centering half-frames, would have prevented them from spreading as the load of the arch stones was applied; and the spacer unit at the crown would have kept the centering assemblage from becoming dislocated or deformed there. Hence the entire falsework, above and below, was made up of rigid but minimum units, each of which was relatively light in weight and relatively easy to set in place, secure, dismantle, and shift to a new position.

The danger of any vertical slipping of one half-frame on another at the crown (induced by the loading of the haunches during the erection of the vault masonry) could have been forestalled by driving square pins, from the side, into matching horizontally rebated grooves where the cradles abutted. 65 shows details of this condition at the point of juncture between four diagonal half-frames. (There could be a much simpler arrangement, of course, in the case of the transverse ribs, where but two half-frames abutted each other in the same plane.)[231] The square pins could not be driven through at right angles to all four frames because of their mutual interference. Hence the necessity for an abutment block, triangular in plan, to unite the pair of adjacent half-frames that came into the crown, one pair from each side of the nave. These triangular blocks, securely dowelled to a pair of half-frames, received the crown thrusts of the half-frames and combined them into a single resultant which could then be met by the rectangular insert block at the center: here the square pins could easily be driven in to prevent any vertical slipping between the pairs of half-frames.

This insert block was absolutely essential in the case of the diagonal rib frames. We have already commented on the desirability of having a removable separator piece between a pair of opposite half-frames, at their crown, in order to free the

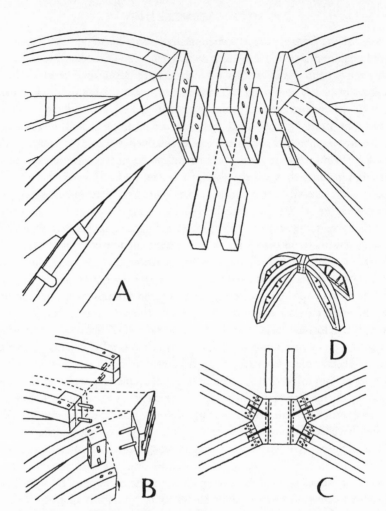

65. *Assemblage and Keying of Four Diagonal Half-Frames of Rib Centering at Their Common Crowns: Scheme with Rectangular Insert Block*

A pair of half-arch rib centerings, each made up of twin frames, are dowel-assembled as at B. The exploded view at A shows the left-hand pair and the right-hand pair separated at the crown by an interval into which a rectangular insert block is placed and secured with large square keys to prevent vertical slipping. The insert block is essential at the time of decentering, for it is the first element of the falsework complex to be removed. This not only allows the formwork to free itself from the soffit of the vault by a wider interval than would otherwise be possible through the retraction of the folding wedges alone. In addition, the interval created by its removal provides

necessary space into which the pegs uniting the double half-frames that converge on the crown can be driven free, so that each pair of half-frames can be disunited. For it is only by means of the separation of all four centering frames at the crown that the falsework complex can be dismantled for removal and subsequent re-use in another bay. C is a plan view at the crown, wherein the heavy lines show the location of the pegs or long dowels that secure each double half-frame to their triangular uniting block (seen isolated above the letter B). D is the complete assemblage of diagonal rib centerings, simplified at small scale. Cleats are not shown in any of these views.

frames more completely from the stone vault than could be done by the decentering wedges alone. We have also noted that dismantling the assemblage of half-frames, for manœuvring and stationing them elsewhere, would have been immeasurably aided by the presence of this insert block at the crown. These advantages could not have been realized in the case of the diagonals if the insert blocks had been omitted. First, it was only by means of the space provided by the insert block (upon its removal) that the converging half-frames, a pair on each side, could be unpinned from their triangular abutment blocks; otherwise the dowels that united each of these triangular blocks to its two half-frames could not have been driven out when the decentering operation took place. Obviously this triangular piece could be attached to the pair of half-frames only after they were placed in their rib-supporting position, in the erection of the vault; and conversely, it would have had to be unattached from them before they could be separated and removed to a new location. For if not, both half-frames would have had to be set up and shifted as a single ensemble: an impossible procedure. Furthermore, these triangular pieces would have had to be removed in order that each half-frame could be moved forward *in its own plane* during the dismantling operation: all kinds of complications would have ensued if the pair of half-frames were to have been moved away from the clerestory wall while they were still attached to each other as a pair.

From the necessity that there be a crown separator piece and from the multiple articulations of the falsework assemblage there (as well as from other factors that have been discussed, such as the cutting and seating of the lagging ends at the groins), it becomes abundantly evident how much the diagonal ribs complicated the centering problems compared to what could have served for the earlier, simpler types of vault. The complication came in the skill and care required on the part of the carpenters in fashioning the assemblage so that the parts would fit together and then be easily removable when they had to dismantle them and set them up in the next bay. By Gothic times, however, as we can see from their surviving permanent structures, the medieval carpenters were eminently able to frame the most complicated and effective assemblages in all-wooden construction.[232] And although the centering frames and the laggings we have described did require highly skilled and knowledgeable design and execution, the advantages—of lightness, manœuvrability, economy, and complete salvageability—were manifestly worth the trouble.

Since the act of decentering the vaults was unquestionably the most hazardous and uncertain operation of the entire building process, it is important to note how many pairs of wedges there were in each bay length of vaulting, and where these wedges were located. Whether in medieval times or the present, each pair of wedges must be manned by a responsible workman at the time of the decentering, so that all the wedges may be retracted a given amount simultaneously.

At first sight, the ideal number of wedges for a rectangular bay would appear to be four pairs, one pair for each corner. But we have already seen the necessity for a break in the continuity of the horizontal timbers at mid-span; where these horizontal bottom timbers were of some length (as in the schemes illustrated in 63 A–D), four additional sets of wedges would have been required for their inner ends, where the break in their continuity occurred. And because of the tas-de-charge's encroachment into the bay's rectangle, its four corners no longer presented simple points but jagged indentations there, in plan. The only likely way, then, by which the centering for an entire bay of quadripartite vaulting could be handled on but four pairs of wedges would be either as a series of transverse horizontal beams whose ends overlapped two heavy longitudinal sleepers, or the reverse of this: a series of longitudinal beams whose ends overlapped two heavy transverse sleepers, the wedges located under the outer corners of the large rectangle thus formed (66 A, B).

Actually, such a layout as this probably wasn't used, in spite of its apparent advantage in making it possible to decenter the falsework of an entire bay of vaulting as a single entity. To be sure, with only four pairs of wedges, there was little risk that differentials in the rate of decentering, between closely contiguous portions, would cause dislocations in some of the vault compartments at this time. There is considerable cause for doubting the medieval use of this scheme, however. It would necessarily have employed additional long and heavy sleeper timbers, which would have been both expensive to obtain and clumsy to move about. But the main reason for doubting this rectangular plan of placing no more than four pairs of wedges is that it would have involved a relatively excessive amount of weight to be concentrated on each of the four pairs of wedges, making their retraction very difficult.

With respect to this latter consideration, it would appear that the more wedges the better, as there would then be less load upon each pair, and their retraction could consequently be effected more evenly and surely, through the agency of much less clumsy and powerful jacking devices, or by driving them with a heavy maul or sledge-hammer. Furthermore, with numerous pairs of wedges, any slight settlement or incipient deformation that might occur during the loading of the frames as the vault was being constructed could be corrected or forestalled to some extent by adjusting the wedges to compensate for the variations at localized points, at the time they became apparent.[233] No such localized adjustments could be made where a bay-length unit of vaulting falsework rested on only four pairs of wedges.

Actually, the number and location of the decentering wedges was dependent upon and influenced by the layout and design of the centering frames; for example, whether supports—and therefore decentering wedges—were needed under the crown or not. In any case, the ends of the centering frames, near the corners of the bay, had to be provided for; and hence the arrangement and location of the decentering wedges there need clarification.

It is normal for simple groin vaults —and for many early rib vaults—of medieval times to abut the clerestory wall directly, without a longitudinal or wall rib to cover the joint there (which, as we have remarked, is often subject to opening and partially closing). Where this wall rib is lacking there had to be, of course, a centering frame as support for the ends of the lagging there, at the time the vault was under construction. This centering frame would have been close to the inner surface of the clerestory wall; hence its decentering wedges would have been somewhat removed, in plan, from those required for the diagonal and transverse ribs, especially as these were displaced from the actual spring of the arches on account of the corbelling of the tas-de-charge. Consequently,

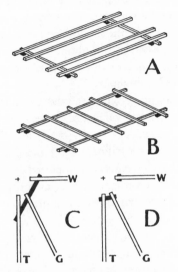

66. *Location of Decentering Wedges in a Quadripartite Vaulting Bay: Provisional Conjectures*

A and B show alternate schemes by which the falsework complex for an entire bay of vaulting could be decentered on but four pairs of wedges. As the text (p. 166) points out, probably neither of these schemes was used in medieval times.

C and D are plan views, near the corner of a vaulting bay, of the centering frames for the wall rib, W, for the groin or diagonal rib, G, and for the transverse rib, T. C shows the situation in which a single sill is sharply skewed so as to support one end of all three frames. D shows the transverse and diagonal rib frames more effectively supported by a short sill set close to the ends of both, and a separate sill for the wall rib's frame, as discussed in the text (pp. 167, 188).

the sill upon which the decentering wedges were located, near each of the four corners of the bay, would have had to be sharply skewed if all three rib-ends were to be accommodated together. This meant that only the diagonal rib's frame could be supported at its extreme end, the other two resting on the sill some distance in from their ends (66 c). Alternatively, the two major rib frames (diagonal and transverse) would have been handled together, and the wall frame separately, on its own independent sill (66 d). The latter appears to be the more logical and efficient scheme, particularly since the level at which the wall centering needed to be set was higher than that for the other ribs due to its stilted springing.

Whatever the number and location of wedges adopted, it is evident that their most careful and evenly synchronized retraction was essential at the time of decentering, in order that the gradual freeing of the forms might take place to the same degree throughout.

This process involved the lowering of the centering frames in absolutely horizontal stages; otherwise, unresolved stresses were set up that could be fatal in bringing about the collapse of the entire structure. Much depended on two factors: the assured rigidity of the falsework substructure under the wedges, so that the level of the centerings supported on these wedges should remain constant throughout the construction of the masonry vault, and the precision with which all the wedges were retracted at a uniform rate, when the decentering operation took place.[234]

It is evident, therefore, that the seating, strutting, and bracing of the supporting substructure required the most experienced and knowledgeable attention on the part of the master carpenter, in its layout, and the most careful and accurate workmanship on the part of the carpenters working under his direction, in its execution.

Unquestionably there must have been not one standard method but more than one scheme for economizing the supporting gantries or falsework assemblages that undergirt the centering frames, depending on (1) the design of the centering frames themselves, (2) the kind of stone employed, (3) the intended thickness and therefore the weight of the vault web, (4) the experience and resourcefulness of the 'architect', and (5) the intensity of the demand for unobstructed floor space on the part of the clergy so that worship would not be postponed or interrupted any longer than was absolutely necessary.

Although this problem of the design of the high-level staging's supporting falsework has already been encountered in connexion with the layout of the rib half-frames (with which it was so intimately associated), nevertheless the problem needs more complete discussion in its own right, even at the risk of some repetition. A few possible solutions whose implications need investigation and evaluation are the following. (1) Fixed pole scaffolding, with standards set on the floor of the nave at regular and frequent intervals.[235] (2) Heavy scaffolding, either fixed or provided with rollers, whose standards started at the floor level as V-shaped legs at either side of the nave, diverging as they rose, so that most of the width of the nave was freed of encumbrance below this gantry-like assemblage of falsework members.[236] (3) Scaffoldings that were hung high up on either side of the nave, supported at one of the passageway levels, so as to free completely the floor of the nave and consequently reduce very much the amount of timber-work required, as compared to the high staging that took its rise all the way up from the floor of the nave.[237]

The first thing to note is the excessive height of the vault above the pavement of the nave in most of the great French Gothic churches. A glance at photographs of the interior of Paris, Chartres, Reims, Rouen, the choir of Le Mans, and Bourges, for instance, not to mention Amiens and Beauvais, is sufficient to make us wonder whether their high vaults could ever have been supported all the way from the floor, during the course of erection. In these churches, as we have noted,[238] the spring of the nave vaults is 80, 90, 110, or even 125 feet above the floor; and the portion of the vault that required centering (that is, from the top of the tas-de-charge) was some 15 feet or so higher yet. Were the supports for the platform to have risen from the pavement, there would have had to be two, certainly, and probably three superimposed lengths of poles, spliced or butted or otherwise firmly attached, one above another.[239]

In connexion with the possibility of two or even three tiers of scaffolding, it is interesting to note that Viollet-le-Duc insists categorically that no metal whatsoever was used in the timber-work of the great Gothic roofs—not even bolts or fish-plates—throughout the entire period of 'pointed architecture'.[240] If there was no use of metal for attachment or tie-rods in the *permanent* timbering, it is highly doubtful that there would have been any of this expensive ironwork anywhere in the *falsework* structure. Indeed, it is probable, as we have seen, that even the lagging was secured to the centering frames by means of pegs or 'tree nails' rather than metal nails, at least in French work.

Viollet-le-Duc's own illustrations of scaffolding assemblages show ingenious combinations of attachment that include wooden pegs and keys, mortises and tenons, and pairs of members that clasp a beam or strut and are secured by wedges. Although he illustrates only one example of lashed bindings,[241] this method of attachment was unquestionably the predominant one employed in the temporary assemblages of medieval falsework, if we may judge by the evidence of many manuscript illustrations and, even in England, by Salzman's quotations from building accounts of the purchase of ropes or of withies for the lashings.[242]

The method of supporting the high staging on numerous vertical poles set at frequent intervals in two or three tiers directly from the floor of the nave would probably have been the least difficult scheme to assemble, structurally. Although this scheme would have required a large number of poles, its assemblage would have been quite uncomplicated and relatively easy to erect; for, in a vertical direction, the poles of the upper tier would have aligned with, and abutted, those of the lower tier, and the close horizontal spacing of these laterally stayed, superimposed columns would have very much reduced if not eliminated the necessity for employing large and heavy timbers up to and including the level of the high staging. In spite of these very real advantages, however, it would seem to be highly doubtful whether the medieval builders would have adopted this scheme except in rare cases, the chief reasons being the excessive amount of falsework this would have involved, and the overwhelming compulsion, almost always, to have the floor of the church free of encumbrance for conducting the services of worship.

A system of falsework using a high gantry with legs straddling the nave would have satisfied the major objection to the above scheme in large part, but it would have required much massive timber-work. It would seem that if the floor of the nave were to be thus freed by having the supporting timbers rise from points near the piers on either side, or even from points between these piers, then the same end —of freeing the floor of the nave—could have been achieved with far less outlay of heavy timber-work. This could have been done by having the legs of the gantry rise from the triforium level rather than from the floor of the nave. In the very lofty interiors of the great Gothic churches there was still a great deal of height between the level of this triforium passageway and the top of the tas-de-charge, where the working platform of the high staging would need to have been established. Consequently, the struts from the triforium ledge would not have had to tilt out over the void at an abrupt angle, but could have been inclined at a fairly steep pitch and yet furnish support to the staging out towards the middle of the void.

The advantage of the steep slope of these supporting struts was the much greater vertical than horizontal component of pressure they developed against their seating on the floor of the triforium passageway: their thrust was more downward than lateral, and hence safer to be met by the existing masonry structure at that level without recourse to any additional bracing there. On the other hand, the advantage of having the upper ends of these struts come fairly close to the center of the void from either side was the resulting shortness of the horizontal span that had to bridge the remaining gap between them, at the platform level: if the type of centering frames adopted by the builders required special strength here, their close juxtaposition would have required much less heavy timbering so as to provide rigid support under the middle of the staging.

Supposing the high-level staging to have been supported by raking poles seated on the triforium ledge, there are three major considerations affecting the arrangement and design of these falsework structures: (1) the design of the rib centering frames they undergirt (for example, see the four schemes—and there are certainly other alternatives—shown diagrammatically in 63); (2) the nature of the lateral bracing and attachment for the inward-tilting poles in relation to the clerestory piers and windows (specifically, whether pairs of these struts were framed on the interior around the clerestory piers and secured to them at intervals, or whether series of parallel frames were attached through the window openings to stable anchorages outside the clerestory wall); and (3) the distribution of the falsework by bays (that is, what arrangements were planned for shifting the temporary structures from one bay to the next).

In regard to the last of these considerations, let us accept the fact that the French, at least, were interested in having the minimum of falsework. Hence the problem arises: how much would have been the minimum? In any event, we can assume that the high vaulting would have been constructed one bay at a time. But it does not follow from this that one bay of falsework would have sufficed. With the triforium-lodged gantry type of falsework we are considering, it would appear that two bays of it would have probably been the minimum requirement. Otherwise, none of the centering could have been shifted at the high level, but would have had to be laboriously dismantled, lowered to the floor, raised up again, and re-erected. With a high platform two bays in length, however, all the falsework it supported for a given bay of vaulting could be disassembled, moved laterally to the next bay, and quickly reassembled there. Then while the new bay of vaulting was under construction, the staging for the previous bay could have been taken down and re-erected in the bay beyond the one whose vaulting was being built.

The nature and sequence of the shifting operation would have varied somewhat in accordance with the location of the platform supports mentioned in (2) above. If we consider the type of centering layout indicated in 64 F that requires no platform-level support at mid-span under the crown, the most economical and minimum arrangement would perhaps have resulted from the gantries being framed around the clerestory piers on either side of the nave (67 A). In this scheme, each gantry assemblage that spans the nave is an independent unit straddling opposite piers on either side of the nave. If the width of its platform in the longitudinal direction were to have been about 7 feet, then there would have been about 13 feet of void separating one gantry unit from the next. These voids of 13 feet would not have been difficult to span with some kind of working platform: either planking, or hurdles resting on light poles set cross-wise to the topmost members

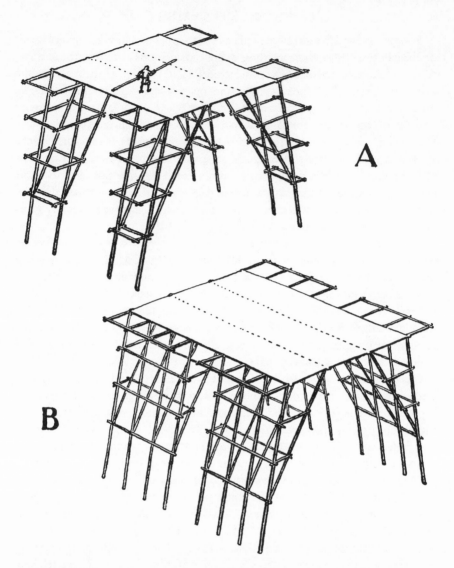

67. *Gantry Schemes for Supporting the Working Platform in High-Level Vaulting*

The hung gantry shown in scheme A is a pier-girdling arrangement (as indicated in 68) supported from the triforium passageway and secured to the clerestory piers. This light scheme would have been quite adequate where no rigid support was required near the center of the bay. A heavier scheme is shown at B, where the multiple frames of the gantry fill a bay and thus provide somewhat more direct undergirding for the rib centerings out in the middle of the bay. This scheme, too, is supported from the triforium passageway, and it could have been similarly braced to the clerestory piers by horizontal ties passing through the window openings and secured from the outside.

of the nave-spanning gantries. On such a platform the workmen could have shifted about and positioned the centering frames, set up their trestles, and kept a ready supply of stones and mortar handy to their work.

On the other hand, if supports for the centering frames (loaded, in their turn, with the lagging units and the weight of the web coursing they were designed to carry) were required at or near the center of the bay, then a much stronger and more direct undergirding would have been needed there. This could have been provided by gantries bridging across the nave in multiple, parallel frames that filled the entire length of the bay from near one pair of piers to near the next, to be secured against tilting inward during the course of their erection by attachment outside the window openings (67 B). In this case, the closeness of the nave-spanning gantry assemblages (with their numerous struts and horizontal ties, some longitudinal some transverse) could have facilitated their sequential dis-mantling and the threading of each member through the assemblage that was currently supporting the vault being erected, to their new location beyond this bay.

In any case, either scheme of high staging could have been made adequately strong and rigid, if properly designed, even though it was composed exclusively of poles lashed together. Only the short lengths of smooth-surfaced sills upon which the decentering wedges were located would have needed to be of squared timber.

Finally, beneath the two bays of high staging, and quite independent of it, there may have been a temporary platform (either extending the length of the nave as a fixed structure, or only two bays in length and mounted on wheels or rollers) which spanned the nave and gave protection to the worshippers from anything inadvertently dropped from above.

With this discussion of the undergirding of the staging for the high vault's erection, we complete our survey of the chief operational equipment and pro-cedures that appear to have been essential in the construction of a great French Gothic church. Although the foregoing detailed analysis and explanation would seem to have taken into account all the major problems encountered, and to offer reasonable solutions for them, there is nevertheless one erectional practice that has not been mentioned. Its adoption by the Gothic masons immeasurably simplified the work of all concerned in the multiple and complicated operations of building the vault. A good deal of what has been covered in the present chapter becomes revealed as obsolete, unnecessary, and needlessly expensive in labour and materials alike when this simplifying practice is understood. The account of it is sufficiently important, and its influence upon the entire operation of erecting Gothic rib vault-ing is so conclusive, that another chapter is needed for its discussion.

68. High-Level Hung Scaffolding: Pier-Girdling Gantry Scheme

This sketch is of the scheme given at A in 67, showing the position of the high-level gantry under the vaulting, to whose erection it has contributed. What is here represented is not a view of the building's state of progress at a given moment, for, in an actual situation, the clerestory walls and the high roof would have been completed before the nave vaulting would have been erected. Rather, this cut-away view presents the

relative positions of such principal features as the timber roof, the high vaulting, and the clerestory windows through whose unglazed voids some of the gantry members pass in order to secure the frames to the clerestory piers. It is evident that the gantries furnish a platform level well above the spring of the transverse and diagonal ribs, as indicated in the elevation view at F in 64.

6

'Given an original problem to resolve, one's first solution will invariably be one of unusual complexity. But the more it is worked over, and thought over, the simpler the solution becomes, until in the end it results in something almost elementary; one is only puzzled why in the world one did not think of the simplest way first.' GEORGE WOODBURY *

ONE READS HERE AND THERE, OR HEARS FROM TIME TO TIME, references to both domes and vaults that have been constructed without formwork or centering. Rarely, however, are these references either complete or specific—perhaps because of the incompleteness of the knowledge held by the writers, who are usually not practitioners of what they describe. We have already seen an instance of this in Porter's expansive but uninforming claim that the early Lombard vaults were built 'virtually without centering'. As in the case of his claim, it seems well to investigate some of the schemes that have been advanced and the suggestions that have been made for eliminating formwork, in order to test the likelihood of their practicality.

Among the earliest writers who have noted one such scheme is William Eton,[243] who writes of it as follows in his *A Survey of the Turkish Empire*:

At Bassora, where they have no timber but wood of the date tree, which is like a cabbage-stalk, they make arches without any frame. The mason, with a nail and a bit of string, describes a semicircle on the ground, lays his bricks, fastened together with a gypsum cement, on the lines thus traced, and having thus formed his arch, except the crown brick, it is carefully raised, and in two parts placed on the walls. They proceed thus till the whole arch is finished; this part is only half a brick thick, but it serves to turn a stronger arch over it.

It would be interesting to know more about this scheme: Why was it 'only half a brick thick', and how could such a thin slice hold together when lifted from a

* *John Goff's Mill*, New York, W. W. Norton & Company, 1948, p. 220.

175

horizontal to a vertical position; what spans were practicable with this system; how were the bricks set, radially or tangentially? When Eton says 'till the whole *arch* is finished', does he mean 'till the *barrel vault* is completed'?

Another scheme, referred to from time to time in the case of domes, is that in which a 'trammel' is claimed as the only piece of falsework required. This trammel is a pole, supported at a point at the center of the hemispherical dome-to-be, and pivoted there in such a way that its free end may be swung about, at whatever level, in full horizontal circles.

Provided no workmen's scaffolding or other falsework was required in the void of the domed space that might get in the way or interfere with the freedom of its operation, the trammel, as here described, is a means of assuring the evenness and regularity of the hemispherical surface. In spite of assertions to the contrary, however, the trammel would appear to be ineffectual as a *support* for the voussoirs, at least at the level of the highest courses near the crown, where the radial angle of the bed joint would be at too steep a slope to expect even fairly stiff mortar to be adhesive enough to prevent the voussoirs from slipping down into the void. But where the material was brick rather than stone, this scheme seems to have been feasible when one or both of two conditions were met; namely, when a large oculus was left at the crown, and when the higher bed joints were kept at a flatter angle than a radial slope would produce. Choisy illustrates and explains the system,[244] but he speaks only of its erection in large flat bricks.

Some schemes for obviating the use of formwork have arisen out of special circumstances or particular conditions. For example (again for a dome), there is the case of the Eskimo igloo, whose construction is described with clarity, accuracy, and completeness, both in the text and in progress photographs, by Stefansson.[245] Here the special conditions that make the scheme work are the relative lightness and consistency of the deeply crusted snow, the spiral procedure followed in setting the blocks of snow (so that each successive block bears against other blocks along *two* of its sides), and the nature of the material itself, which acts as its own adhesive, cementing all the blocks together in a homogeneous mass. The domical snow house whose erection is photographed by Stefansson was built by him to accommodate only three men, and was therefore a small one: 9 feet in diameter and 6 feet high, inside dimensions, the shell being not over 4 inches thick. The process, none the less, is one that requires no falsework whatsoever, and but one tool—a large-bladed butcher knife or a machete.

Another specialized situation—this time, a barrel vault, in which the material is brick—is described and illustrated in some detail by Choisy.[246] The principle here is perhaps most clearly illustrated in the make-up of those underground arched structures used by the Sassanians for their palace drains. Arch rings made up of fairly thin, wide bricks formed slices which were inclined at a considerable angle rather than set vertically, with one of the large flat sides of each brick in a given ring set in mortar against the sloping plane of the previous ring. Each brick was kept from slipping, during the course of erection, partly by the adhesion of the mortar on one of its flat sides, partly by the considerable slope of its setting, and partly by being in contact with what had previously been constructed along two of its surfaces—its flat side, and its lower radial edge.[247]

This system required a solid wall at the starting end of the vault (for the tilted slices to lean against), and produced a thick vault suitable for resisting the earth pressure acting upon underground drains. It was completely inappropriate, however, for the high nave-spanning ceilings of medieval churches.

A primitive scheme of bridging space in stone is that of corbelling. Applied to circular structures, this system has occurred in many regions throughout the world, including Eire,[248] Syria, and even South America.[249] A special case, and one of the earliest, is that of the *tholos* tomb, as seen in the well-known 'Treasury of Atreus' at Mycenae, built in the pre-Hellenic Minoan era. Although of considerable interest because of their size (the Treasury of Atreus has a clear span of $48\frac{1}{2}$ feet), their age, and their technique of erection, these 'bee-hive' tombs or *tholi* do not concern us here because they are underground constructions. The corbelling principle has also been used for structures above ground, however; notably for certain pre-Christian and early Christian Irish buildings, and for many curious dwellings of south-eastern Italy. The latter, called *trulli* and supposedly dating from about 1600, are strikingly illustrated in Kidder Smith's recent book, *Italy Builds*.[250] His excellent photographs clearly illustrate their conical forms, neatly constructed of rough but surprisingly well-fitted stones laid up dry, without mortar. But although it is quite evident that no formwork was required for their execution, this writer has encountered no eye-witness account of their erection.

In general, however, it may be said that all structures using the corbelling system require no falsework support because the bed-joints, instead of being radial or inward-sloping, are flat. Sometimes, in fact, they even slope very slightly downward towards the exterior. Thus each completed course provides a level platform upon which the stones of the succeeding course shelve out slightly over the void within; and in circular structures this platform is stable without any extra counterbalancing because the stones of each horizontal ring prevent each other from tipping downward into the void.

There is, to be sure, some recent photographic evidence that shows considerably more economy in the use of centering for masonry vaults constructed or reconstructed today than we have been prepared, so far, to admit in the case of the original Gothic erections.

One instance of this paucity of falsework was reported in *The Architects' Journal* for 1946 under the title 'Building Vaults without Centering'.[251] The account consists mainly of three illustrations of a constructional brick vault, at a height of some 70 feet and for a span of nearly 40 feet, in the war-damaged church of S. Teresa at Turin, Italy. The brief commentary reads in part as follows:

. . . The first bay of the nave vaulting was . . . in a perilous state, necessitating demolition. The vault consisted of an ellipse 36 ft wide intersecting with a semi-circle 20 ft wide. A light scaffold was erected to provide a platform on which the bricklayer and his mate could work. Two shaped boards were fitted as guide lines under the diagonal intersections, to prevent winding. The vault was then quickly constructed with successive rings of brick, these being hollow-type and set end to end, not on edge as voussoirs. So laid they remain in position because the mortar acts as a dowel, holding the bricks in place until setting is completed. After this one may walk with confidence over the upper surface although the total thickness is only 3 inches. . . . The four flanks are brought in evenly until the remaining opening is finally filled in. . . .

How the groins were interlocked or otherwise secured in this rib-less construction is not indicated in the photographs. In any case, this ingenious and inexpensive method (in which the courses arch across as slices at right angles to the axes of the vaults) could not have been used in the Gothic vaults we are concerned with because of the 'dowel' feature of the mortar keying together its light 'bricks' of hollow tiles. Incidentally, it is worth noting that the coursing in all four panels is designated as having to be carried along together at an even rate, from the bay's outer boundaries inward towards the center at the highest part of the vault.

Another instance of extremely limited falsework support, which appears to be more comparable to the situation in Gothic times, is that shown in two photographic illustrations, figs. 34 and 37, pp. 78, 79, of Chauvel's *Rouen*.[252] The legend for fig. 34 reads: 'The construction of a rib vault, accomplished by the simplest and most reduced means. Here is shown the slightness (*faible importance*) of the centering that was sufficient for the erection of the arch.'

The rib centering that is illustrated appears to consist of a wooden template only one plank thick (although it is two planks wide, in depth) set on edge in a vertical plane under the center of the rib. It is thus what the English call a mere 'turning piece'; that is, employed to support the voussoirs in line and with the proper curvature, but requiring the maximum reliance on the early adhesive action of the mortar and special care on the part of the masons in setting in place and balancing each successive voussoir so as not to disturb either the balance or the alignment of the previous arch stone.

A formwork seating that is only some 2 inches wide for the rib voussoirs seems to put an unnecessarily high premium on delicacy of setting on the part of the mason and, at the least, to cause a slowing down of his procedure. For here, unlike most of the other schemes we have been considering so far in this chapter, there is only one face of each block that is in contact with the masonry that has previously been laid.

Needless to say, it is quite certain that such a thin centering was never used in Gothic times, where approximately *squared timbers*, not *wide flat planks on edge*, were used as segments of the centering arc. In the earlier vaults where the rib voussoirs were very short, there was little tendency for these blocks to tilt out of alignment to one side or another, for the mortar that was spread thickly across their wide flat bed faces largely took care of this eventuality. In later Gothic times, when the rib voussoirs became not only longer but more frequently pointed or narrowly rounded at their intrados, much more care would have needed to be exercised in their setting, perhaps with little blocks or wedges temporarily stuffed in on either side between them and the cradle.

The legend accompanying Chauvel's fig. 37 reads: 'The device of sliding, grooved cerces is not a bookish invention of Viollet-le-Duc but a practical reality that has permitted the rebuilding of the destroyed vault's web panels.' This photographic view shows what appears to be a light template of two spliced boards rather than an extensible cerce (the cut is somewhat obscure in this respect), set radially and apparently hung by metal flanges hooked over the outer edge of the backs of adjacent ribs, the latter being without their centerings. The web course that has just been completed (and under which this template is still in place) is seven blocks in length; and one notes that the length of these blocks is somewhat shorter, on the average, than the thickness of the web. The view given in fig. 37 is too confined to permit an assured estimate of how near the crown the web coursing has been carried, or even which ribs are involved: perhaps the courses near the crown would be twice the length of the longest one shown here.

Both figs. 34 and 37 provide indisputable evidence—being photographs—of how these Gothic vaults have been re-erected in our own day. But it should be noted that the vaults shown are those over side aisles. These, as we have remarked, are not of great span; in addition, they are relatively low and relatively thick compared to their spans. It will be remembered that Choisy doubted whether the cerce could be used for large-span vaults; that is, for those over the naves and choirs of the great churches.[253] And we have already acknowledged that the medieval builders constructed thoroughly Gothic ribbed vaults over side aisles long before they knew how or dared to construct them for the high vaults of wide-spanning naves. Chauvel includes no photographs of the high vaults during the course of their reconstruction. So, once again, we have no sure published evidence, even in terms of modern techniques, of how the centering and formwork for the high vaults of Gothic cathedrals might have been rationalized in medieval times.

There is one device, however, by which centering requirements for stone vaults could in truth be drastically reduced if not largely eliminated. This device is so simple, so characteristic of handicraft practices, and so easy to operate that its use in many vaulted constructions in the past is unquestionable. What is remarkable, under the circumstances, is that such a useful and highly economical device seems to have escaped the attention of architectural historians and technological annotators alike: having been described only once, apparently, it has subsequently been forgotten or at least ignored. This once was in the *Journal of the Royal Institution of Great Britain* in 1831, by M. de Lassaux,[254] as communicated to the *Journal* by Professor William Whewell of Cambridge. Because of the early date and relative obscurity of this article, it would seem to be appropriate and useful to quote extensively from it: first, as to the circumstances of Lassaux's discovery; then, passing along through various vaulting conditions we, too, have encountered and commented on, to the practical device itself.

The title of the article is 'Description of a Mode of Erecting Light Vaults over Churches and Similar Spaces'. It starts out as follows:

M. de Lassaux, of Coblentz, architect to the King of Prussia, is the discoverer and restorer of this process, and gives the following account of his investigations.

He had arrived in various ways at the conviction that what are called the *gothic* and *ante-gothic* styles of architecture (the pointed arch and round arch styles), are not only the most appropriate for churches, but also the cheapest. He had attempted to discover some easy means of erecting stone vaults in such cases, thinking them highly desirable, whenever the funds at the builder's disposal will permit them. Vaults which are at the same time wide and light, belong incontestably to the boldest and most ingenious of human inventions: they are peculiarly suitable in religious edifices; they are secure from the devastations of fire; and, when introduced in public buildings, they correspond to the spirit of the celebrated decree of the republic of Florence, enacted in the year 1294, that all which is executed for the commonwealth should bear the lofty impress of the common will.

M. de Lassaux was also aware, that at Vienna, at the present time, very wide and flat domes are erected almost entirely *free-handed* (i.e. without centering), and that in the neighbourhood of that city, very flat ovens and wide mantelpieces are constructed almost in the same manner, and with the help only of a few slight posts or poles. He endeavoured, therefore, to discover some mode of facilitating, by similar means, the execution of wide vaults in churches.

His attempts for some time led him to nothing bearing on the point in question, except the usual methods of laying down the vaulting lines, and some historical notices, which will be mentioned subsequently. In the old church vaults which are extant, there was little to be seen, as they are in almost all cases covered with a coat of mortar or plaster.

About six years ago, however, happening to go into the space above the vault of the fine church at Ahrweiler, he observed in the *extrados* of the vaults so remarkable a dissimilarity in their height and curvature, that the thought in an instant struck him, that it was impossible these could have been built upon a regular centering. On a closer examination, it appeared impossible to entertain any further doubt on this subject; and in various places, where the rubble work had been laid bare, the whole mode and manner was exhibited of the process which had been employed, and the opinion thus formed was more and more confirmed by subsequent examination of other vaults.

The whole mystery resides in this, that these pointed-arch cross-vaultings consist of separate, generally horizontal, courses; of which courses each has a small concavity, and consequently forms a small vault by itself, as soon as its terminating points have their due counterpoise. Now, as the bed-faces of the individual courses of a regular pointed arch, that is, of one which is described about an equilateral triangle, recede very slowly from the horizontal line, and even at the summit make with it an angle of only 60°, the adhesion of each individual vaulting-stone of moderate dimensions, such as brick and similar stones generally have, to the layer of mortar, is sufficient to prevent the sliding of the stone before the termination of the course; and hence there is no difficulty in executing each individual course *free-handed* and independently, and in locking it against its counterpoise. Against each course already locked, and consequently fixed and immovable, we may begin a new one, and so continue to the final termination of the whole vault. All that is required, therefore, is a solid resistance for the terminating points of each course. Now, such a resistance may be supplied not only by solid obstacles, as the external walls, but equally well by the reaction of a contiguous course. Hence, if the groining-ribs or diagonal lines of the separate compartments are properly supported beneath, the courses which rest on the same point perpetually keep each other in equilibrium, and consequently no further contrivance is needed than to execute the whole

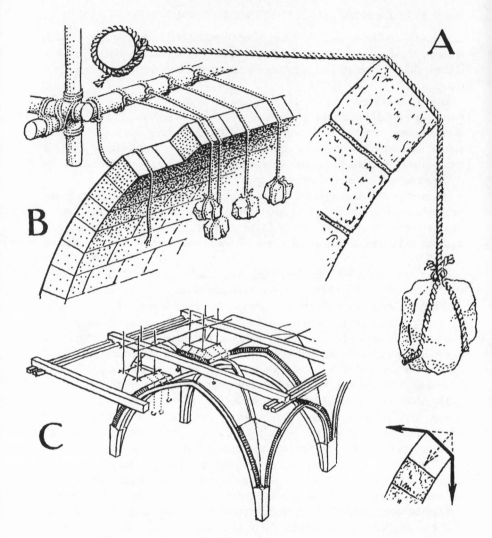

69. *Stone-Weighted Rope Device for Building Web Courses without Lagging or Other Formwork*

The large-scale detail at A shows one end of a length of rope secured around a pole, the other end being weighted by a stone (below which the small diagram indicates the combinaton of forces acting against the block that has just been placed, pressing it against the top of the stone in the course immediately below it). B shows a series of these rope-lengths with their lashed-poles attachment behind the vault and slightly above the level of the course being laid. The nearest weighted rope is ready to be slipped sideways to be in bearing against the next block as soon as it is set in place. The ensemble at C shows the pole assemblages at the far side, supported on light horizontal poles laid across the main tie-beams of the roof, from which they can be braced and quickly adjusted for height as successive courses of the vault come to be laid.

182

courses in the individual horizontal planes at the same time, or nearly at the same time; that is, to carry the courses all the way round; consequently the process in such cross-vaulting is the same fundamentally as in domes, when each *course* is locked by itself as a ring, one ring is gradually laid upon another, and thus finally the dome itself is locked, except that in these domes the upper courses have steeper bed surfaces, and consequently the stones will no longer remain in their places without the application of other auxiliary means, but would slip down as soon as they were laid, if not prevented in some other way. This is now done in Vienna in a very simple manner, *by means of some strong ends of rope, which are fastened above, and somewhat backwards, from the course to be vaulted, and hang down like plummets, being loaded below by some stones tied to the rope. As soon as a stone is laid, and by a moderate blow with the hammer pressed against the preceding stone, one of these ropes is brought over the stone, and the pressure produced by the weight of the appended stone, combined with the adhesion of the mortar, is sufficient to hold the stone till it is sufficiently supported by the contact of the next stone; and this in its turn is prevented from slipping down by the pressure of the cord upon it.*

Although there is much more of interest and value in Lassaux's account, the last few sentences of this excerpt (italics added) describe the device in question. As may readily be surmised, it is applicable to vaults of many sorts, including domes (where it provides that extra feature that makes the trammel operation feasible in the higher—and more steeply sloping—courses near the crown).

What is necessary to make this stone-weighted rope device work is some sort of anchorage to which to secure the ropes 'which are fastened above, and somewhat backward, from the course to be vaulted'. In Gothic construction this anchorage was automatically provided by the tie-beams of the great timber roof which, as we have seen, was almost invariably built before the high vault was commenced. From these heavy, permanent timbers a temporary beam (to which a series of the rope-ends had been fastened) could be securely suspended, its position—in height and in distance from the crown of the intended vault—shifted from time to time in order to achieve the most favourable and effective angle for the functioning of the stone-weighted ropes.

The section diagram (69 A) indicates the mechanics by which a stone-weighted rope held a given voussoir in position: the weight-tightened rope from the upper edge of the arch stone to the temporary beam provided one component of stress, the other component being the vertical downward pull of the loaded free end of the rope. Together, these two components created a resultant pressure (whose direction was approximately that of the dotted arrow, in the little diagram below the pendent stone) against the upper bed of the previously laid course. A series of such stone-weighted lengths of rope hung down from the temporary beam, behind and above the course to be built; and as each new voussoir in this course was set in position, the mason reached for and brought forward one of these ropes and set it dangling over the near face of the voussoir he had just laid, where it remained in line with all the previously utilized rope ends until that course was completed from one boundary rib to the other. Actually, it would doubtless have proved convenient in practice to loop a second weighted rope over a voussoir that had just been set in place; then, when the next voussoir was set adjacent to and in line with the previous one, this second rope merely needed to be shifted laterally a few inches in order to engage and hold the new block at once (69 B).

As in the case of the previously discussed cerce device, each course so constructed became, upon completion, to some extent an arch spanning from rib to rib. But this arch action, to whatever extent it may have operated, was not unduly great even at the moment of completing a new course. For the adhesion of the mortar along the flat side—that is, the bed joint—of a just-completed line of voussoirs prevented longitudinal slipping to a very considerable extent. And with respect to all of the previously laid courses, as the mortar took hold in its first set the arch action would have become predominantly if not exclusively that of the primary vault action: downward and outward towards the spring of the vault, not longitudinally along the web course.

It may well have been a growing awareness of and confidence in the nature of these conditions—the effective role of the mortar in the bed joints of each successive web course in largely eliminating longitudinal arch action, and the predominance of normal vault action even in partial panels of vaulting that had not yet been carried up to the crown—that gradually led the Gothic builders to dare to give less and less camber to their vaults, until many of them eventually came to be built with very little camber, at least at the crowns.

In the early ribbed vaults—at least those of considerable span, such as the high vaults at Paris and the lateral cells of the nave vaults at Chartres—there is what Lassaux refers to as a 'small concavity' in each of the web courses. We have already commented on the stiffening function this created throughout the vault web as a whole. But it is quite likely that the original reason for adopting this bowed form of vaulting panel was a practical erectional one rather than a consciously structural one. Progressing, as they did, from barrel and groin vaults erected from above on a continuous formwork, to relatively thin, ribbed vaults built course by course from the side (as in a wall), where erectional support for these masonry courses was drastically reduced, the masons would doubtless have been hesitant and slow in either recognizing or trusting the full adhesive power of their mortar when they came to construct web courses one at a time. Until their skill had come to be substantially based on considerable experience in constructing these unprecedentedly high, wide-spanning vaults in the new ribbed system, they would have felt more secure if they were to give the web courses a strong camber. Later, as skill and experience lead to increased assurance, they built the web courses with very little camber.

Lassaux goes on to say (pp. 233–4):

The advantage of this kind of vaulting without centering consists, not only in the very considerable saving of boarding, and of the greatest part of the centering arches, but it gives also a firmer vault; since the settling takes place gradually before the usual closing of the vault: indeed, the author almost doubts, whether such thin vaults could be constructed at all upon a boarded centering. Except this is supported by scaffolding to an immoderate degree, the mere motion of the labourers, in the course of the vaulting, must cause a perpetual shaking, and, consequently, separations in the vault after it is begun; and even when the vault is brought to its closing, and it is wished to loosen the centering, which is so extremely advantageous for the uniform closing of all vaults, the inevitable consequence is, bellying and cracking. If, on the other hand, we wish to leave the centering standing till the complete drying of the vault, the wasting of the mortar would cause all the joints to open and crack. But the network formed by the mortar in all the joints, gives to a thin vault of heavy stone a peculiar strength. . . .

The chief reason why the stone-weighted rope device 'gives also a firmer vault' is that the pressure applied to the individual blocks of a web course during its construction operates in the direction of the primary vault action. Thus the squeezing and shrinkage of the mortar as it sets—what Lassaux refers to as 'the wasting of the mortar'—is that of the normal voussoir action of the vault. In the case of web courses individually supported by lagging units, on the other hand, there is no opportunity for slight adjustments in the dimensions or the conformation of the web courses due to this wasting of the mortar, until the falsework supports are eased as the decentering operation starts to take place. It is evident, then, that in the incremental process of building a vault by the stone-weighted rope device, the danger of the vault's deformation and even collapse at the time when the rib centerings are struck is very much reduced. By then, the vault webs are thoroughly consolidated, with each block already established as an integral and interdependent unit of the vault as a whole.

Lassaux sums up his conviction that the stone-weighted rope device was employed in Gothic times on pp. 234–5, thus:

That the old vaults were built *free-handed*, and not upon a boarded centering, no one can doubt. Who would have given himself the trouble, so disproportionate to its object, of making such a boarding vaulted according to each arch of the centering, when he might obtain the same end with one which was quite common? Besides, the unequal convexity of all such old vaults shews that no gage or model was ever applied, but the observation of the proper form was left to the choice and practice of the mason. We often see, as has already been said, a strong convexity pass into a flat one, or reversely; when probably it had suddenly struck the mason, that he was vaulting too round or too flat, and when he set about correcting his mistake too suddenly.

This explains much of the irregularity in the contour of the vault surfaces that has been noted by various writers,[255] and is indeed noticeable in exceptional cases even to the unpractised eye of the lay observer. Many architectural historians have been at some pains to explain or reconcile these irregularities and unevennesses in the conformation of the vault, preoccupied as they have been with the assumption that the webs were constructed on some kind of continuous boarding or lagging of planks. Yet the unevenness of many surviving medieval vault surfaces is too variable, too irregular or intermittent, to be accounted for entirely by settlements subsequent to the original erection; particularly since some of the most striking irregularities occur in areas of the vault which would be the least likely to undergo deformation or settlement, while other more structurally critical areas remain smoothly regular to the present day.

This scheme of stone-weighted ropes—one for each block in a given web course—appears to meet and overcome all the objections we have encountered in assessing the possible use of Viollet-le-Duc's cerce device for high vaults. It also seems likely that the use of lagging frames, as discussed in such extensive detail in Chapters 4 and 5 above, could have been entirely eliminated in French quadripartite vaulting wherever the masons were particularly experienced and skilful.

But there is still the problem of how to close in the highest courses at the crown of the vault. In the construction of a dome by this technique there was no unusual problem, for either an oculus was left open at the apex, or a single block—whose circular bed-joint was cut as a truncated cone—could have been lowered and locked into place from above. But in Gothic vaults, every vault had of necessity to be closed in along the crown. Lassaux does not describe how this was accomplished. Apparently it could only have been managed by some sort of keying-in lagging.

One possibility is that of prefabricating on the ground (somewhat in the manner described in Eton's account, though of much smaller units) a series of units each making up a composite key-block in the form of a pointed arch of say four stones.

This procedure never seems to have been followed, however, at least in French Gothic vaults: if it had been, the joints between one such composite key and the next along the crown would record the procedure, and these tell-tale joints are *not* encountered. Instead, the joints between the stones of one course are staggered with respect to those of the adjacent courses, here at the crown as throughout the vault web elsewhere.

It would seem that the *longitudinal* courses nearest the crown could have been fashioned *crosswise*, none the less, with a minimum of additional falsework. There would have had to be, in any case, a workmen's scaffolding running along beneath the crown, from which a mason could set the stones of the final courses. *Upon this scaffolding*, the mason could establish a small, light frame only a foot or so deep, which he could shim up and then disengage and drag along to a new position as he retreated backwards in the process of filling in the final void along the crown. Such an abbreviated piece of formwork (not unlike the cross-lagging unit illustrated at D in 53, but of taller construction because supported from the scaffold platform rather than from double lagging frames on either side) could have been quite light, easily manœuvrable, and readily adjusted to a given position no matter how uneven the platform surface may have been. For it had very little weight to carry—say, four stones at the most—at any one time; hence the scaffold would not have had to be made any stronger than it would need to have been in any event to support a small stock of stones, a tray of mortar, and the working mason himself.

The saving in the amount of falsework which the stone-weighted rope device effected was considerable. Not only did this device eliminate the use of lagging units for constructing the web courses of the vault; it also made it possible for the rib centerings to be very much simpler and lighter in both design and construction than we have envisioned them to be. For now, with no necessity to provide a seating for the lagging units on each side of the stone rib, the rib centerings could be very thin: as thin as or even thinner than the rib itself. Hence a single instead of a double row of radial poles could be used to support the segmented cradle, which in turn could be cleated or not as desired. This thinness of the centering frames meant that they were much less cumbersome to move about, set up, and install accurately in place: they could be made adequately strong to do the work required of them, without having nearly so much dead weight of their own. And there was, of course, much less notching, fitting, and attachment to work out and adjust, in the labour of assembling them. Being much thinner than the double frames we have heretofore envisaged, the difficulty of their crowding together at the rib springings was not as awkward: as single instead of double frames, the rib centerings could carry down lower, certainly to the top of the tas-de-charge, without that mutual interference that required some special adjustment or modification to the ends of the double frames at their seating.

It is to be noted that in Gothic vaults (as opposed to most Romanesque cross vaults, where the transverse vault cells abut the clerestory wall directly) there is a wall rib or formeret built integrally with, and at the same time as, the windowhead and its enframing wall.

This is another example of Gothic rationality of construction. We have already observed that the clerestory window-heads doubtless utilized their permanent tracery as centering for their arched heads, whose moulded and multiple members came to be concentric with the formeret as part of their complex. Thus the formeret required no timber centering for its own erection. Nor was centering required there when the vault web came to be built, if the practice of stone-weighted ropes was adopted. For no temporary lagging had to be supported; and the curve of the formeret remained rigid and indeformable as the web stones came to be applied on it, without the agency of support from any temporary centering.

Inasmuch as there needed to be no centering for the formeret when the vault web was constructed, the location of the decentering wedges was considerably simplified and less spread out at each of the four corners of the bay.

Previously we have assumed that the wall rib would have required centering— and hence a wedged-up support—that could have been decentered synchronously with the other rib centerings. This would have been somewhat tricky, for two reasons. First, the wall rib was strongly stilted, and hence temporary columns of some sort would have had to be inserted there between the arch centering proper and the falsework sills upon which the decentering wedges rested, in the case of *all* the ribs that sprang from one corner of the bay. Second, because of the tas-de-charge, the centerings would have needed to start (in fact, *could* only start, because of their convergence) at the top of the tas-de-charge, at about the angle of friction. Here where the transverse and diagonal ribs became separated enough to be independent of each other, they were already somewhat launched across the void they bridged; in the meantime there was no encroachment on *its* void by the wall arch, whose plane remained at the inner side of the clerestory wall. Hence any sill supporting the ends of the transverse and diagonal centering frames could be short and effectively oriented to them if they alone were supported by it; but a much longer sill, that had to be skewed at an inconvenient angle to each of the three ribs,

188

would have been required if the wall rib as well as the transverse and diagonal ribs were all supported together from the same wedged-up sill (66 C, D).

Now, however, with the stone-weighted rope device and the consequent elimination of lagging for the stone courses of the webs, each pair of rib centering frames could be put in position and decentered separately. There was no longer any need for long sills; instead, the foot of each half-frame was supported individually on a single pair of folding wedges.

The elimination—made possible by the stone-weighted rope device—not only of all plank formwork (as described for the earlier types of vaulting), but of all lagging units too (as worked out in such specific detail in the previous two chapters), finally achieved that stringent economy of equipment and materials, that complete rationalization of falsework requirements, that had been pursued with such diligence by the French Gothic builders. Now only the transverse and diagonal rib arches needed falsework support in the form of centering frames; and these could be very thin, relatively light, and therefore easily manœuvrable. Rigidity and resistance to deformation were their chief requirements. For they were no longer called upon to support any other falsework, either as continuous planking, or as closely spaced lagging units, or as a series of cerces.

Of course, construction of the vaulting in this 'freehand' fashion presupposes considerable skill on the part of the masons, particularly in such superb examples as Bourges, Amiens, and numerous other major Gothic churches. But by now it must be abundantly clear that the skill and experience of the Gothic masons were more than equal to this assignment. By this time they could be counted on to maintain the proper slope of the bed courses, to give whatever camber seemed desirable to the web courses, and to adjust the width and direction of successive courses so that they came to run parallel to the crown as they approached the crease there from each side.

Not only was an enormous amount of skilled carpentry work cancelled by the elimination of all falsework for the web of the vault. In addition, a corollary advantage was the freeing of the high platform level, and the space immediately beneath the vault, of various carpentry-work assemblages and encumbrances, so that there was more room for the masons to work as the vault rose, and more room for the disassembling and manœuvring of the rib centerings as they were shifted about from a completed bay to the next one to be built.

Again, the exceptional lightness of the rib centerings—due to the fact that they had only the rib voussoirs and none of the web coursing to support—was reflected, in turn, in the size and distribution of the falsework membering that undergirt them. For now, instead of a relatively massive ensemble of heavy timbering that bridged across at about the level of the vault spring, a much lighter platform and staging would have sufficed. Fewer and slenderer strutting suppórts from the triforium passageway or the clerestory sill level were needed, because the platform these struts supported did not have to sustain heavy concentrated loads from double centering frames, either while they were being moved about preparatory or subsequent to the erection of the vault, or while they were in position under the ribs, when they were further weighted with the masonry-burdened complex of laggings.

As with the heavier types of gantry assemblages described in the previous chapter, there still needed to be rigidly undergirt points of support for the rib frames. But now these could be provided by much lighter and slenderer poles. This lightness of the gantry was a real advantage, not only in cost (the heavy beams of earlier schemes of timber-framed falsework were expensive), but also in the largely manual operation of both erecting and dismantling the falsework. Nothing more than simple hand windlasses would have been needed now, instead of the powerful gins or capstans or even great wheels that would have been required in one operation or another when the vault falsework was as extensive as we have previously supposed it to be.

We have finally arrived at the point where, with a certain amount of assurance, we can recapitulate and sum up the procedures and the sequences followed in the erection of a major three-aisled church vaulted in the French Gothic quadripartite system.

The order and progression followed in the building of towers and apse, of transepts and nave, is outside the scope of this study; and in any event, the chronological sequence of the functional parts of the church edifice has been adequately treated by others. Here we are concerned with what might be called the vertical rather than the horizontal progression in Gothic church building in France, with structural and erectional rather than historical or liturgical or functional considerations having the dominant role to play.

After the foundations were laid, the nave arcades and the outer walls of the side aisles, together with their buttress saliencies, were erected (doubtless from light pole scaffoldings supported on standards rising from the ground). These two parallel features were bridged across by the side-aisle vaulting, the inward thrust of which was prevented from pushing the nave piers out of alignment by temporary wooden ties at their springing. With the side aisles vaulted and roofed over,

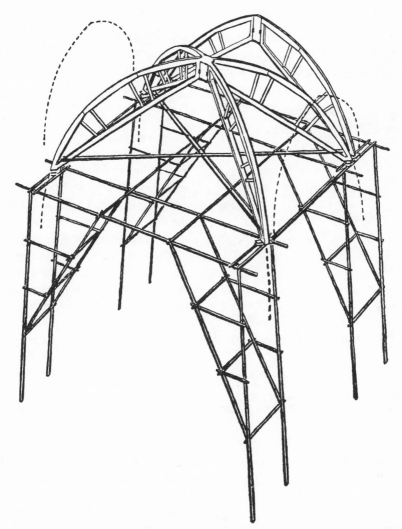

70. *Lightest Scheme of Rib Centering for French Gothic Ribbed Vaulting*

This sketch is of the falsework alone, minus any platform of planking or hurdles, and minus the workmen's trestles this platform would support. Two of the dotted lines, to right and left, show the profile of each wall arch or formeret; other dotted lines prolong the curves of the diagonal rib frames from their wedged supports (near the top of the tas-de-charge, approximately at each rib's angle of friction) down to the spring. The undergirding of the rib frames is that of the scheme shown in 67 A and 68.

What is shown here presupposes a completed

adjacent bay of vaulting, towards the lower left of the drawing; hence, no transverse rib centering frame is needed as the near boundary of the present bay, if the stone-weighted rope device is to be utilized in constructing the web courses. The half-frames for both the far transverse rib and the two diagonals are provided with essential separator blocks, keyed to prevent dislocation by slippage at their crowns; and horizontal ties made up of double poles link opposite feet of the diagonal centering frames.

191

the solid buttress towers and the triforium and clerestory walls were raised aloft, being propped against each other, as they rose, by shores or struts, because of their offset bearing that corbelled out somewhat above the void of the side aisle. Higher up, their separation and mutual support were secured temporarily by the flying buttress centering and eventually (once the roof was built) by the permanent flying buttresses themselves. Thus the void of the nave, transepts, or choir separated two independent, stable structures on either side: the side aisles proper, together with the lofty superstructures above them.

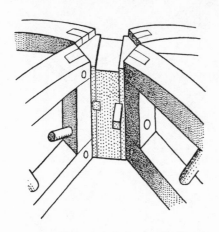

71. *Assemblage of the Diagonal Centering Frames at Their Common Crown: Scheme with Single Frames*

Where the stone-weighted rope device was employed for building the web courses of the vault, the centering frames of the diagonal ribs did not need to be double as would doubtless have been required where lagging was employed. The framing detail here shown is somewhat similar to that in 65; but here, the triangular blocks which a pair of half-frames abut are united at their junction by large hardwood dowels, one of which (on the left) is shown protruding. Square keys, whose slots are gained half from the triangular blocks, half from the rectangular insert piece, prevent vertical slipping during the course of loading the half-frames with the rib voussoirs. The area of intersection of the diagonals is shown somewhat depressed to allow for a boss or slightly pendent keystone, whose rib stems, in some instances, might bear upon the upper extremities of the four half-frames until the mortar in the joints had set.

These twin structures on either side were thereupon united by being bridged across at the level of the clerestory wall-tops, first by the great tie-beams, then gradually by the vast complex of timber-work that made up the steeply pitched structure of the high central roof. All of this timber-work was raised from the floor of the central body of the church; and the main horizontal ties provided at once a foundation from which the rest of the great roof was erected as well as a permanent gantry from which much of the raising, and even perhaps some of the shifting about, of the falsework for the vaulting could subsequently be handled.

The erection of the high vaulting itself—the final and most crucial feature of the construction—began with the establishment of a light but rigid high-level platform that was supported, on each side, from the triforium level. The location, the layout, and the required amount of this platform-supporting falsework were completely contingent upon the nature and the design of the centering for the vault ribs. Since the latter had to be determined before the former

192

could be established (if the maximum of rationality and economy in its construction were to be realized), the design of the centering frames should be noted first.

Each rib-arc was built upon its own centering frame. These were thin and relatively light, for they were required as support only for the rib voussoirs, not for any lagging. Being relatively light, they could have been constructed in the shape indicated in 70. The advantages of such a shape were (1) the concentration they brought about of the loads on the frames at closely confined points, where the decentering wedges could fulfil their function most directly and economically, and (2) the considerable depth that was provided in the frames under the crown, where the assemblage of spacer unit and half-frames could effectively abut each other and be keyed so as to forestall any possibility of slippage as the frames became loaded. Horizontal ties consisting of long poles would have been lashed securely to the opposite feet of a pair of these frames, whether for the transverse or for the diagonal ribs, preventing them from spreading asunder at their wedged-up points of support. This scheme resulted in a very rigid assemblage which was none the less quickly and easily demountable, when the decentering wedges were retracted, into units that were sufficiently light and manoeuvrable to be taken

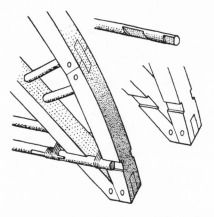

72. *Assemblage of the Double Poles Tying Together the Feet of a Pair of Centering Half-Frames*

Notching of both the poles and the centering frames was carefully done, so that they would fit snugly and accurately when assembled. The pair of poles acted as a tie in tension, preventing the feet of the frames from spreading: they were lashed in place after the half-frames had been placed in position and united at their common crown by some such scheme as that shown in 71. To assure proper tightness in the lashing ropes, a long and slightly tapering wedge was used, approximately half round in section. Such a wedge, though not shown in other drawings, was generally used throughout the Middle Ages to secure and maintain sufficient tightness in the lashing ropes, particularly in scaffolding assemblages.

down, shifted about, and set up again in an adjacent bay, without the need for cumbersome equipment and without the inconvenience of mutual interference.

Such a scheme also simplified and reduced the timber-work requirements of the undergirding falsework. With the feet of the centering half-frames coming down to closely confined areas near the four corners of the bay, their concentrated loads could be carried down almost vertically to the stable support of the triforium passage, and the rest of the falsework for the high-level staging could be assembled out of light poles, some leaning out over the void from this same passage-way level or higher up, some lashed horizontally at convenient intervals up to the level of the platform staging itself. Except for the nearly vertical struts immediately under the decentering wedges, the high-level staging did not need to be absolutely rigid. For, any slight deflexion in this platform, out over the void, did not affect the accurate alignment and contour of the rib arcs: the platform was needed only as a working area on which the rib centering frames could be shifted about and positioned, and where the masons could set their trestles conveniently in order to be able to lay the stones of the vaulting.

On these trestles of various heights the masons would have laid up the rib voussoirs, working from the side (i.e. facing the rib frame). Any large keystone at the intersection of the groin ribs would have been drawn aloft by powerful lifting devices located above the great tie-beams of the timber roof. There it would have been shifted slightly from its line of ascent to a position directly over the spot it was destined to take, then lowered into its key position as the final uniting element of the intersecting ribs.

With the masonry ribs completed, the workmen's trestles would have been re-orientated so as to face the concavity of the vault proper, and the masons would have started to lay up the web courses at an even rate throughout the bay. Until the highest courses were reached, eight trestles would have been needed for each bay: a pair facing outward (i.e. one on each side of the vault) for each of the four units of the bay's vaulting: from clerestory wall to diagonal rib for the two portions of the transverse vault, and from transverse rib to diagonal rib for the two portions of the longitudinal vault. The masons would have stood opposite each other, back to back on separate trestles in each of these portions of the vault, first at some distance apart, then increasingly closer to each other as the two sides of the vault curved together towards the crown.

In this process of carrying up the several panels of the vault web, much skill but no formwork would have been required because the web stones would have been set and secured by the stone-weighted rope device. The accomplished masons who thus erected the web had the boundary ribs to guide their work and control its conformation, for each panel of the vaulting. The centering frames remained in place under the ribs, to reinforce them and maintain their contours intact as the web rose and curved farther out across the void from either side. But there was no lagging to fashion and set in place, or to get in the way or complicate the operation in any way. And when the highest courses near the crown were reached, they were filled in by a single mason working on a high trestle that supported both the mason himself and the short units of cross lagging he kept repositioning as his finished work caused him to retreat along the line of the crown.

Upon completion of such a bay of vaulting, the decentering wedges would have been gradually retracted, the crown inserts between the pairs of half-frames under the ribs unkeyed and removed, then the half-frames themselves taken down. As these separated units of the rib falsework were being moved across the platform of the high staging and reassembled in the adjacent bay, the plasterers would have gone to work on the vault surfaces of the bay that had just been completed, and perhaps the painters would have followed soon after them. Then the falsework staging under this bay of finished vaulting would have been gradually dismantled, to be transferred member by member across the adjacent bay currently under construction to the following bay, and there reassembled so as to be ready to accommodate the succeeding operations. Such a procedure would have involved about two bays of falsework for the high-level platform, or more precisely, three pier-straddling gantries,[256] bridging across the nave and furnishing support for horizontal poles to which the planks or hurdles of the platform proper were secured.

It is evident, then, that with one exception, whatever falsework was required for the construction of the high vaulting consisted of lashed poles, not hewn or sawn timbers. There was little enough undergirding involved in the high-level platform, since it was hung aloft above the triforium level, was only about two bays in length, and was completely re-usable in subsequent bays. With no formwork of planking or lagging required for the erection of the vault web, the one exception to the universal use of poles was the light, thin complex of half-frames and crown insert which made up the rib centerings. With these units accurately fashioned and rigidly secured in place, the thin-webbed Gothic vaults could be erected by skilled masons with no further falsework equipment than stone-weighted ropes tied to poles that were secured to the tie-beams of the roof, from which their height was easily adjusted.

Such appears to be the equipment used and the procedures followed in the multiple operations of erecting a great French Gothic church. If something of the sort really constituted the practices of that era of creative building, it is illuminating to see how thoroughly the structural system, the erectional techniques, the building materials, and above all the aesthetic design, were co-ordinated into a single, integrated work of art of the most transcendent quality and expressiveness. We can be as impressed, today, with the rationale of erection as we are with the visual actuality of these amazing buildings. And it is quite possible that we can even learn something of value, in the twentieth century, from the stringent economy of means, the much that was accomplished with so little, in the thirteenth century.

NOTES AND COMMENTS

1. Moore has written (p. 190): 'Structural and artistic principles find simultaneous expression in every step of the progress of this art. Mechanical invention and aesthetic feeling were never separated in the minds of the French builders. . . . The Gothic movement, though wonderful as a structural organism, is even more wonderful as a work of art.'

Many other writers have expressed similar convictions. For example, Adams's whole book is an eloquent and moving testimonial to the spirit that animated the medieval builders. And Otto von Simson's recent study impressively examines the origins of Gothic architecture 'as the singularly sensitive response of artistic form to the theological vision of the twelfth century' (p. viii).

In his inspired chapter on French Gothic, Lethaby (*Architecture*, p. 201) says: 'It is impossible to explain in words the content of perfect Gothic art. It is frank, clear, gay; it is passionate, mystical and tender; it is energetic, clear, sharp, strong and healthy. It would be a mistake to try to define it in terms of form alone; it embodied a spirit, an age. The ideals of the time of energy and order produced a manner of building of high intensity, all waste tissue was thrown off, and the stonework was gathered up into energetic functional members. These ribs and bars and shafts are all at bowstring tension. A mason will tap a pillar to make its stress audible; we may think of a cathedral as so "high strung" that if struck it would give a musical note.'

2. This concept of Gothic architecture was asserted particularly by Bond (*Gothic Architecture*, pp. 10–11), but was denied by Lethaby (*King's Craftsmen*, pp. 357–9).

3. Although this matter is of more particular concern to the social, economic, and political historians, nevertheless the architectural historians also have given consideration to it: e.g. Enlart, *Manuel*, pp. 73–77; and Porter, *Medieval Architecture*, vol. ii, pp. 160–79.

4. The definitive account of these, as well as many other economic and organizational aspects, is given by Salzman, *Building in England*.

5. *Vide* Knoop and Jones, *The Mediaeval Mason*; and Moles, *Histoire des charpentiers*, chaps. ii–vi.

6. The principal scholar in this phase of medieval history is John Harvey. Among his numerous books, of particular value in this study is *The Gothic World*.

For France alone, a brief summary of French medieval architects whose professional activities took them outside France occurs on the last two pages of Anfray, 'Les Architectes des cathédrales'.

7. One of the first to cover this topic adequately was Brown, *From Schola to Cathedral*. It is still an excellent account.

Scores of scholars, including Conant, Panofsky, Puig i Cadafalch, Lefèvre-Pontalis, and many others have dealt with this problem either locally, regionally, or with respect to the entire western world of medieval times.

8. One of the most recent writers to discuss this matter, and to review the sometimes conflicting assertions of other writers, is du Colombier, *Les Chantiers des cathédrales*. He lists a short but useful bibliography on p. 70.

9. For example, Ward, *Mediaeval Church Vaulting*. This mentions English and one or

two German and Italian examples, but concentrates almost exclusively on French forms.

An earlier survey of vault types, prepared by Professor Babcock and illustrated by many plan, section, and isometric drawings, appeared in *The American Architect and Building News* in ten instalments. There are a number of errors in the drawings.

In England, Sir Gilbert Scott's *Lectures on the Rise and Development of Mediaeval Architecture* include two lectures on 'The Principles of Vaulting' (vol. ii, pp. 161–227), but these are little more than an illustrated cataloguing of different English forms.

A comprehensively thorough coverage of the forms, as well as the stress analysis, the stone or brick coursing, and many other phases, of all kinds and shapes of vaults is given in two nineteenth-century German books: (1) Breymann, vol. i, as chap. iii, pp. 132–273; and (2) Ungewitter, vol. i, as chap. i, pp. 1–121. Both of these books are voluminously illustrated with many drawings and diagrams. Much briefer accounts occur in such volumes as Hasak, sec. 4, pp. 62–82; and in Sturgis, chap. iv, sec. ii, pp. 154–74, and chap. v, sec. i, pp. 186–207.

More recently, two foreign books on medieval vaulting forms have been published. A very thorough and analytical treatise on the vaulting systems of a late era in a limited region appeared in German about 1939: Schulze, *Die Gewölbesysteme im spätgotischen Kirchenbau in Schwaben von 1450–1520*. This specialized treatise concerns itself primarily with the complicated patterning of the multiple ribs on the surfaces of vaults which are, for the most part, of basically simple forms. A more general book dealing with domes and vaulting of all ages, including medieval examples, appeared in Flemish a few years later: Emile Goethals, *Bogen-Gewelven Koepels* (with a French-language edition entitled *Arcs, voûtes, coupoles*). This book, though brief, attempts to cover aesthetic design and proportion, engineering theory, structural varieties, and even a little, pictorially, on erectional techniques. (For example, *vide* decentering devices sketched on plate 80; and progress photographs reproduced on plates 81 and 82 showing, respectively, centering for a wide-span roof of corrugated barrel-vault shape, and brickwork being erected in herringbone fashion on the formwork of this structure.)

For the design development of square or rectangular bays of vaulting in England, including an analysis of the changes, as well as the reasons for these changes, with respect to both the rib curvatures and the contours of the vault surfaces from the earliest forms, the clearest and fullest step-by-step treatment is given in Watson's monograph of the double choir of St. Mungo's Cathedral, Glasgow.

Much the most thorough and comprehensive book to date on most of the phases and all the significant eras of vaulting is Thunnissen, a major work published in Dutch in 1950. Its historical coverage includes oriental and near-eastern examples; and there is much about domes. Thunnissen supplements his text with a great many revealing drawings and diagrams as well as some photographic illustrations, the latter mainly of examples in brick masonry.

10. *Vide* Willis, 'On the Construction of the Vaults of the Middle Ages'.

11. *Vide* especially the important works by Viollet-le-Duc, *Dictionnaire raisonné de l'architecture française du XIe au XVIe siècle*; and Auguste Choisy, *Histoire de l'architecture*.

There have been certain years when an interest in medieval vaulting and vaulting problems appears to have been stronger than at other times, judging particularly by the articles in professional periodicals that deal with the subject, as well as by actual books that have been published. The most recent of these years of special emphasis was 1934, when Pol Abraham's controversial ideas challenged the received opinions of the established historians.

It is interesting to speculate on the possibility of a connexion between this interest and the waves of rebuilding and reconstruction of the fabric of Gothic churches that have occurred during the past century or so. Possibly the

1934 spate of articles was a more or less direct outcome of the reconstructions following upon the destruction of the First World War. A hundred years before, the investigations and analyses of the late 1830's and early 1840's regarding medieval vaulting were doubtless occasioned by the rise in wealth and the consequent re-establishment of ecclesiastical foundations and fabrics that began to be manifest at that time. This movement was certainly reflected in the institution of various architectural and archaeological societies, in France as well as in England. Engineering societies began to multiply at this time or a little later, also; and their journals, too, occasionally dealt with vaulting problems (*vide* Gottgetreu, Rheinhart, &c.).

Reconstructions of the fabric of churches, large and small alike, were undertaken widely and persistently throughout the second half of the nineteenth century, as may be seen from the reports of renovations and major repairs in such periodicals as the *Architectural Societies' Reports and Papers* and the *Ecclesiologist* in England, and the *Congrès archéologique* and the *Bulletin monumental* in France. Indeed, major reconstructions were still taking place in the twentieth century up to the time of World War I.

In the meantime, a number of architectural societies were active in Germany also; and some of these were concerned at times with vaulting problems. For example, in the *Deutsche Bauzeitung* for 1889, vol. xxiii, p. 39, there is a précis of a lecture given by a Herr Hacker at the 21 Nov. 1888 meeting of the Architekten- und Ingenieur-Verein zu Hannover, 'Über praktische Konstruktion der Drucklinien in Kreuz- und Sterngewölben': p. 203 gives a résumé of another lecture by the same man on 'Spannungen in Kreuz- und Sterngewölben', delivered at the 6 Mar. 1889 meeting of this Society. In general, however, any technical (as opposed to historical or comparative) discussion of vaulting practices in the engineering periodicals of the nineteenth century deal with arched bridges for railroads rather than with vaulted churches.

12. *Vide* the pioneering work in this field: William Harvey, *Models of Buildings*, chap. iii, pp. 44–54.

13. *Vide* Roger Gilman, 'The Theory of Gothic Architecture and the Effect of Shellfire at Rheims and Soissons'.

14. One of the most recent books on this subject is Caroe, *Old Churches and Modern Craftsmanship*, which followed by twenty years Powys's informative *Repair of Ancient Buildings*.

15. What relatively little has been attempted on this matter will be noted and commented on in the ensuing pages.

16. In this connexion Moore (p. 58) has this to say: 'Such written records of building as have been preserved are wholly devoid of information respecting architectural forms and methods of construction. We are compelled therefore to rely upon independent study of the buildings themselves.'

17. Some of these trade secrets came to be disclosed only at the end of the medieval period, particularly in Germany, at a time when interest in and knowledge of medieval practices were being superseded by the imported ideas and building concepts of the Renaissance. With the advent of the Renaissance, which repudiated the traditional methods both of training and of building itself, these craft guilds of the Middle Ages died out, their models and patterns were broken and destroyed or lost, and their mysteries forgotten. *Vide* Harvey, *Gothic World*, pp. 22, 33.

18. Gervais's Latin text as translated by Willis appears in his *Canterbury*; and with some condensation in Salzman, pp. 369–75. Other medieval writers quoted in Salzman's appendix A show us how little use they are in revealing the building practices of the times. Similarly, for all their extensive coverage of contemporary excerpts, the two volumes of

Mortet and Deschamps include nothing about the technical problems of building save for one or two very brief, oblique, and incidental references.

19. Suger's treatise is entitled *De consecratione ecclesiae Sancti Dionysii.* Latin text and corresponding English translation, together with scholarly commentary, are given in Panofsky, *Abbot Suger on the Abbey Church of St-Denis and Its Treasures.*

20. *Vide* comments in Colombier, pp. 72, 73.

21. *Vide* the *Album de Villard de Honnecourt.* Colombier (pp. 63 f. and 86–89) reviews and comments significantly on the scholarly studies that have been made of this precious collection of drawings.

22. Andrews, *The Mediaeval Builder and His Methods*, p. 85.

23. *Vide*, for example, Didron, *Annales archéologiques*, vol. vi, plate opp. p. 138; and Willis, *Vaults*, figs. 6, 7, pp. 7–8.

24. Probably the most useful and readily available collections of medieval manuscript illustrations in reproduction that have to do with architectural construction are those published in Andrews and in Colombier. Colombier's 'Notes on the Plates' (pp. 117–33) include references to many other miniatures, paintings, stained glass panels, &c., besides those that are illustrated in his book.

25. Emil Lacroix winds up his argument for the widespread use in the Middle Ages of flying scaffoldings—those consisting of horizontal, cantilevered beams alone, without vertical standards or even diagonal brackets—by citing illustrations from late medieval times, and writing of them (p. 221) that 'An inaccuracy on this point would be very strange, considering the usual exactness in regard to technical descriptions. And as a crane is de-scribed with all its details, why should an artist fail to represent the details in the paintings of scaffolds?' [Present author's translation.]
Some of the reasons why these representations cannot be taken at face value are suggested below.

26. Illustrated in Andrews, plate xii; also in Salzman, plate 7 facing p. 49. Another instance of this point is explained in Lethaby, *Medieval Art*, p. 190: 'In miniatures and reliefs, when the action of the figures represented was taking place within a building, it was usual to indicate gables and domes and towers along the top margin, and to carry down pieces of wall or columns on the sides. . . .'

27. *Vide* Andrews, plate iii, where cf. figs. 1 and 2.

28. From the Bibliothèque Nationale, French MS. no. 1537, fol. 93 verso.

29. For a technique of cradling a column, *vide* Viollet-le-Duc, *Dictionnaire*, article 'Étai' vol. v, p. 339, fig. 5.

30. As long ago as 1842 Willis deplored this lack of accurate information on the geometrical methods really employed in setting out the work and on how the necessity for these methods gradually arose. In making a plea for the assembling of structural data on ribbed vaults, he wrote (*Vaults*, p. 3): '. . . Most of the facts required are of such a nature that they can only be derived from the existing buildings by the aid of scaffolding, minute measurement, and close observation, which it is not often in the power of mere travelling observers to obtain.'
'Now professional men are so commonly entrusted with the repairs or restoration of these old structures, that if they would take the opportunity of making the required observations in every case where scaffolds were erected about a building, and if such observations were transmitted to the [Royal] Institute [of British Architects], a few years would

suffice to bring together a body of examples from which general rules might be deduced. It is only by comparing many examples that this can be done, for general rules deduced from single instances are commonly worthless.'

'Next to complete buildings under repair, Ruins afford the most valuable information upon construction. The best instructor of all, perhaps, is a building which is being pulled down, but such opportunities are always to be regretted. In ordinary cases, the upper surfaces of the vaults are so often covered with courses of rubble and concrete, rubbish and filth, and the lower surfaces with whitewash and paint, that when every facility has been obtained for examination, the jointing of the masonry and actual construction of the vault still remain an unfathomable mystery.'

31. Cf. the astonishing construction of an ancient Chinese bridge, in Liang's Jan. 1938 *Pencil Points* article, where there are no less than twenty-eight thin, separate rings of stone making up the arch of this still-extant early seventh-century span.

32. Note how these problems were handled in the case of the masonry bridge of much smaller span that is covered by the Specification quoted in Appendix H.

Compare the framing employed in the somewhat analogous situation for the viaduct over the Esk River at Whitby in England, as given in three diagrams on p. 156 of *Centralblatt der Bauverwaltung*, vol. vii, 16 Apr. 1887. Here, practically the full semicircle is centered; four double frames are utilized at once (instead of only one that is shoved sideways for re-use); and the 65-foot span is undergirt at four instead of five points. Furthermore, because of the loftiness of the piers, the intermediate supports for the falsework are provided diagonally from the piers lower down (instead of vertically from the roadway level, as in the Pont du Gard scheme).

In the Esk Viaduct, the four parallel centering frames are built up of pairs of timber-work

quadrants mounted on and braced from long stringers set slightly above the spring of the arch. Each frame is undergirt with four pairs of folding wedges (at the ends and at approximately the third points of the stringer). Support for these is given by a heavy timber that is housed at either end in the masonry of the piers and is strutted at the third points by diagonal braces raking up from projecting beams that had been run all the way through the masonry of the piers at a level nearly 20 feet below the arch spring. The plan and the sectional view for one arch of the viaduct's falsework indicate how it was braced laterally by means of diagonal guys that ran from above and below to the ends of a long beam set at right angles to the span of the arch midway between the piers.

Except for these guys, the entire construction was of timber, though all joints were secured with metal straps or fishplates, and bolts. Nevertheless, these latter, in conjunction with the scheme of framing, make it evident that the dismantling process could have involved disassembling the framework member by member, directly upon decentering, without first having to lower either large portions or the whole of it to the ground.

Another example of arch centering, this time for a rather flat arch of nearly 100 feet in clear span and only $11\frac{1}{2}$-foot rise, appears as a rather large-scale, dimensioned elevation of the bridge over the Murg River at Heselbach in the same German periodical, vol. vii, p. 341. The location, sizes, and metal fastenings of the individual members of the falsework framing and its supports are shown. There are no less than ten unevenly spaced sets of folding wedges in this span, whose positions conform to the distribution of the framing members. Perhaps the most interesting feature of this example for our purposes, however, is the extensive use made of unsquared timbers for a large number of the falsework members, including even the sills on which the decentering wedges are set.

Vide Appendix I for some comment on the medieval use of unsquared timber.

33. Moles, pp. 340, 341, and figs. 483, 484, gives a striking eighteenth-century instance of this in the case of the alarming deformations of the falsework during the course of constructing the bridge at Neuilly.

34. Choisy, *Histoire*, vol. ii, pp. 150–1. Cf. Choisy's fig. 6, p. 151. [Here, as elsewhere in these pages, all translations from the French have been made by the author of the present work unless otherwise noted.]

35. *Vide* Appendix A for an annotated bibliography of writings that deal with falsework.

36. Viollet-le-Duc, *Dictionnaire*, article 'Échafaud', vol. v, pp. 113–14.

37. This practice of raising materials from the interior, directly and vertically, is corroborated convincingly and in some detail in Watson's independent and valuable monograph, pp. 118, 122–4, including his fig. 46. *Vide* note 221.

38. Viollet-le-Duc, *Dictionnaire*, article 'Échafaud', vol. v, p. 108. Indirect evidence of economy in the materials used for falsework, tending to corroborate Viollet-le-Duc's contention of the leapfrog practice of re-using localized scaffolding, is perhaps suggested by the small number of hurdles purchased in each of the instances quoted by Salzman, p. 320.

However, it is Emil Lacroix, 'Die mittelalterlichen Baugerüste', who has pressed most for recognition of the fact that the medieval builders used 'flying scaffolding'; that is, scaffolding without standards or even wall brackets, having only horizontal beams set in the masonry as supports for successive platform levels. Lacroix makes a very convincing brief for this kind of scaffolding, and reproduces a number of contemporary representations of it, including miniatures from the fourteenth, fifteenth, and sixteenth centuries. Nevertheless, the fact that all seven of the illustrations he gives involve structures with continuous walls makes one hesitate to accept this scheme completely, in the mature skeletonized structures of the great Gothic churches of France, for the construction of the piers of the nave arcade and of the lofty clerestory.

39. *Vide* Appendix B for commentary on putlog holes.

40. For example, *vide* Andrews, plates ix and xi.

41. The photograph, 5, taken in 1953, is of the fourteenth-century south chapel of the church of Notre-Dame at Mantes. (A perspective drawing of this chapel, taken from a somewhat similar station-point, is found in Viollet-le-Duc, *Dictionnaire*, article 'Chapelle', vol. ii, p. 454, fig. 24.) The rope lashings are similar to the medieval practice. In the modern view, however, planks for the staging have replaced the medieval hurdles described in Andrews, Salzman, *et al.*

A modern example of light pole scaffolding, raised on standards about a pier, is shown photographically in Houvet's plate 56, of the interior of the north transept of Chartres Cathedral.

42. *Vide infra*, however, with respect to the seating requirements and attachments of the flying buttress centerings.

43. *Vide* note 74 *infra*.

44. As in modern usage. *Vide* Cotton, plate 28, which shows an unglazed but otherwise completed window.

45. Harvey (*Gothic World*, p. 19) says: 'The glazing of the windows would normally have been the last work carried out before taking down the scaffolds, to minimize the risk of breakage of the glass.' In regard to 'taking down the scaffolds', however, Andrews (p. 69) states that 'Cradles or swinging scaffolds were also occasionally used for repair work'; and Salzman (pp. 321–2) enlarges on

this scheme of a staging slung on ropes and lowered from above. (*Vide* illustration in Planat, p. 625, fig. 15.) He documents the use of such workmen's cradles for repairs, for plumbers' work, for removing scaffolding, for cleaning windows, &c. It does not seem completely improbable, therefore, that this scheme might sometimes have been employed at the time the glass was first installed.

46. Viollet-le-Duc, *Dictionnaire*, article 'Échafaud', vol. v, p. 108. For medieval manuscript illustrations of scaffolds that profit by offsets, *vide* Colombier, plates 13, 17, and 21.

47. Viollet-le-Duc, article 'Échafaud', p. 112. Emil Lacroix's article seeks to justify the widespread adoption during the Middle Ages of this minimal, suspended scheme of localized scaffolding in which, instead of the customary putlog type of arrangement, independent horizontal beams were set along in a row at not more than one-metre intervals, each passing through the entire thickness of the wall and projecting out on either side far enough to provide support for the workmen's platforms, one on the outside, one on the inside of the wall. Lacroix also cites in some detail the vertical spacings of these beams, and he says that the beams themselves were sometimes round, sometimes square. He mentions the sizes of the holes for them that remain in the walls of existing buildings, and their positions relative to the joints in the stone or brick coursing.

Lacroix neglects to comment on the technique of dislodging these through-members, however, and makes the process of removing them appear the more difficult because he specifically states (p. 218) that when laid in place they were 'firmly embedded in mortar to prevent shifting'. Since he also remarks that 'the bark had not been removed from the lumber, which made it stronger and more durable', the difficulty of drawing the timbers out of their wall-traversing holes is evident, particularly since the whole scheme of the scaffolding involved the minimum of stable lodgement from which the work of either building the wall or dismantling the false-work could be undertaken.

Some of the illuminations Lacroix publishes show the through-wall putlogs strongly tapered to a point at the outer end, like long, horizontally laid stakes. Whether they are delineated as being in this shape or of apparently uniform diameter throughout, it may be that there was enough taper in them, either artificial or natural, to permit these wooden beams to be driven through the wall in the direction of their butt ends, when the time came to remove them. This might have been accomplished by means of a maul handled by a workman who was lodged on the next higher platform level, which Lacroix states as being about 1·17 metres higher up in the case of brickwork, about 1·24 in ashlar masonry. But if this removal procedure were to have been adopted, there would certainly have been real danger that the shock of driving out the through-wall timbers by pounding would have unduly disturbed the as yet somewhat green mortar.

48. Viollet-le-Duc, article 'Galerie', vol. vi, pp. 8–21.

49. This is a prime example of aesthetic and utilitarian functions combined.

50. Andrews (p. 79) insists that 'One at least of the purposes of the clerestory passage in church walls was to allow access to the window shutterings.' By the time these passageways had become a standard feature of French Gothic churches, however, large glazed windows with fixed glass had supplanted the 'screens of oiled linen or frames filled in with sheets of horn, with wooden shutters used for protection' that the English had been using in their church windows.

51. They occur at both the base and the top of the side-aisle roofs in the cathedrals of Chartres and Amiens, for example. There are exterior passageways at no less than five different levels in Beauvais and in the choir of

Le Mans. In addition, some great churches have built-in permanent exterior steps up the slope of the high roof, behind the face of the gables (as at Beauvais, north and south transepts).

52. *Vide* Viollet-le-Duc, *Dictionnaire*, article 'Galerie', vol. vi, pp. 15, 16; also Enlart, pp. 258, 259, and 520. *Vide* Appendix C for a description of passageways in an English cathedral.

53. Viollet-le-Duc, article 'Galerie', p. 14.

54. In as late an example as King's College Chapel, Cambridge, Mackenzie shows, both in plan and section (plates i–iv), the 'doorway and steps communicating with the upper part of the roof [i.e. the vault]. There is a corresponding communication with the passage on the south side, and the same is repeated at each severy. The corresponding panel in each severy is joined in a similar manner to these, supposed to have been left open for the purpose of communication *during the progress of the work*' (p. 19. Italics added).

55. Actually, almost every church of the Gothic era rose on the site of a shrine or an earlier church that had been consecrated and in use for religious services; so that invariably some portion of the former structure had to be maintained in use for a while until an area in the new structure could take over this function.

In this connexion, Watson (pp. 29–32) reminds us that 'In considering the problems and difficulties which the cathedral builders were called upon to meet there is one that is sometimes overlooked. These large churches were not only places of assembly and worship; they were at the same time repositories of the relics of the saints. From a very early period of the Christian era it had been the custom to build oratories or chapels over the places of martyrdom or of interment of those who had died for their faith or who had been distinguished otherwise for piety. At a later date it was the practice to bestow the bodies of those

who had been eminent in the Church within the sacred edifices, either in a crypt beneath the church or within the choir itself "to the intent that they might have their resting-place where they had living ruled in honor". The cathedral of the middle ages was accordingly something more than a church: it was a great reliquary, a place consecrated by generations of religious service at the tombs of the saints whose relics were regarded with peculiar veneration. When it was required to enlarge or rebuild a cathedral, two conditions were imposed on the builders: the daily services of the church had to be maintained, and the tombs and relics of the saints protected against injury or unnecessary disturbance during the operations, frequently prolonged over a long term of years. In the records of several of our cathedrals evidence may be found as to the manner in which these conditions were observed. We have, for example, contemporary accounts of what took place at Canterbury after the fires both of 1067 and of 1174, and during the reconstruction that followed in each case. . . . If, then, we have a shrine to be protected during the construction of the buildings, and daily service to be performed at the altar and tomb of the saint, it follows that this must have been a factor in deciding the order and method on which the work was to be carried out. . . .'

56. One should rule out those galleries, designed solely for military defence, which occur in many churches in the south of France.

57. These spiral stairs are discussed in Choisy, *Histoire*, vol. ii, pp. 177, 394–5; Enlart, pp. 19, 520; and Czarnowsky, 'Escaliers à vis en Alsace'.

58. One of the exceptions is Coutances Cathedral, in Normandy.

59. Like the crawl spaces, cat-walks, &c., of modern buildings. Choisy (*Histoire*, vol. ii, p. 210) advances a theory for certain Romanesque churches, and again (p. 431) for certain

important Gothic churches, that the doors to these spiral stairs were placed obscurely on purpose, even when they led to spacious triforium galleries. His idea is that the triforium galleries provided a storage space of security and safe-keeping for the personal treasures of Crusaders while they were away from home on their holy missions. Subsequent writers, however, have questioned this explanation.

60. Just as horizontal passageways, inside and out, are a distinctive feature of Gothic churches, so too the vertical circulation by means of spiral stairs or vices is a specifically Gothic innovation. A quick check of the rather poorly reproduced but numerous plans given in Lasteyrie (*L'Architecture religieuse en France à l'époque gothique*, vol. i) is of interest in revealing the number of vices that start at the ground level.

Chartres and Cologne head the list with nine apiece. Strasbourg, Senlis, Sens, and the old cathedral of Cambrai each has seven. The cathedrals of Amiens, Anvers, Bayeux, Laon, Lisieux, Reims, and Rodez are provided with six vices apiece; and Beauvais, though without a nave and western towers, also has six. Many churches as well as cathedrals have five vices rising from the level of the nave floor. The cathedrals include Auxerre, Bourges, Évreux, Le Mans, Meaux, Metz, Nevers, Noyon, Soissons, Tournai, Tours, and Vienne. Among the churches that have five vices are St-Étienne at Beauvais, St-Maclou at Pontoise, St-Nicolas-du-Port (Meurthe-et-Moselle), both St-Maclou and St-Ouen at Rouen, the Collegiate Church of St-Quentin, and the Abbey Church of St-Denis. Four vices are found in the cathedrals of Paris, Toul, Toulouse, and Troyes; and in the churches of St-Yved at Braine, Notre-Dame at Châlons-sur-Marne, Notre-Dame at Dijon, Notre-Dame at Cléry (Loiret), Notre-Dame at L'Épine, Notre-Dame at Étampes, St-Remi at Reims, and both Notre-Dame and St-Urbain at Troyes. Even the smallest Gothic churches invariably have at least one spiral stair giving access to the tower or the roofs outside and in; and most

churches have two or three of these vices. Indeed, such a small building as the Sainte-Chapelle in Paris has two such stairs; and the chapel of the Château at Vincennes has four vices.

61. Modern examples of timber shoring are illustrated in Schmidt: photographically at figs. 344, p. 234, 352, p. 238, 355, p. 239, 362, p. 244, 363, p. 245, 364 and 365, p. 246, 367–9, p. 248; and in careful orthographic drawings at figs. 353, p. 238, 359 and 360, p. 243, and 361, p. 244.

62. *Vide infra* with respect to the effect of the nave roof in weighting the clerestory masonry.

63. Explained in Choisy, *Histoire*, vol. ii, pp. 311–13; in Enlart, p. 573; and in Viollet-le-Duc, *Dictionnaire*, article 'Construction', vol. iv, pp. 142–4. (In Huss's English translation of Viollet-le-Duc's entire 'Construction' article, the original's pp. 142–4 correspond to Huss's pp. 189–93.)

William Harvey (*Models of Buildings*, p. 52) explains and demonstrates the signal importance of eccentric loading in medieval vaulted churches. Such 'false bearing' used to be condemned by architectural historians (committed to and preoccupied by the Classical tradition) as being an indication of improper and unsound stability. But Harvey calls attention to the fact 'that designers of arched buildings purposely employed the corbel to apply a violently eccentric load in order to control the still more dangerous arch thrust'. It is because of this eccentricity of loading, particularly in the case of the side-aisle-encroaching clerestory piers and their corresponding buttresses in the lofty French churches, that some shoring of these towering elements was indispensable during the course of erection.

64. Illustrated in Viollet-le-Duc, article 'Construction' at fig. 81, p. 143, and fig. 96, p. 171 (pp. 190 and 225 in Huss).

65. Illustrated in Viollet-le-Duc, article 'Construction', at figs. 43, p. 78, and 101, p. 178 (Huss, pp. 108 and 234).

66. Marcel Aubert ('Les plus anciennes croisées d'ogives', note, p. 220) observes that 'In the twelfth and thirteenth centuries, and again in the fourteenth and fifteenth, the builders had relatively mediocre resources at their disposal, even for building churches of some importance, which explains the slowness of their erection. These churches sometimes take more than a century to build, and many of them are actually never able to be completed.'

On the other hand, Watson (pp. 26–27) asserts that '. . . Where no pecuniary or other difficulty was experienced, nothing is more remarkable than the rapidity with which the buildings of this period were constructed: a rapidity such that it is doubtful whether it could be exceeded appreciably at the present time. Several important churches of the thirteenth century in France were built within five years. . . . If the labours of an age were sometimes required to compass the erection of a great cathedral it was not usually the builders who were at fault. . . .'

Harvey (*Gothic World*, p. 17) is more explicit. He says: 'The rate of progress of Gothic buildings was governed by the available finance rather than by technical considerations, but precautions were taken where heavy work such as towers was concerned. The surviving contracts suggest that a height of about ten or twelve feet per year was considered the best for tower building. . . . Caution was also necessary in arranging the order of operations in a building provided with vaults and flying buttresses, for the flyers and vaults had both to be allowed to set firmly before the centerings could be struck.'

It should be noted, however, that in his 'De Rebus in Administratione sua Gestis' Abbot Suger records that the chevet of his abbey church of St-Denis (comprising the upper choir, ambulatory and apsidal chapels) was completed in the incredibly short time of three years and three months, 'from the crypt below to the summit of the vaults above . . . including even the consummation of the roof' (Panofsky, *Abbot Suger*, pp. 49 f). If Suger's statement can be believed, this would indicate that, in those exceptional cases where sufficient money and outstanding administrative energy were present, the work did not need to be delayed or done slowly on account of technical or erectional considerations.

Vide note A: 'On the Time Required for the Erection of the Different Parts of York Minster', in Willis, *York*, pp. 54–57.

67. This was definitely a factor, although by no means the dominant one, in the builders' adoption of the practice of roofing the nave before they vaulted it. The protection provided by the roof to the scaffolding, the centering, and whatever vaulting formwork may have been used, was insurance against a too rapid deterioration of the extensive falsework involved in constructing the high vaults.

68. *Vide* Chapter 5 *infra*, including note 201, for further discussion of the strutting role of the flying buttresses.

69. Guadet, in fact, emphasizes the point (vol. iii, p. 318) that 'In every vaulted church there must be an area above the vaults, called the loft or garret (*comble ou grenier*): a considerable space occasioned by the timber-work of the roof. . . . This space is valuable, not as a catch-all as it is too often employed in spite of the fire hazard, but for inspection and maintenance of the vaults, for permitting access to the roofs, the gutters, &c.' He goes on to say that these lofts should be aired and lighted, and he mentions the fact that 'In some roofs of churches foresight has even prompted the establishment, at mid-height, of a series of horizontal beams, variously disposed, that can serve to support scaffolding for repairs, in case the need for them should arise.'

70. *Vide* Fitchen, 'A Comment on the Function of the Upper Flying Buttress . . .' pp. 79, 82, 85.

71. The main horizontal tie-beams in the timber roof of Paris Cathedral have no less than five vertical members rising from them, although the outermost posts on either side obtain additional support from the doubly-bracketed hammer-beams reinforcing the ends of these heavy horizontal ties (*vide* Deneux's drawing of one of the great transverse frames, reproduced as fig. 380, p. 353, in Lasteyrie).

For horizontal tie-beams in England, Brandon reports (p. 12): 'In roofs of low pitch, which appear to have been in use at a very early period, the beam was made to bear the whole weight of the roof. . . .'

A modern instance of the use of large timbers not only to span a wide gap but also to support a heavy superstructure in the form of concentrated loads at regular intervals throughout their length, is to be seen in the large photographic illustration on p. 1205 of the *Engineering News*, vol. lxix, no. 24, 12 June 1913. The view is of a railway bridge over the Baker River in the State of Washington, consisting of the bridge proper (at half the height to the track, 180 feet above the river) on which is framed a timber trestle of more ordinary construction. 'Both lower and upper structures are built of round timber. The length of the central span or beam portion of the bridge is about 80 feet, and the beams of this central span are 48-inch-diameter logs. . . . It is stated that the erection of the timberwork complete required only four weeks' time after the foundations were ready. . . . This bridge was built as a temporary structure; when the time comes to replace it, it is to be used as falsework for the permanent bridge. . . .'

The point here is not so much the use of unsquared timber (although that is reminiscent of medieval intentions in its economy of workmanship) as it is the employment of simple beams, as opposed to braced frames, to support heavy concentrated loads. One can the more readily believe, in view of this modern instance, that the medieval carpenters trusted the main tie-beams of their nave roofs to support both the timber-work of the roof itself while it was being framed, piece by piece, and

the great wheels used as lifting devices there (*vide* note 73 *infra*).

72. Moles (p. 170) mentions that Deneux cites 'certain reconstructions of the timber-work where these tie-beams have been put back in place upside-down, in order to correct their previous sag' (quoting Deneux, *L'Ancienne et la nouvelle charpente de la cathédrale de Reims*).

In England, on the other hand, sagging appears to have been forestalled from the start by employing horizontal beams that bowed up naturally. Thus, according to Brandon (p. 12), 'In the churches of the Middle Ages, a perfectly horizontal tie-beam is of extremely rare occurrence: where a tie-beam is used, we almost invariably find it cambered, as are also the collar beams; even the hammer-beams will be generally found, on close inspection, to incline upwards from the walls.'

73. Salzman (p. 325) cites examples of 'great wheels' turned on the treadmill principle by the feet of men climbing inside them, and placed high within a tower or some other lofty part of the building. He illustrates two of these treadmill wheels in plate 17 *a* and *b*, opposite p. 320. Rackham (p. 42) mentions one in Westminster Abbey as 'standing above the vaulting of the nave and being shifted, with the scaffolding, from bay to bay'. Manuscript illustrations of these great wheels are reproduced in Colombier: plate xv, no. 26, shows one located on the ground, with two men inside it; plate xvii, no. 28, shows one high aloft above the west front of a cathedral whose uppermost story is still white, indicating how recently it has been built; plate xxi shows one at the base and one at the top of a many-storied Tower of Babel. Vogts, 'Das ehemalige Karmeliterkloster in Köln', reproduces a section drawing (fig. 266, p. 239) showing a wheel-windlass in place high up in the roof structure of this Convent. Drawings of post-medieval structures in which great wheels are featured appear in Moles, fig. 483, p. 339, and fig. 526, p. 367. There is a great wheel

(reconstructed, to be sure, but unquestionably modelled on a medieval prototype) that is still operational in the abbey of Mont-St-Michel. Illustrations of additional examples are encountered in various other publications.

It is interesting to note that great wheels of this sort were also used in Roman times. In Singer *et al.*, *A History of Technology*, vol. ii, are illustrated two examples: fig. 578, p. 637, which is designated as a 'Roman hoist for raising blocks of stone, operated by a man in a squirrel cage', from a relief at Syracuse, first century; and fig. 603, p. 660, 'Part of a relief from a Roman sepulchral monument of *c.* A.D. 100', where five 'tramping men' are seen inside 'an enormous treadmill' wheel.

The most complete and informing account of these great wheels, however (replete with accurate drawings and even clear, large-scale photographs of some of them *in situ* and still capable of being operated), is found in Czarnowsky, 'Engins de levage dans les combles d'églises en Alsace'. Not only details of construction, location, and secure bracing of these great wheel-windlasses are demonstrated, but also their operation and multiple uses are described. Along with this largest type of lifting device, capstans which were located in the roofs of side aisles are also cited and fully described. Czarnowsky also makes note of examples that are known to have existed but are no longer extant (p. 15); and, in addition, describes and illustrates other medieval and early Renaissance types of lifting machines. Even the relatively late examples that are still extant employ almost no metal in their construction; and in this respect they approximate the true medieval machines whose wooden construction throughout, like the timber roofs that sheltered them, were entirely without straps or pins of metal (cf. note 206).

74. This device of concentric arch rings, begun in early Romanesque times, becomes universal throughout the medieval period. In Gothic times the chief distinction in its appearance is the elimination of the separate planes of the arch faces due to their multiple mouldings that produce a generally splayed effect rather than the stepped offsets of the earlier examples.

In either case, each successive arch ring was prevented from settling or shrinking unduly at the time of its erection by the already completed arch ring that supported it when it was being built.

But not only did each arch ring find permanent support from the previously built one. It is also demonstrably true that, for the wide-spanning arched heads of their great clerestory windows, the builders dispensed altogether with temporary centering. Here the voussoirs of the innermost arch ring itself were supported, at the time of their erection, by the carefully cut and intricately jointed membering of the stone tracery that filled the window-head. The spans of this tracery are half, or a third, or even a smaller fraction of that of the window-head as a whole, depending on the number of slender mullions (permanently held in alignment at their tops by a bar of iron) that divide the total window opening into separate lights. Thus each mullion acted as a permanent shore or vertical strut holding up the patterned complex of tracery, whose upper boundaries, in turn, created a stone centering on which the lowest ring of arch stones was erected.

Proof of this procedure appears to be conclusive on two specific counts, in addition to the persuasive probability based on historical development (from the heavy plate tracery of early times). One is the fact that the individual stones of the tracery are so jointed and fitted together that they could not have been erected in any normal fashion subsequent to the turning of the window arch above and around them. Possibly one or two blocks of the tracery could have been slipped in sideways. But this seems most unlikely, for they are so keyed together and interlocked (for permanent stability) that many would have had to be propped up temporarily until these final key blocks were slipped into position. (*Vide*, among the many drawings indicating the pattern of the tracery stones and their jointing, those in Hazak, figs. 240, p. 158, 241, p. 159;

in Viollet-le-Duc, article 'Fenêtre', vol. v, figs. 18, p. 386, 19, p. 387, 20, p. 390, 24, p. 394; Deneux, 'Signes lapidaires . . .', p. 105, figs. 6 and 7; and elsewhere).

The other, even more conclusive proof that the slender Gothic tracery acted as permanent centering for the innermost arch ring of the window-head is that the tracery was housed into the soffit of this arch ring. Viollet-le-Duc records many instances of this practice of having a channel cut out of the intrados of the voussoirs of the innermost arch ring, into which the upper boundaries of the tracery were let. Obviously, the tracery stones could not have been inserted into this channelled sinkage *after* the arch stones were in place. (For details of this sinkage *vide* Viollet-le-Duc, article 'Fenêtre', vol. v, p. 377, fig. 13, at A for Soissons; p. 381, fig. 15, at C for Chartres; p. 387, fig. 19, at E for the Ste-Chapelle, Paris. Also article 'Meneau', vol. vi, p. 321, fig. 2, at A for Reims; p. 324, fig. 3, upper left-hand corner, for Amiens; p. 326, fig. 4, at C, also for Amiens; and p. 331, fig. 6, at x′ for St-Urbain at Troyes. Also Ungewitter, vol. ii, p. 493, figs. 1145, 1148–1148c; and Deneux, 'Signes lapidaires . . .', p. 109 and fig. 12, p. 110, which clearly indicates the deep rebate of a tracery voussoir that is destined to receive one of the lobed and voided elements of the window's stonework rose.)

75. The problem and the possibilities of reduction in centering requirements, in the case of the ribbed vault, are considered more fully below. Here it is appropriate to note, however, that in connexion with the carriage of stones by pack-horse, slung on either side of the animal, Andrews (p. 68) says: 'Where the transport of stones had to be done in this latter manner, the stones in the building are never of any great cubic content, weight precluding the use of large pieces; indeed, it has been reasonably suggested that the receding "orders" of arches etc. were evolved by this necessity as well as the economy in centerings. It is also very probable that the development of vault ribs was suggested, at least in part, by

a like difficulty in the matter of scaffolds and centerings. Some of the ribs were set with a very simple turning piece which could be adjusted for varying spaces.'

A more general statement is made by Jackson, *Byzantine and Romanesque Architecture*, vol. i, p. 205, on 'the part played by problems of construction in the growth of architecture'. 'No great advance in the art', he says, 'was ever made without a reason outside the art itself; and this reason is generally to be found in some novelty in construction that recommended itself or some facilities that presented themselves for doing things before impossible. It is to suggestions derived from construction that we must look for the origin of all great movements in the history of the art.'

76. Choisy (*Histoire*, vol. i, pp. 33–38) covers aspects of this practice of filling rooms with sand as they rose, in the section on Ancient Egypt entitled 'La Manœuvre des pierres'. *Vide* particularly his fig. 22 (p. 35) of the placing of stone lintels on columns whose interspaces have been filled to their tops with sand. The practices he cites (and documents) for the Egyptians—including the use of long ramps of sand on which stones were hauled up to their ultimate position on a building—are well known and accepted.

Less well known are similar ancient practices used elsewhere in the world. For example, as quoted from *Cassier's Magazine* in the *R.I.B.A. Journal* (14 Jan. 1899, 3rd ser., vol. vi, p. 136), J. Elfreth Watkins writes in part as follows: 'During a visit to the Island of Jersey (Channel Islands) in 1878, while wandering over the hills, I noticed, among many dolmens scattered about, one which seemed to have never been finished. The sides stood erect, and leading up to them were inclines over which such heavy weights as the roofing slabs of the dolmens could have been raised to the positions in which we find them. It was evident that cords and rollers, with a sufficient number of sturdy savages, would have been amply sufficient for the purpose in the case before me. The thorough manner in which the clay of the inclined plane had been consolidated was evident when it was considered that the denudation of it by the elements during unknown centuries had been insufficient to noticeably reduce its level or conceal its evident purpose.

Vide also A. C. Smith, 'On the Method of Moving Colossal Stones, etc.'; and Thomas Inman, 'On a Means Employed for Removing and Erecting Menhirs'.

77. Rivoira (vol. i, p. 212) even claims, for the eleventh-century side-aisle bays of San Flaviano at Montefiascone, that it was the stone ribs of the vaults rather than pole-supported platforms that sustained the earth formwork. He notes that 'the ribs, . . . which . . . were constructed quite independently of the cells, . . . served as centring when the latter were made. The compartments of the vaulting, which geometrically form parts of a cylinder and were originally plastered over, were constructed by first placing a rough wooden centring on the ribs; next, by modelling up the surface in earth or in clay and water to receive them, and then arranging upon this layer lumps of tufa of various sizes, one next to the other, set in mortar, after the Roman fashion, thus producing a kind of coating intended to make the centring firmer. Above this came the backing of the rubble concrete.'

Rivoira does not reveal how he knows that the ribs supported this formwork, nor does he offer any explanation or detail of the way this could be managed in actual practice. As we will see, this part of his reconstruction of the erectional steps is undoubtedly erroneous; the rest of his account may well be true.

78. *Vide infra* for explanation and discussion of the domed groin vault.

79. There is a diagram of this scheme, sometimes called cocket centers, in Séjourné (*Grandes voûtes*, tome i, p. 147), showing the centering for the central arch of the five-span masonry bridge built across the Thames at London in 1824–31. Another example is figured by Rondelet and reproduced in Moles as the lower left-hand example in fig. 271, p. 218. Two examples are illustrated in Rees (Plates, vol. i, figs. 1 and 3 of plate lxviii). Here, fig. 3 represents one of the centering frames for the London bridge referred to as the Blackfriars Bridge. The timbers of this diagram are lettered throughout (as copied from Baldwin, plate vii), and the article on 'Centers' (Text, vol. vii) gives the names of these timber members. Three examples are clearly illustrated in Eric de Maré, *The Bridges of Britain* (pp. 136, fig. 82, 150, fig. 92, and 182–3, fig. 119), each taken from earlier works.

An illustration (fig. 5, p. 60) and description (pp. 74–75) are given in McMaster, who writes as follows: 'In cocket centers the folding wedges are replaced by a *striking plate* placed at each end of the rib, and sustained by strutting or raking pieces which abut either on off-sets at the foot of the pier or on sills placed on the ground. Each plate consists of three parts, a lower and upper plate and a compound wedge driven between them. The upper of these plates is of wood made fast to the base of the rib, and is cut into a series of off-sets on its *under* surface. The lower plate is likewise of wood cut into off-sets, but on its *upper* surface, and is firmly attached to the raking pieces which sustain it. The compound wedge consists of a beam cut into off-sets both upon its upper and lower sides so as to fit those of the two plates, and when driven between them is held in place by keys driven behind its shoulders.'

80. There are detail drawings and a brief explanation of one such scheme in connexion with the Palmgraben Railroad bridge in Austria, built in 1904–5, which appear in Séjourné (tome ii, p. 166). McMaster (p. 75) speaks briefly of this scheme as follows: 'Another method, at one time much in use among French engineers, is to cut off the ends of the chief supports of the rib piece, an operation which cannot be accomplished with much regularity, nor without much danger.'

81. Illustrations of these towers are given in Viollet-le-Duc, *Dictionnaire*, article 'Architecture militaire', vol. i, p. 363, fig. 15, and p. 365, fig. 16; article 'Château', vol. iii, p. 98, fig. 14; and article 'Engin', vol. v, p. 265, fig. 32.

82. Innocent's valuable and detailed study mentions (pp. 86, 87) many instances of the moving of *buildings*, including continental examples, covering a wide range in time from the days of the Norsemen to the seventeenth century. Andrews mentions (p. 74) a case in which a timber house was moved bodily during the later medieval period. Rees (Plates, vol. i, plate i, fig. 5) gives an early nineteenth-century illustration of a 'Dutch moveable barn' mounted on wheels. And Salzman states (p. 248) that as early as 1238 Henry III 'ordered the construction at Winchester of a house of deal running on six wheels . . .'.

Moles reproduces many of Rondelet's drawings of rolling *scaffolding*. Although these were for buildings of Renaissance times or later, it is quite possible that mobile falsework structures analogous to these schemes were employed in the Gothic era. Schmidt discusses modern instances of rolling scaffolding, and presents illustrations of a number of examples (*Die Baugerüste*, pp. 147–55, figs. 210–20 inclusive) not only in photographs but also in elevation, section, and detail drawings.

83. Later, in the Gothic era, this elimination of the voussoir action in the lower portion of the rib arches (and therefore the curtailment, at either end, of the span of the supporting formwork needed to build these rib arches) was undoubtedly one of the many advantages of the Gothic tas-de-charge device (*vide* Chapter 3 *infra* for explanation of the tas-de-charge).

84. Choisy (*Histoire*, vol. ii, p. 168) states flatly that for the Romanesque period 'the abacus plays a double role: it receives the start of the arch and, at the time of erection, it acts as support for the centering'.

However this may have been in Romanesque structures, it is most unlikely that the abacus acted as a seat for the centering frames in Gothic churches, where the ribs crowd out close to its edge. The Gothic tendency was to make each abacus no larger than need be in order to use up practically all of its top surface for seating the ribs that rose from it. Moreover, in late Gothic work the abacus, along with the entire capital, was usually omitted altogether.

85. *Vide* Appendix D for comment on the probable falsework assemblage in the single bay of an early crossing tower.

86. Medieval examples are cited in Aubert, notes, pp. 15, 215.

87. In *Les Mosquées de Samarcande* it is stated (p. v) that 'In his own country, that is, in western Turkestan, Tamerlan [Tamberlaine or Timur] had at his disposal only second-rate artisans, lacking in initiative, who had to be directed by foreigners. The art that we admire in the monuments of Samarkand had to be imported from abroad.' Tamberlaine's ruthless and overwhelming conquests were very widespread, and we read further that 'Whenever a city was taken by assault, orders were given to spare architects, painters and qualified workmen whom Timur subsequently employed in the execution of his projects. . . .' More specifically, in 'The Origin of the Persian Double Dome', Creswell states that 'This explanation of the origin of the Persian dome is borne out by the fact that Timur imported artisans from Damascus. . . .'

88. *Vide* Colombier, chap. iv; and Harvey, *Gothic World*. A thoroughly documented monograph on a single medieval 'architect', including his travels, is that of John Harvey, *Henry Yevele*.

89. *Vide* Harvey, *Gothic World*, pp. 12–15; also Salzman, chaps. i–iv inclusive.

90. *Vide* Enlart, pp. 88, 89.

91. If indeed the earlier structures had not already collapsed on account of 'insufficient foundations, unskilful handling, or bad workmanship' (Salzman, pp. 25 and ff.).

Moreover, a primary incentive to rebuilding was the changed emphasis in the church's purpose, with the advent of Gothic times. West (*Gothic Architecture in England and France*, pp. 27, 29) states it this way: 'In the latter part of the twelfth century, at the rise of the great popular communal movement, what was required was a large open hall, not a pilgrimage church like St. Martin or Cluny. . . . In the two great cathedrals of Paris and Bourges the expression of the religious purpose of the building has become almost secondary to that of the popular use. . . .'

The degree to which the secular aspect of the medieval church was sometimes carried, in England, is remarked upon by R. B. Hull, 'On All Saints' Church, Northampton', p. 73: 'Here it must be remembered that in these early days the nave of the Parish Church was not merely the place for the worship of Almighty God, but the Common Hall of the Parishioners; in fact the nave of every church served as the Town Hall for the parish, and was used for many secular purposes; the chancel being more strictly reserved for the celebration of religious rites. It is well known, for instance, how in St. Paul's Cathedral even horse fairs were held in the nave. And it is only in comparatively speaking late days that men have learned to see the utter impropriety of such doings. However, even in these early days, men were beginning to feel that such arrangements could not be permitted; and in 1236 a Royal Mandate was issued from Henry III commanding the removal of the fair to some open place.'

92. 'Another fact to be noted in the beginning of Gothic is that the introduction of ribs seems to have been due to the desire to find a safe means of vaulting the nave alone. This is demonstrated by the numerous examples of churches that have ribbed vaulted naves and side aisles still covered with groin vaults. The

great churches set the fashion and were followed in turn by the smaller foundations' (quoted from *American Journal of Archaeology*, 1912, 2nd ser., vol. xvi, p. 295, in a résumé of E. Gall).

93. *Vide* Strzygowski, *Early Church Art in Northern Europe.*

94. In this connexion, Choisy's significant observation quoted above, about the stiffening action of the transverse arches, should be recalled (*vide* note 34).

95. Although the transverse arches had to be constructed before the vault proper was built, it would have been possible to erect first an arch, then the portion of vault between this arch and the last one, from the same bay-length platform.

96. These diaphragm divisions of masonry, moreover, are said to have retarded the spread of fire from bay to bay in the side-aisle roof. *Vide* Choisy, *Histoire*, vol. ii, p. 193.

97. Choisy (op. cit., p. 221) says that 'In France, churches with the central nave groin-vaulted occur only as isolated examples, as true exceptions.' By way of accounting for this rarity of simple groin vaults above naves, he cites the case of St-Eutrope at Saintes where there is a banded barrel vault over the nave, but a groin vault in the crypt below. He says (p. 207): 'The simultaneous employment of two kinds of vaults and the circumstances under which each of them is applied clearly show why the groin vault was outlawed from large buildings for so long a time: the effect of its thrusts was feared. Groin vaults were admitted for a crypt where the springs were below grade, but the builders didn't dare install them at the top of the piers in a high nave.'

It may be, however, that it was not so much the fear of the central vault's thrust alone that postponed or prevented the adoption of groin vaults over the nave, but rather the technical difficulties of constructing vaults of such wide span at such heights.

98. *Vide* Choisy, op. cit., p. 151, fig. 6, and p. 154, fig. 9.

99. Bond, *Church Architecture*, vol. i, pp. 279–384. Cf. drawings on p. 293.

100. Bond's two lower drawings on p. 293 are copied from Ungewitter, vol. i, plate iii, fig. 16 opposite p. 10, and fig. 327, p. 120. The first, at least, of these appears to have been copied in turn from a much earlier source; namely, *The Cyclopaedia; or, Universal Dictionary of Arts, Sciences, and Literature*, which appeared early in the nineteenth century. In the first American edition of this work, edited by Rees, this drawing is given in Plates, vol. i, as fig. 1, no. 1, of one of the plates numbered lxxiv, along with other views, diagrams, and details of the same falsework arrangement for groin vaults in series. Here, the boarding of the formwork is continuous for the longitudinal vault, with separate falsework subsequently constructed for the transverse vault compartments. In the text of this *Cyclopaedia*, vol. xvii, there is a long article entitled 'Groin' in part of which (the pages are not numbered) an explanation of the setting out and construction of the formwork illustrated in the plate figs. is given, the lateral compartments being termed 'ungula' in reference to their separate claw-like shapes.

101. For example, a somewhat analogous scheme, for a barrel vault with penetrations, is described by Brodtbeck, 'Les Voûtes romanes de l'église de Romainmôtier', pp. 479 ff. Brodtbeck paraphrases Zemp, 'Die Kirche von Romainmôtier' (p. 100) as follows: 'The principal barrel vault was built on a continuous centering. The laggings of the penetrating vaults in turn were laid on the lagging of this centering and on the cradles of the lateral lunettes, after which a mould of tamped earth was made and the masonry of the vaults was built in rough-hewn rubble set in thick beds of mortar.'

102. A drawing illustrating this arrangement for a semicylindrical barrel vault of small span appears in Quicherat (p. 424, fig. 36) where, moreover, there is no provision of any sort indicated as to how the decentering might be managed.

103. The occurrence, here and there, of rings of stone surrounding a void at the common crown of the high vault's diagonal ribs proves that, in Gothic vaults, the rib centerings could not always be constructed as single frames spanning all the way across the nave in one rigid unit (*vide infra*, including note 204).

104. We are sometimes told that, in the earliest groin vaults of the Middle Ages, the difficulties of cutting the groin voussoirs to proper shape were so great that the masons cut them to conform to only one of the two intersecting vault surfaces, and that then, after the vaulting was up, they came back to hew off the portions that projected beyond the other vault surface.

This is probably nonsense. Whether the practice was ever followed or not in the oldest medieval groin vaults would have depended, for one thing, on what kind of formwork was employed. (For further discussion of the groin voussoirs, *vide infra*, including note 176.)

105. For the relatively less complicated but still difficult job of hewing out voussoirs for a simple arch that curves in plan (rather than occurring in a vertical plane), *vide* Branner's explanation of the procedures followed by the medieval stonemasons (Branner, 'Three Problems ...').

106. A fuller if somewhat turgid account of why the groins are the weakest part of the vault is given by George Tappen, architect, in Rees (Text, vol. xvii, article 'Groin'). To be sure, the vaults Tappen writes about carry both floors and superincumbent live loads of considerable magnitude, for his analysis is confined to the case of continuous groin vaulting

in brick masonry in a tobacco warehouse at the London Docks. However, many of the objections he cites are also applicable to unsurcharged vaults, and are therefore perhaps worth quoting. Here, in part, is what he writes:

'It has long been experienced, and universally acknowledged, that the present established method of erecting groined arches is a weak and imperfect construction. . . . In the first place, it must be manifest to every observer who examines them, that a very material part of the substance of the bricks, forming the groined angle, is pared and cut away, with an intent of producing additional length to the curve of that angle by which the joints of all the brick-work are preserved on an exact level line, as well as from the unavoidable necessity of uniting and bonding the same into the face of the arch with which it is immediately connected.'

'Secondly, the slanting or oblique direction in which the bricks are cut and bedded at the angles of the groins, with an horizontal line at top, render them extremely liable to be thrust out of their situations by any sudden momentum, or extraordinary impulse operating on the crown of the arch.'

'Thirdly, were the groins viewed in a sectional representation, they would present the poorest and most feeble of all forms thus applied, that of a wedge placed vertically on its blade; and at the same time discover so small an area, and consequently such a want of solidity, as to appear incapable of sustaining, so securely as they ought, the combined lateral pressure of the contiguous arches.'

'Lastly, the groins (being the parts where the greatest resistance should be made), instead of springing from a broad substantial base, have nothing else to rest upon, than the most flimsy of all supports, namely, an extreme corner of a square pier. Again, what may be urged, not only as a confirmation, but as an augmentation, is, that when the crowns of these arches are loaded with stores and merchandise, the superincumbent weight has been found, by experience, to act chiefly in the direction of the groins, although they are allowed to be the weakest parts of the arch; therefore it follows, as a natural conclusion, that the stronger these parts are made, the better the whole arch will be able to counteract the tendency of a fracture, and consequently the greater burthen it will be capable of supporting without the danger of giving way.'

107. Along with many other writers, Choisy (*Histoire*, p. 153) notes that 'The diagonal arc, instead of consisting of an elliptical curve as in Roman vaults, is obviously a semicircle.' Because of this, the laying out of the groin centerings was greatly simplified (*see also* note 134).

108. For the practice of cambering or bowing the courses of the vault masonry, by which a longitudinal concavity was imparted to the vault cells, *vide* Lassaux (pp. 227–9, including his diagrammatic drawings, figs. 3–6). He writes, in part, that '. . . in ancient vaults no horizontal line whatsoever occurs, and each course is laid in a line somewhat curved outwards; and consequently incomparably less thickness and less labour is requisite, and yet a far stronger arch is produced . . .'.

109. This was perhaps one of the earliest instances of formwork that made possible the herring-bone type of web coursing illustrated in the drawing, 24. The medieval builders sometimes adopted this pattern of stonework, particularly in the domed groin vault, where it obviated the necessity to cut the voussoirs to conform to the widening and narrowing of the stone courses running through as continuous arcs.

110. Instead of being partially embedded within the rubble masonry of the vault shell, the ribs of some of the earliest rib vaults, at least in England, were completely independent of it to the extent of having diaphragms of thin walling on their backs, up to the level of the vault proper (*vide* note 173).

111. For example, Enlart says (p. 36) that 'in practice, not only the Romans but above all the Romanesque architects sought to avoid the difficulties of stereotomy and the cost of labour required by a groin vault properly coursed. . . . Their vaults were often only concretions of rubble maintained not by their shape but by the solid adherence of the thick mortar which enveloped them.'

112. Thus Guadet (vol. iii, p. 315), speaking of Roman vaults, writes: 'These rubble vaults with excellent mortar form true monoliths which thrust only if they are broken. . . .'

113. For example, Bond (*Church Architecture*, pp. 288 f.) has this to say about cohesion in the four cells of a bay of early groin vaulting: 'On the wooden centre, a thick layer of mortar was laid, and in this mortar were packed on edge thin rough pieces of rubble (i.e. undressed stone); by means of these, with the aid of more mortar and smaller pieces of rubble, the arched form of the centre was reproduced. When the mortar had set, the centre would be removed and then could be re-used to erect another section of vault. A vault constructed in this way was practically a homogeneous mass of concrete; and being but to a slight extent arcuated in construction, had but small lateral thrust, and therefore needed but little abutment. On the other hand, since the rubble mass was thick and heavy, it needed very strong supports.'
Incidentally, Bond's bland assumption that the centering, as described here, could be re-used in subsequent bays, is at once made to seem doubtful by his accompanying note: 'When the centre was removed the top planks sometimes stuck to the mortar and were left imbedded in it; this may be seen in the staircase chamber in the northeast transept of Lincoln Minster [illustration on p. 287]; also in several crypts.' In his earlier work (*Gothic Architecture*), Bond writes in a note (p. 295): 'Sometimes portions of the boarding stuck to the layer of mortar on their upper surfaces, and were left there. Fragments of the original

centering may still be seen adhering to the mortar in Lastingham crypt' (illustrated in Bond, *Church Architecture*, p. 82; and noted also by Bilson, 'Norman Vaulting in England', note, p. 291).
All these examples are early, crude, and of very small span, and hence reveal nothing to us of the practices followed in the erection of wide-spanning high vaults.

114. Only within the past few years have articles on thin shells started to appear in the architectural press. One of the best is by Professor Salvador in the July 1954 *Architectural Record*.

115. One of the very few writers who seems to have recognized the thin shell aspect of the Gothic vault is Conant, according to his characterization of it (op. cit., p. 127) as 'a thin sheet of small cut stones arranged in courses to form warped surfaces which are strong because of double curvature . . .'.

116. *Vide* Choisy, *L'Art de bâtir chez les Romains*, fig. 28, p. 61, fig. 30, p. 63, figs. 31–34, pp. 64–67, and fig. 43, p. 76. The illustration, fig. 1, in Viollet-le-Duc's article 'Voûte' (*Dictionnaire*, vol. ix, p. 466) is a single drawing that presents the features in question as well as various other significant practices that were followed in the construction of a typical Roman barrel vault of concrete.
Gottgetreu (p. 102) has a brief explanation of how the Romans conserved scaffolding in their great barrel vaults by means of constructing a cellular complex in brick, into which the mass of the vault proper was locked, so that 'the wooden scaffold served more as a model than as a support'. Viollet-le-Duc's drawing shows how this was accomplished.

117. In Guastavino, *Theory and History of Cohesive Construction, vide* particularly p. 51 on the advantages of the cohesive system, p. 53 on the action of the mortar joints, pp. 56–57 on the setting time, and p. 134 on centering requirements.

118. A highly technical analysis of this ZD system is given in Molke and Kalinka, 'Principles of Concrete Shell Dome Design'. Among the many less technical accounts of this system are Klyce, 'The ZD System of Shell Roof Construction', and Kalinka, 'Monolithic Concrete Construction for Hangars'.

119. *Vide* the remarkable article by Severud, 'Turtles and Walnuts, Morning Glories and Grass', *Architectural Forum*, Sept. 1945.

120. The engineer, Henri Masson, comments in 'Le Rationalisme dans l'architecture du moyen âge' (p. 35) as follows: 'The assertion [that medieval masonry is unable to undergo tensile stresses] is not accurate, for only bodies that are unprovided with cohesion, such as liquids or pulverized solids, are without resistance to tension. Even the masonry of the Middle Ages always has a little resistance to tension, but it rarely exceeds one or two kilos per square centimetre [$14\frac{1}{4}$ to $28\frac{1}{2}$ lb./sq. in.], while its resistance to compression can attain ten or twelve times as much [$142\frac{1}{2}$ to 342 lb./sq. in.].'

121. *Vide* Roger Gilman, 'The Theory of Gothic Architecture and the Effect of Shellfire at Rheims and Soissons'. Note particularly the photographs reproduced at figs. 1, 4, 5, 6, 18 for Soissons, and 13 for Reims.

122. In regard to the cambering of vault surfaces, *vide infra*, including note 155.

123. Cross-sections of a number of ribs whose stems penetrate their vaults are illustrated by scale drawings in Aubert (p. 142). Since he refers to these as diagonal ribs (*ogives*), they must have occurred in *square* bays of quadripartite vaulting (*vide* discussion *infra*).

In mature English vaults, on the other hand, except in those rare instances where a strongly rectangular bay of French-type quadripartite vaulting produced the 'ploughshare twist', it

was not only possible but normal for all the ribs to have vault-penetrating stems between rebated shelves, to receive the web panels. Thus Willis says (*Archaeological Journal* for 1863, p. 111, note): 'The system of building vaults with the surfaces resting on the backs of the ribs was, with very few exceptions, abandoned at the end of the Early English period. . . .'

124. The reason for the almost universal adoption of rib stems in English vaulting, including the diagonals, resulted from the technique of stone coursing the builders of that country often adopted. In plan view, instead of having the beds of the stone courses (at least those in the higher portion of the vault) practically invariably run parallel to the crown, the English frequently made them run perpendicular to the bisector of the angle formed by a pair of ribs as these ribs departed from their imposts at the corners of the bay (*vide* diagrams 28 C and D, p. 71, in Watson; also Bond, *Church Architecture*, pp. 322–7, including figs. 2 and 5, p. 325; and elsewhere). Thus the angle formed by a given pair of stone courses, one from each of two adjacent panels of vaulting on either side of the *diagonal* rib, was about the same as the angle which a similar pair of stone courses made on either side of the *transverse* rib. In neither case was this angle acute, nor did any of the courses run parallel to the plane of the diagonal rib, as they did in the lower half of the cross vault in French quadripartite vaulting (*vide* 26). Hence there was always room for webs of normal thickness to rest upon the 2-inch-wide rebates of the ribs, in English vaulting, whether these ribs were transverse arches or diagonals, or, later on, tiercerons.

125. Modern recognition of the rigidifying function of the transverse rib is evident in the way by which the rebuilding of war-damaged medieval vaults has come to be handled. One of the first instances of this new scheme occurred in the rebuilding of the nave vaults of St-Remi at Reims in 1930. Here the thinness

of the clerestory walls and the maladjustment of the flying buttresses militated against reconstructing the vaults in heavy materials. Yet the architect, M. Deneux, devised a system by which the vaults were rebuilt in stone without modifying the former appearance of the structure or compromising its security. He writes: 'We conceived of a reinforced concrete skeleton with its members running across the nave on the back of each transverse rib. . . . This skeleton . . . constitutes so many rigid, indeformable beams on top of the transverse arches. This reinforced concrete armature . . . is like a corset which laces together the vaulting. Thanks to the employment of the new material . . . the nave has been able to recapture the old appearance of its early stone vault' (Deneux, 'La Restauration de la basilique Saint-Remi', p. 31). A photographic illustration of this reinforced concrete armature at St-Remi, seen from below before the vaults proper were rebuilt, is given as fig. 322, p. 501, in Léon, *La Vie des monuments français*.

This kind of rigidification through the use of reinforced concrete has well-nigh become standard practice in the repair or reconstruction of churches and other medieval buildings since World War II (for example, *vide* the illustrated article by Trouvelot, 'De la restauration des monuments historiques').

126. There is considerable photographic evidence, from partially collapsed examples, that in French Gothic vaults there were no rib stems in the case of the diagonal arches, even over square bays. The following photographic illustrations constitute some of this evidence:

Aubert, fig. on p. 209: Reims, high vault bay next to crossing, plus crossing vault.

Id., fig. on p. 219: Reims, high crossing vault.

Id., fig. on p. 221: St-Quentin, high vault.

Id., fig. on p. 225: Noyon, porch. (This is particularly clear.)

Id., fig. on p. 226: Noyon, nave vault.

Léon, fig. 313, p. 496: Reims, high vault, choir bay next to crossing.

Porter (*Lombard and Gothic Vaults*), figs.

32 and 35: abbey church of Longpont, sideaisle vaults.

Trouvelot, top fig. p. 45: Rouen, south sideaisle bay next to crossing.

127. *Vide* the classic example of this situation in the ruined church of Ourscamp (Oise), photographically illustrated in Aubert and Maillé, tome i, p. 263, fig. 136.

128. Moore, *Development and Character of Gothic Architecture*, pp. 130–3.

129. In this connexion, Pol Abraham (*Recherche*, p. 49) has emphasized the fact that 'One of the essential characteristics of Gothic architecture, a characteristic that has been ignored in official instruction until recently, is the exclusive employment of vaults on discontinuous supports.'

130. Moore (p. 108 including note, and p. 110) states that 'The belief that the sexpartite form was the first developed, and that it was gradually superseded by the quadripartite, does not appear correct. . . . It is true, however, that in the older cathedrals the sexpartite vault is the more common. . . . With the closer study of the smaller extant monuments, in which the real beginnings of the style may be traced, this misconception . . . respecting Gothic art will be dispelled.' However this may be, we are here concerned with the high vaults of the great Gothic churches, not the small monuments that went so long unstudied and whose analysis was less often systematic. It seems to be recognized that, although sexpartite vaults were not entirely superseded by quadripartite vaults in the great cathedrals of the thirteenth century, the latter were certainly the more characteristic form.

In this connexion it may be noted that in the cathedral of Noyon, clearly designed for and originally covered by sexpartite vaults, the reconstruction following upon the disastrous fire of 1293 involved the erection of *quadripartite* high vaults throughout (*vide* Seymour, pp. 69, 70 ff.).

131. The clearest and best illustration of this tas-de-charge device is in Viollet-le-Duc, *Dictionnaire*, article 'Construction', vol. iv, p. 93, fig. 48 *ter* (p. 129 in Huss), along with which is his explanation of its advantages.

About the same time, and quite independently, Willis wrote about the tas-de-charge under a different name, in the *Archaeological Journal*, 1863, p. 111, partly as follows: '. . . I have shown elsewhere (*Vaults*, p. 6) that in the construction of the ribbed vaults of the Middle Ages, the lower portion, which projects but slightly from the walls, is built as a solid block of masonry, in horizontal courses, forming an integral part of the wall, and carried up with it; but that the upper portion, which is detached from the wall and covers the space, is of a different and lighter construction, and was erected subsequently to the completion of the walls. This solid part of the vault may be called the "springing block".'

Other writers who have illustrated and commented on the tas-de-charge include Choisy (*Histoire*, vol. ii, pp. 272–3, figs. 4 B and 5, also p. 294, figs. 1 D, 1 E); Enlart (op. cit., p. 506, fig. 245, and p. 550, fig. 275); Bond (*Gothic Architecture*, p. 302, figs. 1, 2); and West (op. cit., pp. 99–102). The latter follows Viollet-le-Duc's account very closely, using his illustrations. A sketch showing the modern practice of duplicating the tas-de-charge scheme is shown in Warland, *Modern Practical Masonry*, p. 229, fig. 591.

One misconception about the medieval practice of working the rib mouldings on the tas-de-charge springers should be noted. Although he gives no reference or authority for the statement, Scott (*History of English Church Architecture*, p. 180, note 'q') confidently asserts that 'We must remember that the springers of the vaults were always built "in block", and were worked into the required forms upon the completion of the groining, often many years subsequent to their erection'. Willis (*Vaults*, pp. 7–9) has conclusively proved that this was *not* the case in the instances he was able to examine. Instead, the mouldings were outlined by templates, both on the top and the

bottom beds of each springer, which proves that the rib mouldings were cut on the banker before they were raised aloft and set in place.

Lethaby gives some figures for the French-type vaulting conoid of Westminster Abbey in England. He says (*King's Craftsmen*, p. 130): 'The clerestory windows are pushed high up into the vaults (Fig. 49); they spring 10 ft. above the springing of the vaulting and consequently the fillings of the vault, between the windows, are little more than vertical strips of walling on the back of the transverse ribs. This portion of the work is jointed horizontally for about 16 ft., and the sheaf of ribs is jointed horizontally for about 6 ft. above the caps. . . .'

132. Fitchen, op. cit., pp. 78–80, 82–85, and 90.

133. It is only in recent modern times, largely due to the supplementary role of reinforced-concrete armatures tying the walls together above the vault, that the vaulting has sometimes been rebuilt before the roof—burned or destroyed by bombardment—has been reconstructed. For example, *vide* the photographic illustration dated 1937, given as fig. 23 opposite p. 94 in Seymour, entitled 'Extrados of vaults of the choir as restored after their fall in 1918', where the roof above these vaults is as yet completely absent.

This is quite a different situation from that of the roofless Spanish churches of the medieval period, such as those of Barcelona. According to Street (p. 302), all these churches originally had timber roofs, though at the present time the extradoses of their vaults are all 'covered with tiles or stone neatly and evenly laid on the vault, in such a way as effectually to keep out the weather'. As we have seen, such timber roofs would have been essential stabilizing adjuncts at the time the original construction was taking place, until the high vaults came to be finished.

One of the very few instances, in medieval times, of the construction of a high vault before the roof was built is that of King's

College Chapel, Cambridge, according to Mackenzie (op. cit., note p. 18). If his information is correct, the explanation from a structural standpoint would include such considerations as the following: (1) the building is without side aisles; hence, the deep buttresses are attached to the wall and not separated by a gap requiring flying buttresses; (2) heavy, lofty pinnacles were constructed before the vault was commenced, thus weighting the vault-supporting piers from above; (3) the vault is excessively thin, producing the minimum of lateral thrust, while the buttresses are deeply salient; (4) the vault, though over 40 feet in clear span (Howard, 'Mediaeval Roofs', p. 13, says 'about 44 feet'), is nowhere near as lofty as in the French examples we are here chiefly concerned with.

134. In many Gothic vaults with semicircular diagonal ribs, the transverse ribs came to be set out as pointed arches whose twin arcs are of the same curvature as that of the diagonals. Thus, as Watson points out (p. 67): 'The same face mould would serve for both, and the voussoirs or arch stones as they were wrought might be used indifferently for either. ...In points like these we recognize a designer versed in the technicalities of his craft, and capable of applying the labour at his disposal to the greatest advantage.'

135. As we will see in Chapter 5, the difficulties encountered in the problems of fashioning, erecting, decentering, and dismantling the intersecting frames of the diagonal rib centerings were formidable. However, their solution was simplified somewhat through the customary adoption, in Gothic vaulting, of semicircular groin ribs. For, because of the employment of semicircular rather than pointed diagonal arcs, the extradoses of the rib frames met in approximately a common plane instead of a four-sided ridge or irregular pyramid. Thus the relative flatness at the crown produced much more stable seatings for the higher lagging units where, during the course of erection, the pressure of the stone courses on them would have been greatest.

136. Conant (op. cit., p. 127) says 'the pointed arch is an approximate catenary, and it is a fact that unless an arched structure has the catenary form, extra strength is needed in the arch to keep the arch itself intact, quite aside from the thrusting action generated in an arch of any kind'.

It is precisely because no Gothic arch or vault *did* describe an actual catenary curve that the medieval builders had to resort to the various adjustments and devices here explained, in order to prevent their vaults from deforming.

Vide discussion of the catenary principle applied to Gothic churches in England, in Mackenzie, pp. 17, 18.

137. The fill is shown in the cross-sectional drawings of Viollet-le-Duc (article 'Construction', vol. iv, p. 172, fig. 98, for the choir of Amiens, and p. 178, fig. 101, for Beauvais (pp. 227 and 234 in Huss)). In de Baudot and Perrault-Dabot (vol. ii, plate 47) a transverse section taken through the flying buttress shows a very high fill in the case of the old cathedral of St-Samson at Dol-de-Bretagne (Ille-et-Vilaine).

Among those who note the function of this fill is Aubert (op. cit., pp. 222 and 167) who says: 'From a very early time, and doubtless from the start in most cases, the extrados of the vaults was charged with masonry at its supports, thereby preventing the haunches from rising, uniting the springers to the clerestory wall, and lowering the curve of the line of pressure by their own weight.'

It was only at the end of the Gothic period, in the flattened and carefully cut ashlaring of English fan vaulting, that the rubble fill was sometimes dispensed with. But even in the case of as late an example as the sixteenth-century vault of King's College Chapel, Mackenzie (p. 14) speaks of the conoid 'being filled with rubble and mortar to the height of 16 feet above the spring-line'. He says that 'this was probably done rather for the sake of additional security than as an essential part of the work', for, in this wide-spanning fan vault of late date and small rise, he demonstrates that 'the architect no doubt designed the construction upon the most perfect principle independently of any extraneous aid . . .'.

138. 33 is a drawing of fissures that are characteristic of Gothic vaults, from Abraham, *Viollet-le-Duc et le rationalisme médiéval* (p. 32, fig. 15). *Vide* also Caroe's sec. 6, entitled 'Cracks which are not Serious' (op. cit., pp. 20–24); particularly his observations on the normality and 'healthiness' of cracks that so often exist where the transverse vault panels meet the clerestory wall. Powys and Wilson, 'The Repair of Vaulted Buildings', provide the most authoritative account of those cracks that are not dangerous to the stability of a vaulted structure.

139. In speaking of the early adoption by the masons of the Île-de-France and Picardy of vaults of ashlar instead of rubble, by which they were able to reduce the thickness of the web from some 12 inches to 6 inches or even much less, and hence to reduce the weight of the vault by at least half, Bond (*Church Architecture*, p. 318) says: 'At first, however, the weight of the vault was often actually increased by covering the ashlar web with a layer of concrete. . . . The later vaults dispensed with this layer of concrete' (*see also* Bond, *Gothic Architecture*, p. 304).

On the other hand, Lethaby (*King's Craftsmen*) readily accepts the overlay of concrete as a praiseworthy feature. He says (p. 129): 'The method of making the courses of filling fall on the diagonal ribs appears to have brought about the English fashion of rebating the ribs; and that, in turn, led to covering up our vaults with a second layer, usually of concrete, which bound all together' (*vide* his drawing, fig. 49, showing the concrete overlay of the vaulting at Westminster).

A century and a half before Lethaby's book appeared, Price (*Salisbury*) made the same error of ascribing to the concrete overlay the advantage of greatly added strength. Price says (p. 24): 'The groins, and principal ribs, are of Chilmark stone and chalk mixed, on top of which is laid a coat of mortar and rubble of a consistence, probably ground in a kind of mill, and poured on hot, while the lime was bubbling; because of this, the whole is so cemented together, as to become all of one substance. This composition is very remarkable, somewhat resembling the pumice stone, being porous and light, by which it contributed prodigiously to the strength of the whole, and at the same time the least weight of any contrivance that was perhaps ever used.'

Simpson (op. cit., p. 84, including note 2) comments as follows: 'The web is generally of the lightest material available, Clunch (i.e., hard chalk) being not uncommon, although courses of harder, heavier stone are sometimes introduced at intervals, as in Westminster Abbey. It varies in thickness from 4 to 8 inches, although in some early vaults a kind of concrete is laid on its extrados, as in Chichester Cathedral and Westminster Abbey nave vaults. In later work this is omitted, partly because it was found that the added strength was dearly bought by the additional weight. In Chichester Cathedral the concrete is a foot thick, the chalk below 6 inches. In Westminster Abbey the vaults over the eastern part of the church and over about two thirds of the nave have about nine inches of concrete above them. The remaining bays to the west, which are a century or two later in date, have none. The Roman tradition of layer upon layer of concrete may possibly have suggested this covering; but it is more probable that the old traditions were lost, and that the early mediaeval builders added the layers because they were afraid of the strength of their thin shells.'

140. *Vide* Appendix E for statements on web thicknesses.

141. Bond, *Gothic Architecture*, p. 304.

142. This structural function of the large decorated keystone has been recognized by many writers, among them Aubert, op. cit., pp. 149, 169.

143. Choisy (*Histoire*, p. 261) says that 'What the monuments teach us is the pains taken by the Gothic builders to simplify the installation of their works. Thanks to the light weight of the stone they placed in the structure, they were able to get along with inexpensive apparatus and, above all, with light scaffoldings. For reasons of economy they were obliged to make the construction itself, as far as possible, carry these scaffoldings.'

144. *Vide* Salzman's entire chap. vii, which begins with the sentence: 'A large part of the cost of masonry lay in the expense of carriage of the stone.'

145. In speaking of the rebuilding of Canterbury Cathedral after the devastating fire of 1174, Andrews says (p. 21) that 'large parts of the stonework were actually prepared in the Caen quarries (patterns being sent over) and, as custom was, practically finished ready to be put into the building before it was sent to England'.

146. Choisy (*Histoire*, p. 270) says: 'Not only does the vault on ribs permit the isolation of forces which the complications of stereotomy made impossible in all other systems, but it permits the reduction of the forces themselves. A groin vault is necessarily heavy because the groin voussoirs present an assured overlapping only under the condition of a sufficient thickness, and this thickness involves that of the entire vault. There is nothing of the kind when one builds on ribs, for the vault, whose compartments are nothing but infillings, becomes extremely light; along with the weight the thrusts lessen, and the abutments can be accommodated to a less massive structure. . . .'

147. Cf. Lefèvre-Pontalis, 'Les Voûtes en berceau et d'arêtes sans doubleaux', pp. 71 ff.

148. For example, the Romanesque Cross Vault diagrammed at B on the plate entitled 'Comparative Diagrams of Vaults' in the chapter on 'Gothic Architecture in Europe', in Banister Fletcher. Here the voussoirs adjacent to the upper left-hand pier are numbered in the sectional views of both the larger and the smaller vaults that intersect with their crowns at a common level. The joint between voussoirs 1 and 2 of the larger vault is of course radial; that between blocks 1 and 2 of the smaller vault is drawn as a horizontal because of the stilt. Yet the vertical height of the extrados (as well as that of the intrados) *must* be the same for block 1 in both sectional views It is not so shown in the drawing.

149. In general, cut stone vaults of accurately jointed ashlar were not constructed until the end of the Middle Ages. Actually they were an innovation, or at least a foreshadowing, of the Renaissance return to supposedly Classical patterns and practices. Thus all but one of the very large number of vaulting forms and conditions illustrated and described in Derand, *L'Architecture des voûtes ou l'art des traits et coupe des voûtes*, are of ribless vaults, with at times extremely complicated and geometrically arrived-at shapes with respect to the individual voussoirs. The one exception is of a rather simple quadripartite ribbed vault with tiercerons and ridge ribs over a square bay, to which Derand devotes only part of a plate (the upper half of p. 393) and two and a half pages of explanation (part iv, chap. 24, pp. 392, 394, 395). In this example of what he calls 'voûtes modernes ou à ogives', unlike his procedure in the case of so many of the other vaults he illustrates and explains, he does not bother to prescribe the stereotomy of the voussoirs. (*Vide* Willis, *Vaults*, pp. 14 and 15, for comment on Derand's and other early writers' misunderstanding of the nature and shape of Gothic vaults, due to their exclusive preoccupation with geometrically projected forms.)

150. In discussing the church of St-Maclou at Pontoise, Moore (p. 81) says that 'All survival of forms growing out of ancient modes of vaulting by interpenetrating geometrical surfaces have disappeared, and the skeleton of

ribs wholly determines the shape of the vault. Aubert (p. 62) speaks of very slender torus-moulded ribs that constitute 'no more than a skeleton facilitating the construction of a vault whose curvature they determine'.

151. As in the case, for example, of a conical vault surface intersecting the annular vault of each bay of the ambulatory aisle; which is a condition that may be seen in a number of Romanesque churches such as Conques, Selles-sur-Cher (Loir-et-Cher), Issoire, Notre-Dame-du-Port at Clermont-Ferrand, and St-Nicolas at Blois (Loir-et-Cher).

152. For a brief classification, *vide* Ward, *Mediaeval Church Vaulting*, chap. iv: 'Ambulatory Vaults', pp. 158–84.

153. The heavy vault of Durham is an early exception (in alternate bays where the transverse rib is omitted entirely); Bourges is a later French exception to the use of deep and heavy transverse arches.

154. Howard ('Fan-Vaults', p. 21) says that 'In the case of the thirteenth-century vault . . . the permanent function of the ribs is to stiffen the vault and prevent buckling, and the popular idea that they are arched girders carrying the webs is incorrect.'

Where exceptions to the presence of relatively heavy transverse ribs occur, there is invariably some explanation. For example, according to the architect in charge of reconstructing Soissons Cathedral after it was so badly damaged in World War I, the transverse ribs of the nave are identical in depth and in cross-section with those of the diagonals. Here the explanation is to be found partly in the excellent workmanship throughout, partly in the very massive and powerful abutments, but mostly in the considerable thickness of the vault: some 30 to 35 centimetres, or from 12 to 14 inches, in a clear span of about 38 feet (*vide* Brunet, 'La Restauration de la cathédrale de Soissons', pp. 92–93, including the dimensioned drawings in fig. 16:

'Profile of the rib-arches of the nave and of the side aisles').

155. The large photographic view, plate 82 in Houvet, which is taken looking directly up at the vault over the crossing at Chartres Cathedral, shows very clearly the excessive amount of concavity in each of the vaulting cells, particularly in their lower portions.

Vide Appendix F for some accounts of camber in Gothic vaults.

156. Watson (p. 48) clarifies this point as follows: 'We have seen that the diagonal or groin of the Romanesque vault was elliptical in outline; when, however, we substitute an independent arch for the angle of intersection of two curved surfaces, we may give the arch what form we please within certain limits. . . . The process of designing the vault is reversed, and in place of setting out the surfaces and leaving the groins to result from their intersection, we proceed by setting out the ribs and leave the surfaces largely to take care of themselves.'

Thus Aubert (p. 218) observes that 'The diagonal ribs . . . would always guide the masons charged with the job of building the vault webs'.

157. Viollet-le-Duc, article 'Construction', vol. iv, pp. 105–8 (pp. 144–7 in Huss).

158. Transversely from the formeret to the intersection of the groin ribs, or longitudinally along the crown in sexpartite vaults.

Choisy, who generally accepts the principles and follows the theories of Viollet-le-Duc, asserts that often the span of the courses turned out to be too great, and their rise too slight, for a movable cerce to have sufficed (Choisy, *Histoire*, p. 274). He does not, however, offer an alternative scheme.

159. In order to find a rough approximation of the weight of stonework imposed on one of the longer lagging units during the course of erection, the following assumptions

might be made: 20-foot length, average 9-inch thickness, and 9-inch width of web course near the crown; no support from contiguous course below; 150 lb./cubic foot for weight of limestone set in mortar. Using these data, a lagging unit near the crown of a transverse vault compartment would have to support $20 \times \frac{3}{4} \times \frac{3}{4} \times 150 = 1,687\frac{1}{2}$ lb., or considerably more than four-fifths of a ton.

160. Viollet-le-Duc, article 'Construction', vol. iv, p. 106, fig. 58 at A and B (Huss, p. 145).

161. Ibid., p. 107, lines 8–9.

162. A table giving the pressure of the vault stones against the formwork, depending on the angle their beds make with the horizontal, is given for intervals of every two degrees, from 34° to 60°, in both Tredgold (p. 187) and McMaster (p. 41). Tredgold goes on to say that 'When the plane of the joint becomes so much inclined that a vertical line passing through the centre of gravity of the arch-stone does not fall within the lower bed of the stone, the whole weight of the arch-stone may be considered as resting upon the centre, without any material error. . . . It is evident from an inspection of the table that the pressures increase very slowly till the joint begins to make a considerable angle with the horizon; and it is of importance to bear this in mind in designing centres, because the strength should be directed to the parts where the strain is greatest. For instance, at the point where the joint makes an angle of 44 degrees with the horizon, the arch-stone only exerts a pressure of one-fourth of its weight upon the centre; where the angle of the joint is 58 degrees, the pressure exceeds half the weight; but near to the crown the stone rests wholly upon the centre. . . .'

163. *Vide* Appendix G for discussion of the setting time of medieval mortar.

164. Salzman, plate 10, *a*, opp. p. 112.

165. Andrews, plate ix, with a commentary on p. 92.

For sixteenth-century examples, note the minutely detailed *Tower of Babel*, painted by Pieter Brueghel the Elder about 1565, which shows many erectional practices of the time, together with the equipment employed. For example, on the lowest level to the left, stacks of scaffolding poles are shown leaning against the foundation wall. To the right of this, a staged scaffolding is surmounted by a number of centering frames for an annular vault that is about to be built. Farther to the right, on the next story, are shown centering frames in face view, each with a support at mid-span which consists of a tall pole. Again, to the right of this and at the next level, are to be seen centering frames of larger span, also shown in frontal view and with central support. Farther to the right, and up another story, is a centering complex for a ramping barrel vault with some of its lagging in place. Scattered about the huge building elsewhere are centering frames that are still in place although the masonry has been completed above them. Spidery pole scaffoldings are to be seen here and there at all levels. There are a number of tall T-shaped cranes, as well as two great wheels—one, a huge double wheel with thick boom between—which are in process of raising large blocks. Ladders, wagons of various sorts, a windlass, suspended scaffoldings, baskets, levers, and other tools and equipment are depicted, along with a number of 'lodges' (and presumably 'tracing houses') for the workmen and the designers.

166. These little wedges may possibly have been used in the case of the much more carefully jointed rib voussoirs, especially in later Gothic work where these rib voussoirs came to be long, with many fewer joints around the arch ring than occurred in the web. Nevertheless, it is doubtful whether this practice was ever followed by the medieval masons, since the rib voussoirs would have been in place for a much longer time than the web stones, and

they would have been undergirt all this time by the rigid support of the rib frames.

167. Arthur Kingsley Porter, *The Construction of Lombard and Gothic Vaults*, p. 2.

168. Ibid., p. 2, &c. This assertion is reiterated no less than ten times on pp. 11–15 inclusive.

169. Ibid., p. 10. Porter's fig. 9 shows the vaulting of the choir in the church of St-Léger, Soissons.

170. Bond, *Gothic Architecture*, pp. 296–8, including the figs.

171. Bond, *Church Architecture*, p. 296.

172. Viollet-le-Duc, article 'Construction', vol. iv, p. 23, figs. 12 and 12 *bis* (p. 33 in Huss). These drawings have been reprinted or copied by many writers, including Bond, *Church Architecture*, p. 285, figs. 18, 19.

173. Willis (*Vaults*, pp. 3, 4 ff.) illustrates and comments on an early ribbed vault in which the rib sections are full and complete down to the springing. Because of differences in the spans of the longitudinal, diagonal, and transverse ribs, stilting of various amounts occurs; and some ribs (particularly the diagonals) are backed up by diaphragms of walling, with the spring of the vault webs at a much higher level.

Thus, although the formwork for the webs could not have been supported on the rib centerings, nevertheless these rib centerings could have been removed by the time the webs came to be constructed, because the diaphragm walling would have prevented any appreciable deformation of the stone ribs under gradual loading by the web courses as the vault was being built.

174. Viollet-le-Duc, 'De la construction des monuments religieux en France', *Annales archéologiques*, vol. vi, pp. 194 ff.

175. Something akin to this scheme of Viollet-le-Duc's appears to be indicated along the intrados of one of the vaults over the north side aisle in the ruined church of Longpont (Aisne). Here a rib has fallen away, revealing a zigzag interlocking of voussoirs. The blocks do not fit well, however, and there are large wedge-shaped joints where the blocks fail to abut each other, necessitating (1) stuffing these joints with mortar (which has fallen out, if it ever existed) and (2) covering them from view by means of the rib. The close-up photographic view given by Porter (*Lombard and Gothic Vaults*, fig. 35) is too faint, however, for the facets of the blocks to be discernible in revealing to what extent they were cut to fit against the extrados of the rib.

176. *Vide* Appendix H on the difficulties of stereotomy as illustrated by nineteenth-century oblique arches.

177. Aubert, op. cit., pp. 216–17, including notes.

178. For example, St-Léger, Soissons: vaults of choir (fig. 9 opp. p. 10 in Porter); La Madeleine, Vézelay: vaults of choir (fig. 66, p. 140 in Ward); St-Leu-d'Esserent: vault over tribune (illustration on p. 164 in Aubert).

179. Occasionally the beds of the lower courses slope the other way; that is, *upward* from diagonal to clerestory wall. This appears to happen sporadically and without systematic uniformity even in the same bay, let alone the same church. (This condition occurs, for example, above the spring of the south-east crossing pier of Sens Cathedral, in the left-hand vaulting compartment, looking west.) In this respect it perhaps reflects that restless inventiveness and experimentation so characteristic of medieval work, whether structural or decorative. That it was accidental or due to miscalculation appears unlikely in the case of high vaults, since too much was at stake there for there to have been haphazard or careless workmanship.

If there was a deliberate reason for this scheme it may have been that the courses were tilted so as to have them run more at right angles to the direction of the thrust in the lower portion of the vaulting conoid. In this way, the thrust of the main vault—the nave-spanning longitudinal one—would have been directed somewhat lower down and focused more positively against the solid block of the tas-de-charge. Where the courses of the lateral compartments followed the more frequent scheme of sloping *downward* towards the exterior, the tendency would have been, to some extent, to allow the thrust's resultant to pass towards the exterior *above* the tas-de-charge, thus aggravating the disruptive condition illustrated in Paquet, 'La Restauration de St-Leu-d'Esserent. Problèmes de stabilité', fig. on p. 14, where the lower or vault-resisting flying buttress impinges much too low against the clerestory wall.

180. *Vide* Appendix I for discussion of scaffolding: planks *v.* poles.

181. Somewhat akin to this scheme, though using metal, was one advanced in Heck (Text, vol. iv, division x: 'Technology', plate 8, figs. 35–40, &c.) as a complete innovation of the time. The text account reads in part as follows: 'A new system of bridge building recently come much into use should be here mentioned; it was invented by Laves, chief architect to the Court of Hanover. Laves had already invented a peculiar method of building beams, by which he had attained great strength at comparatively small cost. The girders were sawn longitudinally each way from the centre to within two feet from the ends, as seen in Fig. 35. At each end where the cut commences the girder is bound with iron rings, *a*, two inches wide and half an inch thick, to prevent the entire splitting of the timber. The two portions of the bridge were then driven apart by wedges, *b*, and a girder was obtained, having all the strength of a flat arch without the thrust, only wall plates *AB* being required to give the ends an even bearing. Shortly afterwards the inven-tor carried the idea further and constructed his girders of two timbers notched together at the ends, Fig. 36; as in the former case no abutments were required and no thrust was exerted. . . .'

See also the article 'Bow and String Beam' in the Architectural Publication Society's *Dictionary*, p. B-122.

182. We shall see subsequently, in the account of the rib centering frames, how the highest and longest of these lagging units could have been removed intact.

183. For example, Bond (*Church Architecture*, pp. 312–13) 'substantiates' his statement that sometimes vaults and their abutments were built before the roofs were constructed by *mis*-quoting Choisy (*Histoire*, p. 338), where just the opposite sequence is noted and discussed.

184. Fol. 31, verso (plate lxii, *Album de Villard de Honnecourt*).

185. Choisy, *Histoire*, pp. 337–8. There is a paraphrasing of Choisy's account of erectional procedures and their sequence, for Gothic churches, in Sturgis and Frothingham, *A History of Architecture*, vol. iii, pp. 20–21.

For Salisbury Cathedral, Price has analysed the sequence of the constructional steps for various parts of the building in considerable detail. One of his briefer passages reads as follows (p. 25): '. . . All the springing stones of the vaultings were inserted into the walls at the time of their being erected, and so left till the whole church was roofed and covered in; and then being defended from rains, etc. they fixed their principal ribs and groins, and turned over the vaultings, as having the weight of the superstructure to act instead of a buttment. . . .'

186. A modern example of one of these heavy, nave-spanning compression members is shown in the photographic illustration, fig. 254, p. 442 of Léon, as a temporary stay against

inward collapse, before restoration, in the case of the war-damaged church of Triel (Seine-et-Oise).

187. *Vide* Appendix J for discussion of tie-rods.

188. Viollet-le-Duc, article 'Chaînage', vol. ii, pp. 396–404.

189. Ibid., pp. 397–8.

190. Viollet-le-Duc, article 'Construction', vol. iv, p. 145, fig. 82 (p. 191 in Huss).

191. Another case of temporary wooden ties from spring to spring of the side aisles was found to have occurred in Soissons Cathedral. The head of one such tie was discovered intact at the time of rebuilding this badly damaged church after the First World War. Scale drawings of it and of its emplacement in a respond pier of the south side aisle, together with a brief account of it, are included in Brunet, 'La Restauration de la cathédrale de Soissons', pp. 81–83 and fig. 15.

In connexion with his discovery, the architect in charge of the work of reconstruction (doubtless paraphrasing Viollet-le-Duc) comments in a note (p. 82): 'In the twelfth and thirteenth centuries these ties were generally of wood, subsequently sawn off flush with the stone; later they were composed of an iron rod furnished with eyes arranged to fit over strong hooks anchored in the masonry.' Brunet further takes note of 'primitive iron *chaînages* 0·05 × 0·05 metres square [2 inches by 2 inches] with forked anchorages, dating from the beginning of the thirteenth century in Laon Cathedral; and also some iron anchorages sunk in the masonry and sealed in lead, in the cloister of St-Jean-des-Vignes at Soissons. The two dispositions, wood and iron, had been adopted in Soissons Cathedral; the first in the twelfth and thirteenth centuries; the second in the fourteenth, in the north arm of the transept.

Square voids at the springing, left by the removal of these temporary wooden ties of the side aisles, are evident in many of Houvet's photographs of Chartres Cathedral, such as plates 58, 60, 63 to 79 inclusive, and 89.

192. Viollet-le-Duc, article 'Chaînage', vol. ii, p. 402. The archivolt ties would have been useful in stiffening the structure longitudinally during erection. One of the reasons why the centerings were made double was so that they would not interfere with the tie-beams, which were in place both before the centerings were raised into position and long after they were struck.

For further discussion of iron as well as wooden ties, *vide* Appendix J.

193. Around the turn of the century, William H. Goodyear made studies of these departures from the vertical and other variations in the strictly geometrical and rectilinear layout of medieval churches, in such articles as those listed in the bibliography. Although few authorities have agreed with Goodyear's conclusions, his carefully measured data, substantiated by photographic illustrations, provide a record of the dimensional discrepancies encountered in some Gothic cathedrals.

Vide statement in Caroe (p. 24) regarding internally battered walls; also Powys and Wilson; and William Harvey, *St. Paul's*.

It would seem that most of the dimensional discrepancies and departures from geometrical accuracy in the existing structures of almost every medieval church in France are due in large part to the nature of the mortar and its excessively slow setting time (*vide* Appendix G). Thus Abraham (*Bull. mon.*, p. 71) remarks that 'The Gothic masonry was essentially deformable because the mortar employed remained plastic for a long time; but these deformations were permanent....' Later (p. 83) he explains that 'The "frightening deformations" noted by Viollet-le-Duc could take place without rupture because they were acquired progressively and insensibly during the slow period of the hardening of the mortar. The Gothic masonry, in its youth, was a soft wax wherein the imprint of the successive stresses resulting from the slow rate of construction was recorded for the future.'

194. Innocent (p. 78), in speaking of the erection of timber houses in the Middle Ages, says: 'The elaborate numbering of the mortice holes in many ordinary buildings is an indication that the mortice holes were cut and the timbers framed together provisionally on the ground.'

It seems reasonable to assume, in the case of the nave roofs of churches, that the same practice was followed in the preparation of the work as was done in the case of timber houses; namely, the wooden members were cut and notched, and then large sections of the framework were test-assembled on the ground; subsequently these sections were taken apart and the component members were hauled up to the roof level individually, where they were quickly and permanently reassembled.

195. *Vide* Appendix K for comparable problems encountered during the erection of the nave of Westminster Abbey.

196. Gilman, fig. 2, p. 50, fig. 6, p. 54, and fig. 18, p. 70.

197. Another example is photographically illustrated in Lasteyrie (vol. ii, p. 11, fig. 592), showing the ruined abbey church of Longpont (Aisne). Here the westernmost of the two western bays of the nave retains its high vault, but the eastern pier of the second bay is a lofty isolated pile, unstayed by either roof or vaulting, against which both an upper and a lower flying buttress remain intact.

198. For example, in the case of Notre-Dame at Dijon, noted at т, fig. 79 *bis*, in Viollet-le-Duc, article 'Construction', vol. iv, p. 139 (p. 185 in Huss); for Beauvais, at figs. 101 and 101 *ter*, pp. 178 and 181 (pp. 234 and 238 in Huss). *Vide* also, for St-Denis, article 'Arc', vol. i, p. 66, fig. 55.

199. It is possible that a temporary wall of masonry, constructed of bricks or small stones,

may have been employed to support the voussoirs of the flying buttress arches in lieu of wooden centerings during the course of their erection. A modern example of a thin diaphragm wall of masonry used as temporary formwork for the reconstruction of a flying buttress at Reims Cathedral is pictured in Léon, *La Vie des monuments français*, p. 497, fig. 314.

As may be seen in Léon's photographic illustration, this scheme dispenses with cradles and permits the minimum use of poles in a situation where poles would find little in the way of ready-made bearing on account of the sloping side-aisle roof, which would already have been built to protect the side-aisle vaulting from the weather. What few poles are used in this scheme are braced and tied into the temporary masonry—just as though it were a regular wall—by means of horizontal putlogs which could occur at any convenient intervals of height, to provide working platforms from which the masons could construct (or reconstruct, in the example illustrated) the flying buttress arches. Furthermore, such a diaphragm wall of masonry acts as a transverse stiffener, uniting clerestory wall to buttress mass and thus preventing any tendency of these two elements to lean towards each other during the course of erection, and assuring stability against any deformation, transversely with respect to the axis of the building, due to high winds or to any other causes.

Whether this scheme was ever used in Gothic times is impossible to determine at this distant time. Although its adoption entails certain distinct advantages, as indicated above, it would seem to be more appropriately employed for major repairs, as with a damaged or badly decayed building, than at the time of the original construction.

200. As indicated above, it seems quite clear that nave-spanning tie-rods would not have been needed during the course of construction, originally. It should perhaps be noted, however, that if they ever were used they would probably not have interfered completely

with the erectional operations there if, in accordance with our assumption, the bottom of the centering frames were set at a level just above the top of the tas-de-charge. Actually, any tie-rods would have been placed not at the spring of the vault (as is so often said) but at the bed joint of the highest of the tas-de-charge courses. In other words, they would range with the platform level, and would therefore be just below the area in which the centering frames would have been manœuvred, wedged up into position, decentered, and repositioned. They would nevertheless have been a nuisance with respect to the framing of the high platform's timber-work which would have had to be kept free and clear of them.

201. *Vide* Appendix L for comment on the pertinent passages in Suger's account of the construction of St-Denis.

202. The approximate heights, in feet, of some of the great Gothic cathedrals, from nave pavement to the top of the clerestory abacuses where the transverse and diagonal ribs took their springings, are as follows: Soissons 77, Paris 79, Chartres 79, Le Mans 88, Reims 88, Amiens 110, Beauvais 125½.

However, it should be noted that it was only at the top of the tas-de-charge, often many feet above these levels, that the joints became radial and the active vault commenced. In Reims, for example, where there are as many as ten courses of varying height in the tas-de-charge, the vault proper begins considerably more than 100 feet above the pavement.

203. Aubert (op. cit., p. 58) notes that '. . . most of these vaults were covered from the beginning with a coating on which false joint-lines were drawn . . .'; and (p. 160) '. . . the intrados of the vault was covered from the start with plaster on which was drawn in red paint a perfectly regular stone-jointing, whose beds are rigorously parallel to the ridge line'. *Vide* also his note, p. 218. An English account, describing much more lavish enrichment of the walls and vault sur-

faces by painting and gilding, is given in Lethaby (*Reëxamined*, pp. 204–7).

This customary medieval practice is not to be confused, however, with the nineteenth-century procedure reported in 1881 by G. G. Scott (*English Church Architecture*, p. 174), as follows: 'I cannot help observing here that the beauty of these wonderful French works is being systematically destroyed by the process, now in vogue throughout France, of *painting* the joints of the internal masonry in black or gray. This is as though one were to outline upon an antique statue (say, the Venus of the Capitol) the forms of the sub-cutaneous muscles. I can only account for this barbarous fashion by supposing that the sketches of M. Viollet-le-Duc are taken as the standard of beauty; and as these do not resemble the old work, the old work is to be made to resemble them.'

This latter practice is also noted, more recently, in Brunet (p. 88), where he speaks of 'The stone-jointing painted black, as executed some thirty years ago.'

204. A partial and occasional exception to this obvious inability of the falsework, below, to have been handled by any lifting devices located *above* the vault, may have occurred in those fairly frequent situations in which the common key of the two diagonal ribs was fashioned as a pierced block. This circular perforation through the single key-block should not be confused with the large openings rimmed with a ring of voussoirs which occur in tower vaults and sometimes in the center of the crossing vault, for raising bells through and above the vault. The pierced key-block nevertheless provided a fair-sized hole through which ropes could be let from above the vault; and these may have been utilized for helping to shift and lower the falsework assemblages, below.

205. Moles (*Histoire des charpentiers*, p. 335, fig. 475) illustrates a modern scaffolding of this type installed in the church of St-Jacques at Amiens, complete with a high

228

floored staging; showing how unencumbered the nave can be while work goes on above.

Vide also the photograph reproduced on p. 257 of 'Notes on the Historic Stained Glass Windows of Northern France', *Art and Archaeology*, vol. xxiii. This illustration shows one of the large timber trusses for this type of scaffolding being raised into position in Reims Cathedral, from a floor of planking laid on the nave pavement as protection while the work is in progress.

206. Viollet-le-Duc (article 'Armature', vol. i, p. 461) says: 'For carpentry-work, iron was employed only very late, and during the whole period of pointed architecture no use of it was made whatsoever. The carpenters of the Middle Ages up to the end of the sixteenth century did not seek any other combinations but those provided by a judicious employment of wood, without resorting to ironwork. All the great carpentry-work of old, including that of spires, is constructed without a single piece of iron: the tie-beams, the ridge-beams, the pendant keys, the armatures, all are solely of wood, without any bolts or metal plates. Even though the art of the iron-worker was called upon to co-operate with the masonry construction, it was absolutely excluded from carpentry-work, appearing solely in association with decorative lead-work.'

This non-use of metal, even for nails, is corroborated in England in the case of the sixteenth-century King's College Chapel roof, concerning which Mackenzie writes (p. 19) of '...the original work, in which no iron or nails were used'. His plate ii indicates the framing details of this collared and bracketed roof, with the tongued and multiple-pegged assemblage of its heavy members.

With respect to the open timber roofs of the Middle Ages, Brandon states (p. 32) that 'The material used for these roofs were either oak or chestnut, and the different timbers were always morticed and tenoned together, and fixed with wooden pins—no iron ties or straps, or even nails, being used in any part....'

Howard ('On the Construction of Mediaeval Roofs', p. 299) states that, at least for England, 'no iron-work is used in mediaeval roofs, save nails to fix the boarding to the rafters. The joints are made with the mortise and tenon, the slot and tenon, the halved or the notched joint, and are secured with wooden pegs only.'

Still another instance of the non-use of iron in a medieval example of English timber-framing is that reported by Willis with his customary accuracy and thoroughness. Speaking of the Sextry Barn at Ely (p. 6) he says: 'No ironwork of any kind was employed in the original framing; the ends of beams were united to the pieces against which they abutted, by mortice and tenon, and secured by pins from one half inch to an inch in diameter, as usual in this class of constructions. Whenever two beams crossed each other, they were half-notched together, greatly diminishing the strength of both. The long rafter *CD* is curiously employed in this framing, and by crossing and notching into the entire system of timbers, serves to bind together and stiffen the whole frame, in the absence of iron ties, in a very effectual manner.'

Although he mentions (p. 308) 'tree nails' (i.e. wooden pins or dowels), Salzman has much more to say about metal nails and spikes of many different sizes (pp. 304–16), including '*brags pro le scaffold*', 'scaffoldnaill', 'florneyl for planks', &c. It does not appear, however, that metal nails were customarily used in medieval France to anywhere near the extent they may have been employed in England, and especially not for falsework structures.

207. Practically the only exception to this non-use of the truss in medieval times was the so-called hammerbeam truss that was frequently employed in England, particularly in the open timber roofs of East Anglia. It would seem that the truss as such, however, was not clearly understood even here. Rather, the hammerbeams appear to have been conceived as short, diagonally braced beams projecting inward from the top of the nave walls in order to reduce the central span of the timbering, whose full-length rafters, from ridge to wall-

top, probably unintentionally and perhaps fortuitously gave rise to the truss action.

A more compelling structural reason why the medieval English builders adopted the hammerbeam 'truss' for their open timber roofs was that its particular scheme of framing provided a means of lowering any lateral pressure of the roof so that it acted as far down as possible against the lateral walls. For in England, as opposed to France, horizontal tie-beams stretching directly across from one wall-top to the other were rare, even in great cathedral roofs whose timber-work was hidden from view by the interposition of the stone vaulting. Lacking a direct tie, these roofs inevitably created a certain amount of spreading action that was brought to bear on the wall-tops precisely because the structure was *not* framed as a true truss.

This is doubtless the condition referred to as the 'thrust' of the roof by many writers. Theoretically, there is no structural thrust against the wall-tops in a properly designed roof truss when the bases of the rafters are prevented from spreading by the presence of indeformable triangles throughout the roof assemblage. Nor is there such a 'thrust' in the French Gothic roofs, where the heavy tie-beams link one wall-top directly to the other. Lateral thrust from wind action against a high-pitched roof, however, is quite a different matter, as we have seen.

The fact that there is no lateral pressure of a structural nature at the wall-top is amply demonstrated, in the case of Westminster Hall, by the models illustrated in figs. 21–23, p. 45, in William Harvey, *Models of Buildings*. The oblique thrust in this particular example (due to the composite arch) only 'enters the wall at corbel level', many feet below the wall tops.

In his excellent, detailed, and copiously illustrated article 'On the Construction of Mediaeval Roofs', Howard makes pertinent comments on the joints and the framing of timber-work, indicating (p. 300) that the carpenters designed their trussless roofs so that 'as many members of a mediaeval roof as possible are arranged so as to be in compression or cross-strain', not

in tension. This came about due to the essential weakness in tension of medieval pegged joints, for 'without ironwork, trussing is practically impossible'. With regard to the triangulation basis of modern trusses, Howard writes as follows (p. 302):

'It is a well-known fact that a rectangular framework is a deformable structure, while a triangular framework is absolutely rigid. Therefore modern roof principals [i.e. the transverse frames] are divided up into triangles to insure rigidity. It is generally accepted that elasticity of structure and the balance of opposing thrusts are the leading principles of mediaeval construction, and it is not surprising to find that no such principle of triangulation was employed by the mediaeval carpenters, who preferred to stiffen their roof timbers with the aid of angle-brackets, braces and struts.'

208. An almost universal instance of this scheme of doubling members for stiffness occurs in countless medieval roofs, where the principal rafters are doubled in the direction of their vertical plane.

209. Viollet-le-Duc gives a plan view of the carpentry assemblage for a spire in fig. 11, a section view in fig. 12, and a perspective detail in fig. 15, article 'Flèche'.

210. *Vide* Bartlett, p. 279; and Thatcher, p. 88.

211. Cf. Moles, Trouvelot, Schmidt, *et al.*

212. Vol. cvii.
An interesting example of another 'primitive' structure of wooden members is that reported in *The Engineering News*, 1 July 1909, vol. lxii, p. 19, figs. 1 (a photograph) and 2 (an elevation drawing). It is a 140-foot bridge over a gorge in British Columbia, said to have been built by Indians. A correspondent writes about it: '. . . The bridge is built of round poles fastened together with telegraph wire and wooden pins, the floor being

the only part where nails are used to any extent. . . . Looking at it from a distance it seems to be nothing but a collection of poles and wire stuck together any way, with no particular reason for its not falling; the floor is very uneven and the joints of the different members are made by lapping and binding them with wire; . . . no two joints are made alike. . . . [But it has served] as a means for pack trains to cross the Bulkley River. . . .'

213. Brigham (*The Ancient Hawaiian House*, p. 84) remarks that 'In most of the woods enumerated as preferred for house building it was important to cut away all the sap-wood to insure durability of the posts.' Caroe (pp. 129–30) discusses the reasons why sap-wood should be removed.

214. For example, Ricketson, 'American Nail-less Houses in the Maya Bush'; Brigham, op. cit., particularly pp. 77–78, 79, 85–86, 102, also fig. 82 and plates xxvi, xxvii; and, with commendable clarity and in considerable detail via text, drawings, and photographs, in Wauchope, *Modern Maya Houses*, as follows: text, pp. 57–60; drawings, p. 31, fig. 12 *a–d*, p. 59, fig. 17 *a–j*, p. 62, fig. 18; plates 9 *b, c,* and 10 *a–e.*

215. An example of primitive framing for an arch centering is shown photographically in *The National Geographic Magazine*, Nov. 1940, vol. lxxviii, p. 640. This view is of a culvert-like masonry bridge of perhaps 30-foot span, built in 1938 along the Burma Road in China at a time when no modern equipment was available. It shows seven heavy, unsquared struts fanning up from a horizontal bottom timber that spans the semicircular arch at its springing. The cradle's curving rib segments are thin compared to the struts, and these segments appear to be fitted into a notch cut out of the top of the struts. The number of parallel frames is not evident in the photograph, but there must be many of them set quite close together, for the lagging (whose ends protrude) is light compared to the thickness of the arch ring.

Vide Appendix M for a nineteenth-century analysis of methods of framing timber centerings for simple arch ribs.

216. Detail drawings of criss-crossing centering frames are given in *The Engineering News*, 14 Apr. 1910, vol. lxiii, p. 424, fig. 4, for the concrete formwork of an extensive groin-vaulted underground water filter plant. But these modern centering frames are for the sides and diagonals of only 12-foot-square bays, and they make use of metal bolts, plates, and tie-rods.

Photographic illustrations in Brunet (p. 79, fig. 11) and in Rauline (p. 19) show centerings in place for the diagonal ribs of side aisles during construction, but these do not reveal the scheme of their framing on account of their small size, the distance at which the photographs were taken, and especially the angle of vision.'

Warland (fig. 228 between pp. 74 and 75) gives a photographic illustration of the converging centering frames for a half-dome of cut stone some 35 to 40 feet in diameter, with approximately radial strutting. But the condition at the converging crowns is not disclosed.

One of the most impressive photographs of converging and criss-crossing centering frames is given in Cotton, *Liverpool Cathedral*, as plate xxx, entitled 'Wooden Centering for the Under-Tower Vault'. This is such a huge and intricate complex of timber-work, however, that it is hard to decipher in the unfinished state of the carpentry assemblages it illustrates; that is, not all the rib centers are presently in place, some are without their cleats, and modification for projecting bosses at the rib intersections is as yet unprovided for.

217. *Vide* Appendix N for comment on the tower vault in the medieval church at Lärbro, Sweden, and its still existing original centering.

218. *Vide* Appendix O for comment on the need for non-continuous rib frames and the probability of their having been worked out via models.

219. The half barrel vault over Roman-esque side aisles is evidence of the medieval builders' familiarity with the use of half-arch frames and half-arch formwork from a time long before the Gothic complications of false-work came about.

In this instance it should be noted that the lower portion of the vault—probably up to the angle of friction, roughly—would have had to be built integrally with the outer wall; that is, before the formwork for the half barrel vault was set in place. A full quadrant of false-work could not have been employed here (if of wood rather than of tamped earth), because there would have been no clearance for its removal, upon completion of the vault. To allow for the decentering and removal opera-tions, the span of the formwork structure had to be made less than the span of the void to be vaulted (analogous to 21 c). Consequently, as

frames for centering the intersecting diagonal ribs of Gothic vaulting.

220. It is perhaps at least partial corrobora-tion of this gap between the two units of a pair of half-frames that late French Gothic vaulting sometimes has a deeply pendent key-stone at the intersection of the diagonal ribs. This would of course have been impossible to manage if the rib frames had been continuous without a break under the crown.

221. *Vide* Appendix P for Watson's dis-cussion of raising building materials in medieval times.

222. In the lining of tunnels, where the con-finement of space necessitates such a procedure, we read as follows in McMaster (pp. 94–97): 'Tunnel centres again differ from those of

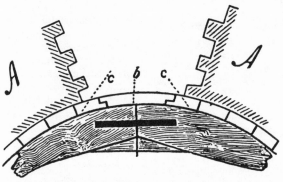

Figure 73

a factor in determining the less-than-quadrant extent of the formwork structure, this decen-tering requirement was quite as significant as either the desire to economize on falsework or the practical need to lighten the weight of the temporary erection as much as possible.

This obvious use of less-than-quadrant frames at an early date in Romanesque vault-ing suggests that there could not have been any great unusualness or unprecedented inno-vation on the part of the builders when they were subsequently called upon to employ half-

bridges in that the laggings are very differ-ently adjusted. In the latter case it is the custom in practice to place all the laggings on the ribs before commencing to turn the arch, by which means no small degree of stability is given to the ribs. In tunneling, however, where only a few inches of space remains between the back pieces of the frame and the poling which sus-tains the earth, it would be utterly impossible to turn the arch if *all* the laggings were put in place before the brick-work is begun. To over-come this difficulty, only a few laggings, say five or six, are placed at a time. Thus, starting at the springing line, we adjust six laggings on each side of the frame, and carry the arch up equally on both sides. When it has reached the upper bolster, we add six more, and the masonry continued as before, and proceed in this way until very near the crown as shown in Fig. 8 [73 above], where AA' is the brickwork. At this stage of the work the two laggings CC' are placed on the ribs, the top of their inner edges being first rabbeted as shown in the figure. In these rabbets "*cross*" or "*keying-in*" laggings B, consisting of stout planks 18 or 20 inches in width, are laid one at a time beginning at one end of the centring. The brick-layer whose duty it is to key-in the arch stands with his head and shoulders between the brick-work A, A, and starting at the end of the last piece of completed arch places the first *cross* lagging, and keys in the arch over it; then a second, and in like manner keys in the arch over it, and thus retreats along the entire opening until the whole length of the arch is keyed in.'

223. Cf. note 192.

224. Only a single frame would have been needed, of course, for each flying buttress arch, for here there were no vaulting compartments to be sustained.

225. The often reproduced photograph of falsework high up under the vaulting of St-Vulfran, Abbeville (appearing, for example, as fig. 516, p. 357 in Moles), is a curious and untypical instance in modern times of some of the points under discussion.

First, there is a continuous planked floor, but this appears to be supported on the lower chords of the centering assemblages and on other horizontal beams framed into these bottom chords. Contrary to this arrangement, we have assumed that in medieval times the flooring would have provided a working staging on which the rib frames could be manœuvred into position, set up on wedges, and subsequently shifted to a new position.

The frames of this example are double, to be sure, but they and their laggings continue all the way down to the spring of the arches, below the floored staging. In contrast to this, we have noted how the medieval builders could have economized on centering by providing frames only from the level of the angle of friction, above the top of the tas-de-charge. (This is doubtless explained by the fact that at St-Vulfran the modern centerings were installed primarily to prevent further deformation or collapse in the transverse arches of the high vault until permanent steps could be taken to abut and tie the clerestory piers. Thus the problem illustrated is one of preservation and reparation rather than of original construction.)

As the illustration reveals, only the transverse ribs are provided with centering frames, and these are so wide that there is obviously no possibility of seating a diagonal frame for the groin rib. Hence these transverse centerings appear to be part of a temporary reinforcing system inside the church—a kind of shoring up of the transverse arches, as it were—installed so as to relieve the strain on the temporary tie-rods below, and so as to maintain the vault shape while the external abutment undergoes repair and strengthening.

This latter assumption regarding the function of the centering frames is perhaps corroborated in this instance by the serried assemblage of very heavy lagging blocks which constitute the cleating of the timber frames. It would seem that they do not need to be so heavy, since apparently they are not destined to support lagging for the vault webs.

Another modern instance of the shoring of a Gothic vault while repairs and replacements of its foundations were undertaken is described and illustrated in Bartlett's article on 'Shoring' in vol. xxiv of the *Encyclopaedia Britannica*, 11th edn. The brief descriptive account, on p. 1007, together with the revealing pen-and-ink illustrations (fig. 7 for the exterior view showing raking shores; fig. 8 for the complicated supports of the vaulting) are concerned with the replacement and reconstruction of the foundations for the retro-choir and Lady Chapel of Winchester Cathedral in England, which were works carried out in 1906.

For another high continuous floored staging of modern times viewed from above, *vide* the photograph in Cotton, *Liverpool Cathedral*,° plate xxxi, entitled 'Under Western Transept Crossing'. Here the vault has been finished, and its falsework has been dismantled and removed, revealing the continuous flooring at the level of the vault spring.

See also the photograph on p. 17 of Paquet, 'La Restauration de St-Leu-d'Esserent'.

226. For the stonework itself (the lagging is not indicated), even the careful drawings of Forsyth show the bias cut of the web stones as they come in to meet the groin rib, but no dihedral (that is, no bevel, below).

227. Williams and Williams (*Old American Houses and How to Restore Them*, p. 131) state that 'Some houses of 1700 have the floor boards fastened to the joists with pegs, but by that time the use of nails was becoming common.'

228. The structural or supporting lagging (as opposed to mere guiding members to facilitate the alignment of the stones in certain web courses) would not have had to commence as low down in the lateral cells as it had to in the longitudinal cells, because of the high stilting of the window arches or formerets.

229. *Vide* note 162.

230. Not all of these full-sized working drawings (*épures*) were laid out on a level plastered surface on the ground. We read in du Ranquet, *La Cathédrale de Clermont-Ferrand*, p. 73, that the architect planned to have the usual sloping roofs over the side aisles and their chapels, but that these roofs 'were kept as flat terraces in order to make use of their areas as a table where working drawings were traced out at full size: some

of them are still visible and deserve to be examined with care'.

At Reims and at Limoges there are other full-sized drawings incised in the permanent fabric of the building. For example, *vide* H. Deneux, 'Signes lapidaires et épures du XIIIᵉ siècle à la cathédrale de Reims', *Bull. mon.*, 1925, pp. 99 ff.; and Félix de Verneilh, 'Construction des monuments ogivaux: Épures de la cathédrale de Limoges', *Annales archéologiques*, 1847, vol. vi, pp. 139–44. Other examples are to be found in Willis, *Vaults*; Viollet-le-Duc, *Dictionnaire*; and elsewhere.

231. This method of securing two quadrant arcs of centering, as applied to nineteenth-century tunnelling operations, is illustrated in McMaster (p. 86, fig. 6) and described on pp. 84–85. Although the author indicates how the two half-frames are keyed against slipping vertically under the crown, he does not explain how the two frames are removed, for relocation elsewhere. This would have to be done, after the decentering, by sliding one of the two half-frames a foot or so longitudinally (at right angles to its span); that is, by displacing one of them out of their common vertical plane, so that it no longer abutted its mate in this plane.

This procedure is easily managed in barrel vaults of any form, but it could not have been done in the case of the diagonal frames of Gothic ribbed vaulting. For, because of the closely adjacent seating of a transverse rib frame (and perhaps a wall rib frame as well), there was no room at the springing to move one of the half-frames of the diagonal rib at right angles to its span. The most that could have been done in this instance (provided there was clearance enough at the crown, due to the size and arrangement of the crown cradle unit) would have been to pivot the half-frame at its lower end and swing it horizontally free of the other converging half-frames at their meeting under the crown, in the direction of the transverse arch.

At least in some instances, the clearance would not have been sufficient to free one of the diagonal half-frames in this fashion; and the procedure seems too indirect and complicated to have been adopted by the builders of the high Gothic vaults.

232. Viollet-le-Duc (article 'Charpente', vol. iii, p. 57) acknowledges that 'Timber framing is an art to which modern perfectionings have added little: it was during the fifteenth century that it reached its consummate development.' He says: 'One of the special characteristics of the art of timber framing in the Middle Ages was its freedom of action, its knowledge of different kinds of wood and its respect, we might say, for their properties. The timber-work assemblages of the Middle Ages merit scrupulous study. They are uncomplicated and well-proportioned to the strength of the wood or to the particular purpose they have to perform. The foresight that made provision for some reinforcement in a long timber, some buttressing support by which the strength of the assemblage might be augmented; the choice of timbers or their location with respect to the position they were to occupy; the care lest they should be engaged within the masonry instead of being left exposed for the air to circulate around them: all these considerations indicate, on the part of the master carpenters, a perfect understanding of their art, a study of and attention to the qualities of the materials they used.'

'So, too, the rightness and the proper proportioning of the assemblages indicate a long-established habit of good building practice. The medieval carpenters did not call upon the aid of the iron-worker in order to bind together, stay, or fasten the wooden members he assembled in the work, except in certain particular and rare cases. On the contrary, the carpenter was sufficient unto himself, and iron did not have to make up for the inadequacy or the weakness of the assemblages, as in modern timber-work.'

233. Heck (vol. iv, division x: 'Technology', p. 40) states that 'Fig. 23 [plate 7] represents Westminster bridge in process of building, together with its centrings. The latter are supported upon a great number of wedges,

that any particular portion requiring it may be tightened, and ultimately to facilitate the removing of the centrings when the work is completed.'

In connexion with the levelling and the alignment of the centering frames in a Gothic cathedral, vide W. A. Nicholson for a description, and J. B. Papworth for a possible explanation, of the slender stone arch of very slight rise between the western towers of Lincoln Cathedral in England.

234. McMaster explains in detail both the nature of the decentering wedges and the way in which they can minutely control the decentering process, provided the supports for them are unyielding. Here, in part, is what he says (pp. 71–74):

'. . . The folding wedges are, perhaps, most commonly met with in practice, and are finely suited for arches of small span, as a sill stretching from abutment to abutment may then be used to rest them on. They consist of two hardwood wedges, about 15 in. long, right angled along one edge, and placed one upon the other, thus making their surface of contact an inclined plane. These wedges are placed under the tie beam of the rib and on the sill. It is evident that by driving the upper wedge up along the inclined surface of the lower, the rib which rests upon the upper one must rise, so that by placing a number of these folding wedges under each rib it may easily be keyed up to the desired level, and by driving the upper down the inclined surface of the lower, the rib may gradually be lowered.'

'To keep the under wedge in place, it is usually made fast to the sill, and the surface of contact of each wedge well greased with soft-soap and black lead. When the wedges are in place under the rib, it is good practice to mark each wedge at the point where contact ceases, so that when the centers are being lowered we may be able to know whether they are lowered uniformly or not. For instance, let the lower wedges of three pair of folding wedges project two inches beyond the end of the upper ones, and mark with chalk on the *side* of each lower wedge the point where contact ceases; namely, two inches from its end. Now, if in striking the centres the upper wedges have *all* been driven back so that the *end* of each instead of being *at* the line is one inch *beyond* it, then the frame has been uniformly lowered; but if some are one inch and some ¾ inch from the line, the frame has not been lowered uniformly, and the difference must be corrected by driving *all* the wedges till they are one inch from the chalk line.'

'It is evident that such an arrangement of folding wedges can be of but little use unless the horizontal beam or sill on which they rest is rigidly supported from beneath, as any yielding of the sill would be followed by a separation of the wedges and rib. In constructing bridges of wide span over creeks or rivers on which there is no navigation to be interrupted, it is usual to make use of the folding wedges and support the sill by a row of piles driven into the river bed, and it then becomes especially necessary to watch the wedges lest by some settling of the piles and sill they have separated in the smallest degree from the tie beam of the rib.'

235. Photographic illustrations of modern examples of pole scaffolding that is continuous throughout the whole interior are given in Schmidt at fig. 169, p. 120 (for a cinema); and at fig. 328, p. 224 (for a church).

236. *Vide* note 205.

Examples of modern rolling scaffolding furnished with a high platform of one bay length are shown in Schmidt, both photographically and in drawings, at figs. 210 and 211, pp. 146, 147 (for a church); figs. 212–14, pp. 149–51, as well as figs. 215 and 219, pp. 152, 155 (for an auditorium in a museum); figs. 216, 217, 218, and 220, pp. 153–5 (for a manufacturing plant).

237. Very few illustrations seem to have been published of interior scaffoldings hung from the walls of the nave on either side without taking support from the floor below. One isolated example that appears to be little more

than a bridge walk-way set above the clerestory sill level, and less than one bay in extent, is photographically illustrated in Bumpus, opposite p. 260, in Troyes Cathedral.

Another isolated example of lofty hung falsework—this one, of arch centering alone —is shown in the vertical upward view of a double frame of falsework straddling one of the transverse arches of the high vault of St-Vulfran, Abbeville, in Simpson, vol. ii, fig. 18 opp. p. 121: in this case the diagonal struts at either side are bracketed out from a level well above the clerestory string.

But apparently only Brunet ('La Restauration de la cathédrale de Soissons', plate opp. p. 80) shows a scaffolding of the sort we have suggested: a number of bays in extent, with a high platform about the level of the clerestory sill, and supported by raking struts from the triforium passage.

238. *Vide* note 202.

239. This condition may be what is referred to as 'the three scaffolds, the lower, higher and highest', mentioned in Rackham (p. 68), although this, being an English example, would undoubtedly have used much more extensive falsework than in French practice. The photographic view in Moles (fig. 475, p. 335) shows a modern two-tier scaffolding for the fairly small church of St-Jacques in Amiens, with a high platform completely floored over, and supported below by canted legs that free practically the entire width of the nave from all falsework encumbrance. For heavy, many-tiered underpinning construction, rather than high-scaffolded working platforms, see the photographic illustrations of falsework employed under the main crossing arches of Rouen Cathedral during the reconstruction of that badly damaged church: these appear in Chauvel, 'Les Destructions, le sauvetage', figs. 20, p. 68, 27, p. 74, 30, p. 76, and 31, p. 77.

240. *Vide* note 206 and the last paragraph of note 232.

241. Viollet-le-Duc, article 'Échafaud', vol. v, p. 109, fig. 5, indicates a few lashed connexions on an otherwise keyed and framed assemblage of squared members.

242. For example, Salzman writes (p. 320) that 'For the scaffolding at Windsor in 1368 as many as 185,000 'twists' of withies were bought.' Compare with this the small quantities of hurdles mentioned in similar documents: the numbers quoted by Salzman are 24, 6, and 4.

Although Salzman specifically states (p. 318) that 'on these short logs [the putlogs] lay the platform, composed of hurdles, instead of the planks now used', there appears to be some confusion and uncertainty with respect to this interpretation. A number of the medieval manuscript illustrations distinctly show the elevated platforms on which the masons are working to be of *planking*. (*Vide* Salzman, plate 14 opp. p. 209, where two such are clearly illustrated; also Colombier, plate ix, no. 16; xii, no. 20 (where a ladder is supported from one of the platform levels); xv, no. 25 (a repetition of Salzman's plate 14); xx, no. 35; xxv, no. 42; and xxxii, no. 56). Other illustrations that show scaffolding (e.g. in Colombier) are at too small a scale or at too flat an angle of view for one to be able to determine the nature of the material making up the scaffolding platforms. Only one (Colombier, plate xix, no. 34) gives clear indication of a hurdle of rods and woven wattle (*vide* Appendix K for other uses to which hurdles were put in building construction, in England).

There is a very clear indication of planks used for workmen's scaffolding platforms in the late medieval example given in Phleps, 'Mittelalterliche Gerüstbauten', p. 112, fig. 123. This illustration reproduces part of the very realistic and detailed painting that embellishes the 'Pacherscher Hochaltar in St. Wolfgang', and shows long, wide planks supported only by poles set horizontally through the wall, unaided by diagonal struts or any kind of bracing from below.

Not all of this should be taken literally, however. For instance, the stone frame and tracery of a rose window are shown completely finished although the wall that is being constructed in horizontal courses below this window has risen as yet only up to the base of it! As for this latter, it was apparently not unusual for painters, particularly in the Renaissance period, to leave unfinished certain portions of a painting which they had sketched out only in terms of ruled lines and light under-painting. This example from St. Wolfgang may be a case in point, but it none the less indicates that not all the pictorial evidence in a contemporary drawing or painting can be accepted at its face value.

It is just possible that the small number of hurdles mentioned by Salzman (about which one of his quotations reads 'for the masons to stand upon') were additional, free members that could be set up on some sort of blocks or 'lifts', a foot or so higher than the scaffolding platform of planks or hurdles that supported them. By their means the masons would not have had to lay stones above the level of their heads at each stage just before another stage was reached; and perhaps, in the case of pole scaffolding, the platform stages themselves could have been established at greater intervals than they would otherwise have needed to be. (More than normal spacings seem to be indicated in some of the manuscript illustrations: e.g. Colombier, plates xiii, no. 22, and xxi, no. 37; also Andrews, plate xi.) In modern times where fixed scaffoldings are still used rather than tubular steel scaffolding or adjustable stagings hung from above on cables, it has been common practice to raise the worker somewhat above the platform level, as occasion warrants, by supplementary planks set up on blocks or low horses.

243. William Eton, *A Survey of the Turkish Empire*, 2nd edn. 1799 (quoted in Lassaux, note on p. 224).

244. Choisy, *L'Art de bâtir chez les Byzantins*, fig. 66, p. 61 &c. Described also in Lassaux, p. 240; Hess, p. 86; *et al.*

245. Vilhjalmur Stefansson, *The Friendly Arctic*, 1921, pp. 172–9.

246. Choisy, *L'Art de bâtir chez les Byzantins*, figs. 31–39, &c., pp. 33–37 ff.

247. Somewhat analogous to this scheme, apparently, is that described in the *Architectural Dictionary*, p. G-91, under the term 'Gueesh': 'In Minorca a species of gypsum called gueesh is used, which indurates so very quickly that, in turning arches with it, the use of regular centering is dispensed with, each set of arch-stones being supported by reeds or wooden rods until the keystone is introduced, after which those temporary props, extending throughout the whole width of the arch, are removed and used for supporting another set of arch stones. Thus the arch, which is commenced at one end, is continued in portions, until the whole is completed. In using this cement, the outside joints of adjacent stones being secured with common mortar, the gueesh in powder is stirred up in a bucket with water, until it becomes well mixed but in a fluid state, after which it is poured into all the joints, which are previously scored for the purpose crossways. This cement sets almost instantaneously, and eventually becomes harder than the stone itself, but it must be carefully secured from wet, which renders it useless by reducing it to a pulp. For arches or partition walls protected by a roof nothing can be better;. the latter are often built with stones only 3 or 4 ins. thick set on edge, which are sufficiently strong when cemented in the manner that has been described; Pasley, *Outline of Pract. Arch.*, 4to, lithog., Chatham, 1826, p. 16. It is not stated whether there is any difference between this and the ordinary plaster of Paris.'

248. Among the many published illustrations of circular houses of dry-wall stonework in Ireland, one of the clearest photographs, taken close up, is that in *Art and Archaeology*, Mar. 1923, vol. xv, p. 133, fig. 9, labelled 'Beehive Huts at Fahan, County Kerry'.

The Irish use of this system appears to ante-

date the introduction of Christianity there by some two centuries. *Vide* Stokes, *Early Christian Art in Ireland*, part. ii, pp. 29–33, including the drawings: fig. 69, p. 31, 'Oratory, Gallarus', the best preserved of all rectangular examples in Ireland; and fig. 75, p. 37, 'Monastic Cell, Skelling Michael', a circular example of dry-wall corbelling with intermittently projecting stones in the upper portion of the exterior. Both of these examples are found in south-western Ireland, in County Kerry.

Vide the article 'Clochan' on Irish structures of this corbelled type, in the Architectural Publication Society's *Dictionary of Architecture*, C-103, 104.

249. *Vide The National Geographic*, Jan. 1955, vol. cvii, p. 142, where the caption reads 'Windowless houses in beehive shape shelter Aymaras in the Rio Ramis region. Built of sod [?], such houses can endure 50 years. . . .'

250. G. E. Kidder Smith, *Italy Builds: Its Modern Architecture and Native Inheritance*, 1954, pp. 32–33. See also photographic illustrations of south Italian *trulli* in Glück, figs. 135–9, opp. p. 216.

251. Anonymous article in *The Architects' Journal*, 11 Apr. 1946, p. 284.

252. Albert Chauvell, 'La Cathédrale de Rouen: Les destructions, le sauvetage', *Les Monuments historiques de la France*, avr.–juin 1956, nouv. sér., vol. ii, no. 2.

253. *Vide* note 158.

Quite recently the following statement regarding the use of the cerce has been made by J.-P. Paquet, 'Structures des monuments anciens et leur consolidation', p. 174: 'Again, nothing can replace such a simple technique as that of the cerce, which is always employed nowadays because by its use the most important vaults can be built without centering.' Yet the 'most important vault' he illustrates (fig. 19, p. 173) is that of a side aisle, not a nave. Moreover, there appear to be two cerces side by side in his photograph, as though one were left in place under its completed row of web stones while those of the current course are being laid; and the cerces are hung radially instead of vertically, in opposition to Viollet-le-Duc's specific instructions. Thus there would still seem to be some misunderstanding about the way in which the cerce is hung and operated, and some confusion about the extent to which it is applicable to wide-span vaults.

254. This is apparently an attempt to give a French form to, but is also a misspelling of, the name Johann Claudius Lassaulx.

According to the author himself (*vide* pp. 159–60 of his 'Notes on the Churches of the Rhine', in Whewell's *Architectural Notes on German Churches*, 3rd edn.), the descriptive account of his rediscovery of the technique of building light vaults without formwork was published that same year (1831) in Paris, in the *Journal du génie civil*, and it also appeared in the fourth part of Crell's *Architectural Journal*. Thus it is all the more surprising that this extremely significant account, having appeared in three languages, made no impact upon the architectural literature of the time, but apparently dropped out of sight immediately and has had to be rediscovered and exhumed these many generations later.

Occasionally, in the mid- to late-nineteenth-century books, there is an obscure citing of this method of vault erection (as in the one-sentence reference in Breymann, I, pp. 191–2), but only in connexion with dome construction in brick, never for vault construction in stone.

255. With respect to the irregularity of the vault surfaces in one specific building, *vide* Bond's statement (*Gothic Architecture*, p. 299) quoted in Appendix F, about the extraordinary 'twisting and contortion' of the vaulting in St-Quentin.

It may well be that some of the 'frightening deformations' in vaulting that were noted by Viollet-le-Duc were largely if not wholly

irregularities of the masonry web coursing from the start, rather than subsequent distortions due to uneven settlement or some such cause. Certainly the unsymmetrical contours, the exaggerated concavities, and the conspicuous irregularities of the crossing vault at Chartres Cathedral (shown in Houvet's photographic plate 82) could have resulted *only* from the 'freehand' practice of constructing the vault webs, as described by Lassaux. For here, as also in the early vaults cited in note 178, the stone courses are far from being perfectly regular: they are sometimes, in Porter's words, quite 'irregularly disposed . . . , one stone being cut to fill an odd-shaped opening between two others, courses twisting and dying away, at times frankly broken'.

It is hard to believe that any of these irregularities could have happened except in a freehand scheme of laying the masonry courses of the vault, as with the stone-weighted rope device. The significant change, as we have noted elsewhere, would have come about when the critical shift was made from laying the vault masonry from above, on continuous formwork, to laying the web courses from the side, without formwork. From the earliest vaults constructed by the latter technique we can follow the progressive improvement in the experience and skill of the masons, through their less clumsy efforts, to those mechanically expert and visually regular web coursings of such accomplished high vaults as those of Bourges, Amiens, Rouen, and the choir of Le Mans.

256. Actually, because all the falsework needed to construct a bay of vaulting above these stagings (thanks to the stone-weighted rope device) was now only the light centering for the diagonal and transverse ribs, these could be accommodated on one of the 7-foot-wide gantry platforms that have previously been noted (64), when the time came to shift the rib centerings from one bay to the next. Stacking these pairs of quadrant frames side by side on one such gantry would have freed the adjacent gantry so that its members could

be dismantled and reassembled at the next pier interval. A new bay-length platform that included this 7-foot-wide unit could then be established, the centering frames set up as before, and the erection of first the ribs then the web of another bay of vaulting undertaken.

However, this takes into account only the *construction* of the vault, not its plastering and decoration. If these latter operations were to have been done without the subsequent erection of separate scaffolding, the three gantry units as described above, rather than the two units as suggested here, would have been required.

APPENDIX A

Annotated Bibliography of Falsework Literature

W H A T makes the lack of coverage of falsework subjects so incomprehensible today is the modern practice of letting contracts on the basis of competitive bids. For, since all the bids submitted are computed from the same working drawings and the same voluminous and highly detailed specifications, it is largely on the matter of the temporary structures by means of which the project is brought into being that success in submitting the lowest bid, and therefore being awarded the contract, is won. It is in the organization of the sequence of the work, the efficiency of the various operations, and, above all, in the economy of materials and labour involved in the design of the temporary structures, that real brilliance in planning and the imaginative solutions to sometimes unprecedentedly difficult problems of layout and operation pay off. Yet although there are brief case histories on how these problems have been solved in certain specific instances, there are no books that deal substantially with the general principles or even the practical methods to be followed in working out the most efficient and economical solutions to the kind of problems that are likely to be encountered, either today or for the past. And apparently the engiheering schools, if they deal with the matter at all, give only the most token and cursory attention to falsework problems in their curriculums.

In his stimulating and optimistic discussion of contemporary design, Walter Dorwin Teague (*Design This Day*, p. 229) reminds us that 'the solution of any problem is good only for that problem, but the method of working out the solution may have a lot to teach us'. What is unaccountably lacking in our libraries, periodicals, and reference books is any treatise or analysis that deals with 'the method of working out the solution' to problems of scaffolding and centering.

There are very few books indeed that deal specifically with the subject of falsework structures. Unless Krafft's collection of plates is included, there are apparently only two books devoted to *scaffolding*. The more recent of these is Karl Schmidt, *Die Baugerüste*, 1949, with 382 pp., 406 photos and drawings. This book, which covers the contemporary scene in Germany, is neither an historical account nor a treatise on how to solve problems of layout and arrangement, but a technical handbook concerned with all practical aspects of scaffolding and shoring from the standpoint of modern usages, materials, quantities, safety regulations, local ordinances, &c. Although the examples

241

and solutions are all recent—of the post-World-War-II era—some of the schemes are applicable, with modifications, to what may have been the practices of the Middle Ages. In any case, the many drawings and photographs of details and ensembles alike are interesting and illuminating, particularly the numerous examples that illustrate pole scaffolding with its various connexions and means of attachment.

In 1904 was published the only book, it seems, to appear on this subject in English; namely, Thatcher's *Scaffolding*. There are chapters on Scaffolding, Scaffolds for Special Purposes, Shoring and Underpinning, and Scaffolding Accessories and Their Use, along with Cordage and Knots, Timber, The Stability of a Scaffold, and The Strength of a Scaffold. The date of publication makes the chapters on The Transport of Materials, The Prevention of Accidents, and Legal Matters Affecting Scaffolding of little use to our present study. But there is much of information and explanation, including the 146 detail drawings, that disclose the nature of falsework problems and clarify their solution at a time when wood was still very generally the material in common use. There is nothing whatsoever on centering practices, however; and the book, being designed 'for the use of contractors, builders, clerks of works, etc.', concerns itself exclusively with contemporary problems and practices: there is no historical coverage. But it is thorough and detailed as a handbook of early twentieth-century materials, equipment, and falsework procedures. (Bartlett's article on Scaffolding in the *Encyclopaedia Britannica*, 11th edition, is based almost exclusively on this book.)

Closely related to the subject of temporary falsework is that of *underpinning*, on which two books have recently been published, both dealing in part with shoring. One is L. E. Hunter, *Underpinning and Strengthening of Structures*, 1952, 162 pp., 110 diagrams. Chapter ix: 'Shoring' (pp. 131–8) is the only portion that is concerned, even remotely, with the kind of problems that are comparable to what might have been encountered in the building of medieval churches. The other is E. A. Prentis and L. White, *Underpinning: Its Practice and Application*, 2nd edition, 1950, 374 pp., 200 illustrations.

This latter book explains generously and in detail the solutions to some of the most difficult foundation problems of modern times: the underpinning of very tall skyscrapers in connexion with the construction of subways through 'quicksand' and other hazardous subsoil conditions on Manhattan Island, New York City. The experienced author-engineers cover their subject admirably, citing a wide variety of problems, with their solutions clearly explained and accounted for. However, the subject is primarily concerned with the present, and with permanent, not temporary, installations. And although there is, of necessity, much in the text and illustrations alike that describes temporary erectional equipment and practices, very little of it is comparable to the kind of problems encountered by the medieval builders, or the kinds of materials they used. It is a pity that no book to date deals as thoroughly with falsework structures as this one does with the closely related field of underpinning.

Earlier books in English on underpinning and temporary shoring include: C. H. Stock, *A Treatise on Shoring and Underpinning* (three editions; 1882, 1893, 1902); G. H. Blagrove, *Shoring and Its Application*, 1887; idem, *Dangerous Structures* (two editions; 1892, 1906).

Modern books on masonry, which deal exhaustively with masons' tools and stone-cutting machinery, with the types of stone commercially employed, with the geometry of their setting out, with mortars and lifting devices and estimating and the like, nevertheless have little if anything to say about falsework practices. For example, E. G. Warland, *Modern Practical Masonry*, 1929—a thick, sumptuous, and voluminously illustrated volume which purports to be a comprehensive treatise—mentions scaffolding only on parts of two pages (69 and 70), centering on pp. 74–76, and shoring not at all.

It is the carpenters—those who actually erect the scaffolding, place the shoring, and assemble the centerings—whose books might be expected to include some coverage of falsework structures. But what they do report on this subject is almost invariably brief and extremely rudimentary. Thus W. B. Douglas, *Carpentry and Joinery*, 1937, 137 pp., 205 figs., has a chapter (vi: 'Centring, Shoring and Scaffolding', pp. 30–36) which does little more than define and illustrate the most basic and common terms. Similarly, J. O. Cave and R. A. Earthrowl, *Construction and Maintenance of Buildings*, 1947, 191 pp., 312 figs., has a brief exposition (chapter ii, pp. 13–18) which consists mainly of the explanation and illustration of terminology.

An earlier handbook on this subject is Tredgold's *Carpentry and Joinery*. (Thomas Tredgold, *Elementary Principles of Carpentry* . . . and E. Wyndham Tarn, *A Treatise on Joinery* . . ., 14th impression, 1942. Accompanying one of the earlier editions was a volume of plates: Robinson and Tredgold, *An Atlas of Engravings to . . . Illustrate 'Elementary Principles of Carpentry . . .'*, 2nd edition, 1878. The 8th edition, 1892, revised and partly rewritten by T. J. Hurst, combines text and 48 plates in a single volume.) The material of this work, first published in 1820 (Tredgold died in 1829), was significant enough in its day to have been repeatedly incorporated not only in many subsequent editions but also in various compilations, such as the *Encyclopaedia Britannica*, 7th edition, 1839, articles on Masonry, Joinery, and Carpentry; and in a book entitled *Principles of Construction in Carpentry and Joinery of Roofs*, 1859, by J. Robinson, F. Price, and T. Tredgold. The fact that this alone of the early nineteenth-century treatises has had a 1942 printing reflects the accuracy and the practical usefulness to the carpenter of this work. However, Tredgold's discussion of centering deals exclusively with simple arches; nothing whatsoever is said about vaults. *Vide* particularly chapter iv, section 1, on 'Centerings' (pp. 185–97), and part of section 4, on 'Scaffolding, Shoring, etc.' (pp. 237–41).

In German, Breymann's large thick textbook on Wood Construction, vol. ii, with its wealth of clear drawings of details and ensembles alike, has a brief final chapter on scaffolding (xiv: 'Die Gerüste', pp. 341–55), only about two-thirds of which is concerned with this topic (the rest dealing with the hanging of bells). There is but one text-figure (no. 821, p. 351) of a scaffold; but plates 117, 120, and 122 are drawings of scaffoldings, 121 and 123 are of rolling scaffoldings, and 113 to 116 show bridge centerings. No vault formwork or centerings are given.

A book with a promising enough title is Owen B. Maginnis, *Practical Centring*, 1891. However, this volume is well-nigh useless, for it is extremely rudimentary, deals almost exclusively with but simple arches of 3- to 5-foot span, and wanders off into such 'hints and suggestions' as how to set mortice locks and the relative merits of iron and wood planes. Chapter v, pp. 33–34, is on 'Centring Circular Windows'; chapter viii, pp. 42–47, on 'Flaring or Splayed Centres'; but many more questions come to mind than are answered, and there is nothing about intersecting vaults of any sort, or the problems encountered in lofty installations.

Blake's excessively documented book on *Ancient Roman Construction* has a chapter (v, pp. 192–226) on 'Arch and Vault Construction in Cut-Stone Work', but only the last page and a half of this are about 'Vaults' and 'Technical Considerations'. Both its documentary historical emphasis and the earliness of the period covered (previous to Augustus) prevent this monograph from contributing any original or useful information on the erection of the great arcuated structures of the Romans, which might have some bearing on medieval practices.

Perhaps the nearest thing to a treatise on the specialized problem and the solution of certain centering installations is John B. McMaster, *Bridge and Tunnel Centres*, 1875. This vest-pocket-size practical handbook presents 'the rules and principles, in as brief a manner as the nature of the subject will allow'. Much of the general part of the book appears to be based upon and merely to paraphrase Tredgold. Only the last portion deals specifically with tunnel centerings. It gives four methods of estimating the load on a center; briefly describes the make-up of centering frames; and explains in some detail the various schemes that may be used to decenter these frames. It is part of this latter explanation—on decentering techniques—that alone could illuminate possible medieval practices.

Probably the best general statement on centering, although brief and unillustrated, is the article entitled 'Centre of an Arch or Vault' by the engineer George Rowdon Burnell, in the Architectural Publication Society's *Dictionary of Architecture*, C-57, 58.

In French, an early but detailed and specific account of centering, including the necessity for it, its difficulties and hazards, its problems of design, and its nomenclature, is to be found in Gautier, *Traité des ponts et chaussées*, chap. xv, pp. 71–77.

For an up-to-date treatment of the subject, Thunnissen's Chapter ii (pp. 28–58) discusses the problems of construction in vaults of many types, and gives diagrams of some modern centering installations for masonry vaults. But his coverage of the special conditions and problems of Gothic ribbed vaults is very limited.

Drawings and photographic reproductions of impressive *modern* examples of centering and formwork appear in all manner of publications today, but these are exclusively concerned with reinforced concrete: they almost never treat of stone or brick masonry. (For example, *vide* the illustrations, pp. 35, 43, 56, 65, 87, 93, 98 of the falsework for Maillart's exciting and marvellously expressive bridges of reinforced concrete, in Max Bill, *Robert Maillart.*)

The engineering periodicals in the United States (for example, the weekly *Engineering News*, and the monthly *Construction Methods*) have always published photographs from time to time of striking or unusual examples of falsework. But, like Schmidt, they almost never analyse the factors which led to the particular design solution adopted, nor make more than a passing comment on the problems or difficulties encountered, and why they came to be disposed of in the way they were.

One outstanding work of the early twentieth century should be mentioned, however, though it deals almost exclusively with bridges of 40-metre spans (130 feet) and over. The work is Paul Séjourné, *Grandes voûtes*, 6 tomes in 3 vols., 1913–16. This is a lavishly illustrated, remarkably detailed, and thoroughly documented catalogue of data —a synopsis of vital statistics, in fact—and not a treatise on the problems encountered and the reasons why they were solved the way they were. But although the author is concerned with bridges that support roadways of various sorts rather than with unsurcharged vaults (and with spans many times the width of Gothic vaults), the work is of value to us in our present study for some of the comparative data it assembles. For example, (1) the materials (the source and kind of stone, ingredients of the mortar, &c.) are carefully designated; (2) the thickness of the arch ring is given, together with the span; (3) the scheme of centering is described and almost always diagrammed, along with the cubage of the materials employed in the falsework; (4) the time interval is usually recorded between the keying of the arch and the striking of the centerings; and (5) the amount of deformation occurring after decentering is often given. Séjourné's vol. iii, livre ii, tells 'Comment on exécute un pont en maconnerie': titre ii covers 'Cintres', pp. 132–57; titre iv, 'Décintrement', pp. 171–8.

With the very brief exception of Thunnissen, not one of the recent publications cited above covers the falsework problems or practices of the Middle Ages as such, however. The primary reason why there is nothing here, at least in the case of *centerings*, that would explain or illuminate our present study, is that Gothic vaults have intersecting ribs; whereas the falseworks illustrated, whether of small or of extraordinary span, whether for tunnels or bridges, for hangars or exhibition halls, invariably have centering frames set in parallel planes. The complications that arise as a result of different span lengths and the different angles at which the centering frames are set, together with the fact of their intersection, are discussed in Chapter 5. Here it is sufficient to note that the centerings for high, nave-spanning Gothic vaults are never illustrated, perhaps because of their extreme visual complexity, perhaps because those few who do understand the multiple technical problems involved are practitioners rather than writers of illustrated handbooks of explanation and instruction.

Both Powys and, more recently, Caroe illustrate and discuss some modern scaffolding, shoring, and centering practices as applied to the repair or reconstruction of medieval buildings in our own day, and explain many of the conditions and the special problems encountered in this highly specialized work, where the aim is to maintain as much as possible of the original fabric of the building.

The French architectural periodical *Techniques et architecture* for November 1950 is a monograph on the restoration of historical monuments, including medieval buildings damaged during World War II, and shows among other examples the shoring used in restoring the badly damaged Gothic cathedral of Rouen. However, the well-illustrated principal article (by Jean Trouvelot, Chief Architect, National Commission for Historical Monuments, entitled 'De la restauration des monuments historiques', pp. 38–50) is concerned less with the actual practices of restoration and repair than it is with considerations of effectiveness in the replacement of original materials with modern materials, and the appropriateness of the alterations to a building, as originally planned, in making its usefulness up to date.

Occasional articles in the *Bulletin monumental* and in *Monuments historiques* give illustrations of the falsework used today in the repair or restoration of medieval buildings, even though they rarely if ever analyse the solutions adopted.

Phleps's article on 'Mittelalterliche Gerüstbauten' does not carry the subject into the Gothic problems of lofty skeleton construction, but is content to comment on, and to illustrate, a few examples of wall construction (not of vault construction) wherein windows are secondary in importance and extent to the solid wall. Nor is Lacroix's article on 'Die mittelalterliche Baugerüste' very helpful in dealing with the problems of vault erection in Gothic times.

As for nineteenth-century writers who have dealt at length with the Middle Ages, Viollet-le-Duc devotes an article to scaffolding ('Échafaud', vol. v, pp. 103–14) and one to shoring ('Étai', vol. v, pp. 332–45); and he discusses some aspects of these subjects, and of centering, in connexion with other articles on various subjects in his remarkably encyclopedic *Dictionnaire*.

Choisy, Breymann, and Ungewitter also make, and illustrate, some observations from time to time with respect to the problems and probable solutions of medieval falsework. The various comments and speculations of these important writers are assessed elsewhere in this work as the occasion arises, along with those of the early twentieth-century English writer, Francis Bond, and others.

In recent years a good deal of documentary material has been accumulated on the tools, materials, and equipment of the medieval builders, and these sometimes reflect building operations, including falsework. The outstanding and definitive work in this field is Salzman, *Building in England Down to 1540*, whose chapter xx (pp. 318–29) deals with 'Scaffolding, Cranes, and Other Machines'. Here, and in his chapter xvi on 'Timber', there is much detailed but frustratingly incomplete information on such items as scaffolding poles and their wedged lashings, on hurdles that often made up the workmen's platforms, and on the sizes and species of the wood scantlings. There is also interesting documentary evidence of this sort scattered through the pages of Andrews, *The Mediaeval Builder and His Methods*, and Colombier, *Les Chantiers des cathédrales*.

Finally, there is the lavishly illustrated recent volume by Moles, *Histoire des charpentiers*, whose chapter xvii (pp. 339–70) is devoted to temporary structures, including scaffolding, shoring, and centering. He also has a chapter (viii, pp. 150–81) on the carpentry-work of the Middle Ages; and many of his illustrations, not only in this chapter but elsewhere throughout the text, are of medieval subjects. He reproduces a number of Villard de Honnecourt's drawings, and many of the carefully drawn plates on scaffolding that were published in the early nineteenth century (e.g. in Jean Rondelet, *Traité théorique et practique de l'art de bâtir*, 1812) although the latter are generally for a period considerably later than the Middle Ages. Mole's book, written by a highly successful and outstanding practitioner, is valuable both in its text and in the wealth of unusual illustrative material it assembles. Its chapter on temporary structures probably deals as much as any modern book does with centering and shoring problems as applied to the repair and reconstruction of medieval buildings in France; but the plan of the book is too comprehensive to have allowed more than a general introductory coverage of these matters, though the photographic illustrations are exceptionally fine.

APPENDIX B

The Occurrence of Putlog Holes and the Location and Extent of the Scaffolding They Reveal

IN connexion with putlog holes and the kind of evidence they can furnish of building activity, it is worth quoting in part some of the observant detective work, mainly by Mr. F. Mackenzie, that is presented in G. G. Scott (*English Church Architecture*, pp. 180–6, and figs. 1–5, plate xxxvi) concerning the interrupted work on 'the great church of the college royal of St. Mary and St. Nicholas' (King's College Chapel) at Cambridge, England.

There were three periods of activity in the building of this remarkable chapel, which were separated by intervals of some twenty years; namely, 1446–62, 1480–4, and 1508–45. In demonstrating that the original design did not contemplate a fan vault, but a sort of lierne vault of Welsh-groin form, Scott notes that 'The works executed between 1446 and 1462 are readily distinguishable from those of the later builders by the use in them of the magnesian limestone from the Thesdale and Huddlestone quarries. By the application of this test we ascertain that, at the cessation of the works in 1462, the building had been carried up as far as the transoms of the side-windows for five bays from the east end, while at the west end it stood but some four or five feet out of the ground.' Furthermore: 'The evidence of the stone employed is confirmed by these two points: (1) The angel corbels of the quire which range with the transoms are alike, and of the first date, until we come to the sixth pier (always numbering from the east), where they are of much larger size and of quite a different design. These two corbels clearly belong to the second period (1480–4). (2) When the scaffolding was struck upon the cessation of the works in 1462, the holes which had been left in the ashlar for the putlogs were made good (at any rate in the interior). When, therefore, the operations recommenced, in 1480, it became necessary either to draw these stones, or, as in practice would be found much simpler, to cut new ones. Accordingly, in the interior of the quire we may trace the putlock-holes thus formed by the second architect in the ashlar-work erected by his predecessor, as far up as the window-transoms. Above this level he would naturally form the holes by simply leaving out a stone here and there, as had been done by the earlier builders, and thus above this level no such cuttings are to be traced.'

In most medieval buildings the presence of unplugged putlog holes is quite evident, especially where they occur in large areas of plain walling. Where the putlog holes have been plugged up, however, they are often not easily discernible. And in the case of piers or window jambs, especially where there are clusters of mouldings or panel-work, one has to look carefully for them with a practised eye. High up on the building they are often invisible even with a pair of field glasses, but must be observed face-to-face close at hand at their own level, as from a scaffolding. Detection of their existence depends somewhat, of course, on how recently they were inserted, how well and incon-spicuously the work was done, and whether the same kind of stone was used for the plug as that of the original masonry surrounding it. (Note, however, that not all stone inserts mark the presence of putlog holes. In this connexion, *vide* Appendix J.)

With respect to the indication of putlog holes in *drawings* of medieval buildings, it is not certain how trustworthy in all details are the large-scale pictorial sketches of Shaw, for example, a trained architect. Thus the putlog holes shown in his plate 64, on the west side of the porch of Erfurt Cathedral, are not indicated in plate 65, a more foreshortened view of the same subject. But many of his drawings—and those of other careful draftsmen—do show putlog holes whose darkly shadowed locations, whose irregular spacing and characteristic size, and whose occurrence in some examples and absence from analogous positions on similar buildings, lend them an air of authenticity (*vide* Shaw's plates 17, 19, 34, 39 for French examples; and plates 64, 81, 84, 92, 100 for Germany and Belgium). It is highly interesting to note, moreover, the occurrence of unfilled putlog holes remaining on the *interior* of some buildings, as in plates 10 (ambulatory of Beauvais Cathedral) and 85 (nave of St. Sebald's, Nuremburg), as well as in some of the concentric arch orders of the deep porch of Erfurt Cathedral (plate 64).

Other examples of the occurrence of putlog holes are to be found in the collection of drawings that are reproduced in the five large volumes of *Archives de la Commission des Monuments Historiques*, under the editorship of de Baudot and Perrault-Dabot, by such accomplished draftsmen as Boeswilwald, Louzier, Pettigrand, Selmersheim, Simil, and Viollet-le-Duc himself. One of the largest and clearest of these drawings is a close-up north-west view of the chapel of the Château de Vincennes (Seine), which appears as plate 80 in vol. i. This tall, aisleless structure corroborates one of Viollet-le-Duc's statements (about the fact that hung scaffolding began above the level from which building operations could be conducted from scaffolding set on the ground) in that the putlog holes commence only about the height of the spring of the bay-filling window-heads.

Perhaps it is safe to conjecture that, in drawings where putlog holes are unmistak-ably indicated, the draftsman would not have included them had their presence not been obtrusively evident to him.

There is ample evidence of putlog holes in the more trustworthy record of photo-graphs, of course; but their recognition requires more careful seeking out because so many photographs of medieval churches are taken at a considerable distance from these holes, and under lighting conditions that frequently render them difficult to detect. Replugged putlog holes are clearly shown at close range in the window spandrels of the apse clerestory at Reims in the photograph that appears as plate 124 in Moreau-Nélaton, *La Cathédrale de Reims*. Similar holes are shown left *un*plugged in plate 76 of the same work, in the analogous spandrels of a bay on the south side of the nave. Photographic evidence of the occurrence of putlog holes on the *interior* is given in Gall, *Die gotische Baukunst*, plate 87, p. 189. This view of the priory church of St-Leu-d'Esserent clearly shows unfilled putlog holes in the spandrels of the apsidal arcade, and two filled putlog holes at similar locations in the last choir bay, south side.

It is certainly true that even comprehensive photographs of some churches reveal a much greater number of putlog holes than are apparent in other churches. This comes about from the practice of leaving the putlog holes unplugged in certain churches (such as the western towers of Paris Cathedral) so that they do not have to be recut every time repairs are undertaken, and of filling them up in other churches (such as parts of Reims Cathedral) each time repairs have been made, so that the masonry surfaces appear smoothly finished and continuous.

In general, putlog holes, filled or unfilled, are largely confined to smooth ashlar surfaces such as the lateral faces of buttresses and the spandrels of clerestory windows. For where decoration occurs, there are often projections or indentations already existing as part of the fabric of the building to which the scaffolding can be secured; or else the scaffolding takes its support at less frequent intervals where substantial bearing can be had upon gallery platforms or passageways, thereby eliminating the need to attach the temporary falsework to more fragile portions of the building.

What has been written on medieval scaffolding practices (with the exception of Viollet-le-Duc's account of spire scaffolding) is concerned almost exclusively with that for continuous walls, or at least for structures wherein areas of plain walling predominate over window openings. (Thus Viollet-le-Duc himself, article 'Échafaud', vol. v, pp. 103–14; Salzman, chap. xx, pp. 318–29, and elsewhere; Forsyth, pp. 117 and 125–32; and Phleps, pp. 111–16, figs. 121–31). Forsyth, for example, has carefully measured and analysed the spacings, both horizontally and vertically, of the putlog holes that occur in the solid tower walls of St-Martin's at Angers. And Phleps has made conjectural drawings of two types of Romanesque suspended scaffolding (p. 113, figs. 125, 126): one type wherein the putlogs go through the wall to support platforms on both sides, the other wherein the putlogs are deeply inserted brackets on one side only, strutted by diagonal braces.

Since there appears to be nothing at all written on the probable methods used for scaffolding the isolated members of the great Gothic churches (that is, the nave and clerestory piers, &c.), it would seem to be necessary to work deductively from the practices followed in the nineteenth and early twentieth centuries, when wood scaffoldings were still generally employed. The schemes there represented, however, must be re-interpreted in the light of some of the factors known to have governed medieval falsework practices: for example, their virtual non-use of metal, their lack of knowledge about the truss whose rigidity is based on the non-deformability of triangles, and above all their stringent economy of material, uninhibited by the requirements of modern building codes with respect to strength, and the safety of the workmen.

For example, the post-World-War-I scaffolding around the north-east crossing pier to the spring of the vault in Cologne Cathedral (which is shown in the full-page photographic illustration, p. 199, fig. 224, of Güldenpfennig, 'Sicherungsarbeiten an den Vierungspfeilern des Kölner Domes'), has built-in stairs connecting its sixteen stages, instead of the ladders that would unquestionably have been used in Gothic times.

A much more striking example of prodigality in falsework structures is what was used in the late nineteenth century for the building of the Sacré Cœur church on the hill of Montmartre in Paris. The architect, who himself wrote an account of the building when it was nearly finished (Henri Rauline, 'The Church of the Sacred Heart at Montmartre: Its Origin and Construction'), boasts (p. 23) that 'No wood or iron is used in the construction of the monument. The walls, the arches and the roof are in dressed stone.' He describes the advantages of lifting all the stones into place by means of the so-called 'ram's head' (an obsolete term for a kind of pincer-like hook). The use of this device, he says, 'requires fewer men to put the stones in place, but necessitates the construction of solid timber scaffolding, at a heavy cost, to carry the cranes employed in lifting. On this account, up to the first of January, 1893, the amount expended for timber from the commencement of the work was 2,200,000 francs . . . while . . . to the same date the amount spent on masonry was 16,000,000 francs.'

A number of the photographic illustrations in Rauline's article reveal some of the massive and extensive falsework structures for this all-stone building. The one appearing on p. 15, for example, shows a tall tower-crane travelling on tracks at one side of the interior of the nave, for raising the deep voussoirs up on to the double centerings for one of the great lateral arches, where there are many tiers of workmen's platforms, probably needed for the subsequent glazing. But the most amazing illustration is that on p. 19, entitled 'View over Apse, September 27, 1885'. This shows a wide and continuous planked platform, located outside the side-aisle walls above the level of the semi-domes of the apsidal chapels, on which traveller cranes moved on railroad rails along the flanks of the building and made the circuit of the apse, their booms long enough to reach across the side-aisle gap to the nave walls. Such extravagant use of falsework would have been unthinkable in the Gothic era.

Although there are coming to be some large collections of architectural photographs, including medieval buildings in their war-damaged state and during the course of reconstruction (such as the National Building Record, in England), no comprehensive corpus of photographic illustrations of scaffolding has yet been published. It would be a great service if someone would undertake to assemble and edit these for publication, at least for those medieval buildings damaged in World Wars I and II, or from natural causes, that have subsequently been rebuilt or restored. For much that is interesting and informing to the student of medieval architecture is revealed only as the buildings or parts of them are seen in actual section, when they are in their damaged state.

Probably the clearest and most numerous photographs of scaffoldings that have been published in a single volume are those to be found in Moles, although this excellent book is perhaps too early (1949) to have included many examples of buildings during their reconstruction after World War II. Léon's book gives a number of interesting illustrations—unfortunately they are either from poor photographs or are not well reproduced—of scaffolding, shoring, and of reconstruction generally. Many of his exterior views of buildings reveal putlog holes.

Schmidt's compact and thorough little volume—one of only two books dedicated exclusively to scaffolding (with some treatment of shoring but none on centering)—is extensively illustrated with drawings, details, and photographic cuts, although the latter are usually small and the paper on which they are printed is of rather indifferent quality for them to be of as much value as they might be. However, Schmidt's pictorial presentation of scaffolding includes a varied assortment of situations where practically nothing but unsquared poles are employed in the falsework assemblages. One of the chief values of this book is that it shows photographs of actual installations, often accompanied by working drawings, in elevation, of these installations. Furthermore, the various connexions and methods of attachment for pole scaffolding are shown in close-up, large-scale detail; and some of these (either because they are lashed or because they make use of metal only in such fashion that lashing could replace the metal device) might well be comparable to medieval practices. For example, *vide* his figs. 6, p. 18, 52, p. 47, 57, p. 49, 112 and 113, p. 83, 116 and 117, p. 85, 126, p. 88, and 127, p. 89.

APPENDIX C

Passageways in Lincoln Cathedral

THIS essentially Gothic feature of built-in service passageways is found in English churches, too. In his book on Lincoln Cathedral, J. C. Buckler, the careful architect in charge of the restoration of the towers, 'pronaos', and western façade of this great church in the 1860's, has this to say of them (p. 163):

'The Norman builder formed blank passages in the front of the Church, between the outer wall and that of the towers, communication therewith being opened by stairs in the angles. But the galleries in the thickness of the walls, the recesses, and the blank passages, are so numerous, irregular, and so frequently connected by precipitous steps and narrow links, dark, crooked, and fearful to pursue, that no description can here be given of them. Suffice it to say, that the builders in the thirteenth century saw good reason to augment the number, and that he of the fourteenth century approved the system; and if he did not add to the extent of these darksome passages, he assuredly maintained them in the walls with which he interfered. In the way through these singularly connected and circuitous passages, ascending and descending with different degrees of steepness, and at the foot of the archways either open or guarded, the work executed under Bishop Alexander is seen to advantage.'

Again (p. 164): 'Among the number of the most accessible, straightforward, and efficiently illuminated galleries, are those in the front of the Church, over each aisle of the pronaos. They are one over another, but lead to nothing; and are vacant spaces opening upon the staircase, as well formed and windowed as if designed for purposes of frequent use....'

Finally (p. 180): 'The recesses, the passages, and the stairs are numerous and intricate in almost every part of this remarkable building. Many of these narrow, steep, and crooked ways are due to the original arrangement; others have been formed subsequently, and, owing to the nature of the plan, have no outlet. Others again are joined with greater ingenuity than convenience to pre-existing ways in the thickness of the walls, to the great increase of their length and irregularity, rendering the passage and the footing hazardous. To these references to artificial chasms should be added a remark upon those formed in the arches of the front recesses: They sever the arch in a vertical direction, between its broad members, in the manner so commonly seen in the parapets of military architecture. The gap is carried up through the thickness of the wall, but for what purpose, and to what height, are particulars which were unconsidered in the thirteenth century, and are now unknown.'

APPENDIX D

cA Tower Vault of the Eleventh Century

THE erection of a single high central vault over the crossing, as built in the last quarter of the eleventh century, is described by Forsyth, *The Church of St. Martin at Angers*. As he reconstructs the erectional operations, a floor was built at the sill level of the tower windows on large beams and joists let into the heavy walls. This platform thereupon supported the entire falsework for the vault, without any of it being built up from the pavement of the church, whose services could thus proceed without interference from scaffolding.

Although Forsyth's account of erectional techniques is confined almost exclusively to the tenth and eleventh centuries, when walls were generally massive, thick, and pierced only occasionally with openings, he nevertheless has much of interest and value to say about medieval scaffolding, including the quoting and translation of contemporary references to it (p. 114). He has noted with great care the position and spacing of putlog holes in walls constructed from suspended scaffoldings. Moreover, unquestionably no one else has treated in such circumstantial detail the equipment involved (lagging, centering frames, and supporting falsework) and the various steps that may have been followed in the erection of a specific eleventh-century vault over a crossing (pp. 117, 125–32). Although his illustration (fig. 199 e: 'Conjectural Centering of Dome of Tower') and his account (p. 128) of how the lagging was supported (the carpenter 'only had to erect two arch-like wooden cradles which would join the centers of opposite walls, crossing each other at right angles above the middle of the space to be vaulted, and then he could lay boards horizontally on top of these cradles') makes the falsework appear to be precarious, insufficiently braced, and incompletely accounted for at the rounded corners of the vault, nevertheless most of Forsyth's treatment of the erectional procedures in this tower vault is very carefully studied and reasoned out, and therefore makes an important contribution to our understanding of early medieval constructional practices.

However, this tower vault he discusses in such thorough and informing detail is (1) an early example, when masonry structures were built massively of coarse rubble; (2) of modest span, relative to the great Gothic cathedrals (Forsyth gives (p. 124) the clear spans of the nearly square vault as *c.* 6·60 metres by 5·95 metres, or about 21 feet 6 inches by 19 feet 4 inches); (3) a single, isolated unit, enclosed on all four sides within heavy walls, rather than one of a series of vaults along nave or transept; and (4) of a

254

completely different type from those of the mature Gothic system. Unfortunately this author does not give a detailed explanation of the techniques of erection followed in the twelfth-century ribbed vaults over the nave, which occur in this very church he studies so painstakingly. Even if he had done so, however, neither their height nor their width would make the account of their construction comparable to that of the great Gothic churches.

It is regrettable that this writer has not undertaken to treat of the construction of the high vaults of one of the great cathedrals. For his monograph of St-Martin's is a model—worthy of the most thorough emulation—of an expert, exacting, and minutely observed investigation of a medieval church, replete with penetrating and knowledgeable interpretations.

APPENDIX E

Medieval Vault Thicknesses

SINCE many vault webs have been repaired at some time or other during the past hundred years or so, one would think that there might be accurate information recorded on their thickness. Yet precise data on the thickness of medieval vaults are hard to come by. Even in those churches damaged in World Wars I and II, where the vaults were broken so that their shells showed in edge view, their thicknesses seem seldom enough to have been published. Moreover, because many vault webs are pierced with small holes through which hangers for lamps have at times been suspended, it would not appear to be unduly difficult to ascertain these figures without scaffolding, from above the vault. Most writers, however, if they mention the matter at all, give only generalizations, and these (like the more easily obtained figures for vault spans and heights, indeed) are sometimes conflicting and contradictory. For example, see the figures given below for the nave vault of Chartres: 11 inches by Bond, and 15 inches by Adams (who is often untrustworthy in regard to details).

Brunet (p. 92) records the thickness of the web compartments of the high vaults at Soissons as '30 to 33 cm.' ($11\frac{3}{4}$ to 13 inches) in a span of 13 metres ($42\frac{1}{4}$ feet) center to center of piers, or about 38 feet clear span.

Seymour (p. 110) states that 'the filling over the ribs' of the original choir vaults at Noyon 'was of average section: under 25 cm.' (about $9\frac{3}{4}$ inches). Here the span is approximately 33 feet 4 inches c. to c. of piers, and about 29 feet 4 inches in the clear.

Pol Abraham (*Viollet-le-Duc et le rationalisme médiéval*, p. 51) asserts that the high vaults at Reims were 'nearly 60 cm. ($23\frac{5}{8}$ inches) thick' [in c. to c. and in clear span, about 47 feet and $40\frac{1}{2}$ feet, respectively]; but that the average web thickness for vaults 'in all eras' was 'from 20 to 35 cm.' ($7\frac{7}{8}$ to $13\frac{3}{4}$ inches), whatever the span might be.

Viollet-le-Duc, article 'Construction' (p. 108), notes that 'many of the webs of the wide-spanning Gothic vaults, especially at the end of the twelfth century, are not over 10 or 12 cm. thick' (4 to $4\frac{3}{4}$ inches). He specifically states in a note that the webs of the great vaults of the choir in Paris Cathedral are 'not more than 15 cm. thick' ($5\frac{3}{4}$ inches). Huss (p. 147) mistranslates this note as 'only 10 cm.' (4 inches); and Simpson, vol. ii, p. 84, perpetuates this mistake.

Aubert, op. cit., mentions specific vault thicknesses in a note on p. 222: '... The thickness of the vaults, which is generally 0·30 ($11\frac{3}{4}$ inches) at the summit—it attains 0·40 ($15\frac{3}{4}$ inches) under the towers of Acy-en-Multien, Noël-St-Martin, and Gaillon;

256

and 0·80 (31$\frac{1}{2}$ inches) under that of Bruyères (Aisne)—reverts to 0·20 or 0·25 (7$\frac{7}{8}$ or 9$\frac{3}{4}$ inches) in the naves of most of our great churches of the thirteenth century. It is only 0·165 (6$\frac{1}{2}$ inches) in Notre-Dame, Paris; 0·24 (9$\frac{1}{2}$ inches) in Auxerre Cathedral; and increases to 0·28 (11 inches) at St-Quentin; 0·33 (13 inches) at Soissons. . . .' On p. 10 he quotes Porter for the early, rather clumsy ribbed vault of Sannazzaro Sesia, Italy, as having a vault thickness of 0·50 (19$\frac{3}{4}$ inches); and on p. 36 he quotes Bilson for the early vaults of Durham Cathedral, England, at 0·35 (13$\frac{3}{4}$ inches) in the western bays, and up to nearly 0·50 (19$\frac{3}{4}$ inches) in the eastern bays.

Conant, op. cit., p. 128, says that the great church at Cluny (begun in 1088) had a slightly pointed barrel vault which 'spanned 10·45 metres in the clear' (34 feet), and that its 'web was of rubble, with a minimum thickness of about 40 cm.' (15$\frac{3}{4}$ inches). Later (p. 131), in speaking of the abbey church of St-Denis, 'that first of all Gothic churches', he says that 'the vaulting had thin webs of small cut stones carefully fitted together, as became usual thenceforth in Gothic vaulting'.

Late Gothic vaults tended to be very thin. A rather special example of this is illustrated in fig. 6, p. 120, of Jullien, 'Clé de voûte de la chapelle de la Vierge à Caudebec-en-Caux', about which it is written: 'In Fig. 6 we observe at the summit of the arches the rebate contrived so as to lodge the in-filling: it is here that the stone was only 7 or 8 cm. thick' (2$\frac{3}{4}$ to 3$\frac{1}{8}$ inches).

For England, vault thicknesses are given for Salisbury by Price, the thorough and knowledgeable eighteenth-century repairer of that great church. Speaking of the vaulting immediately under the tower, he says (p. 50): 'The shell between the ribs and tracery of stone, is not above eight inches thick at a medium; whereas all the others are eighteen inches thick: And besides this difference, the said vaulting under the tower has not the coat of putty, or cement laid upon it, to strengthen it.'

For the carefully cut stone fan vault of King's College Chapel, constructed in 1513–15 and well over 40 feet in clear span, Mackenzie writes (p. 16): 'The panels are laid in rabbets at the back of the ribs. . . . It is remarkable that the panels are found to vary from 2 to 6 inches in thickness. . . . The late Mr. Wilkins, measuring them in two or three places, found them from 4 to 6 inches. And the measurement taken for these plates gave 4$\frac{1}{2}$ inches. And all this difference must occur in the three upper tiers of panels, within the space of about 11 feet (in a line crossing the tiers), the lower panels being covered with rubble, and of course could not be measured. . . .'

For western Germany, Lassaux writes (p. 232) that 'The material of ancient church vaults is, on the Lower Rhine, everywhere, the well-known tuf, which is manufactured as Trass ['an earthy or more or less compact rock, made up in large part of firmly comminuted pumice or other volcanic material'], modelled to the size of common tiles, and 3 or 4 inches thick. On the Upper Rhine, beginning from about Bingen, it is brick of small size: the thickness of the vaults varies from 4 to 8 inches. . . .'

Among the more general writers, Adams (p. 111) says that the vaulting of Chartres

APPENDIX E

'is heavy, about 15 inches thick'. Here the distance c. to c. of piers is about 52 feet 9¾ inches, with the free span of the vault about 43 feet 10½ inches.

Bond (*Gothic Architecture*, p. 304) writes that 'the original rubble vault of the Abbaye-aux-Dames ... was 12 inches thick; ... those of Chartres are nearly 11 inches thick. ... Many French Gothic vaults over naves, even in the twelfth century, are not more than 4 to 5 inches thick; that of Notre Dame, Paris, is 6 inches. ...' (This latter doubtless quotes Viollet-le-Duc.)

Simpson (vol. ii, p. 84) reports that for English vaults 'The web ... varies in thickness from 4 to 8 inches. ...'

Sartell Prentice (p. 155) states that the vaulted churches of the Romanesque period in Italy had vaults that were 'excessively thick—between 16 and 20 inches'; but that the Gothic builder, to the north, 'lightened the weight of his vault by diminishing its thickness, since the panels or "webs", unlike the masonry of the barrel vault which was sometimes nearly two feet thick, could be given a depth of only a few inches' (pp. 147–8).

The thickness of war-damaged vaults is clearly shown in the following photographic illustrations:

Aubert, figs. on pp. 209 and 219 for crossing vault of Reims Cathedral; fig. on p. 221 for high vault of St-Quentin; figs. on p. 225 for porch, on p. 226 for nave, and on p. 228 for apse, all of Noyon Cathedral.

Brunet, fig. 9, p. 77, for the north side-aisle vault of Soissons Cathedral.

Léon, fig. 328, p. 506, for the high nave vault of Soissons.

Seymour, fig. 22, opposite p. 94, for the high nave vault of Noyon Cathedral.

Verrier, illustration on p. 24 for the high nave vault of the church of Gisors (Eure).

A few photographic illustrations of either formerly ruined or war-damaged vault shells seen in edge view are the following. In the main, however, most of these illustrations are at too small a scale, or are taken at too great a distance, or are too darkly reproduced to be as revealing as they might be.

Aubert and Maillé: vol. i, fig. 75, p. 198, for the church of Mazan (Ardèche); fig. 136, p. 263, for south side-aisle vault of choir, church of Ourscamp (Oise); fig. 163, p. 280, for apse vault, church of Chaalis (Oise); fig. 196, p. 288, for north side-aisle vault of choir, church of Fontainejean (Loiret); fig. 200, p. 290, for north side-aisle vault, church of Longpont (Aisne); vol. ii, fig. 408, p. 90, for the high vault of Chaalis; fig. 506, p. 178, for apse vault, church of Fontaine-Guérard (Eure).

Gilman: figs. 1, 2, 4, 5, 6, 18 for Soissons; 13 for Reims.

Lasteyrie: vol. i, fig. 329, p. 316, for high nave vault of Noyon; vol. ii, fig. 592, p. 11, for nave vault of the abbey church of Longpont (Aisne).

· Porter, *Lombard and Gothic Vaults*: figs. 29, 30, 32, and 35 (between pp. 16 and 17), for the north and south side-aisle vaults of the abbey church of Longpont.

Rheims and the Battles for its Possession: p. 31 for nave vaults from above, p. 56 for nave vaults from below. Illustrations on p. 69 show nave vault of church of St-Jacques from above and from below; those on pp. 109 and 112 show the choir and south transept vaults, respectively, of the church of St-Remi.

Reims au lendemain de la guerre: plates xlvii and xlviii for Reims' high vault; lxxii for Archiepiscopal Chapel at Reims; and cxiv for apsidal chapel at St-Remi, Reims.

Trouvelot: top figure on p. 45, for side-aisle vault of Rouen Cathedral.

APPENDIX F

Surfaces of Double Curvature in Gothic Vaults

THE presence of camber in Gothic vaults is variously reported. Here are some of the conflicting assertions:

Enlart (op. cit., pp. 448, 449) states that 'In the straight bays themselves, the first rib vaults are very often bowed up ... [but] the perfected Gothic vault is not at all cambered or is only slightly so. . . .'

Bond (*Gothic Architecture*, p. 310) says: 'In France, east of Normandy, the early Gothic vaults, e.g. at St-Denis, are excessively domical; later on, they are less so, but their ridges seldom become quite horizontal.'

Porter (*Medieval Architecture*, vol. ii, p. 61) says that '. . . up to the very end of the Gothic period, French vaults always continued to be built in a slightly domical form'.

Aubert repeatedly speaks of the crown lines of Gothic ribbed vaults as being 'in a horizontal plane' (op. cit., pp. 137, 161, 170, 222); and he says the Gothic builders raised their high vaults 'with horizontal crown lines' (p. 234). Elsewhere he states that from the second half of the twelfth century 'the longitudinal compartments have their ridge lines horizontal' (p. 231); and again, 'in the thirteenth century, the lines of the crown of the vault become horizontal' (p. 232). But he notes that the oldest rib vaults of the Île-de-France 'have the curvature of the vault accentuated, especially in the lateral compartments' (p. 222); and he sums up by saying: 'All these dispositions did not prevent a certain curvature in the vault, especially in the lateral direction' (p. 164). (The reason for more curvature in the lateral cells, of course, was that in a quadripartite vault the span of the web courses in the cross vaults was roughly twice the length of those in the longitudinal portions of the vault, the maximum being in the neighbourhood of some 22 feet or so, and 11 feet, respectively.)

In contrast to Aubert's somewhat inconclusive observations, Moore (p. 65) makes the clear-cut assertion that 'The vault surfaces are invariably arched more or less from rib to rib, and their ridges are never quite level.' Actually, he goes much farther than this, pointing out that 'Irregularities are, in fact, inherent in the Gothic system, which in this respect resembles nature itself, where a vital principle seems to operate to prevent perfect uniformity in the development of organic forms. . . . The irregularities result, in part, from lack of mechanical precision in laying out plans and carrying up the edifice, but more largely from structural necessities . . .' (p. 84).

Later (p. 111) he enlarges on this latter point, noting that 'Irregularity of surface is a constant and necessary characteristic of Gothic vaults, even of those of the quadri-partite form. . . . In the vaults of Paris, as in all Gothic vaults, the shells consist of successive courses of masonry which are slightly arched from rib to rib over each triangular cell. The beds of these successive courses are not parallel, but are variously inclined according as the mason found necessary or convenient in developing the con-cave and winding surfaces engendered by the forms and positions of the ribs to which they had to be accommodated. These courses of masonry have here in Paris, as they have in most Gothic vaults, a considerable inclination near the springing from the longitudinal rib upward toward the diagonal, and they become gradually more level as they approach the crown of the vault where they are more nearly parallel. But perfectly parallel they can hardly ever be, since each course forms a portion of a surface that is concaved in all directions.'

In this connexion, Bond (*Gothic Architecture*, p. 299) notes that 'In some French churches, e.g. in the collegiate church of St-Quentin, the twisting and contortion of the vault surfaces is something extraordinary; the vaults look most unpleasantly unsafe; yet they have stood since the thirteenth century.'

For a clear and practical explanation of the reasons for and the advantages of camber in Gothic vaults—not only the outward bowing of the web courses but also the strongly defined arching of the crowns—see Lassaux, pp. 227–9, including his figs. 1 to 6.

APPENDIX G

The Slow Setting Time of Medieval Mortars and Its Consequences

IT is curious that some writers make a great point of the slow setting time of medieval mortars (which required the centering for vault ribs, for example, to remain in place throughout many weeks), and yet that these same writers accept, or at least do not question, the cerce device, which obviously is thought of as being able to be retracted and removed from a given web course immediately upon completion of that course.

Aubert (op. cit., p. 217) acknowledges the fact that only 'after many months did they take away the centers', and that moreover 'tie-rods of wood or iron, disposed from the spring of one arc to the other, stiffened the construction while the mortar set and until the building was finished' (p. 218): thus the church 'was able to be used during the drying of the mortar' (p. 220). But Aubert asserts that 'the setting time of the fat lime that was used in the Middle Ages is very slow, and takes a year or a year and a half' (note, p. 214). He goes on to say that the masons first established the voussoirs of the ribs on their centerings, whereupon 'the mortar, whose total set requires many months, begins to harden; then, on this skeleton of stone ribs, still reinforced by the centerings that had served in placing them, they erected the lagging or the movable cerces on which the webs were built' (p. 216).

The whole thesis of H. and E. du Ranquet, 'Origine française du berceau roman', on the originality of French Romanesque barrel vaults over those of the Romans, Armenians, and Byzantines, is based on the slow setting time of the lime mortars native to France, which caused the builders 'to search out a new procedure of construction' (p. 47). The authors state (p. 45) that 'the decentering of the barrel vault takes place as soon as this lime mortar, in drying, has taken on some consistency, but before it has completely dried out in the mass, a condition that requires a minimum of six months and sometimes a much longer time, depending on the quality of the mortar.... In fact, the removal of the timber frames of the centering before the complete drying out of the mortar fatally involved a general settlement of the barrel vault, which ran the risk of producing a rupture at the haunches and thus bringing about the ruin of the entire building, a catastrophe that happened many a time, moreover, in the train of a too hasty decentering.'

Pol Abraham, 'Les Données plastiques et fonctionnelles du problème de l'ogive',

262

goes even farther in speaking of the slow setting time of medieval mortar in France. He says (p. 36) that 'these mortars of aerated lime set only with extreme slowness when they are not directly exposed to the air. In walls of medium thickness the final set can be figured in years, whereas in walls of very great thickness centuries can pass before the final set is acquired.'

In this respect, the progressive development towards leanness and attenuation of the masonry members throughout the medieval period served well in making technically possible the soaring structures of the mature Gothic cathedrals, very much diminishing the latent dangers that had proved so disruptive in the much less ambitious but massive erections of Romanesque times.

In corroboration of this, Lassaux (p. 232) writes that 'in order to make a small thickness of wall suffice, the skilful ancients applied also another effective means; namely, to build very slowly, and to put on the vault late, after the complete drying and hardening of the mortar; and till then, for the temporary use of the church, to cover the roof simply with boards, or perhaps, after the manner of so many basilicae, to leave it quite open'.

The long-continuing greenness of the mortar, not to mention the concomitant shrinkage of the joints, explains the builders' dilemma over the timing of the decentering operation, and their misgivings about its consequences. Knowing from experience that the vaults as well as the walls and every other part of the masonry structure would continue to settle over a period of many years, they would have been tempted to decenter too quickly, since settlement would continue to take place anyway, and the process might just as well begin at once while the mortar was fresh enough for the joints to accommodate themselves to the pressures and adjustments of the vault as a free, self-supporting entity. Yet too quick a decentering was fatal, for then the mortar was still so plastic that its strength and effectiveness were insufficient to take care of the compression developed in the joints when the vault, relieved of its falsework, started out on its independent existence.

It is clear from the above observations that the nature and properties of French medieval mortars had permeating and widespread influence, both immediately with respect to the building procedures and practices that were followed, and ultimately in the settlements and even the fissures that came to manifest themselves in various degrees in practically every church, sooner *and* later. Structurally, the culmination of the entire building—the location and distribution of the supports, the weighting and counterbalancing of lofty piers, the adjustments and proportionings of the abutments—all these, both individually and collectively, found their reason for being in the nave's ceiling, the high stone vault. Yet it was here in the great vault itself (for which all the rest was, in a structural sense, only preparation) that the uncertainties of the mortar became critically focused at the time of decentering, endangering the collapse of all.

Even with the superior mortars of modern times, this matter of the decentering is sometimes disastrous; and it is therefore worth noting some of the things said of it by

APPENDIX G

an engineer. John McMaster (*Bridge and Tunnel Centres*, pp. 69–71) writes: 'Undoubtedly the most dangerous operation connected with the use of bridge centres is the process of striking them. No matter with how much care the arch may have been constructed, the drying and squeezing of the mortar will cause it to settle in some degree when the centres are removed, and this degree of settlement seems to be very largely affected by the time the centres are allowed to stand. By some it has been urged that the centring should never be removed until the mortar in the joints of the last course has had ample time to harden; others going to the other extreme have advocated striking the ribs as soon as the arch is keyed, claiming, not without reason, that the settlement of a *well-built* arch will never be so great as to become dangerous even though the supporting frames be removed when the mortar is green. But possibly the best practice lies not far from either of these extremes. It has, indeed, time and again, been amply demonstrated that to leave the centring standing till the mortar has hardened, and *then* take away all support, the mortar having become unyielding, is to cause the courses to open along their joints. To strike the centre, on the other hand, when the arch is still green will, seven cases out of ten, be followed by the fall of the bridge; but by easing the centring as soon as the arch is keyed in, and continuing this gradual easing till the framing is quite free from the arch, the latter has time to set slowly as the mortar hardens, and the settlement will be found to be very small.'

We have no information, of course, regarding the quickness with which the decentering operation followed upon the keying of the vaults in medieval times. However, thanks to the data assembled by Séjourné, *Grandes voûtes*, it is possible to cite specific modern instances of the time lapse between the keying of the masonry arch and the decentering, together with the amount of deformation, in many cases. The time lapse for decentering the many great masonry arches of wide span which Séjourné describes ranges from $1\frac{1}{2}$ hours, for the mid-nineteenth-century bridge of Nogent-sur-Marne, to 1,145 days, for the late-eighteenth-century bridge of Lavaur, France, with the most usual period somewhere between 21 and 90 days (cf. the 1893 Specification cited in Appendix H).

The amount of deformation occurring while the centerings are in place, at the time of decentering, and afterwards, though not always separately recorded, varies all the way from 'no appreciable settlement' through 5, 10, 25, 33, 50, 65, 83, 97, and even 200 and 290 millimetres, to complete collapse. There does not appear to be any clear-cut pattern for the deformation; and indeed, on p. 57 of Séjourné's tome iii a graph of 'Movements in the key after decentering' is given for a five-year period in the case of the 90-metre ($292\frac{1}{2}$-foot) masonry span at Plauen in Saxony, in the form of a diminishing wave profile, fluctuating from an extreme crest of $20\cdot8$ cm. ($8\frac{3}{16}$ inches) at the start of the decentering operations through subsiding seasonal waves to a trough of $5\cdot55$ cm. ($3\frac{3}{16}$ inches). Nor does there appear to be any clear-cut pattern for the time lapse between keying and decentering, at least as far as the season of the year and the span and rise of the arch are concerned, together with the degree to which the arch is surcharged

264

at the time of decentering. The quality of the mortar and the sequence of the arch loading during erection, however, are definitely significant factors.

In one sense these great masonry bridges that are documented by Séjourné, whether of the past or the present, are much easier to provide centering for, and also easier to decenter, than the high nave vaults of the Gothic era. This is true because the stone bridges he documents are simple arches of greater or lesser depth, whereas the Gothic vaults are masonry ensembles of non-parallel ribs beneath more or less warped webs. Consequently there are different spans, different directions, and different degrees of possible shrinkage because of dissimilar rib and web thicknesses, that have to be contended with as a synchronous ensemble of operations at the time of decentering. All this made the decentering of the great Gothic churches' high nave vaults an especially intricate and hazardous operation: no wonder a number of them collapsed at this critical time.

265

APPENDIX H

Oblique or Skew Vaults of Masonry

THE shapes of the groin voussoirs, if properly cut to key accurately into the web stones of the two vault surfaces whose intersection they form, are very difficult to arrive at. This difficulty unquestionably accounts for the very small number of unribbed, simple groin vaults constructed by the medieval builders over naves. They could 'get away with' approximate shapes in the case of modest spans in the lower vaults erected above side aisles, both because of the greater thickness of the web relative to the vault span there, and because of the thick mortar joints which took care of some degree of inaccuracy in the close fitting of these groin stones. But the builders realized that nave vaults of large span necessitated a high degree of accuracy—especially along the critical area of the groin—which they were either *unable* to achieve (on account of the practical geometry involved in laying out their shapes), or *unwilling* to face (on account of the extra time and expense involved in working these stones to their complicated contours). (For a completely illustrated, step-by-step procedure for working the groin stones of intersecting vaults, *vide* Warland, pp. 103–5, figs. 286–9, and pp. 213–17, figs. 532–49.)

Today, we have nothing comparable in stone masonry to the complexity of cutting these groin voussoirs, because we no longer build structurally in stone. However, a century or more ago, before the introduction of either steel or reinforced concrete in building, the advent of railroads demanded bridges of arched masonry many of which had to accommodate a right-of-way that crossed a stream or a roadway at an oblique angle.

Laying out the complicated shapes and hewing the twisting surfaces of the voussoirs of these oblique arches created masonry problems which, for their day, were comparable in difficulty and cost to those of the determination and shaping of unribbed groin stones in medieval times. The nineteenth-century problem involved not only difficult and specialized engineering calculations but, in addition, a high degree of skill and experienced know-how on the part of the practising masons who built these skewed bridges of coursed stonework.

With the engineering formulas and computations for oblique bridges we are not here concerned. But it is worth noting the nature of the practices, the equipment, and the procedures of the masons who built them. This information is actually on record in a few books: surviving accounts, descriptions, drawings, and, occasionally, early photo-

266

graphs of an art that is practically extinct in our day. They provide our closest contact with the mason's craft at its most accomplished and impressive status in modern times; and thus they put us in touch with the latest—and perhaps final—chapter in its long and splendid tradition of skilful accomplishment. Of the various books on this technical subject, the following five are written in English:

Peter Nicholson, *The Guide to Railway Masonry, containing a Complete Treatise on the Oblique Arch.*

John Hart, *A Practical Treatise on the Construction of Oblique Arches.*

George Watson Buck, *A Practical and Theoretical Essay on Oblique Bridges.*

John L. Culley, *Treatise on the Theory of the Construction of Helicoidal Oblique Arches.*

George Joseph Bell, *A Practical Treatise on Segmental and Elliptical Oblique or Skew Arches.*

(There is also a complete and very clearly illustrated modern account of the working of a single voussoir for a semi-elliptical skew arch given in Warland, p. 90, figs. 254–5, and pp. 188–91, figs. 444–9.)

Not only do all these writers on oblique arches describe formulas and demonstrate the methods the draftsman uses in laying out the stone-jointing of skew arches and vaults in stone or brick, but they are also at pains to present a great deal of practical data, in considerable detail, regarding the ways by which the masons can make the many full-sized templates and moulds and 'squares' they need in order to hew out the winding shapes of the web-course blocks accurately and with precision.

For example, Nicholson describes (p. 8) how 'to construct the templates for working the arch stones', giving methods for forming the arch stones proper (pp. 9–12), the springers (p. 15), and the quoins (pp. 19–24), together with 'a practical method of constructing as much of the development of the oblique arch to the full size, as will be found sufficient for making the templates for the use of the workmen' (p. 36). Nicholson illustrates many of these templates, squares, &c., in connexion with the specific examples of skew arches in stone or in brick that are given in his plates; and, upon the start of actual construction, he says (p. 35) that '... Previous to setting the brick courses, the boarding or laggings should be truly adjusted and fixed; and, for the regulation of the work, the bed lines should be drawn thereon in their true position.'

It is constantly recognized throughout the treatises on oblique arches that the mathematical computations and the engineering data required in the design of these arches is beyond the training or knowledge of the working mason. Consequently, much space is devoted to the practical steps to be taken and the equipment used by the masons in the operation of hewing the stones to proper shape and setting them in place.

As in the case of other writers, Hart (a professional mason rather than a civil engineer) frankly states (p. 40) that 'It is probable that there are many bricklayers who will consider it too much trouble to observe these rules' (regarding the laying out of an oblique arch in brickwork). He continues: 'I will therefore give one more in accordance with their wishes, whereby they will be able to accomplish the work, without making a drawing for any part of it.' Whereupon he proceeds to demonstrate a method of laying out the coursing directly on the formwork of the centering with the aid of straight-edges and squares.

The discrepancy between the engineering knowledge required for the design of skew bridges, and the mason's practical skill and experience in their execution, is acknowledged in Hart's preface, where he states: 'My principal aim throughout has been to simplify the construction of oblique arches as much as possible, which I trust will be seen upon an examination of the plates and their definitions. I have been more anxious to explain them in language suited to the capacities of the men engaged in the execution of them, than to embellish the Work with scientific terms, (which, with many, would require more learning than a knowledge of the work itself,) thus rendering it what it professes to be, a useful reference for practical men:—my own experience, in the superintendence of work and workmen, having placed before me the necessity of adapting the explanations of drawings to the understandings of those engaged in their execution; for much of the value and beauty of a design depends upon the workmen being acquainted with the principles of the construction upon which they are engaged.'

Culley remarks as follows (pp. 92–94) about centering (italics added): 'The centering ribs should be placed in planes parallel to the face of the arch, and, therefore, when so arranged will be elliptical. They are sometimes placed normal to the soffit, or made circular, when, in order to receive the arch under its acute angle, the centering has to be extended beyond the obtuse angle, and there *loaded to prevent any movement in the centering when the voussoirs are set near the actual angle.* Circular centering should not be employed to receive the voussoirs of an oblique arch. The ribs of the elliptical centering being parallel to the arch face, are in the planes of pressure, are easily maintained and *require no more material than is necessary* to receive the voussoirs.'

'The sheeting or lagging should be so put on the ribs that it will have an even and smooth surface, and that the centering will be of the exact dimensions to receive the voussoirs. When so prepared *the soffit coursing joints of every course should be carefully and permanently marked upon the sheeting, as a guide for the placement of the voussoirs in the arch....* As the skew-back stones are generally set before the centering is, no lagging or sheeting will be required on the centering below the intradosal upper courses of the skew-back stones.'

Buck has a whole chapter (pp. 17–28) on the 'Method of Working the Voussoirs, etc.', which explains the manner of determining the dimensions of the twisting rules, or winding strips, and the templates; and a short chapter (pp. 44–46) on the 'Mode of Erection', which describes how the spiral joint lines are drawn on the lagging with a flexible straight-edge.

Bell's preface states that 'This Essay has been solely written for the purpose of making the subject intelligible to the average working mason....'

For our purposes, however, the most valuable feature of Bell's book, other than his photographs of the stonework of an oblique bridge during the course of erection, is a contract he reprints. He quotes (pp. 98–104) in their entirety the contract Specifications, dated 1893, for an oblique bridge 20 feet wide erected at an angle of 45° over the King River in Cumberlandshire, with an oblique span of 56½ feet. The thickness of the arch stones of this bridge is designated as 2 feet, and of course they support a surcharge up to an approximately level right-of-way. Although the problem in many respects is not analogous to that of medieval vaulting, certain practices and procedures indicated in the Specifications are highly revealing and illuminating. This is particularly true in the case of the stipulations and conditions set forth under the heading of Centering, as follows:

'The Contractor shall provide at least 13 centres for the arch, each centre to be of sufficient strength to bear one fifth of the gross weight of the arch, and these 13 centres shall be constructed of and lagged with approved foreign timber, the lagging shall be of battens of suitable lengths, 6½" broad, and 2½" thick.'

'The centres shall be supported in the following manner, that is to say, corbels shall be left in the abutment walls of sufficient substance and strength (to be neatly broken off after the centres are removed), these corbels shall be further strengthened by having stout wooden props placed underneath each corbel, each prop shall rest on a solid footing and wedges shall be driven between the head of each prop and the underside of each corbel, and at a suitable distance below the springer line, to support a beam on which the ends of the centre shall rest, each centre on two hard-wood wedges, as broad on the bed as the beam, and at least 4" thick at the smaller end. The beam and wedges to be well smeared with soft soap, and the beam smeared on the face where the wedges rest and the wedges smeared on both sides so as to facilitate the slackening of the wedges, and to allow the arch to sustain itself. At least four rows of support shall be provided in the bed of the stream between the abutment walls the full width of the Bridge, either of stone or wooden piles as the case may require, and on each of these four rows of stone pillars or wooden piles the Contractor shall place a beam of approved strength and quality on which the above 13 centres shall rest on hard-wood wedges, as broad on the bed as the beams, and smeared with soft soap as above described.'

'After the arch has been closed and properly keyed, each set of wedges shall, on the seventh day after the arch has been keyed, be driven back an inch daily, till the arch sustains itself and the whole of the weight is removed from the centres, when the spandrel walls may be commenced.'

Although the structure involved in this Specification is very different from the Gothic vaults, a number of operational techniques which are pertinent and comparable to those of unsurcharged vaults of the Middle Ages are disclosed, including the following:

The frequency and close spacing of the centers, when the lagging they support is laid flatwise;

Support by means of stone corbels that are subsequently hewn off flush with the rest of the masonry, leaving no trace of their employment;

These corbels undergirt with stout wooden props wedged tightly against the corbel from beneath;

Pairs of hardwood wedges, the narrow end of each being large enough to be engaged by a jack at the time of decentering;

The liberal smearing of both beams and wedges with soft soap, so as to facilitate retraction of the wedges;

The presence of intermediate as well as end supports for the centerings, with substantial bearing for each of these intermediate supports;

The seven-day drying period for the mortar in the joints, after the arch rings were completed;

The very gradual operation of decentering, in which the wedges are to be driven back only an inch per day; and

The delay in constructing the masonry spandrels above the arch until after the arch has become self-supporting.

APPENDIX I

Pole Scaffolding

FROM both documentary evidence and the direct testimony of whatever carpentry work has survived from the thirteenth or late twelfth century, it seems abundantly clear that sawing (at least for structural as opposed to decorative uses) was almost exclusively confined to cutting across the grain; that is, to giving the proper length to a piece of wood, whether timber or board. Long, straight pieces, such as those used for rafters, posts, or beams, were roughly squared by means of an adze; and this was also the practice followed in shaping curved members such as knee braces, crucks, &c. (This is the justification for the formula 'one tree, one plank' explained in Bond, *Church Architecture*, p. 288.) But at least in the case of oak, not only boards, planks, laths, but any other straight pieces whose cross-sectional area was considerably less than that of the log from which they came, were invariably split, by means of wedges. The effort involved in sawing through the length of a tree-trunk 1½ or 2 feet or more in diameter would have been prodigious, especially if the wood were as hard as oak. And although late medieval manuscript illuminations picture this being done (usually on logs of much less girth, to be sure) by the pit-sawing method, it is extremely doubtful that the wood in question was oak.

Certainly such a costly and difficult process would not have been followed for the temporary carpentry work used in centerings. Perhaps the boards of the cerce may have been fashioned in this way. But if the cerce was used only as an extensible pattern for determining the length and shape of the plank forms or lagging frames, as we have suggested above, rather than as the actual form for successive courses, then it would doubtless have been made from the straight-grained wood of some softer species. In any case, the careful workmanship of its smooth sides and accurate faces would have been eminently justified, as applying to a valued piece of permanent equipment. In this connexion it should be noted that the formwork itself—probably of lagging frames set radially, rather than of planking set on edge—could have been quite roughly adzed or split, since only the narrow upper edge (on which alone the stone courses rested during the vault's erection) would have required planing to a smooth and regular curve. Hence such a scheme of formwork would have been much easier and less expensive to produce than that of continuous formwork with planks set flat-wise.

To be sure, in certain early vaults, usually of very small span, we have the unequivocal evidence of somewhat irregularly shaped boards, laid flatwise, for forming the vault.

271

(*Vide*, for example, those mentioned by Bond and referred to in note 113 above, and by Forsyth: his p. 113, note 165, for window centering; p. 126 for formwork of main tower vault; and p. 164 for the helical formwork of a vice.) No one has yet thought to investigate the imprint of these boards closely enough to determine whether they were riven or sawn. In any event, the production of smooth boards of conspicuous width and considerable length was as slow and costly a process as any carpentry work the medieval builders undertook, in the preparation of individual pieces.

Most architectural historians, from Viollet-le-Duc down to the present day, have perhaps been far too ready to envisage the members used in medieval scaffolding, centering, and formwork as though they were similar to the power-sawn boards, planks, and timbers of modern times. Yet the whole effort of the medieval period with respect to wooden falsework was quite obviously to reduce the amount of it that was needed and to limit as far as possible the amount of complicated craftsmanship its erection entailed. Certainly it is highly unlikely, for this reason, that a double-curving continuous surface of boarding, such as might be used today for concrete formwork, would have been employed as temporary support for the vault webs in medieval times.

There seems, in fact, to be no good reason to doubt that for vertical and diagonal supports, as well as for horizontal ties and ledgers, the medieval builders used the tall, straight, unsquared poles that are only now coming to be generally supplanted, in Europe, by the tubular metal scaffolding of today. (A stockpile of these poles is shown in the photographic illustration, fig. 1, p. 14, in Schmidt.)

Because the pre-eminent wood used throughout the medieval period was oak, whether for structural members or for carved finish work, it does not follow that temporary falsework was often, or even occasionally, fashioned out of this hard and heavy wood (*vide* Crossley, *Timber Building in England*, 'Introductory Note: The Royal Oak', pp. 1–4). Obviously, oak would not be appropriate for most scaffolding, where tall, straight, slender members, not short, thick ones, are what is needed.

Tall, straight poles whose natural taper is very slight have been used and re-used throughout Europe for untold generations. In this connexion Salzman (p. 318) speaks of alder, especially, and of fir (p. 248). Thatcher, writing about scaffolding materials and practices at the beginning of the twentieth century, says (p. 69) that pine or northern fir, white spruce or white fir, and larch are used for scaffolding poles, with the first named the best. Being of fir or some similar softwood, scaffolding poles grow naturally long and straight, with numerous but small branches, instead of the great limbs of oak or beech; and this makes their preparation for use as scaffolding members quick, easy, and cheap. They need only be felled and their small branches lopped off with an axe, for the debarking can often wait until weathering and the natural process of seasoning bring this about almost automatically.

In the past, as in more recent times, there were other advantages of scaffolding that was made up of poles lashed together, besides those of cheapness and availability. For example, each member was light enough to be handled by one or two workmen: hence, derricks and machinery for lifting and setting them in place could be dispensed with (*vide* last paragraph, p. 29, of Thatcher). Because of this relative facility of handling the scaffolding poles, there was also less danger of damaging existing work when the time came to dismantle the falsework. For instead of the big trusses made up of massive timbers pinned together at the joints and spanning the entire distance of the arch ribs they were destined to support (which most architectural historians have envisaged), it is much more likely that the medieval builders erected a scaffolding of poles which were framed into a complex of relatively short spans. Thus the whole temporary structure was light, being made up of slender members lashed together at frequent intervals. Even the lateral ties occurred at frequent intervals, too; and these secondary, horizontal members often provided support for platforms, spaced conveniently for a man's height, from which the workmen could perform their jobs, whether in connexion with the erection of the building as the scaffolding was going up, or in connexion with the plastering and painting of the vaulted surfaces as the scaffolding was being dismantled.

A further advantage of pole scaffolding is that the poles are completely salvageable; that is, the scaffolding may be taken apart by unlashing the ropes, and then re-erected in the same or some other pattern, as needed elsewhere. More than this: because the members are lashed together instead of being nailed or bolted, they are not subject to cutting, notching, or other mechanical injury that would weaken them or impair their life expectancy. Hence their use and re-use, again and again, may extend throughout many years. (Thatcher, p. 74, speaks of six to ten years for exposed positions, depending on the care exercised in their use.)

It would seem, therefore, that the falsework members used by the medieval builders were usually of unsquared timbers. (For substantiation of this practice, even today, note the many examples depicted in Schmidt, for most of the scaffolding poles he shows in photographic illustrations.)

As for shoring, it is worth noting that the very extensive work of reconstruction that went on for some years in Rouen Cathedral after World War II involved heavy interior shoring which consisted mainly of very thick poles, bolted together to be sure, but the full diameter of the original tree, and *with the bark still on* (*vide* illustrations in *Techniques et architecture*, pp. 44, 45; also Chauvel, *Rouen*). Photographic illustrations of *exterior* scaffolding assemblages of poles with their bark still on are shown in close-up detail in Schmidt, pp. 47, 80, 88, figs. 52, 105, and 126, respectively.

Unquestionably the medieval builders, like their successors in the modern instances just cited, were at pains to limit the expense and the time involved in preparing and shaping falsework members, wherever and as often as they could manage to do without this expenditure. Indeed, Innocent notes that even the permanent members in the roofs of medieval buildings in the north of England presented a similar saving in workmanship. He says (p. 89): 'Originally the rafters were natural poles, then split poles were used, probably to give a better hold for the laths, then these were roughly squared, and so old rafters came to be laid on their flat sides, as the builders knew nothing of mathematical formulae of the strength of materials. In South Yorkshire old roofs with rafters of split poles still remain, and old roofs constructed with natural round poles also; while in Surrey the rafters of old roofs were either pit sawn or squared with the adze.' Elsewhere (p. 101) he notes that 'Some of the older buildings of South Yorkshire, however, still retain pieces of the bark on their timbers. . . .' And Colson (p. 18) even reports that, in the work of repairing the original timber assemblages of the great roof over Winchester Cathedral in the late 1890's, 'many pieces of timber were discovered on which the bark and lichen still remained'.

Although Innocent's book is concerned primarily with buildings other than those of the first class, what he has to say regarding carpentry work is worth noting, even in connexion with the major class of ecclesiastical buildings he does not discuss; for, the great tithe barns and granges, which he *does* comment on, were often framed in a fashion very similar to the roofs of the great cathedrals.

APPENDIX J

Arch and Vault Ties in Medieval Construction

IT is perhaps worth noting that not all the iron hooks that remain in medieval churches were necessarily placed there for the attachment of tie-rods or tie-beams. For example, in Bourges Cathedral to this day there are two tiers of strong iron hooks that project on the nave side of many of the very tall piers of the nave arcade, the lower ones at about the level of the sixteenth course above the base of the cluster shafts, the upper ones some eleven courses higher but still about fourteen courses below the capitals, and consequently far below the springing of the nave ribs.

In addition, we have already seen that Viollet-le-Duc, Choisy, and Enlart each speaks of the service passages as being useful at the time of great ceremonies in providing a place from which festive hangings could be conveniently suspended: hooks and rods were sometimes used for the attachments of these hangings.

Moreover, G. G. Scott (*English Church Architecture*, p. 156), in discussing the significance of the Lenten Veil in the medieval ritual of England, mentions the fact that 'In many of our ancient churches the hooks by which this Lenten curtain was supported may still be seen'; and he goes on to say that 'At Salisbury Cathedral the winch by which the veil was raised remains, affixed to the south-eastern pier of the crossing of the lesser transept. In the quire of Arundel Church, Sussex, the pulleys still exist by which the curtain cord was tightened. The hooks remain in the cathedrals of Winchester and Durham, and I have observed them in many of our unrestored old churches, as at Alfriston, Sussex, and Skirlaugh in the East Riding of York. In a "restoration", of course, they most commonly disappear, but their position may often be traced by the pieces of new stonework which their removal has necessitated....'

An early reference to iron ties is given in Richard Brown, *Sacred Architecture*. This book by Professor Brown, who designated himself an architect, is uneven and not very significant for our purposes. But on p. 107, in speaking of the construction of Beauvais Cathedral in the thirteenth century, he says: 'At this time, the pillars being placed too far apart, the vaulted roof threatened to fall in, which actually took place after means had been adopted to support it *by iron braces and chains*, to hold the side walls together' [italics added].

Lethaby (*King's Craftsmen*, pp. 145 f.), speaking of the 'new work' of Henry III at Westminster Abbey, which began with the eastern and three northern bays of the apse together with the corresponding chapels, says that 'To this same portion of the apse, across the springings of the arches, and across the aisles, are wooden ties, whereas throughout the rest of this work iron ties occupy similar positions [his fig. 62, I, II, III]. It might be thought that the wooden ties were comparatively recent stays but there has been no reason for their insertion at any time subsequent to the first erection of the tall pillars, and such wooden ties were frequently used in the erection of French works. Moreover, a further proof of their being a part of the first scheme is to be seen in the capitals of the columns between which they stretch. These capitals are of a curiously plain profile, the bell not being undercut as is the case in the neighbouring capitals where the iron rods are used. . . . The next portion of the work comprised three bays on the south side which have iron ties which pass *through* the caps of the piers. Later it was found better to build in only hooks, to which the ties might be attached afterwards. This third plan continues throughout the *first work*. In the later work of the nave no permanent ties were used.'

Elsewhere (pp. 139 ff.) Lethaby calls attention to the fact that 'Within the church the whole construction was, from the first, laced up with iron to an extent which is without parallel. At Vézelay the high vaults had iron transverse ties, the hooks for which still remain. In William of Sens' work, at Canterbury, the arcade around the eastern transept is stayed with iron. At Westminster there are not only continuous longitudinal ties to the arcades, but others pass across the aisles, so that in some perspectives four or five bars may be seen crossing at different angles [his fig. 58]. At the triforium there are two continuous iron bands which pass along at the springings of the double planes of tracery. Certain rods which stand clear of the glass at the back of the windows of the chapels are also, I believe, ancient and continuous. Other ties thread the end windows high up in the aisles of the north transept. The Chapter House had eight rods passing from the central stem to the ribs, just like those in an umbrella, but of these only the hooks remain.'

'It is certain that the iron ties were part of the first construction. Wren speaks of the original architect having tied the arches every way with iron; but many of them, he says, had been "unhooked". Some are shown in position in the engraving in Sandford's "Burial of the Duke of Albemarle" (1670). There are several of them which are not attached by hooks, but are built into the work directly. . . .'

'The long Fabric Roll of 1253 shows that in that year a large quantity of iron was brought from Gloucester for the works; and in this year there were no less than nineteen smiths at one time engaged on the building. The shorter summary for 1253, also at the Record Office, gives a special item to the iron used for "nails and other purposes". . . . In this, nearly three tons of iron, we must, I think, have the material from which many of the ties were made.'

For evidence of the widespread use of iron embedded in the masonry of Salisbury Cathedral, to tie it together, *vide* Price, whose discoveries have been corroborated recently (nearly two hundred years later) by the architect, W. A. Forsyth, in charge of the work of conservation in this building (reported in the *Journal of the Royal Institute of British Architects*, vol. liii, Jan. 1946).

In his later book (*Westminster Abbey Reëxamined*, pp. 103–5 and notes, p. 297) Lethaby has more to say about the use of iron in the Chapter Houses at Salisbury and Westminster, and includes a perspective drawing (fig. 58) of the interior of the latter with the tie-rods showing. He notes (p. 105) that 'Besides the eight ties mentioned above, the windows are threaded by three tiers of strong iron bars, which are still wholly or largely original. One may assume that they link up at the angles and form bands right around the octagon. Scott found, from the fact that the round bars were beaten square where they passed through the mullions, that the western window originally had four lights like the others.'

It appears from these and similar accounts that iron was used far more extensively to tie together the masonry members in the great English churches than it was in those of France. Lethaby's evidence from Westminster would seem to indicate that the English builders progressed from wood ties (probably because they were so much cheaper than iron), to continuous through-the-pier iron ties, to eyed iron ties attached to projecting iron hooks, to no ties at all: as though the builders' proficiency grew along with their increasing confidence. On the other hand, the *wooden* ties of the nave arcades of as maturely Gothic a structure as Amiens Cathedral would indicate the French builders' intention, right from the start, to use these ties as only the most temporary of erectional devices, to be cut off and dispensed with as soon as possible, as the higher portions of the superstructure came into operation and thus came to supersede the temporary function of the ties.

Photographic illustrations of ties that have had to be installed in *modern* times because of alarming deformations and settlements are given, for example, in Lasteyrie, vol. i: fig. 30, p. 49, for the choir of St-Julien-le-Pauvre, Paris; fig. 48, p. 77, for the church of Taverny (Seine-et-Oise); fig. 91, p. 125, for the collegiate church of St-Quentin; and fig. 148, p. 178, for the great abbey church of Abbeville (Somme), where both iron ties (in the nave) and wooden ones (in the choir) had to be inserted under the high vaults.

With respect to the presence of ties that were placed in churches at the time of their construction and that remain in place to this day, a sharp distinction should be drawn between those of western Europe and of the eastern Mediterranean area. Lethaby (*King's Craftsmen*, p. 361) seeks to establish the widespread use of ties throughout the ages by recalling that 'In old schools of architecture the use of iron and wood ties for binding arches was quite general. The most important Byzantine buildings—S. Sophia, Constantinople, and S. Demetrius, Salonika—have such ties throughout. Of the early Arabic school, the Dome of the Rock and the Aksa mosque have series of ties at the springing of the arches....'

But it should be noted that arch ties in these and other Byzantine and eastern Mediterranean churches were invariably of wood, not of iron. This was not solely, or even primarily, a matter of original expense, wood being so much cheaper than iron. Actually these eastern ties fulfil a quite different function from the ties of Gothic buildings in France and even those of England, as indicated both by their being exclusively of wood and by their being permanent installations. The arch ties of Byzantine and other eastern churches are conspicuous and practically universal features of these buildings, large and small alike, *because the lands in which they are found are subject to earthquake tremors.* Hence, from the start as well as ever since, these buildings have needed to be strutted by ties that are resistant to both tensile and compressive stresses (cf. Choisy, *L'Art de bâtir chez les Byzantins*, chap. x, 'Les Chaînages', pp. 115–22).

As for French Gothic windows, Viollet-le-Duc gives many carefully executed detail drawings of them in such articles of his *Dictionnaire* as 'Fenêtre', vol. v, pp. 365–419, and 'Meneau', vol. vi, pp. 317–45. But only once (article 'Meneau', p. 335, fig. 8 at T) does he indicate unequivocally that the iron bars pass through the slender mullions from one jamb to the other without a joint or break. He writes (p. 336): 'At s is shown one of the capitals of the mullions, and at T the dowels that thread the iron bars that were set at the spring of the window lights in order to maintain both the colonnettes and the compartments of glass in a vertical plane. These fastenings of dowels and of all the joints of the stone-jointing are cast in lead, a precaution that became necessary by the time the cross-section of the mullion became reduced to a very small surface. . . .'

So much for the single case at the spring of the window lights. But in windows of even quite small span, bars that support the lead cames of the glass occur at frequent and regular intervals. In regard to the windows of the Sainte Chapelle in Paris, Viollet-le-Duc observes (article 'Fenêtre', p. 388, referring to fig. 19, p. 387): 'K is a sketch of the whole window, which is three times its width in height. At L are ties of iron which preserve the deviation of the buttresses, link them to each other, and prevent the mullions from becoming displaced from the plane of the window. Moreover, the mullions are no longer built up in courses, but are cut into long stones set on edge with respect to their natural beds; and this allowed them to be given less width so that there could be more glass area. . . .' Judging by the stone-jointing of the mullions shown in fig. 20, p. 390 (clerestory windows in Amiens Cathedral), only two out of twelve of the iron bars pass through the slenderest of the mullions, only one through the stouter central mullion.

Various French examples of war-damaged or previously ruined churches show windows denuded of their glass but still preserving their horizontal metal bars. For instance, Lasteyrie (vol. i, fig. 98, p. 132) gives a photographic illustration of the Wernerkapelle in Bacharach (Alsace); fig. 329, p. 316, portrays some clerestory windows of Noyon Cathedral; and fig. 363, p. 339, shows windows of the choir in the church of Etain (Meuse). The continued presence of these iron bars long after the buildings have become exposed to all the inclemencies of the seasons, is evidence of how securely they are affixed, and perhaps suggests that the tall slender center mullions would not still remain in place were it not for their being firmly anchored into the window jambs from the start by iron rods that pass through them without a break. It seems probable that, at least in French work, whatever bars may have been made continuous through the mullions, from one window jamb to the other, occur only at the level of the joints which separate the long erect mullion stones; in which case the intermediate bars (which occur at much more frequent intervals than do the mullion joints) would be let into the sides of the mullion stones and their housing sealed with lead, as in many iron-barred windows today.

The reason for speculating on this matter here is in connexion with any scaffolding ties that had to pass through the window opening from exterior to interior during the course of erection. Threading these into place, and later removing them, would have necessitated considerable care in order not to knock them against the iron bars that held the slender mullion stones in alignment. But much of the work on mature Gothic buildings required similar care in seating and handling the scaffolding, because so much of the building and its decoration was relatively fragile and easily damageable. Hence the necessity for exercising the greatest care in handling the scaffolding members merely underlines the probability that these members were light in weight and easily manœuvrable, as suggested above (in Appendix I).

APPENDIX K

Medieval Falsework Practices in England

PROBABLY the most completely documented account of the building of a major portion of a specific church of the first magnitude is that dealing with the nave of Westminster Abbey. Rackham does an eminently scholarly job in presenting the story of the erection and sequence of the work, together with its cost and the means of financing it, based on a long series of fabric rolls covering this portion of the building, the *Novum Opus*. Because of vicissitudes of various sorts, the work extended over a period of 152 years, from 1376 to 1528. The late date of this undertaking—the vaulting, in particular, was constructed only towards the end of the fifteenth century—is less significant than might appear, since the design that was followed adhered to the original pattern and style of the thirteenth-century work previously established in the eastern part of the church: the presbytery, choir, and transepts.

The fact that Westminster Abbey is a structure built on English rather than on French soil accounts for certain differences in the execution as well as in the form and the details of the building. For example, the means of protecting unfinished walls from the ravages of the weather, both over the wintertime and throughout the long periods of building inactivity when no work was in progress, were apparently far more thorough (and expensive) in rainy England than in France. In the latter country, judging by the evidence of manuscript illustrations, this was accomplished by thatching. Thus Andrews (plate x, with commentary on p. 93) reproduces a fifteenth-century French or Flemish miniature where a whole temporary roof has been constructed to shelter the not yet full-height choir, north transept, and one bay of the nave; and the unfinished west wall has a coping of thatch, too. Colombier (plate xii, fig. 21, with a commentary on p. 126) gives a mid-fifteenth-century Flemish miniature of the construction of the church of the Madeleine at Vézelay, where thick tufts of thatching (Colombier calls it straw or stable litter) crown the unfinished tops of the piers between the windows.

In the case of Westminster Abbey, on the other hand, Rackham finds (p. 66) that 'Two carpenters are paid for "covering the walls of the new work" (5*s.* 4*d.*), and two tilers are occupied in the same business. Lead is also used for this purpose *super muros novi operis*. This covering of the walls (*coopertura murorum*) with tiling and lead becomes almost an annual charge.' (Earlier, in the accounts of Henry III's time which are abstracted and put into English in Scott's *Gleanings*, less expensive care seems to have been taken. For we read (p. 254, *Pipe Roll of 1267–8*) of 'hollowed (or fluted?) tiles, litter, reeds bought for covering the walls of the works aforesaid'; and in the *Pipe Roll of 1269–70*, 'Hollowed (?) tiles, litter, stubble for covering the walls of the same church'.)

Rackham's excerpts for Westminster nave are paralleled in other accounts. For example, a much more detailed listing of these provisions for protecting unfinished work, along with the itemization of installations for the protection of the workmen themselves, are given in Brayley and Britton (pp. 154–67) in connexion with the work on St. Stephen's Chapel, Westminster. Not only were temporary coverings constructed over unfinished work, whether gables, walls, towers, or even individual carved stones; there were also penthouses, hoardings, and enclosures walled and roofed with hurdles, to protect the workmen from the weather. One does not come across such lavish provisions for temporary structures of this sort in French accounts. Hastings (*St. Stephen's Chapel*, p. 47) observes that 'when a pause takes place in the work it is covered up to protect it from the weather'. In some of the items extracted from contemporary fourteenth-century accounts by Brayley and Britton, and quoted below, we will see how extensive, and how expensive, this protection was in the case of St. Stephen's Chapel.

Another and much more significant difference between French and English practices is in the relatively prodigal amount of scaffolding used by the latter. Here are some of the instances mentioned by Rackham from the fabric rolls of Westminster:

(1) (p. 59). '. . . Between March and September 1457 four carpenters are working *super le scaffold' pro rosa ad finem australem ecclesis*. In 1460–1 five carpenters are engaged in raising the great scaffold (*erigent' magnum scaffold'*), for which timber had been cut down at Knightsbridge. In particular three carpenters were at work cutting down and framing (*framant'*) timber *pro ancora rose in ecclesia et pro nailing tabul' magnam scaffold'*, and six labourers raised the timber *de le anker*. In all, the scaffold cost £11/5/8. The restoration of the window was completed next year (1461–2). A carpenter spent 160 days in "setting up five scaffolds within and without the church about the rose and in taking down the same"; and also making a "great wheel". . . . Eighty ells of canvas were needed to protect the church from "wind, rain, and other misfortune".'

(2) (p. 62). 'In the roll for 1468 we find masons employed at an average of ten or eleven a week. But the chief feature of the account is the building of a great scaffold. Richard Pache and others receive £17/11/- for work *circa scafold' et gynnes et tect' novi operis et circa mer[emium]*, etc. In all, £36/3/3½ is spent on the scaffolding and the carpenters' work. Timber is cut down and brought from Hendon, Kensington, and Endyth; the sawyers saw 13,947 feet of elm and oak planks and "quarters"; the necessary implements are brought, e.g. ropes and *cordes de baste*, ladders, two new *pavones*, and two "great veils" (*magnam vela*) to protect the masons from wind and rain. . . . A payment is made *pro clausura in ecclesia ad finem chori*; and eight labourers are employed *circa magnam scaffold fiend' et circa mundac' magn' fenestr' in navi ecclesie*. . . .'

281

In the next year's account (1468–9), 'three carpenters are paid £12 for work on the scaffolds, etc., and *circa le framyng et erectionem tecti ecclesie in novo opere.*'

(3) (p. 68). 'In 1472–3, while preparations are being made for the roofing, we find that there are three scaffolds—the lower, higher, and highest (*inferior, superior,* and *supremus*); elsewhere we read of the great scaffold and the small scaffolds (*magnum* and *parva*). The great wheel and the ginnies, with their pulleys of brass or iron, which hauled up the stones and timber, are of corresponding importance and require a good deal of tackling and constant repair . . . ; (p. 69). By 1476–7 the scaffolding seems to have reached the west end, for that year the carpenters' work is *circa tria scaffoldia et situac' gynnorum in campanilibus et magnum scaffoldum ac parva scaffoldia* (£4/8/-). . . . That the roofing is finished [by 1477–8] is shown by the advance of the carpenters who now begin to work on the centres and scaffolds for the flying buttresses.'

(4) (p. 74). 'In these past eight years (1482–90) the carpenters had been occupied chiefly in moving the scaffolding from severy to severy as the work advanced. The scaffolding was elaborate. Each portion of the great scaffold, upon which the centres stood and where the masons worked, was floored and shut off by partitions from wind and weather. With the scaffolding the great wheel and the ginnies had also to be moved from bay to bay. Above the "beams" and the vaulting, and stretching beyond the centres, there was a scaffold or boarding on which the great wheel was placed so as to raise up the great keys. Pains were taken to exclude the wind and the pigeons; and the great windows of the new work were all boarded up. Incidentally we learn that the new work was separated from the old church, at least in the upper storey, by canvas stretched upon a wooden framework.'

'In 1490, the year which we have reached in the vaulting, there is a great increase in the carpentry bill, which amounts to £60. It is thus explained. Richard Russell was making *lez grete scaffoldes in summitate navis ecclesie* and moving the centres to the next bays: then he was occupied . . . in making *le newe scaffoldes pro lez syde yles* of the church . . . and he is also making the scaffolds for *lez batilments.* . . . The vaulting of the side aisles is in progress, and . . . carpenters are occupied in "excluding the wind *in lez round wyndowes desuper les voltes*", that is, in the triforium windows, which are just above the side aisle vaulting. This work seems to be still going on in 1493–4, for the wind has still to be excluded from the round windows in that year.'

[An earlier reference to canvas is cited in Lethaby, *Reëxamined,* p. 85, who says of work being done in 1252–3: '. . . The entry to the Chapter House from the Cloister was being built, and canvas for the windows of the former was obtained. On this last item, Professor Willis remarked: "The mention of canvas for the windows of the Chapter House shows that these windows were so far completed in 1253 as to require to be closed with canvas until the glass was ready for them."']

(5) (p. 75). 'In 1491–2 . . . Richard Russell is engaged in making and removing *les scaffoldes in occident' fenestr' ecclesie.* . . . Next year 300 feet of great oaken quarters are bought for the centres for the west window (3*s.*), and planks and "slyttingwork"

for "the great centres" (? for the vaulting of the tower) 10*s*.; Russell also . . . raises and takes down the centres and scaffolds there, i.e. at the window. Other centres and scaffolds remain through the years 1493–5. . . .'

Roughly a century and a half previous to the period covered in Rackham's study, there is a considerable amount of documentation for the extensive employment of scaffolding in another Westminster structure, that of St. Stephen's Chapel. Hastings is convinced that this building was not vaulted in masonry. He says (p. 90): 'As to the roof itself, there appears no doubt that it was of wood: all references to it are for carpenter's work. . . .' Nevertheless, St. Stephen's was a most important building, wide and lofty. Though not of major size and extent, as was Westminster Abbey, it was none the less an outstanding work due to its lavish decoration, its stylistic innovations, and the intense interest which the King himself showed in its establishment and progress. The contemporary building accounts of its erection are therefore worth quoting with respect to their many references to scaffolding as well as their occasional mention of other operational materials and equipment. Here are some of the items dealing with scaffolding during the years 1330–52 that have been extracted from contemporary accounts by Brayley and Britton, pp. 150–67. Although the dates of payment do not necessarily correspond to the dates of use or employment, it is interesting to note the time of year when the scaffolding materials were received and put to use.

'1330, Jul 15.
To three scaffold-makers, for erecting a scaffold at the east end of the Chapel, etc. for five days, @ 3½*d*. per day, 4*s*. 4½*d*.

——, Jul 23.
To the scaffold-makers, for four days, 3*s*. 6*d*.

——, Jul 29.
For 25 beams of alder tree, for the scaffold at the east end of the Chapel, @ 2*d*. each, 4*s*. 2*d*.
For 24 hurdles for the same scaffold, @ 2*d*. each, 4*s*.
For 500 thongs to tie the scaffolds, @ 4*d*. per 100, 1*s*. 8*d*.
For 100 nails called Spikyng, for the Scaffold, 10*d*.

1331, Mar 15.
To two scaffold-makers, for working 6 days, @ 3½*d* per day, 3*s*. 6*d*.

——, May 4.
For 100 poles of alder, for the scaffold at the east gable of the new chapel, 16*s*.
For 12 large poles for standards for the scaffold, @ 10*d*. each, 10*s*.
For 24 hurdles for the scaffold, @ 1¾*d*. each, 3*s*. 6*d*.
For 1000 thongs, as before, 3*s*. 4*d*.

For 2 long poles, for standards to the scaffold, @ 12*d.* each, 2*s.*

For 6 beams of alder, to make centres, @ 2*d.* each, 1*s.*

——, Jul 20.

For a large cable of hemp for drawing up stones by a windlass to the top of the chapel, weighing six score great pounds, @ 1¾*d.* per lb., with porterage and boatage, 17*s.* 6*d.*

——, Dec 2.

For 2½ hundred of reeds, for covering the new house for the stone-cutters and workmen, @ 10*d.* per hundred, with boatage to Westminster, 6*s.* 3*d.*

For 4½ hundred of reeds, for the same purpose, 3*s.* 9*d.*

For 2000 nails for laths, @ 10*d.* per thousand, 1*s.* 8*d.*

For 1000 of iron nails for an inclosure in the above house, 7*d.*

For 300 of hert-laths for the said house, @ 5*d.* per hundred, 1*s.* 3*d.*

For 500 beech-laths for the said house, @ 2½*d.* per hundred, 1*s.* 0½*d.*

1332, Mar 15.

For two oak boards, for covering two tabernacles at the east end, @ 3*d.* each, 6*d.*

For 100 beech boards to cover the *soursadel reredos*, in the east gable, 6*s.* 8*d.*

For two boards to cover the said gable, 1*s.*

——, Jul 19.

For 50 beams of alder, for the new scaffold at the gable of the front of the new chapel, 8*s.*

For thongs and hurdles for the scaffold, 5*s.* 2*d.*

——, Aug 9.

For half a hundred of beech boards, to cover the stone-masons during their work in the front of the chapel from wind and rain, etc. 4*s.* 6*d.*

——, Aug 23.

To John de Hungerford, carpenter, for working and making timbers for the scaffold to be erected afresh round the towers of the front of the chapel, for six days, @ 5*d.* per day, 2*s.* 6*d.*

To two scaffold-makers, for erecting and tying the scaffold, five days @ 3½*d.* each, 2*s.* 11*d.*

——, Nov 9.

For 500 reeds, for covering the walls of the chapel, and the stones and timber, @ 11*d.* per hundred, with boatage, 4*s.* 7*d.*

——, Nov 23.

To two workmen covering over the walls of the chapel, @ 3*d.* per day each, 2*s.* 6*d.*

1333, Mar 21.

To John de Hungerford, carpenter, for two days' work on a penthouse on the gable, where the masons began that week to lay the stones on the said gable, @ 5d. per day, 10d.

——, Apr 11.

To two scaffold-makers for erecting a new scaffold round the tower on the north part of the gable, six days' work, @ $3\frac{1}{2}d$. per day each, 3s. 6d.

——, Oct 18.

For 150 beams of alder, @ 2d. each, £1/5/–.
For 1000 beech-laths, @ $2\frac{1}{2}d$. per hundred, 2s. 1d.

——, Oct 25.

For 300 reeds, to cover the penthouse over the gable, @ 10d. per hundred, 2s. 6d.

1333–1337, Jan 23.

For 400 reeds, to cover the gable, oratories, etc., 4s.

——, Apr 18.

To Michael le Disser, for half a hundred of alder poles, for a new scaffold round two towers of the gable of the chapel, @ 2d. each, 8s. 4d.

——, Dec 12.

To John de Lincoln, for 800 beech laths, for covering and preserving two oratories, viz. the King's, between the new chapel and the Painted Chamber, and that in the west gable where the Bell Tower is to be, @ $3\frac{1}{2}d$. per 100, 2s. 4d.
To Tho. Clyp, of Greenwich, for 800 reeds, to cover the walls of the gable of the chapel and oratories, @ 1s. per 100, with boatage, 13s.

1341, Oct 24.

To Agnes le Disshere, for six pieces of alder timber, for a scaffold to the chapel of St. Stephen, near the Receipt, to repair and mend the wall on the south side with plaster of Paris afresh, @ 2d. each, 1s.

1347, Jul 14.

To Agnes Dishe, for 100 hurdles, to put on the top of the chapel to cover and preserve it, 14s.
To the same for seven large hurdles, 2s. 4d.

——, Jul 21.

To William Beynes, for 600 nails, for the ceiling of the chapel, and for the scaffolding, 1s. $6\frac{1}{2}d$.

1351, Aug 1.

To Rich. Euer, for 200 Ryngholt boards, for the scaffold of the upper chapel, £3/6/8.

1352, Jan 9.

To the scaffold-maker, for erecting a scaffold to glaze the windows of the chapel, 2s. 3d.'

For the King's Works at his Palace at Westminster, in 1365, the following items are among those noted in Brayley and Britton, pp. 190 ff.:

'For 50 boards, bought for the masons to make centring, price per foot 4*d*., 16*s*. 8*d*.

For 14 plaunch boards, bought for the same, 7*s*. 3*d*.

For 355 scaffold logs, @ 3*d*. per foot, £4/8/9.

For 150 crates or hurdles ["crat"], bought to make the scaffolds, @ 4*d*. per foot, £2/13/4.

For 5450 thongs [scortic'], bought for the same, @ 7*d*. per 100, £1/11/9½.

For 10 bundles of *warroks*, for the same, @ 2½ per bundle, 2*s*. 1*d*.

For 11,500 spykyngs, for the same work, @ 5*s*. 6*d*. per 1000, £3/3/3.

For one cord "pro Wyron", for a windlass, 9*d*.

For one great cord, bought for a certain engine, weight 42 lbs., at 1¾*d*. per lb., 6*s*. 1½*d*.

For the boatage of 160 hurdles, from Deptford to Westminster, at two trips, 5*s*. 4*d*.

For the carriage of timber, boards, scaffold logs, and other necessaries, from London to Westminster, £1/-/-.'

These and other extensive and seemingly redundant instances of scaffolding from one or another of the Westminster accounts suggest the need for some explanation: why should the English have been so elaborate in their falsework structures in comparison with the French frugality? Even though we have no positive assurance that *all* French examples exercised the most stringent economy of means, nor that *all* English examples were prodigal in their use of falsework structures, there appear to be substantial reasons for these discrepancies in outlay besides the general but deep-seated ones of different national character and attitude.

First of all, there had long been, and there continued to be, a strong national tradition of wood construction in England: we need only cite the countless open timber roofs, including those remarkable hammerbeam and double hammerbeam structures culminating in Hugh Herland's great roof over Westminster Hall, that are unique to England. Again, in connexion with the vaulting (apparently of wood) in St. Stephen's Chapel, erected before the middle of the fourteenth century, Hastings (p. 91) cites the contemporary wooden vaults at St. Albans, York, and Selby to draw the astonishing inference that 'the imitation of stone vaulting in wood is a fashion of the time'. Second, there was a great deal more timber of stout and lengthy proportions at hand in England than in France: we may note what difficulty Abbot Suger had, before the middle of the twelfth century and long before many of the great Gothic buildings were even begun, in locating as few as twelve great beams for the 'ceiling' of his new choir (*vide* Panofsky, pp. 95 ff.). Third, with respect to the falsework in the nave proper, the English nature of the vaults, with their huge keystone bosses, would help to account for the massive scaffoldings there. For it is noteworthy that various entries covering the purchase of 'great stones' for *lez keyes* occur during the 1480's at Westminster Abbey; and that in 1491-2, twenty great stones 'each too big for a cart' were bought (Rackham, p. 75).

It is significant in the Abbey accounts, moreover, that when the *roof* is being erected, three levels of scaffolding are mentioned (cf. (3) above); whereas when the high *vaulting* is in progress there is mention (cf. (4) above) only of 'the great scaffold, upon which the centres stood and where the masons worked'. From this distinction it seems likely that the roof construction involved smaller, though more numerous, units of scaffolding than did the vaulting; and this is logical enough since the latter had to be far more rigid, stable, and strong to carry the weight of the centers and their burden of vault masonry.

The Abbey accounts for 1482–90 make it clear that the great scaffold for erecting the vaulting occupied a single bay at a time, and was moved to the next bay as each such unit of the vaulting was completed. (This was apparently not true in King's College Chapel, where a separate scaffolding was used for each bay of the vaulting; doubtless because here, untypically, the roof was constructed only after the vaulting was completed.) How the moving operation was accomplished is not entirely clear. But it is significant that the tie-beams of the roof, including those beyond the bay being vaulted, were utilized to support planking on which 'the great wheel was placed so as to raise up the great keys' (*vide* section (4) of the quotations from Rackham, above). Thus it would appear that these heavy stones were raised vertically to the level of a temporary plank staging laid across the tie-beams of a not-yet-vaulted bay, and were then shifted or dragged horizontally on this staging to a point directly above the intersection of the groin ribs in the bay under construction, where they could be lowered a few feet carefully and accurately into place.

There is a paucity of detail in regard to the nature of the centers and the formwork that supported the masonry of the vault web. However, another passage is worth quoting in this connexion, pertaining to the erection of the two bays of the high vaulting that were the last to be built. Rackham writes (p. 79): 'The carpenters' bill continues to be heavy in the following years [1501–5], but full details are not given as hitherto. They are working *circa les scaffoldes*; centres are also mentioned. . . . The carpenters receive £18/17/-; timber is bought for scaffolding, and over 17,000 "quarters" of "elmenbord" and "Slyttyngwork" are sawn *pro nova volta ecclesie.* . . .' (*Vide* Salzman, p. 243, for a possible explanation of 'slyttyngwork' or 'slitware' that is sawn.) This very large number of wooden pieces apparently destined for the formwork of but two bays of the nave vaulting would seem to be one of the very few contemporary references we have of the amount of material used for carrying the masonry of the high vault during its erection, as practised by the English builders of the later Middle Ages.

Another apparent discrepancy between English and French building practices is that of the sequence of construction with respect to the flying buttresses. To be sure, they were finished before the high vaulting was started, but they appear to have been undertaken immediately *after* rather than before the nave roof was erected. This in spite of the danger of high winds, one of which blew out the great rose window of the south transept in 1362, a hundred years after it had been built (Rackham, p. 60). Apparently the builders took a chance, as contractors nowadays often do, on the unlikelihood of a great wind occurring. And there may well have been some shoring of the clerestory walls to make this chance they took less of a gamble.

But intrinsically in the building itself there was less need for the precaution afforded by either the flying buttresses themselves or their rigid centerings alone. For example, there appears to be no false bearing, either above the side-aisle wall responds or above the piers of the nave arcade, which would necessitate, as in various French examples, cross bracing or strutting to prevent the clerestory piers and the buttresses proper from leaning towards each other. For all its height—some hundred feet to the vaulting, which is unusual for an English cathedral—this church is far more massive than the great French churches of the thirteenth century. For example, the high windows of the nave do not take up anywhere near all the space they could, between the clerestory piers. And there is also the heavy, permanent timber bracing, furnished by the slightly pitched roofs over the side-aisle tribunes, that abuts the walls of the nave at a level more than two-thirds of their total height. Actually, the naves of about half the English cathedrals have no flying buttresses at all, a few have them at intermittent and seemingly haphazard intervals, and in one or two others they impinge at so low a point against the clerestory wall that they are obviously needed, if at all, for abutting the vaults rather than for stabilizing the whole superstructure against wind action.

These great English churches are very different, then, from the lofty, skeletonized French structures that would surely have collapsed—either at the time of their erection or subsequently—without the flying buttresses the French themselves were the first to adopt.

One further matter needs to be noted. There are a number of items in the accounts that mention (1) canvas to keep out the weather (and the pigeons), and (2) the boarding up of the windows. A few of these are quoted above. When we read that 'the great windows of the new work were all boarded up' at the very time the vaulting was in progress, we wonder how there could have been light enough, under the shelter of the lead-covered roof, for the masons working on the vaulting to be able to see what they were doing. When we also read that 'each portion of the great scaffold, upon which the centres stood and where the masons worked, was floored and shut off by partitions from wind and weather', it is evident that very little natural light could penetrate to the scene of operations, either from below or from the side.

Perhaps a series of small louvred dormers, of the sort shown in the earliest photographs of Paris Cathedral (which preceded and have survived its restoration by Viollet-le-Duc), sufficiently took care of this matter.

APPENDIX L

Abbot Suger on the New Work at St-Denis: A Reinterpretation

IN the light of these considerations—the strutting function of the flying buttresses together with tie-beams of the great roof, and the order of sequence in their erection as here suggested—it is perhaps worth reconsidering and speculating upon that well-known passage in Suger's *De Consecratione* in which the abbot describes the 'miraculous' survival of his unfinished choir when a great storm arose.[1]

The theories and speculations of the nineteenth-century writers on the function of the ribs in Gothic vaulting, and the controversies that have flared up in our own century on this subject, are doubtless responsible in large part for colouring the interpretation that has been given to this oft-quoted passage. Because of this preoccupation with the ribs, everyone up to the present day has read this admittedly difficult and somewhat equivocal passage as the classical recognition of the skeletal independence of the ribs at the time of the vault's erection and prior to the construction of the webs or panels of infilling. Some writers have gone farther, interpreting Suger's account as corroborating the supporting function of the ribs in Gothic vaulting, wherein the compartments of the vault are thought merely to rest upon the permanent stone skeleton of the ribs, which alone are thought to receive and transmit all the vault pressures.

Whatever the degree of these interpretations, however, there are still unresolved difficulties and unsatisfactory speculations to account for, as Panofsky's two full pages of commentary on this passage demonstrate.[2] Of course, it should be emphasized that Suger's primary purpose in writing this passage was to demonstrate or prove a miracle; and for this reason the whole passage is suspect as an accurate description of the state of the building at the time, and of just what did happen. However, if we assume the trustworthiness of the account (which all writers appear generally to have done), it is nevertheless possible to interpret certain words and expressions in the passage somewhat differently, in the light of the more comprehensive frame of reference, structurally speaking, we have been pursuing, from the way in which they have hitherto been interpreted by previous writers, however painstaking.

Two of the key expressions in any interpretation of Suger's meaning are 'cum necdum principales arcus singulariter voluti[3] voltarum cumulo cohaererent' and, some

[1] *Vide* Erwin Panofsky, *Abbot Suger on the Abbey Church of St-Denis and Its Treasures*, Princeton, Princeton University Press, 1946, pp. 108, 109.
[2] Ibid., pp. 224–6.
[3] *Vide* Panofsky's own correction of the

9 lines later, 'nullis renitentes suffragiis'. A more literal translation of the latter would appear to illuminate the meaning of the former. This would make the pertinent portions of the translation go something as follows (italics added):

'When the work of the new addition was being carried forward with capitals and upper arches to the peak of its height, but the principal arches, having been separately turned, were not yet *consolidated by the piling up of the vault*, [. . . a terrible storm arose . . . during which] such a force of opposing winds buffeted against the aforesaid arches, which were neither undergirt by any platform *nor favoured by any resistance*, that they threatened destructive collapse at any moment, trembling miserably and swaying back and forth as it were. The Bishop became greatly alarmed by this vibration of the arches and the roofing [. . . but . . . the tempest] was unable to dislocate these isolated, recently built arches wavering up aloft. . . .'

With respect to the structure he is describing, Suger appears to use layman's terms throughout, and terms for the most conspicuous or recognizable features at that. Thus he speaks of capitals, arches, vault, and roof. When it comes to technical terms for the falsework or for the action of the stresses, he appears either not to know these terms or to prefer not to use them, since his treatise is not addressed to an audience of technicians. It is almost as though the abbot were echoing an explanation of the structure made to him by the master mason, but in his own words, using his own figures of speech, his own ecclesiastical equivalents. For example, the word *suffragiis*, which Panofsky would read as 'centering', does not appear to be used by any other writers in this sense, as a builder's technical term. Gervase uses the term *machines*, which comes much closer to the sense of 'centerings', although this Latin word is a very general term that could cover almost any equipment or artificial contrivance for performing work. Doubtless *suffragiis* should be taken in a much more literal sense, as suffrage, favour, support, vote, interest.

Much of the confusion in the interpretation of this passage appears to be in the double use of the word *arcus*, first in the expression *arcubus superioribus* (l. 6), and next as *principales arcus* (ll. 7–8). It is to the 'principal arches' that the subsequent uses of this noun logically refer, first in the expression *praefatos arcus* (l. 17), then in *quorum* (l. 20), and later (l. 27) in the phrase *recentibus arcubus*. It is these *principales arcus* that were 'not yet consolidated' by the piling up or massing of the vault, although they had already 'been separately turned'; they are the ones that had already been freed of their centering, although as yet they were receiving no abutting 'resistance' to their thrust; they are the ones that were in full view, 'isolated up aloft'. Clearly, these arches had been completed. The *arcus superiores*, on the other hand, along with the capitals, were 'being carried forward'. They constituted part of the work in hand, which was in process of being raised 'to the peak of its height'.

It should be remembered that the Gothic structural system was a very novel thing at

Latin word *veluti* to read *voluti*, with his accompanying commentary, in 'Postlogium Sugerianum', *The Art Bulletin*, June 1947, vol. xxix, p. 120.

the time Suger was building his new work, the upper choir. The most conspicuous features of this new structural scheme were certainly the flying buttresses, those isolated external props which to the layman would readily be thought to be the principal arches. Whether these were double-tiered, as in the still existing ones dating from the reconstruction of the thirteenth century, or single-tiered and of more rudimentary type, in any case the nature of this unprecedented structure with its innovation of full bay-sized clerestory windows and lofty ribbed vaulting seems to argue incontrovertibly the presence of some sort of flying buttresses from the start.[1]

[1] To the objection that the existing flying buttresses of St-Denis date from the thirteenth century and therefore do not necessarily reflect Suger's original construction, it should be recalled, first of all, that there is general agreement among scholars that this church is not a Romanesque but a definitely Gothic structure. No less an authority than Professor Conant calls it 'that first of all Gothic churches' (K. J. Conant, 'Observations on the Vaulting Problems of the Period 1088–1211', *Gazette des Beaux-Arts*, series 6, July–Dec. 1944, vol. xxvi, p. 131).

Previously in the same article (p. 128), Conant speaks of the great early nave of Cluny as being covered with a banded barrel vault that 'collapsed in 1125', only to be 'rebuilt with archaic flying buttresses soon after', which were such effective props that the structure 'remained secure until the demolition (1798–1811)'. He goes on to say (p. 130) that 'the narthex bays at Cluny seem appropriately dated not far from 1130', and that 'the narthex was completed in the Burgundian half-Gothic style of the late twelfth or early thirteenth century, and the original bays were strengthened by flying buttresses at the time *if not before*' (italics added). Yet with respect to the abbey church of St-Denis (begun about 1134; the choir finished and consecrated in 1144), Conant states (p. 131) that 'the St-Denis vaults employed ramping penetrations on ribbed structure, and (as obviously in the Cluny narthex) the thrusts were received into the walls without flying buttresses'.

In view of his previous discussion of essentially Romanesque Cluny, however, this latter denial of flying buttresses at early Gothic St-Denis is further confused by his statement (p. 133) that 'Gothic structure, achieved in large measure at St-Denis, for the first time allowed vast windows in a fire-proof mediaeval church'. It is difficult to see how such an accomplishment could have been secured without the agency of flying buttresses.

Crosby, whose excavation and thorough study of St-Denis have covered so many years of patient and persistent effort, frankly states that 'L'élévation de la nef et du chœur doivent rester dans le domaine des hypothèses. Le chœur était achevé, mais la reconstruction des parties hautes au XIIIᵉ siècle a détruit toute indication concernant l'état du sanctuaire au temps de Suger' (S. McK. Crosby, 'Fouilles exécutées récemment dans la basilique de Saint-Denis', *Bulletin monumental*, 1947, vol. cv, p. 175). In other words, this scholar who has made St-Denis his special subject for prolonged and concentrated investigation cannot tell us what the original disposition of abutment for the high vaults of the choir may have been; but neither does he preclude the possibility of flying buttresses in either one or two tiers.

Actually, however, there is a certain amount of positive presumptive evidence in favour of the presence of flying buttresses from the start, in a later article by Crosby ('Early Gothic Architecture: New Problems as a Result of the St-Denis Excavations', *Journal of the Society of Architectural Historians*, July–Dec. 1948, vol. vii, pp. 13–16). 'It is surprising to note', he writes (p. 15), 'that the buttresses between the radiating chapels jut out from the adjacent masonry at angles which do not coincide with the perimeter of the chevet as a whole. If the lines of the buttresses are continued inward, however, they meet at a point several feet to the east of the center for the radii of the outline of the chevet. This point could very easily have coincided with the keystone for the ribs of the semi-circular, or upper choir, vaults. Such a system for choir vaults is not at all unusual, but we have not taken into account how this divergency of centers created counter-tensions in the

In this connexion, an examination of Viollet-le-Duc's drawings of the thirteenth-century system of St-Denis that appear in his *Dictionnaire* will help to clarify the meaning of Suger's text,[1] and show how conspicuously prominent these flying buttresses (or rather, their pre-thirteenth-century predecessors) would have been from any view-point. Seen from the exterior, the early Gothic superstructure, whatever its membering may have been in detail, had been built by the time the tempest struck (this we know from the fact that the roof was in place); and, with the constructional falsework removed, it would have been clearly evident to all: a source of both amazement and admiration because of the height of the unscaffolded *arcus principales* above the side aisle, and because of their remarkable novelty.

The interior, on the other hand, would not have been open to the public, nor would the work going on in the superstructure there have been either observable or intelligible if it had been. Work on the high vaulting (the *arcus superiores*) was going forward 'to the peak of its height', from the capitals to the crown, and the choir would have been filled with scaffolding, workmen's platforms, and the centering framework. This is what Forsyth refers to as 'the general clumsiness and dense confusion of the support-ing framework' (the *multiplex lignorum strues* of a Latin text of *c.* 1095, which he translates (p. 127) as 'the labyrinthine aggregation of timbers').[2] Here was a con-glomeration of requisite paraphernalia with which the final structural operation—building the high vault—was being consummated, all in the dim light high up beneath the shelter of the roof. What was going on there would have been difficult to see, from down below, in any event; and the layman would have found it quite impossible to differentiate the timber-work of permanent roof and temporary falsework in the clutter of beams, struts, platform staging, and scaffolding poles.[3]

It will be noted that Suger's account of what happened during the storm is second-

masonry. Nor have we given, perhaps, enough credit to the far-sightedness of the Gothic master-mason, or architect, who from the very beginning of his construction was able to compute and allow for these tensions, which increased the stability of his skeletal, stone framework.'

On the basis of these observations it is pos-sible that the only reason for this unexpected angle the buttresses make with the periphery of the chevet was to conform to the direction of flying buttresses spanning the void of the am-bulatory, in line with the ribs and hence the thrusts of the high vault. The 'skeletal, stone framework' would seem to have made these flying buttresses inevitable from the start.

[1] E. Viollet-le-Duc, *Dictionnaire raisonné de l'architecture française du XIe au XVIe siècle*, Paris, Libraires-Imprimeries Réunies, 1854–68, 10 vols. *Vide* article 'Arc', vol. i,

p. 66, fig. 55; and article 'Fenêtre', vol. v, p. 394, fig. 24.

[2] G. H. Fòrsyth, Jr., *The Church of St. Martin at Angers*, Princeton, Princeton Uni-versity Press, 1953, p. 129.

[3] In speaking of the work of reparation to Winchester Cathedral in 1896–8, which in-volved, along with much other falsework, 'the lofty and graceful travelling bridge scaffolding spanning the nave, running on tram rails sup-ported on cantilever brackets projecting from the triforium arches', Colson speaks of 'the fact that, as seen from below, the full extent of the work that has been carried out, the magnitude of the undertaking, and of the difficulties that had to be overcome cannot adequately be con-ceived' (*vide* J. B. Colson, *Winchester Cathe-dral: A Description and Illustrated Record of the Reparations of the Nave Roof, 1896–8*, Winchester, 1899, p. 6).

hand: it was not he who saw the arches 'trembling miserably and swaying back and forth as it were'. It was the Bishop of Chartres, celebrating a conventual Mass at the main altar, who was there at the time. And it is quite understandable that, in reporting to his host, the abbot, his profound uneasiness over the stability of such a towering, skeletal structure during the storm, and his belief in its miraculous preservation due to the power of the sacred relic he held extended in expiatory faith, he would have perhaps unconsciously exaggerated the circumstances because 'the grace of God and the merit of the Saints' were glorified thereby. The main altar was not within the choir, but just to the west of it, in the transept-crossing of the existing Carolingian church to which the new work was attached. Whether the bishop could actually *see* the arches trembling at the time (possibly through the voids of as yet unglazed windows) is not stated. He was certainly aware of and alarmed by the strong 'vibration of the arches and the roofing', for he 'frequently extended his blessing arm in the direction of that part' where the structure, being farthest from its fixed and stable anchorage in the ground, was most exposed or most 'isolated', and therefore appeared to be and doubtless was actually 'trembling'.

There would have been many arches in Suger's new choir: for example, those in the choir arcade and at the triforium level, the ribs of both the side aisle and the high vaulting, the window arches of both side aisle and clerestory. None of these, however, was 'isolated' but was either surcharged with spandrels of walling or (as in the case of the ribs of the choir ceiling) destined to be one of the boundaries of the severies of continuous vaulting. The flying buttresses, on the other hand, were independent arches leaping between buttress and clerestory wall. The adjective *principales* seems a particularly apt one for the flying buttresses since they are free spans (actually, half-arches) that remain in view as free-standing arcs; whereas the arches of rib vaulting are visually no more than projecting linear forms accenting the continuous surfaces of the vaulting. The flying buttress arches can be thought of as the *arcus principales* of Suger's account both because they were the only ones that could have been seen as free-standing, separate spans, and because they had the main job of bracing the entire superstructure.

Incidentally, Panofsky's translation of *singulariter voluti* as 'independently vaulted arches' (those that had been 'separately turned') seems a particularly revealing phrase to convey the constructional distinction between the two types of *arcus*. For, in clearly differentiating what has already been done from what is currently being undertaken, does it not emphasize the prior building and completion of the flying buttresses, before the vaulting complex was taken in hand?

It has been shown elsewhere that the upper flying buttress was employed primarily as a permanent shore to resist the overturning force of the wind.[1] Whether Suger's choir vaults were braced by flying buttresses in one tier or in two tiers, in any event this shoring function seems to have been conclusively demonstrated, even before the

---

[1] J. F. Fitchen III, 'A Comment on the Function of the Upper Flying Buttress in French Gothic Architecture', *Gazette des Beaux-Arts*, series 6, Feb. 1955, vol. xlv, pp. 69–90.

vaulting had come to interpose its own supplementary consolidation across the interior, at the time the tempest struck.

The ribs of the vaulting—the *arcus superiores* of Suger's account—were somewhat higher than the flying buttress arches. If the latter were originally single (as may very well have been the case, since the early examples of this external bracing of masonry that are still extant are invariably single-tiered), they would normally have impinged against the clerestory wall somewhere between spring and mid-haunch of the vault ribs within.

If the above distinctions be granted between *arcus principales* and *arcus superiores* on the basis of their referring to flying buttress arches and to the ribs of the vaulting, respectively, then the difficulties Panofsky and other writers have wrestled with—as to the sequence of the ribs' erection and the presence or absence of centering—are no longer troublesome. For now Suger's account can be read as not referring to the falsework of the vaulting in any way. Quite simply, the slender flying buttress arches, having been finished, were no longer supported or undergirt by any centering, but the entire complex of the rib vaulting was then in process of construction, with whatever scaffolding, centering, and workmen's platforms may have been needed for this final, major, erectional undertaking.

Panofsky is certainly right in thinking that the duplication of effort involved in constructing and decentering the transverse arches alone, then constructing and decentering the diagonal ribs of the high vault, would never have occurred. But, by the same token, the builders would not have tolerated the dangerous and totally impractical situation in which the nave-spanning ribs were all decentered before the construction of the webs began. In view of their high-vault spans and their relatively small cross-section, vaulting ribs that were *un*-supported by their own centering frames would surely have collapsed when their haunches alone became weighted by the web masonry as it rose course by course towards the vault crown.

At the time of the great storm, only the roof with its weight and its tie-beams linked the wall-tops together, thereby uniting them in resistance to the shuddering blasts. The 'piling up of the vault', within, which had not yet occurred, would become the permanent stabilizing feature that would brace the superstructure internally against pressures from without; that is, against the crown thrusts of the flying buttress arches and, of much greater seriousness, the live load of wind against roof slope and clerestory wall. Not until the completion of the vaulting would the stability of the whole superstructure become assured, through the consolidation it furnished high in the interior against both the constant pressure of the flying buttresses and the greatly increased pressures exerted from time to time because of the wind.

A very free paraphrasing of the pertinent portions of Suger's account, where modern terminology is used and the literal constructions of the Latin are augmented so as to make the meaning, as here proposed, unequivocal, might run somewhat as follows:

'When the work on the capitals and the high vaulting of the new addition was being carried out to its full height (but before the flying buttresses, which had been separately erected, were consolidated across the choir, within, by the interposition of the vaulting), a violent storm arose during which these flying buttress arches, neither supported by their falsework nor abutted by the thrust of the vault, were so buffeted by contrary winds that they trembled and appeared to sway, threatening imminent collapse. In spite of this alarming vibration of both the roof and the arches, the tempest did not succeed in dislocating these lofty, free-standing flying buttress arches that had but recently been erected.'

APPENDIX M

Strutting Systems Used in Centering Frames

McMaster gives the following description and analysis of the types of timber-work assemblages used in fashioning centering frames for masonry arches.

'As the sole object of the framing', he says, 'is to uphold the voussoirs and transmit the strains it receives as directly as possible to firm points of support, the beams must be so arranged as to do this with the least tendency to change the shape of the rib, by their bending or breaking. The conditions will be best fulfilled by giving each beam a position such that it shall offer the greatest possible resistance, and this will be accomplished when the direction of the fibres of the beam and the direction of the strain are one and the same . . .' (p. 27).

'Applying this fact to the framing of the ribs, it follows that the greatest stiffness and strength will be gained when the principal pieces are placed in the direction of the strains, or in the direction of the radii of curvature of the arch to be upheld. This deduction, unfortunately, is under certain restrictions placed upon it by the imperfections of the timber, and demands of economy and the circumstances of construction, which make its practical application quite limited . . .' (pp. 28, 29).

'There are, therefore, three methods of arranging the principal pieces or struts of a centre frame:

(1) They may be placed in the direction of the radii of curvature of the arch, thus giving a figure of invariable form as the strain at any one point is received by the beam in the most favorable position, and transmitted through its axis directly to the fixed point of support.

(2) They may be placed in a vertical, or in vertical and horizontal directions.

(3) The curve of the arch may be divided into a number of arcs, and the beams placed in the direction of the chords of these arcs.

(4) To these three we may add a fourth, which embraces by far the largest number of centre frames, and is based on two or all of the preceding methods. In this class the beams are not arranged in accordance with any one system, but several; as, for instance, the second and third, in which case, as we will see hereafter, several straining beams span the arch at different points, and are sustained by inclined struts; or if all three systems are used, we may use the straining beam and inclined struts, and strengthen them by bridle pieces in the direction of the radii . . .' (pp. 32, 33).

'Theoretically, the first method will in all cases afford the greatest amount of strength

296

and stability with the least amount of material, since the beams are then capable of resisting the most severe strains. Nor can there be any doubt that, within moderate limits, this result actually is attained in practice, and that of two ribs constructed with the same number of beams, of the same quality of wood and similar dimensions, in one of which the pieces are placed radially, and in the other vertically or inclined, the rib arrangement on the former plan will be decidedly the stronger of the two. But, unfortunately, the impossibility of always obtaining firm points of support at the centre of curvature, the difficulty of finding sound, well seasoned timber of such length as would be required in arches of large span, and the relation which exists between the length and strength of beams under longitudinal compression—the strength varying inversely as the square of the length—restricts its application to centre frames of very small span and rise. In semi-circular arches of twelve, fifteen or even twenty feet span, when a horizontal beam can be used at the springing line this arrangement can be used with great success. The frame then consists of the tie beam and two, or if great strength is required, three radial struts which support the back-pieces and abut against the horizontal beam at the centre of curvature. These struts, when two are used, should be inclined on the right and left at a little less than 45° to the horizon, so as to meet the back-pieces at the point where the voussoirs first begin to press on the rib. A vertical strut is in such an arrangement of little or no use, as no strain of any consequence can possibly reach it; the voussoirs almost ceasing to press on the frame when the keystone is driven down. As these supports are struts and not bridle pieces clamping the back-pieces and tie-beam between them, the joints, especially in the larger and heavier arches, must be secured by pieces of iron placed across them and bolted to the backpieces and struts, to prevent the joints opening in consequence of the bulging at the crown as course after course of stone is laid on the frame' (pp. 34–36).

'Frames arranged on the second method, with the principal pieces all vertical, afford centres of great simplicity of structure and of almost as much strength as one with radial struts—supposing, of course, that the number and dimensions of the struts are the same in each case—and of much greater strength than one constructed with inclined beams, since the nearer the angle the direction of the strain makes with the fibres of the wood approaches a right angle the less becomes the resistance of the beam. . . . The objection to this vertical bracing of the frame is that it requires the use of a horizontal tie beam, unless the rib is constructed as a girder resting upon framed abutments of its own. If the former arrangement is used, the struts should be placed from five to eight feet apart, depending on the strength required, and mortised to the tie beam and backpiece. When the beams are of such length that there is danger of their bulging or curving under the load laid on them, they may be strengthened by diagonal braces or horizontal wales. Of the two, the diagonal braces are to be preferred as they not only give stiffness to the posts, but sustain a portion of the load on the backpieces in case any of the piles under the horizontal tie beam should give way . . .' (pp. 52–54).

'The third and fourth systems of arranging the principal pieces afford an almost.

unlimited number of designs for centre ribs, which are especially worthy of notice, in that they are applicable to every possible shape and span that can be given to stone arches, and may be constructed with or without intermediate points of support, according as circumstance will admit. The principles which control such arrangements are few and simple. The beams should as far as possible abut end to end: they should intersect each other as little as may be since every joint causes some degree of settlement, and halving destroys fully half the strength of the beams halved. When the framing is composed of a number of beams crossing each other, pieces tending toward the centre should be notched upon and bolted to the framing in pairs; ties should also be continued across the frame at points where many timbers meet. Particular attention must, furthermore, be given to the manner of connecting the beams so that there should be no tendency to rise at the crown under the action of the varying load.' An instance is given of 'a simple method of arranging the timbers for arches of small span', wherein 'the inclined struts abut against horizontal straining beams placed at different points on the soffit; and, to add greater strength to the framing, and to prevent the horizontal beam from sagging, bridle pieces are placed in the direction of the radii of curvature. The chief difficulty with such arrangement as this is, that as they require beams of great length they can be used to advantage only in small span arches . . .' (pp. 56, 57).

APPENDIX N

An Instance of Vault Centering that Survives from the Gothic Era

THE Lärbro vault is an irregular octagon in plan, about 8·50 metres (27½ feet) from side to side, with cells somewhat similar to Gothic apse vaults but with their crowns sloping downward to pointed lunettes of solid walling which are practically devoid of any window openings (*vide* Curman and Roosval, *Sveriges Kyrkor: Konsthistoriskt Inventarium*, figs. 150,.152 (pp. 95, 97); text, p. 100; notes viii and x, p. 114).

According to the text illustrations (which are transverse and longitudinal sections through the tower, reduced from carefully delineated drawings at larger scale), it appears that this is not a ribbed vault but one of coarse rubble throughout. The nature of the masonry is disclosed in the upper portion of the western severy (fig. 150), where the planking formwork has fallen in or been removed. Both cross-sections show the vault to be very thick, averaging about 1·30 metres (4 feet 3 inches) at the walls and tapering to about 0·60 metres (2 feet) at the center where the crowns converge.

Apparently the planking was left in place for two reasons, one negative, the other positive. The negative reason would be that there was no point in bothering to remove it, since it could not be seen: the ground story is similarly vaulted, so there is no possibility of the upper vault being open to view from the church's interior, below. Moreover, the 'window' openings in the tower are so minute—practically nothing but small vents—that this high vaulting complex is in almost complete darkness and obscurity.

The positive reason stems from the nature of the vault: a massive rubble concretion, but with salient groins. (Due to these salient groins, the Lärbro vault is fundamentally different from the cloister vault with rounded re-entrant angles that is set in the crossing tower of Saint-Martin's at Angers, although Forsyth (op. cit., p. 127) attempts to link the latter's technique of erection closely to that of Lärbro.) Since there appear to be no stone ribs, the lagging of continuous planking would have needed to remain in position for a long time—even for a number of years, perhaps—until the mortar in this thick vault had thoroughly consolidated. The vault below is so similar, except for its somewhat more steeply sloping crowns, that it is quite possible this same centering may have been used for it and then transferred, frame by frame and board by board, to the high location with but little modification. At any rate, both lower and upper vaults make use of approximately Gothic *shapes* of vault, although the masonry of these vaults is anything but Gothic in *execution*. Indeed, the thick mass of coarse rubble is early Romanesque in character, and it is perhaps only the centering for it that shows some Gothic lightness of technique. The centering frames do indicate, however, how intersecting assemblages of timber could be built without any metal. And the late date of construction (given as 1522) could reflect both the apparent anomalies of execution and the time lag that might well have occurred for the thirteenth-century building practices of the great *chantiers* at the centers of creative activity to travel to this rather distant locale.

APPENDIX O

Intersecting Centering Frames, and the Use of Models to Solve the Difficulties Encountered

JUDGING by the evidence of some of the earliest rib vaults, the adoption of ribs under the groins was at first complicated by the difficulty of fashioning the formwork for them. (This was doubtless the reason, also, for the long delay in rib-vaulting the apse, which remained—perhaps partly for strong traditional and liturgical reasons—a simple half-dome, until the builders became proficient with the technique of erecting rib vaults.) Unlike the vault-stiffening arches of both the banded barrel vault and the simple groin vault with transverse ribs bounding each bay, ribs along the groin had to intersect; and this involved the intersection of their centering frames, too, at the time they were constructed. The evidence of a number of illustrations—mostly photographic —of the stone jointing at the crown of early vaults with intersecting salient ribs (as given in Aubert, op. cit., for example) suggests the scheme of their erection: one diagonal rib was built as a complete arch, and the other as two half-arches abutting the first at its crown.

This appears to have been the case as far back in time as the small atypical Roman example of the irregularly shaped room at Setti Bassi, figured in Aubert, p. 11 (from Rivoira's work on Roman architecture). It is clearly apparent in the photograph (p. 14) of the porch at Moissac (in spite of Porter's denial in *Lombard Vaults*, p. 12, fig. 17, where his version of the stone jointing differs somewhat from Viollet-le-Duc's, article 'Porche', vol. vii, p. 292, fig. 26 at N). It is also evident in the following illustrations in Aubert: Tower vault at the old cathedral of Sisteron (p. 17); Tower vault of St-Hilaire at Poitiers (p. 19); Choir vault in the church of St-Paul at Rouen; and in the Cloister vaults with ribs at the re-entrant angles, at Cormery (p. 41) and at Mouliherne (p. 45).

These indications that the centering frame for one of the two groin ribs was non-continuous from spring to spring would suggest the technique (of using approximately half-span frames for diagonal ribs and for apse ribs) that had to be mastered by the medieval builders before they could reap the significant benefits of the rib vault system. The fact that these early examples of criss-crossing ribs—invariably of broad, heavy arches—intersect at right angles (at least in French and Italian examples) demonstrates clearly the trials and hesitations the builders underwent in their first essays with the new system. Not until they had thoroughly mastered the multiple problems of juncture for the half-frames of rib centering at their common crowns, could the builders fashion the truly Gothic vaulting on slender ribs that is found in trapezoidal ambulatory bays, in the many-celled complexes of apse vaulting, and in the great nave and choir bays of strongly rectangular quadripartite vaults. In none of these was it possible for the rib frames to intersect at right angles; and, except for the ambulatory, there was the concomitant problem of erecting and decentering them high up in the lofty interior, which ruled out centering frames that spanned the whole width of the central void of the church in one ponderous assemblage of timber-work.

In order to work out these complicated requirements, the medieval builders resorted to models. So it is that Percy J. Waldram, in a thoughtful and informing letter to the editor of the *R.I.B.A. Journal* published under the title 'Science and Architecture: Wren and Hooke', reminds us that 'When Hugh Herland, Master Carpenter to Richard II, designed Westminster Hall roof ... his text books and stress diagrams were his innumerable models, which as we know occupied so much space that rooms in the King's palace had to be reserved for them. ...' This, to be sure, was a supreme example of the carpenter's art at the end of the fourteenth century. But there is much evidence that models were used extensively throughout the Gothic era for working out difficult and unprecedented structural problems. Unquestionably there must have been widespread use of models also in solving the practical problems of erection.

William Harvey (in the *R.I.B.A. Journal* of 12 June 1924; in his *St. Paul's*; and especially in his *Models of Buildings*, chap. iii) is the first, and possibly the only one to date, to have revived this practice with respect to buildings of the past. The illustrations he provides, and the comments he makes on his own carefully executed analytical models of Gothic structures, give us some insight into the probable practices of former times.

APPENDIX P

Medieval Lifting Devices and Procedures

WATSON remarks (pp. 117 ff.) that the thirteenth century 'had the means of raising considerable loads in a vertical direction, but it had no appliance that would swing a weight even of half a ton for some distance horizontally at a height of 50 or 100 feet above the ground. As the stones had to be built all round the clerestory, each course at a different level, it would have required a mass of heavy scaffolding, and involved great and unnecessary labour, to raise them outside the aisle walls and convey them to their places. But the mediaeval builder never employed heavy scaffolding, or scaffolding of any kind in great quantities; his appliances were few and his methods as simple and direct as possible. What, then, were the means available, and what must have been the method employed to raise the large stones of the triforium and clerestory?'

'To answer that question we may consider for a moment the nature and extent of the scaffolding used in the middle ages, the mechanical appliances that were employed, and the process followed in conveying and raising heavy loads.'

'We have said that the mediaeval builder worked without heavy scaffolding, and it may be added that he used the smallest amount even of light scaffolding and gangways. The buildings themselves amply demonstrate that the walls were their own main scaffolding, and supported the light wooden brackets and planks which the builders used and moved from place to place as the work proceeded. The wooden scaffolding used in the construction of the upper walls of a high building, even that used in the erection of towers and spires, was not as a rule carried up from the base of the building, but was bracketed out from the walls. It was used for the circulation of the workers and the movement of such loads only as they could carry, never to support the heavier materials, which were raised directly from the ground on to the walls.'

'As the walls were almost always built from the inside, it was necessary that the heavier stones should be wheeled into the building on the level of the ground. The absence of heavy scaffolding and of far-reaching cranes made it imperative that they should be brought as near as possible under the position which they were to occupy on the walls, and the appliances at the disposal of the builders required that they should be hoisted vertically. The process implied a roadway into the interior of the building; it required that the stones should be wheeled in by this roadway on such hand-carts as

303

APPENDIX P

that figured in Viollet-le-Duc (vol. v, p. 218, fig. 6), and that they should be hoisted directly into their places on the walls. . . . It is an obvious conclusion, therefore, that the middle vault was delayed in order to admit of the heavy material of the upper walls and pillars being directly hoisted into position from the level of the ground. . . .'

'With regard to the nature of the machinery employed at this time, it is to be noted that up till the latter part of the XII century only small stones were used in building in this country, and it may be inferred that only the simplest mechanical appliances were employed in transporting or raising them. The stones were, indeed, such as could be handled by the unaided efforts of the workers. With the advent of William of Sens at Canterbury in 1174, or at all events about that date, improved methods and new machinery were introduced into England. At the very outset of his work, as we are informed by Gervase, "he constructed ingenious machines for loading and unloading ships and for drawing cement and stones". The work of the Frenchman at Canterbury is in evidence, and is distinguished from that of his predecessors, not only by its design, but by the greater size of the stones of which it is constructed.'

'In the XIII century the advance of mechanical skill was such as to make the use of comparatively large material general in the more important buildings. . . . The mechanical appliances of the XIII century included the windlass, pulley, and screw, with a variety of adaptations of the lever and the inclined plane. The motive power was chiefly manual, though draught animals were also employed. . . . The hoisting apparatus in use was mainly of the windlass and pulley type, and was capable of a direct vertical lift only; it could not transport a load horizontally for some distance above the level of the ground without heavy scaffolding. There was no means open to the builder of raising a heavy load to a considerable height except in a direct vertical line, and it thus became a matter of necessity that the middle of the [church] should be left open from the ground upwards until the clerestory walls were finished. . . .'

'We do not suggest that Vilars' "most powerful engine known for raising weights" was employed at Glasgow or in the majority of the churches of the period. Had it been in common use the probability is that Vilars would not have thought it necessary to depict it. But it is certain that a hoisting apparatus of some kind was employed—some application, it may be supposed, of the windlass wrought by men on the ground, and directed by a foreman or by those who were to receive and set the stones on the wall. The rope would pass over a pulley on the jib of a short crane or attached to a beam or bracket at a suitable height, one end would be wound on the drum of the windlass, and the other would terminate with a "lewis" for grappling the stone to be raised. . . .'

Viollet-le-Duc (*Dictionnaire*, article 'Engin', vol. v, p. 218), writing shortly after the middle of the nineteenth century, says that 'Only in the last twenty years or so have notable improvements (*perfectionnements*) taken place in the basic design and the composition of machines employed in building construction: up to that time the apparatuses that had served in the thirteenth century were similarly employed, whether to

304

transport materials from one point to another, or to raise them vertically. The gin (*chèvre*), that admirable and simple invention that goes back to earliest antiquity, is still in use today; and it is likely that it will continue to serve us for a long time to come.'

Most of Viollet-le-Duc's article deals with 'Engines of War', but his pp. 210–18 illustrate and comment on various machines utilized in construction; i.e. devices or equipment for transporting loads such as stones either vertically or horizontally. For example, he illustrates and comments on the great wheel device, as well as other more complicated machines. And he illustrates (p. 217, fig. 4 at F) the *louve*, a pincer-like linkage of three pieces of iron for grasping a stone to be lifted. In this free assemblage, the lower ends of the two curved pieces are inserted in a dove-tailed sinkage in the stone, while their upper, outward-curving ends are linked together by the third piece which locks them against the sides of the hole when the weight of the stone comes into play.

In the *Architectural Dictionary* (p. F-74) there is a detailed account and explanation of the term *Forfex* as used by Vitruvius (x. 2) for part of the apparatus by which large stones or other weights were raised. The minute and documented description is of a contrivance that was undoubtedly used in medieval as well as Roman times.

We have already noted the widespread use of the great wheel (*vide* note 73). These machines were indispensable in those cases where more mechanical power was required than could be achieved by the light and much less bulky windlasses. A striking instance is that recorded by Rackham, from the late fifteenth-century fabric rolls of Westminster Abbey (*vide* Appendix K): here it is expressly stated that it was on the tie-beams of the roof, including those beyond the bay presently being vaulted, that 'the great wheel was placed so as to raise up the great keys', some of which, in their transport to the building site, were 'too big for a cart'. It would have required the heavy, permanent timber-work of the roof construction, rather than the temporary gantries of the falsework, to support the raising of such heavy loads.

As indicated in Appendix A, it is not in the older books on masonry but in those on carpentry that one is most likely to find some information about falsework, together with the apparatus and the gear by which the buildings of the past were raised. Some of these books—mainly of the nineteenth century, and mostly by French writers—are cited in the Bibliography under the following authors' names: Adhémar, Blanchard, Breymann, Christy, Degen, Deneux, Denfer, Douglas, Douliot, Émy, Fourneau, Frezier, Heinzerling, Jaggard and Drury, Jousse, Krafft, P. Lacroix, Mazerole, Moles, Oslet, Perronet, and Tredgold.

Another general source from which information on the falsework structures and the erectional practices of the past may sometimes be gained is that of the older architectural or engineering or scientific dictionaries, encyclopedias, and 'compendiums of useful knowledge'. Some of those that are pertinent to this study, along with a few more recent works, are cited in the Bibliography under the following authors: Ashpitel, Bosc, Bruyère, Bullet, Cresy, Debauve, Delaistre, Exchaquet, Franklin, Heck, P. Nicholson, W. Papworth, Parsons, Planat, Rebolledo, Rees, Rondelet, Singer *et al.*, Straub, and of course Viollet-le-Duc.

Individual chapters in otherwise general books, and separate articles or monographs, on the means of moving heavy loads either horizontally or vertically, are cited in the Bibliography under the following authors: Barré, Barry, Choisy (*Histoire*, vol. i, pp. 33–38), Czarnowsky, Gibson, Inman, Perronet, Planat (vol. v, pp. 369–98), Salzman (chap. xx, pp. 318–29), A. C. Smith, Watkins, and Viollet-le-Duc, article 'Engin' (vol. v, pp. 210–69).

The cranes and derricks of more recent times could not have been used anywhere on the great French Gothic cathedrals (except perhaps in the construction of towers up to the level where the spire began) for a very simple reason: the walls on which they would have stood were much too thin to accommodate their wide-straddling legs. As Watson has emphasized, stones had to be hoisted vertically very close to the position they were destined to assume, and this precluded all but the slightest amount of overhang on the part of any boom or jib.

Undoubtedly the largest and heaviest stone to be raised, while the clerestory walls of a great Gothic church were going up, was the highest of the tas-de-charge blocks, which often went through the wall, projecting on both sides. The raising and careful setting of this block would have required exceptional skill and ingenuity on the part of the medieval builders, although they may well have been able to count on both support and lateral stability for their hoisting apparatus from the flying buttress centering. This particular piece of falsework, as we have seen, would have been in place at this time, as a temporary strut rigidly bracing the clerestory wall to the towering masonry of the buttress proper.

When the stonework of the clerestory walls had been carried all the way to their tops, and the great tie-beams stretched across, the massive timber-work of the nave roof became a permanent gantry for a great wheel: this could now be sufficiently supported and braced to afford very powerful means of lifting the sometimes huge keystones of the vault ribs. Until the timber-work of the great roof came into use, however, it would seem that very simple and relatively slight hoisting apparatus was all that could be employed for raising stones and beams onto the thin and lofty walls of the towering, skeletonized churches of Gothic times.

GLOSSARY

Terms with multiple meanings are defined or explained here only with respect to the meaning or meanings they have in the context of the subject of this book.

Abutment: The generic term for any structure designed to receive or resist the lateral thrust of an arch or vault, such as a wall buttress, wing wall (when so used), or a buttress proper (with or without its flying buttress link).

Aggregate: The coarse or fine ingredients, such as crushed rock or sand respectively, which, when combined with cement and water, make concrete.

Alternate system: A regular alternation of size and design in the piers or columns of the nave arcade, reflecting the greater or lesser loads they carry as supports for the normal or the intermediate transverse ribs, respectively, of the sexpartite vault.

Ambulatory bay: A unit of space into which the curving or semipolygonal aisle surrounding the apse is visually divided. In Gothic churches such a unit division is usually trapezoidal in plan.

Angle of friction: In a masonry arch or vault, the maximum slope that the bed of a voussoir or web course can make with the horizontal without the need for centering or some other kind of temporary support for the arch stones.

Annular vault: A vault that curves in plan, such as the annular barrel vault that covered many an early ambulatory.

Apse: The eastern termination of the nave or main body of a church: it is semicircular or semipolygonal in plan. Small apses or absidioles projected eastward from the transept arms in Romanesque times; Gothic churches usually have absidioles ringing the apse proper, exterior to the ambulatory, that function as chapels.

Arch order: A ring of voussoirs, either plain or decorated on its face, that is thought of as an architectural feature.

Arch ring: An assemblage of voussoirs in a self-supporting arch, thought of in its structural sense.

Arris: The continuous edge or ridge of an external angle.

Ashlar: Masonry in which the stones are all squared so as to present a pattern of exclusively vertical and horizontal joints. In true ashlar construction, all the horizontal joints are continuous throughout the length of a course, and thus all stones in a given course are of equal height.

Banded barrel vault: A barrel vault whose semicylindrical shape is stiffened at intervals by previously-built transverse arches that project beneath its under surface.

Barrel vault: The simplest of all vault forms, basically semicylindrical in shape, and therefore everywhere semicircular in cross-section. Sometimes barrel vaults are slightly pointed in section.

Bay of vaulting: A unit of vaulting whose extent is determined by some sort of architectural boundaries. Whether these be the salient arches of the banded barrel vault or the transverse arches of the ribbed vault, a bay of vaulting normally corresponds to the square or rectangular area, in plan, that is defined by opposite pairs of piers.

Beam: The generic term for a one-piece horizontal structural member. Simple beams may support only themselves, but more often (e.g. wooden floor beams, or the stone lintel of a door or window opening) they carry a distributed load. Beams that support concentrated loads at one or more points are called girders.

Bearing: In contemporary architectural terminology, bearing is the amount or length of the area that furnishes vertical support at one end of a structural member such as a beam, girder, or the base of a column; the area such a member rests upon.

Bed (of a stone course): In masonry, the joint at the base of a row or course of stones; the surface on which these stones are laid or bedded. Normally it is horizontal, but in stone vaults the beds are tilted at a greater or lesser angle.

Buttress: A rectangular block of masonry—either attached to a wall in its entirety, or attached to the wall throughout the lower part of its height, or free-standing—which receives and grounds the lateral thrust of a vault. In large Gothic churches the buttresses are rectangular towers, deeply salient from the side-aisle walls below, and free-standing above, which act as the solid anchors of the entire superstructure, resisting vault thrusts and wind loads alike.

Camber: The upward bowing of something that is normally horizontal, such as a tie-beam or a lintel, or the crown of a pointed vault. The term is also sometimes applied to the outward bowing or convexity of the normally straight stone courses of Gothic vaults.

Capstan: An apparatus working on the principle of the wheel and axle, used for raising weights or applying power. It consists of an upright concave barrel around which the rope is wound a few turns. The head is pierced with holes through which long bars are inserted which act as horizontal levers by means of which the barrel is revolved. At the bottom of the barrel a pawl arrangement prevents the barrel from unwinding due to the strain on the rope. A capstan differs from a windlass in having a vertical instead of a horizontal axis.

Catenary curve: Loosely, the curve assumed by a freely suspended chain or flexible cable under the action of gravity, the center-line of the links being the line of tensile stress. In an inverted catenary (as in an arch, where the voussoirs correspond to the links of the chain), the units along the line of stress are in compression.

Centering; centers. Centering is the falsework support for the ring of voussoirs in an arch, during construction; thus the contour of the top of a centering frame conforms to the curve of the intended arch. In arches of large span the centers sometimes consist of more than one unit, requiring intermediate points of support as well as end supports at or near the two springs of the arch. The masonry of vaults is often laid upon planking or lagging, which stretches between, and is supported by, arch centers that are spaced at appropriate intervals. In any case, the centering frames must be both strong enough to support the arch structure and rigid enough to prevent any appreciable deflexion in the contour of its curve as it becomes weighted, during

the course of erection, by the incremental load of the voussoirs, up around the curve from either end.

Cerce: An extensible device, proposed by Viollet-le-Duc, for supporting the stones of successive web courses in the construction of rib vaults. As described by that writer, it consists of two boards set side by side on edge, having throughout most of their length a slot that is curved to conform with their curving top edge. To align the boards, and to permit them to act as a single extensible unit, wedged pieces are secured through the slots; and there are metal flanges at either end of the unit by which it is hung from the backs of the stone ribs. Set in position at a given level, it supports a bowed course of stones across the void from one boundary rib to another, one course at a time, up the curve of the vault.

Clerestory: A wall, or story, that rises above a roof and is consequently pierced by windows that light the inner portion of a building by natural means.

Cloister vault. In appearance, a cloister vault is a four-sided dome. It consists of those portions of two barrel vaults, often pointed, that span between opposite sides of the square area it covers. It differs fundamentally from a simple groin vault in that the voided portions of the latter's intersecting barrel vaults are the very portions that are retained in the cloister vault, where their junctions are re-entrant corners instead of salient groins. Like a true dome, the thrusts are continuous along the entire circuit of the supporting walls, rather than confined to the corner piers as in the groin vault.

Cocket centers. Cocket centers are supported at either end on a striking plate, usually canted up at an angle. The striking plate replaces the more usual pairs of simple folding wedges, and consists of three parts: a lower and an upper plate each of which is notched to conform to the compound wedge driven between them. Thus a considerable area at either end of the centering frame rests upon an extensive and substantial decentering device.

Column: The generic term for a major structural member that is vertical and supports loads in compression. Of the two terms, column and pier, the former is usually applied to a cylindrical form, in medieval architecture, whereas the latter refers to a member that is either square or rectangular or composite in plan.

Compartments (of a vault): In rib vaulting, the divisions or areas of the vaulting proper that are defined and bounded by the ribs. Also called severies.

Compression member: Any structural element, horizontal, vertical, or sloping, that is subject to stresses that tend to compress or shorten it.

Concentric arch rings: A series of arches, one within another, either in the same plane or more often stepped or offset on their faces, whose curves are struck from the same center (or centers, in the case of pointed arches).

Conoid, vaulting: The expanding masonry funnel whose shape is defined by the sheaf of ribs as they rise from their common springing and diverge in arcs that terminate at the vault crown. The horizontal section of the vaulting conoid at mid-height is significant as an index of the character of different vault types and as a key to the direction and magnitude of the vault's action in the structural system.

Corbel; corbelling. A corbel is a stone that projects beyond the face of the wall in which it is set, usually in order to give support to some feature or structural member. Corbelling is a structural scheme for reducing the span over a void by shelving out in successive courses beyond the face of the one below. Because the beds of corbelled courses are horizontal, no lateral thrust is created.

Course; stone coursing. In masonry, a course is a line or row of blocks, ordinarily thought of as being ranged horizontally. Broken courses are those whose beds do not carry through on a single plane, but step up or down to different levels.

Cradle; cradling. The term cradle is sometimes applied to a centering of small span whose assemblage of transverse cleats on an arching sequence of wooden ribs, together with their horizontal straining piece below, suggests the inverted form of a baby's cradle. 'Cradling a column' is to support and partially surround it with falsework, as when one of its drums is being replaced.

Crossing: The central, usually square, area in a cruciform church where transepts and nave intersect.

Cross, or keying-in, lagging: The short units of wooden formwork which are used to support successive blocks of stone in the final, highest courses of the vault while it is being built. They are set cross-wise to the normal, longitudinal

laggings, a pair of which often supports them, and are repositioned along the crown of the vault, by a single mason who retreats backwards while setting stones to fill the narrow void between the two webs of the vault as they converge on the crown.

Crown of arch or vault: The highest part of the curve of an arch or vault, whether pointed or not.

Crown thrust. Any true arch, being made up of wedge-shaped blocks, has a lateral thrust, and this action operates in all parts of the arch: there is lateral pressure not only at the spring and throughout the haunch but also at the crown. Consequently, the half-arches of flying buttresses, for example, press against the clerestory wall with the thrust at their crowns.

Dead load: The weight of the structure itself. Thus the dead load of a roof, for example, consists of the weight of the timber-work (transverse frames, rafters, purlins, struts, sheathing, &c.) plus the covering (tiles or slate or sheets of lead); whereas the live load is any weight that is unfixed or transient or intermittent, such as the wind load, or the snow load, or the weight of workmen climbing about on the roof.

Decentering: The occasion on which, or the process by which, the centers are 'struck'; that is, freed from the arched masonry which the falsework has until then been supporting. This may be done in various ways, the commonest of which is by retracting pairs of folding wedges. In any case, decentering is the most critical and dangerous of any operation in connexion with the building of an arch or vault.

Dome: A hemispherical structure of masonry; a vaulted construction spanning a circular or polygonal area, wherein all sides curve upward and inward towards a single high point.

Domed groin vault. In a simple groin vault, the profile along the groin is a semi-ellipse, being produced by the right-angled intersection of two barrel vaults of equal span. In a domed groin vault, the profile along the groin is arbitrarily made to be a semicircle. Consequently, the two vaults that meet each other along the groin are bowed upward and outward; their crowns are strongly arched; and the center of the bay they cover is much higher than that of the arches that bound this bay.

Dowel: A cylindrical pin, usually of wood, used to unite two members and prevent them from being displaced laterally in relation to each other.

Drum, column: One of the cylindrical blocks making up the shaft of a stone column.

Dry-wall construction: A masonry wall or other structure in which the stones are laid up without mortar.

Eccentric load: A load that is applied to a column, or other member, parallel to but out of alignment with its axis.

Elevation: A geometrical projection on a plane perpendicular to the horizon; a representation of the upright portions of a building or part thereof in which every part of every feature is indicated as though seen at eye level.

Extrados: The upper or convex surface of an arch or vault.

False bearing: The structural condition in which the location of the support for some load does not continue directly beneath or in line with the load all the way to the ground. This was often intentional in Gothic churches, as for instance the frequent case of clerestory piers that did not carry all the way down to the pavement in a direct line, but instead, received corbelled support for part of their area, in plan.

Falsework: Any of the temporary structures utilized in the erection of a building, such as scaffolding, shoring, centering, or formwork.

Flying buttress: The masonry strut from clerestory wall to buttress top. It transmits the vault thrusts across the side-aisle gap from the point at which a group of these thrusts are collected (following the lines of the ribs) to where they are met and grounded by the buttress proper. The normal flying buttress is built as a half-arch usually surmounted with masonry that is finished off in a straight sloping line of blocks.

Formeret: The longitudinal or wall arch, where the transverse vault abuts the clerestory wall, in rib vaulting.

Formwork: In the erection of vaulting, that portion of a falsework structure by which the vault is given its shape and is supported while it is being built. In simple, early vaults, the formwork was sometimes of mounded earth. Planking and lagging are other means by which vaults have been formed.

Frame; framing: A general term for any structural assemblage of members, usually of wood,

that are fitted and united together in an open-work ensemble; the sustaining parts of a structure fitted and joined together, either in a permanent assemblage as a roof framing, or in a temporary one as a centering frame.

Gantry: A framed structure raised on side supports so as to span a void, and usually of large dimensions. It is used to support something, such as a centering, a working platform, or a crane.

Gin: A machine used for raising weights, consisting essentially of three tapering poles 12 to 15 feet in length. The feet of the poles are set 8 or 9 feet apart where they rest on a platform or on the ground; but the poles are united at their upper extremities, from which a block-and-tackle is suspended. The gin is usually furnished with a windlass fixed between two of the legs and turned by hand spikes.

Glazing is the collective term for the sheets or pieces of glass that fill a window opening. As a verb, glazing is the act or process of installing glass in a window.

Great wheel: A powerful device for raising weights, that works on the principle of the revolving squirrel cage. A wheel of large diameter in the form of a short length of hollow cylinder was made to turn by one or more men tramping inside it, causing the rope to wind or unwind about the axle (or a small-diameter drum fixed to the axle) at one side of the wheel. Sometimes great wheels were paired, one on either side of the winding drum.

Groin: The solid, continuous angle or curving intersection formed by the meeting of two simple vaults that cross each other at any angle, growing obtuse as it approaches the summit. In a simple groin vault over a square bay, as seen from below, the groins are the salient ridges that arch across above the diagonals of the square. In rib vaulting the groin is hidden from view by the diagonal or groin rib that covers the actual intersection of the two vaults.

Groin vault or groined vault: A compound unit of vaulting formed by the crossing of any two simple vaults. The commonest groin vault —often called the simple groin vault—is that formed by two barrel vaults of equal span intersecting at right angles above a square bay.

Grout: A rich concrete without large aggregate and of very fluid consistency which can be poured into the joints of masonry.

Hammerbeam: A short horizontal beam projecting inward from the top of a masonry wall and strutted by a diagonal or curving brace at its projecting end. An opposite pair of hammerbeams effectively lessens the span of the transverse members in some roof frames.

Hammerbeam truss: An ensemble of timber members making up a transverse roof frame that employs the hammerbeam as a characteristic element.

Haunch: That portion of an arch or vault that lies between spring and crown, on either side.

Herring-bone stone coursing: Masonry in which all the stones of one course slant uniformly in one direction, alternating with courses in which all the stones slant uniformly in the other direction. Such masonry consists of rectangular blocks, but none of the joints is either horizontal or vertical.

Hung scaffolding receives its support from the permanent structure of the building itself, either by struts rising up at an angle from some ledge or offset, or by beams temporarily threaded through the wall, or by brackets attached to the building in one of various ways.

Hurdle: A movable mattress or panel of wickerwork made of rods or sticks interwoven with similar but more pliable materials such as willow withes. Hurdles were much used in medieval times for all sorts of purposes, including that of serving as platforms on scaffolding, in lieu of planks.

Impost: The level at which an arch or vault rests on a pier or wall. This place is usually marked by some architectural treatment, such as a capital in the case of a pier, or a string course of projecting mouldings in the case of a wall.

Intrados: The concave or inner surface of an arch or vault.

Jack: A portable device, utilizing leverage or the screw, for exerting great pressure or for lifting a heavy body a short distance.

Jamb: The side of a window or door opening.

Keystone; keying. The keystone is the central or topmost voussoir in an arch; it is also known as the key. Keying, or keying in, is the act of inserting the final voussoir or line of voussoirs at the crown of an arch or vault, respectively, by which such a structure is completed.

King post: The central vertical member which reaches to the apex of a triangular roof frame.

Lagging: The temporary wooden members on which the stones rest, in forming a masonry vault. Lagging is often of thick but narrow planks or battens that are set parallel but some inches apart, so that air can circulate freely to the mortar joints to facilitate their setting.

Lashing: The joining or securing together of two or more poles or other wooden members by ropes or cords, binding them in many turns or windings; the rope bindings themselves.

Lath (roof): The slender wooden strips, set horizontally across the rafters, to which the roof covering (of slates, tiles, or sheets of lead) is attached. In medieval times these laths were half an inch thick, of split oak, and were set parallel but an inch or so apart.

Lean-to roof: A roof of one slope, whose upper edge abuts a wall. Also called a pent roof.

Ledger: A horizontal pole secured to the uprights of a scaffolding and used to support the outer ends of the putlogs.

Live load: The weight of, or pressure exerted by, any transient feature, intermittent force, or movable body that is not part of the permanent structure. Unlike the dead load, the live load, as in the case of wind against a sloping roof, does not always act vertically downward.

Masonry: Anything constructed of stone (or brick or tiles), usually involving mortar. More specifically, as opposed to brickwork or brick-masonry, walls, vaults, &c., of stones that have been shaped or dressed, arranged and united by the mason.

Mortar: A material used in masonry for binding together stones (or bricks) so that the mass may form one compact whole. Mortar consists primarily of lime, water, and sand in various proportions, according to the 'fatness' of the lime. The more there is of lime, the more workable is the mix while the mortar is in its plastic state, but the more shrinkage occurs as it sets or hardens. Mortar made of ordinary lime sets not in water but in air, and the process is slow. The adhesive quality of medieval mortar was not great, although with the passage of time bringing about the thorough drying out of the mortar, its strength and adhesive power increased.

Nave: The main body, or middle part, lengthwise, of a church interior, extending from the principal entrance to the choir or chancel. Normally the nave is flanked by an aisle on each side, these being much lower and narrower than the nave.

Neutral axis: That level or plane, in a simple beam for example, at which neither compressive nor tensile forces are operative.

Oblique vault: A vault spanning between supporting walls that are parallel but not directly opposite each other. The end faces of such a vault are not at right angles to its axis, as in the case of a masonry arch bridge supporting a roadway that crosses at an angle to a stream. For stability, the masonry of such a vault must run in helicoidal courses. An oblique vault is also called a skew vault.

Oculus: The circular opening which sometimes occurs at the top of a dome. An oculus may be of any size, since a true dome is stable at the completion of any horizontal ring.

Pendentive: One of the triangular segments of the lower part of a hemispherical dome, used to effect a transition at the angles from a square or polygonal base below to a circle above, on which a complete dome may rest.

Pier: The solid support from which an arch springs; an upright structure of masonry, usually square or compound in plan, which serves as a principal support; one of the solid parts between openings in a wall.

Plan, or plan view: The horizontal cross-section of a building, that is taken at some revealing level and viewed vertically downward. A reflected plan is one that is viewed vertically upward.

Ploughshare twist: The characteristic warping of the lower portion of the transverse vault surfaces in Gothic vaulting that is brought about by the stilting of the wall arch.

Pole scaffolding rises from the ground on vertical standards. It is of two varieties: one, quite independent of the permanent building, having standards set in two parallel rows, with working platforms supported on short beams crossing between them; the other having platforms supported on putlogs, the inner ends of which rest in cavities in the wall of the permanent building, the outer ends being supported on a ledger secured to a single row of standards.

Purlin: A structural timber in roofs, running horizontally from frame to frame at one or more levels between the top of the wall and the peak of the roof, as intermediate support for the common rafters.

Putlog: A short horizontal beam used to support the platform of a scaffolding, one end resting in a voided cavity in the wall (the putlog hole), the outer end resting on the ledger.

Quadripartite vault: A usually rectangular bay of rib vaulting in which two transverse, two diagonal, and two wall or longitudinal ribs divide the vault into four compartments.

Rafter: One of the canted beams that make the slope of a roof, and to which are secured the laths for supporting the roof covering. The common rafters extend from the eaves to the ridge of the roof; and in medieval roofs they abutted at their upper ends against corresponding rafters rising up the other slope. The principal rafter was larger in section than the common rafter, and, as part of the transverse roof frame, a pair of the former was attached at their lower extremities to one of the main tie-beams. The principal rafters supported the purlins, which in turn carried the common rafters: thus the whole weight of the roof was sustained by the principal rafters (often called simply the principals).

Ramping vault: a vault that spans between imposts one of which is at a higher level than the other. Also, a vault whose axis is not horizontal but sloping.

Rebate or rabbet: A longitudinal space or groove that is cut back or sunk into a member to receive the edge of another.

Respond: A half pier attached to a wall and set opposite a complete, free-standing pier, used to support one end of an arch.

Resultant (of forces): A force that is equal in effect to the combination, in direction as well as magnitude, of two or more component forces.

Rib: One of the salient stone arches that visually divides a Gothic vault into compartments. In a bay of French quadripartite vaulting there are six ribs: a pair of transverse and a pair of longitudinal ribs plus the intersecting diagonal ribs. A rib is also often referred to, not as the entire salient arch, but as one of the two halves of such an arch, extending from spring to crown.

Rib stem. Where ribs are cut in such a fashion that the webs or panels of the vaulting rest on shelf-like rebates cut along the sides of the ribs,

GLOSSARY

instead of resting on the backs of the ribs, the rib stem is that portion that projects up into or through the vault webs.

Rib vault or ribbed vault: The characteristically Gothic system of vaulting, in which independent ribs are first constructed and then the thin web of the vault proper is built in the panels or compartments they define, the conformation of each such web being determined by the contour of the ribs that bound it.

Rise: The vertical distance, in an arch or vault, from spring to crown.

Rolling scaffolding was perhaps used more often for repairs than for any original construction, at least in the lofty naves of the great Gothic churches. Except in the case of domes, rolling scaffolding was usually a form of independent pole scaffolding mounted at the floor or ground level on wheels or on rollers.

Roof pitch: The degree of inclination of the plane of a roof. French Gothic roofs over the high vaults usually had slopes of around 54 to 57 degrees with the horizontal; the roof of Reims Cathedral is somewhat exceptional at 65 degrees. On the other hand, side-aisle roofs were occasionally almost flat.

Rubble masonry: A term of very imprecise designation, applied to various types of stonework. Sometimes it refers to masonry of broken, untrimmed stones completely without coursing; sometimes to stonework with predominantly vertical and horizontal joints similar to ashlar except that the stones are somewhat less carefully dressed, or in courses that vary in height, or in courses that occasionally break to a higher or lower level.

Scaffolding: A temporary structure for supporting one or more platforms by means of which the workmen and their materials are brought within reach of their work. (For various types of scaffolding, see the adjectives Hung, Pole, and Rolling.) Where employed in the original erection, as opposed to repair work, scaffolding was ordinarily constructed on the outside of buildings so as to be free of the interference of floors and to facilitate the supplying of the workmen with materials. An exception to this, in medieval building practice, was the case of the central body of a church, which was constructed from scaffolding established within the nave.

Seating: The area on which any member,

whether vertical or horizontal, rests. This is a much more general term than Bearing.

Section: The aspect of a building or other object when projected on an imaginary plane that cuts through it at right angles to its axis. The normal, or transverse, section of a building is how it appears when it is viewed at right angles to the plane that cuts it cross-wise and vertically. The longitudinal section of a building presents the structure's aspect when it is cut lengthwise and vertically through its center. A horizontal section is known as a plan.

Setting (of mortar): The hardening of the mortar after its plastic state. Mortar, like concrete, sets in two phases. The first set, which takes place in a few hours, is that in which the material can no longer change its shape appreciably: it is still 'green' in the sense that the crystallization involved in the hardening process has hardly begun. The second or final set does not take place for at least a month, and usually not for a much longer period, depending on the thickness and depth of the mortar's mass. Setting is not complete until the water, whose presence is necessary in the process of crystallization, has done its job and has completely evaporated from the interior of the mass.

Sexpartite vault: A square bay of rib vaulting in which, besides two transverse, two diagonal, and two wall ribs, there is an additional transverse rib, dividing the vault surfaces into six compartments, that arches across through the point in the crown where the diagonal ribs intersect. As a consequence of this intermediate transverse rib there are two cross vaults per bay, their axes criss-crossing, with neither one being at right angles to the axis of the longitudinal vault.

Shear: The action or stress that tends to force two closely united members, or, more often, two contiguous parts of a solid body, to slide on each other, parallel to their plane of contact. For example, horizontal shear occurs near the ends of a simple rectangular beam, under a load, as its lower half (which is in tension; that is, trying to lengthen) tends to slide along its upper half, which is in compression. Again, the same beam, if heavily loaded near one of its supports, may tend to shear through, transversely, as the downward pressure of the load on the beam is resisted by the close support.

Shoring: Collectively, the temporary buttress-like props set against the side of a structure to

313

prevent its collapse, or its tilting out of the vertical. In buildings, shores are usually sloping struts, either simple or compound, that are set upon a firm base and maintain the structure, or some part of it, in an upright position.

Side aisle: The portions of a church, usually one on each side, that flank the main body and are separated from it by a row of columns or piers. Typically, in French Gothic churches, the side aisles are about half the width of the nave, and vaulted at a much lower level in order to allow for clerestory windows above their roofs, to light the nave directly.

Sill: A horizontal piece of timber or stone forming the lowest member of a frame, or supporting a structure (as a door or window sill). More specifically, in carpentry work, the lowest horizontal member of a timber assemblage, such as the double sills at the top of the clerestory walls, upon which the whole complex of a church's high roof rests.

Skewback: The bevelled supporting stone at either end of a segmental or flat arch.

Skew vault. *See* Oblique vault.

Soffit: The finished under side of an architectural member. It is usually horizontal, as in the case of a lintel or the overhanging portion of a cornice, but it also applies to the concave under side or intrados of an arch or vault.

Span: The distance between the supports of a beam, an arch, or a vault. The clear span is the dimension of the actual void from face to face of the supporting members; the span center-to-center is the dimension from the axis of one column or pier to that of another. In cantilevers, the span is the length of the projecting arm.

Spandrel: In arch construction, the wall surface at either side of an arch between the extrados of the arch and two imaginary lines, one horizontal through the apex or crown of the arch's extrados, the other vertical through the extrados at its spring. In adjacent arches, as in an arcade, the spandrel is the surface of walling between the two arches from spring to crown.

Spring or springing: The point or level at which the actual curve of an arch or vault begins.

Springer: The lowest of the voussoirs; the arch stone whose lower bed is horizontal.

Stereotomy: Literally, the cutting of solids. In masonry, the three-dimensional form or shape of stone blocks; or, the proper hewing and shaping of such blocks so as to accommodate

them to their destined position in a wall, arch, or vault.

Stilt; stilting. Stilting is the condition in which the actual spring of an arch occurs above the level of its impost. The stilt of an arch or vault is the length of the vertical intrados above the impost.

Stone-weighted rope device: A method of constructing the web courses of thin rib vaults without formwork. It consists of lengths of rope, one for each stone in a given course, that are secured above and behind the course being built, passed over the stone, and weighted at their free lower ends in such fashion as to press the stone temporarily against its tilted bed and thus prevent it from slipping down into the void.

Striking (of centers): The action or process of freeing the centering frames from the soffit of the arch or vault they have been supporting during the course of erection. In Gothic times this was usually accomplished by retracting the wedges upon which the centering frames rested.

String course: A continuous horizontal band, either plain or moulded, on the face of a wall.

Strut: A secondary structural member, whether vertical, horizontal, or diagonal, that is subject to compression longitudinally.

Superstructure: A higher, and always visible, portion of a structure. Thus, all of a building that occurs above ground is the superstructure in contradistinction to the foundations; while the whole complex of the timber roof of a Gothic cathedral is the superstructure as distinct from all the masonry that lies below it.

System: A combination or assemblage of things adjusted and connected in such fashion as to make one complex whole; the organized and purposeful arrangement of interdependent parts in accordance with some definite scheme, as, the rib vault system.

Tas-de-charge: In rib vaulting, the multiple-coursed block of masonry that constitutes the lower portion of the vaulting conoid, wherein all the courses have horizontal beds and hence no lateral thrust. Each course of the tas-de-charge normally consists of but a single stone; and the whole complex extends upward, following the curves of the clustered ribs, from the impost (usually the top of the capital) to about the angle of friction, where the radial joints begin.

GLOSSARY

Template: A pattern used to indicate the shape any piece of work is to assume when finished; a thin piece, cut to the profile outline of a member, to be used repeatedly as a guide in shaping many similar pieces, such as the voussoirs of a moulded rib.

Thrust (lateral): A force tending to push outward, as in an arch, vault, or dome; the disruptive pressure at either side of an arch, which tends to push apart or overturn the supports. Because of the wedge action of its voussoirs, every arch construction has a lateral thrust, downward and outward from the crown, that must be met or countered by one means or another.

Tie-beam: The main horizontal timber that spans the void, in the framing of a roof, tying together the feet of opposing principal rafters.

Tracery: The permanent, jointed stonework that divides the upper part, or in circular windows the whole, of a window into an openwork pattern of separate voids. In Gothic times the tracery became highly decorative, its stone members being slender and moulded, curving and branching or intersecting in complex and intricate geometrical or flowing patterns.

Trammel: As claimed to have been used in the construction of domes, a device for assuring perfect regularity in the spherical surface of the intrados. It consists of a pole pivoted at the center of the spherical void in such fashion that its free end may be swung through a full circle horizontally at any and all levels within the dome.

Transept: Either of the lateral arms, at right angles to the main axis, in a church of cruciform plan.

Trestle (workmen's): A frame consisting of a short beam fixed at each end to a pair of spreading legs, for use as a support for a raised platform; a sawhorse.

Triforium: A second-story gallery or a passageway above either of the side aisles that flank the nave, and opening into the main body of the church through a range of arches above the arcade bounding nave or choir or transept. The triforium is sometimes called the blind story because its height within corresponds to the lean-to roof over the side aisle without, and therefore normally receives no direct daylight.

Undergirding: A binding together beneath something; a general term for a supporting structure, temporary or permanent, whose strength is due to the combining of its individual members into a rigid ensemble which acts to secure a higher structure.

Underpinning: A solid structure, such as a new foundation or other support, temporary or permanent, introduced beneath a wall, a building, or other structure that has previously been built, as when the original foundation has proved insufficient or has been impaired from any cause.

Vault: A masonry ceiling based on the arch principle, in which the stones or bricks of which it is composed mutually sustain themselves in their places between the abutments by being wedge-shaped, with radial joints. For some of the many varieties of vaults, see under the adjectives: Annular, Banded, Barrel, Cloister, Domed, Groin, Oblique, Quadripartite, Ramping, Ribbed, Sexpartite.

Vibration: Repeated motion back and forth, which is one of the most serious causes of failure in a structure. In medieval times, disruptive vibration was caused primarily by two separate agencies: the wind action of violent storms, and the ringing of bells. Both of these were the more serious because they acted upon the building high up in its superstructure.

Vice: A spiral stair.

Voussoir: One of the wedge-shaped blocks that make up an arch or vault.

Wall buttress: An abutment that consists, throughout its entire height, of a saliency in the masonry of a wall, to give it stability and to ground any lateral thrust against it.

Web; web coursing. In a ribbed vault, the web is the vault proper, as opposed to the ribs. In French practice, the web courses normally run parallel to the vault crown. In English vaulting, the web courses of the separate vault compartments often run perpendicular to the bisector of the angle, in plan, formed by a given pair of adjacent ribs as they depart from their common springing.

Wedges (folding): A pair of broad hardwood blocks, each some 15 inches long, cut so as to taper to about 4 inches at the thinner end, and facing in opposite directions, one on top of another, their top and bottom faces being parallel, with their surfaces of mutual contact on a slant. Such folding wedges were 'struck' or retracted when an arch or vault was finished and the falsework they supported was decentered.

Wind-bracing: In medieval roofs, various members collectively, such as diagonal struts and arched or criss-crossing timbers in a plane parallel to the slope of the roof, whose function was to secure the framed structure against longitudinal deformation due to wind action.

Windlass: A device for raising weights in which a horizontal spindle or axle, around which the rope is wound, is turned by levers or handspikes inserted in holes at either end of the axle and projecting from it radially.

Wind-pressure: A kind of live load exerted by the wind on any object in its path. The pressure of the wind blowing against a roof is considered as acting perpendicular to its windward slope, and is based largely on the wind's velocity.

ZD system: A method, devised by Zeiss and Dywidag in the mid-1920's, for spanning space by means of a thin reinforced concrete slab that is curved, in section, to the form of a segment of a circle. Spanning consists of a longitudinal beam action, not a transverse vault action; the resistance to bending is due to the rise of the slab's arc; and the imbedded reinforcing rods are located so as to follow the curving lines of the stresses.

BIBLIOGRAPHY

ABRAHAM, POL, 'Les Données plastiques et fonctionelles du problème de l'ogive', *Recherche no. 1: Le Problème de l'ogive*, Paris, Centre International des Instituts de Recherche, 1939, pp. 29–51. 7 figs.
—— *Violet-le-Duc et le rationalisme médiéval*, Paris, Vincent Fréal et Cie., 1934. 116 pp., 49 figs.
—— 'Viollet-le-Duc et le rationalisme médiéval', *Bulletin monumental*, Paris, A. Picard, 1934, vol. xciii, pp. 69–88. 1 illus.
ADAMS, HENRY, *Mont-Saint-Michel and Chartres*, New York, Houghton Mifflin Co., 1913.
ADHÉMAR, J[OSEPH], *Traité de la coupe des pierres*, Paris, V. Dalmont, 5e édition, 1856.
—— *Traité de charpente*, Paris, Carilian Goeury et V. Dalmont, 2e édition, 1854. 1 vol. text; atlas, 48 plates.
AINGER, ALFRED, 'Centering for Large Stone Arches', *Transactions of the Society, instituted at London, for the Encouragement of Arts, Manufactures, and Commerce*, London, 1825, vol. xliii, pp. 183–94. 1 plate.
ALEXANDER, ARSÈNE, *Les Monuments français détruits par l'Allemagne*, Paris et Nancy, Berger-Levrault, 1918. 218 pp., 242 small photographic illus.
ANDERSON, ROBERT R., 'Notice of Working Drawings Scratched on the Walls of the Crypt at Roslin Chapel', *Proceedings of the Society of Antiquaries of Scotland*, Edinburgh, 1875, vol. x, pp. 63–64. 1 plate.
ANDREWS, FRANCIS B., *The Mediaeval Builder and His Methods*, Oxford, University Press, 1925. 99 pp., 3 figs., 13 plates.
ANFRAY, MARCEL, 'Les Architectes des cathédrales', *Les Cahiers techniques de l'art*, tome i, fasc. 2, mai–déc. 1947, pp. 5–16.
Appleton's Dictionary of Machines, Mechanics, Engine-work and Engineering, designed for practical workingmen and those intended for the engineering profession, 2 vols., New York, D. Appleton & Co., 1855.
ARCHITECTURAL PUBLICATION SOCIETY. *See* PAPWORTH, WYATT.
ASHBY, THOMAS, 'Practical Engineering in Ancient Rome', Papers read at the Association meeting of 1925, *British Association for the Advancement of Science*, London, H.M. Stationery Office. [Printed for Eyre & Spottiswoode, 1926.]
ASHPITEL, ARTHUR, Compiler, *Treatise on Architecture, including the Arts of Construction, Building, Stone-Masonry . . . and Strength of Materials* (a collection of treatises reprinted from the *Encyclopaedia Britannica*), [London, 1852], Edinburgh, A. & C. Black, 1867. 55 plates.
ASSOCIATION ÉTRANGÈRE D'ÉCHANGES ARTISTIQUES, 'Notes on the Historic Stained Glass Windows of Northern France', *Art and Archaeology*, June 1927, vol. xxiii, pp. 242–59. 20 illus.

BIBLIOGRAPHY

ATWOOD, GEORGE, *A Dissertation on the Construction and Properties of Arches*, London, Lunn : Egerton, 1801.

AUBERT, MARCEL, 'Les plus anciennes croisées d'ogives, leur rôle dans la construction', *Bulletin monumental*, 1934, vol. xciii, pp. 5–67 and 137–237. 105 illus.

—— and MAILLÉ, LA MARQUISE DE, *L'Architecture cistercienne en France*, 2 vols., Paris, Van Oest (Éditions d'Art et d'Histoire), 2e édition, 1947.

B., R., 'Viaduct über den Esk-Fluß bei Whitby in England', *Centralblatt der Bauverwaltung*, 1887, vol. vii, pp. 325–7, 339–41, 349–50. 3 figs.

BABCOCK, CHARLES, 'Vaults', *The American Architect and Building News*, vol. viii, no. 241 (7 Aug. 1880) to vol. ix, no. 280 (7 May 1881).

BAKER, IRA OSBORN, *Treatise on Masonry Construction*, 10th edn., New York, J. Wiley & Sons, 1909.

BALDWIN, R., *Plans, Elevations and Sections of the Machines and Centering used in erecting Black-Friars Bridge*, London, I. & J. Taylor at the Architectural Library, 1787. 7 large plates.

BANKS, SIR JOSEPH, 'Extracts out of an Old Book relating to the Building of Louth Steeple and Repairing the Church, etc., from about the Year 1500 or 1501 to 1518', *Archaeologia*, 1792, vol. x, pp. 70–98.

BARRÉ, L.-A., 'Déplacement en bloc de la fontaine du Palmier située sur l'ancienne place du Châtelet, à Paris', *Revue générale de l'architecture et des travaux publics*, 1858, vol. xvi, pp. 126–30, 169–73. 8 plates.

BARRY, CHARLES, *fils*, 'Description des échafauds méchaniques employés au nouveau palais de Westminster (Londres) spécialement dans la construction des trois grandes tours', *Revue générale de l'architecture et des travaux publics*, 1857, vol. xv, pp. 129–35, 197–206. 3 plates.

BARTLETT, JAMES, 'Scaffold, Scaffolding', *Encyclopaedia Britannica*, 11th edn., Cambridge University Press, 1911, vol. xxiv, pp. 279–82. *Also*, article 'Shoring' in same volume, pp. 1004–7.

BAUDOT, A[NATOLE DE], and PERRAULT-DABOT, A[LFRED] (editors), *Archives de la Commission des Monuments Historiques*, Paris, Librairie Renouard/Librairie Générale de l'Architecture, 5 vols. [1898–1904].

BEISSEL, STEPHAN, *Die Bauführung des Mittelalters: Studie über die Kirche des heiligen Victor zu Xanten* . . . 2. Aufl. . . . Freiburg im Breisgau, Herdersche Verlagshandlung, 1889.

BELL, GEORGE JOSEPH, *A Practical Treatise on Segmental and Elliptical Oblique or Skew Arches*, Carlisle, Charles Thurnam & Sons, 2nd edn., 1906.

BILL, MAX, *Robert Maillart*, Erlenbach-Zürich, Verlag für Architektur AG, 1949.

BILSON, JOHN, 'The Beginnings of Gothic Architecture: I, Review of Recent Discussion'; II, 'Norman Vaulting in England', *Journal of the Royal Institute of British Architects*, London, 1899, 3rd ser., vol. vi, pp. 259–68 (2 illus.), 289–319 (29 illus.). Plus 'Discussion', pp. 319–26 and 345–9 (2 illus.). *See also* Bilson's 'Reply', *R.I.B.A. Journal*, 1902, vol. ix, pp. 350–6, &c.

—— 'Les Voûtes d'ogives de Morienval', *Bulletin monumental*, 1908, vol. lxxii, pp. 128–36. 6 rib and 9 arch profiles.

BILSON, JOHN, 'Les Voûtes de la nef de la cathédrale d'Angers', *Congrès archéologique de France*, LXXVIIe Session tenue à Angers et à Saumur en 1910, Paris, A. Picard, vol. lxxvii, tome ii, 1911, pp. 203–23. 5 illus.

BLAKE, MARION ELIZABETH, *Ancient Roman Construction in Italy from the Prehistoric Period to Augustus*, Washington D.C., Carnegie Institute of Washington, Publication no. 570, 1947.

BLANCHARD, EDMÉ, *Traité de la coupe des bois pour le revêtement des voûtes, arrières-voûtes, trompes, rampes et tours rondes . . .*, Paris, J. Josse, 1729. 46 plates.

BLAND, WILLIAM, *Experimental Essays on the Principles of Construction in Arches, Piers, Buttresses . . .*, London, John Weale, 1839.

BLOOR, A[LFRED] J[ANSON], *The Architectural and Other Art Societies of Europe*; some account of their origin, processes of formation and methods of administration, with suggestions as to some of the conditions necessary for the maximum success of a national American architectural-art society. . . . Read before the New York Chapter, AIA, 16 Feb. 1869, [New York], Committee on Library & Publications, 1869.

BOND, FRANCIS, *Gothic Architecture in England*, London, Batsford, 1906. (Referred to as *Gothic Architecture*.)

—— *An Introduction to English Church Architecture*, 2 vols., London, Oxford University Press, 1913. (Referred to as *Church Architecture*.)

—— 'On the Comparative Value of Documentary and Architectural Evidence in Establishing the Chronology of the English Cathedrals', *Journal of the Royal Institute of British Architects*, 1899, 3rd ser., vol. vi, pp. 17–29. 5 illus. Plus 'Discussion', pp. 29–35 and 72–73.

BOOZ, PAUL, *Der Baumeister der Gotik*, Berlin, Deutscher Kunstverlag, 1956. 24 line drawings and plans.

BORDEAUX, JEAN HIPPOLYTE RAYMOND, 'Des voûtes en bois et leur reparation', *Revue de l'art chrétien*, 1862, vol. vi, pp. 354–70.

BOSC, ERNEST, *Dictionnaire raisonné d'architecture et des sciences et arts qui s'y rattachent*, 4 vols., Paris, Librairie-Imprimeries Réunies, [1877–80].

BOSSE, ABRAHAM, *La Pratiqve dv Trait à Prevves de Mr Desargves . . . Pour la Coupe des Pierres en l'Architecture*, Paris, Des-Hayes, 1643.

BOUET, GEORGES ADELMARD, 'Nouvelles observations sur les voûtes de l'abbaye de St-Étienne de Caen', *Bulletin monumental*, 1862, vol. xxviii, pp. 57–70.

BOWEN, JAMES H., 'Report upon Buildings, Building Materials, and Methods of Building' (in *U.S. Commission to the Paris Exhibition: Reports of the U.S. Commissioners*, 6 vols., [1868–]1870), Washington, Government Printing Office, 1869, vol. 4, part 6. 96 pp.

BRANDON, RAPHAEL, and BRANDON, J. ARTHUR, *The Open Timber Roofs of the Middle Ages*, London, David Bogue, 1849.

BRANNER, ROBERT, 'Three Problems from Villard de Honnecourt Manuscript', *The Art Bulletin*, Mar. 1957, vol. xxxix, pp. 61–66.

BRAYLEY, EDWARD WEDLAKE, and BRITTON, JOHN, *The History of the Ancient Palace and Late Houses of Parliament at Westminster*, London, John Weale, 1836. 48 illus.

BREYMANN, G. A., *Allgemeine Baukonstruktionslehre mit besonderer Beziehung auf das*

Hochbauwesen, Leipzig, J. M. Gebhardt's Verlag, 4 vols. Vol. i: Otto Warth, *Die Konstruktionen in Stein*, 1896. Vol. ii: Otto Warth, *Die Konstruktionen in Holz*, 1900.

BRIGHAM, WILLIAM T., *The Ancient Hawaiian House*, Memoir of the Bernice Pauahi Bishop Museum of Polynesian Ethnology and Natural History, vol. ii, no. 3, Honolulu, Bishop Museum Press, 1908.

BRITTON. *See* BRAYLEY and BRITTON.

BRODTBECK, SUZANNE, 'Les Voûtes romanes de l'église de Romainmôtier (Suisse): Étude sur l'éclairage direct dans les églises voûtées de la fin du XIe siècle', *Bulletin monumental*, 1936, vol. xcv, pp. 473–505. 8 illus.

BROWN, G. BALDWIN, *From Schola to Cathedral*, Edinburgh, David Douglas, 1886.

BROWN, RICHARD, *Sacred Architecture: Its Rise, Progress and Present State*, &c., London, Fisher, Son & Co., 1845.

BRUNET, ÉMILE, 'La Restauration de la cathédrale de Soissons', *Bulletin monumental*, 1928, vol. lxxxvii, pp. 65–99. 21 illus.

BRUYÈRE, LOUIS, *Études relatives à l'art des constructions*, 2 vols., Paris, Bance aîné, 1823–8.

BUCK, GEORGE WATSON, *A Practical and Theoretical Essay on Oblique Bridges*, London, Crosby Lockwood & Co., 3rd edn., 1880.

BUCKLER, J[OHN] C[HESSEL], *A Description and Defence of the Restoration of the Exterior of Lincoln Cathedral . . .*, Oxford, Rivingtons, 1866.

'Building Vaults Without Centering', *Architects' Journal*, 11 Apr. 1946, vol. ciii, p. 284. 3 photographic illus.

BULLET, PIERRE, *L'Architecture pratique, qui comprend le détail . . . des ouvrages de maçonnerie, charpenterie, menuiserie . . .*, Paris, J.-B. Delespine, [1691], 1722.

BUMPUS, T. FRANCIS, *A Guide to Gothic Architecture*, New York, Dodd, Mead & Co., 1914.

BURN, ROBERT SCOTT, *Building Construction; Showing the Employment of Brickwork and Masonry* (Collins' Advanced Science Series), London, 1876. 1 vol. text; atlas, 38 plates.

BURNELL, G[EORGE] R[OWDON], 'Centre of an Arch or Vault', *The Dictionary of Architecture*, London, The Architectural Publication Society, 1853, vol. i (A–C), pp. C 57–58.

—— 'Sixty Years Since, or Improvements in Building Materials and Construction During the Present Century', *Papers Read at the R.I.B.A. Session 1859–1860*, London, 1860, pp. 28–37.

CAIN, WILLIAM, *Voussoir Arches applied to Stone Bridges, Tunnels, Domes and Groined Arches*, New York, D. Van Nostrand, 1879. 196 pp., 26 line diagrams.

CAMPIN, FRANCIS, *Materials and Construction: a Theoretical and Practical Treatise on the Strains, Designing and Erection of Works of Construction*, 3rd edn., London, Lockwood, 1891 (Weale's Rudimentary Series).

CAROE, ALBAN D. R., *Old Churches and Modern Craftsmanship*, London, Oxford University Press, 1949.

CAVE, J. O[TWAY], and EARTHWROL, R[USSELL] A., *Construction and Maintenance of Buildings*, London, Estates Gazette, 1947. 191 pp., 312 figs.

CESCINSKY, HERBERT, and GRIBBLE, ERNEST R., *Early English Furniture and Woodwork*, 2 vols., London, G. Routledge & Sons, 1922.

CHAULIOT, E., and GÉNERMONT, M., 'Les Travaux d'assainissement et de consolidation de l'église de Souvigny', *Les Monuments historiques de la France*, 1938, 3ᵉ année, fasc. 5–6, pp. 145–50. 6 photos, 5 section drawings.

CHAUVEL, A[LBERT], 'La Cathédrale de Rouen: Les destructions, le sauvetage', *Les Monuments historiques de la France*, numéro spécial, avr.–juin 1956, nouv. sér., vol. ii, no. 2, pp. 55–92. 58 illus. (Referred to as *Rouen*.)

—— 'Étude sur la taille des pierres au moyen âge', *Bulletin monumental*, 1934, vol. xciii, pp. 435–50. 23 illus.

CHOISY, AUGUSTE, *L'Art de bâtir chez les Byzantins*, Paris, Librairie de la Société Anonyme de Publications Périodiques, 1883.

—— *L'Art de bâtir chez les Romains*, Paris, Librairie de la Société Anonyme de Publications Périodiques, 1872.

—— *Histoire de l'architecture*, 2 vols., Paris, Librarie Georges Baranger, [1899].

CHRISTY, W[YVIL] J[AMES], *A Practical Treatise on the Joints Made and Used by Builders in the Construction of Various Kinds of Engineering and Architectural Works*, London, C. Lockwood & Co., 1882.

CLASEN, KARL HEINZ, *Deutsche Gewölbe der Spätgotik* (Series: Deutsche Bauakademie Schriften des Instituts für Theorie und Geschichte der Baukunst), Berlin, Henschelverlag, 1958.

COLOMBIER, PIERRE DU, *Les Chantiers des cathédrales*, Paris, A. et J. Picard, 1953.

COLSON, J[OHN] B[ARNES], *Winchester Cathedral: A Descriptive and Illustrated Record of the Reparations of the Nave Roof, 1896–8*, Winchester, Warren & Son, 1899. 28 pp.

CONANT, KENNETH JOHN, 'Observations on the Vaulting Problems of the Period 1088–1211', *Gazette des Beaux-Arts*, July–Dec. 1944, ser. 6, vol. xxvi, pp. 127–34. 7 illus.

Construction Methods, New York, McGraw-Hill. Monthly.

COTTON, VERE E., *Liverpool Cathedral: The Official Handbook*, Liverpool, Littlebury Bros., [1924], 9th edn., 1936.

CRESWELL, K[EPPEL] A[RCHIBALD] C[AMERON], 'The Origin of the Persian Double Dome', *Burlington Magazine*, 1913, vol. xxiv, pp. 94–99 and 152–8.

CRESY, EDWARD, *An Encyclopaedia of Civil Engineering, Historical, Theoretical, and Practical*, London, Longman, Brown, Green & Longmans, [1847], new edn., 1861.

—— *Practical Treatise on Bridge-Building and on the Equilibrium of Vaults and Arches, with the Professional Life and Selections from the Works of Rennie*, London, J. Williams; New York, Appleton & Co., 1839.

CROSSLEY, FRED H., *Timber Building in England*, London, Batsford, 1951.

CULLEY, JOHN L., *Treatise on the Theory of the Construction of Helicoidal Oblique Arches* (Van Nostrand's Science Series no. 87), New York, D. Van Nostrand, 1886.

CURMAN, SIGURD, and ROOSVAL, JOHNNY, *Sveriges Kyrkor: Konsthistoriskt Inventarium. Gotland, II: Rute Setting*, Stockholm, 1935.

CZARNOWSKY, CHARLES, 'Engins de levage dans les combles d'églises en Alsace', *Les Cahiers techniques de l'art*, Strasbourg, Éditions F.-x. Le Roux, janv.–août 1949, vol. ii, fasc. 1–2, pp. 11–27. 25 illus.

—— 'Escaliers à vis en Alsace', *Les Cahiers techniques de l'art*, mai–déc. 1947, vol. i, fasc. 2, pp. 17–32. 31 illus.

DEBAUVE, A[LPHONSE], *Procédés et matériaux de construction*, Paris, Vᵛᵉ C. Dunod, 1884–8. 4 vols. text; 4 vols. atlas.

DEGEN, LUDWIG, *Les Constructions en bois, avec supplément*, 2 vols., Paris, A. Morel, 1866, 1867. 84 plates.

DELAISTRE, J.-R., *Encyclopédie de l'ingénieur ou dictionnaire des ponts et chaussées*, 3 vols., Paris, J. G. Dentu, 1812.

DENEUX, H[ENRI], *L'Ancienne et la nouvelle charpente de la cathédrale de Reims*, Reims, Matot-Braine, 1927.

—— 'La Restauration de la basilique Saint-Remie', *L'Annuaire-Bulletin de la Société des Amis du Vieux-Reims*, 1931–5, pp. 22–35.

—— 'Signes lapidaires et épures du XIIIᵉ siècle à la cathédrale de Reims', *Bulletin monumental*, 1925, vol. lxxxiv, pp. 99–130. 24 illus.

DENFER, JULES, *Architecture et constructions civiles. Charpente en bois et menuiserie* (Encyclopédie des travaux publics), Paris, Baudry, 1891–7.

—— and MULLER, ÉMILE, *Album de serrurerie . . . contenant l'emploi du fer dans la maçonnerie et dans la charpente en bois . . .*, Paris, J. Dejey, 1872. 100 plates.

DERAND, FRANÇOIS, *L'Architecture des voûtes ou l'art des traits et coupe des voûtes*, Paris, Sebastien Cramoisy, 1643.

DESCHAMPS. *See* MORTET and DESCHAMPS.

DOBSON, EDWARD, *The Rudiments of Masonry and Stonecutting*, exhibiting the principles of masonic projection and their application to the construction of curved wing-walls and domes, oblique bridges, and Roman and Gothic vaulting (Weale's Scientific and Technical Series), London, Lockwood & Co., 12th edn., 1903. 104 illus.

DOUGLAS, W. B., *Carpentry and Joinery* (Lockwood's Modern Handbooks), London, Crosby Lockwood & Son, 1937.

DOULIOT, J. P., *Cours élémentaire, théorique et pratique de construction*, 4 vols., Paris, Carilian-Goeury, 1826–35. 2ᵉ partie: *Charpente en bois*, 1828. 1 vol. text; atlas, 136 plates.

—— *Traité spécial de la coupe des pierres . . . augmentée . . . par F.-M. Jay, . . . par J. Claudel et L.-A. Barré*, 2 vols. (one of plates), Paris, Dunod, 2ᵉ édition, 1862–9.

DOWNEY, GLANVILLE, 'Earthquakes at Constantinople and Vicinity, A.D. 342–1454', *Speculum*, Oct. 1955, vol. xxx, pp. 596–600.

DOYON, GEORGES, and HUBRECHT, ROBERT, *L'Architecture rurale et bourgeoise en France:* Étude sur les techniques d'autrefois et leurs applications à notre temps, Paris, Vincent Fréal et Cie, 1942.

DRURY. *See* JAGGARD and DRURY.

DRY, THOMAS, 'The Skew Bridge at Rimini', *Archaeologia*, 1844, vol. xxx, pp. 530–5. 1 plan drawing and bibliographical notes.

DRYDEN, SIR HENRY E. L., 'Two Barns at Peterborough', *Associated Architectural Societies Reports and Papers*, 1897–8, vol. xxiv, pp. 177–87. 6 plates of plans, elevations, sections.

DUBOSQUE, J., *Études théoriques et pratiques sur les murs de soutènement et les ponts et viaducs en maçonnerie . . .*, 4ᵉ édition, Paris, Imprimerie de A. Broise et Courtier, [1887]. 12 plates.

DUPUIT, J., *Traité de l'équilibre des voûtes et de la construction des ponts en maçonnerie*, Paris, Imprimerie Cusset et Cie; Librairie Dunod, 1873. 398 pp. et atlas de 49 planches.

DURACH, FELIX, *Mittelalterliche Bauhütten und Geometrie*, Stuttgart, Julius Hoffmann, 1929.

EARTHWROL. *See* CAVE and EARTHWROL.

EMY, COL. A[MAND] R[OSE], *Description d'un nouveau système d'arcs pour les grands charpentes*, Paris, Carilian-Goeury, 1828.

—— *Traité de l'art de la charpenterie*, 2 vols. text, atlas, Paris, Anselin, 1837–41; 2 vols., Liège, 1841-2; 2 vols., Paris, [1867]; Paris, Dunod, 1878.

The Engineering News, New York, Engineering News Publishing Co. Weekly.

ENLART, CAMILLE, *Manuel d'archéologie française: I, Architecture religieuse*, Paris, Alphonse Picard et Fils, 1902.

ESSENWEIN, AUGUST [OTTMAR], 'Die Entwickelung des Pfeiler- und Gewölbe-systemes in der kirchlichen Baukunst vom Beginne des Mittelalters bis zum Schlusse des 13. Jahrhunderts', *Austria—Centralcommission zur Erforschung und Erhaltung der Baudenkmale, Jahrbuch*, Wien, 1859, vol. iii, pp. 1–104.

ETCHELLS, E[RNEST] F[IANDER], 'The Evolution of Engineering Institutions', *Journal of the Institute of Structural Engineers* (until 1922, The Concrete Institute), London, [1924].

ETON, WILLIAM, *A Survey of the Turkish Empire*, London, printed for T. Cadell, jun. & W. Davies, 2nd edn., 1799.

EXCHAQUET, HENRI, *Dictionnaire des ponts et chaussées*, Paris, La Grange, 1788.

FITCHEN, JOHN, 'A Comment on the Function of the Upper Flying Buttress in French Gothic Architecture', *Gazette des Beaux-Arts*, Feb. 1955, ser. 6, vol. xlv, pp. 69–90.

FLETCHER, SIR BANISTER, *A History of Architecture on the Comparative Method*, New York, Scribner's, many edns., various dates.

FORMIGÉ, JULES, 'Note sur l'appareil des voûtes en cul-de-four romanes de Provence', *Bulletin monumental*, 1923, vol. lxxxii, pp. 197–201.

FORSYTH, GEORGE H., Jr., *The Church of St. Martin at Angers* (Princeton Monographs in Art and Archaeology, xxviii), Princeton, University Press, 2 vols., 1953.

FOURNEAU, N[ICOLAS], *L'Art du trait de la charpente*, Paris, Firmin-Didot, [1767–70], 1820.

FRANKL, PAUL, 'The Crazy Vaults of Lincoln Cathedral', *The Art Bulletin*, June 1953, vol. xxxv, pp. 95–107.

FRANKLIN, A[LFRED], *Dictionnaire historique des arts, métiers et professions exercés dans Paris depuis le XIIIᵉ siècle*, Paris, H. Welter, 1906.

FREER, Maj. W. J., 'A Beehive-shaped Dwelling in one of the Isles of the Sea, Argylshire…', *Associated Architectural Societies Reports and Papers*, 1902, vol. xxvi, part ii, pp. 462-3.

FRENCH, ARTHUR WILLARD, and IVES, HOWARD CHAPIN, *Stereotomy*, New York, John Wiley & Sons, 2nd edn., 1911. 48 illus. plus xxii folding plates. Chap. iv, pp. 44–78, 'Structures Containing Developable Surfaces'; chap. v, pp. 79–106, 'The Oblique or Skew Arch'.

FREZIER, A[MÉDÉE FRANÇOIS], *La Théorie et la pratique de la coupe des pierres et des bois, pour la construction des voûtes et autres parties des bâtiments civils et militaires, ou traité de stéréotomie à l'usage de l'architecture*, 3 vols., Strasbourg, J.-D. Doulsseker le fils, 1737-9.

FROIDEVAUX, Y.-M., 'L'Abbatiale de Lessay: Les fouilles et les découvertes', *Les Monuments historiques de la France*, juill.–sept. 1958, nouv. sér., vol. iv, pp. 139–42.

FROTHINGHAM. *See* STURGIS and FROTHINGHAM.

GAILHABAUD, JULES, *L'Architecture du Vᵉ au XVIIᵉ siècle et les arts qui en dépendent*, 4 vols., Paris, A. Morel, 1869–72.

GALL, ERNST, *Die gotische Baukunst in Frankreich und Deutschland* (Handbücher der Kunstgeschichte), Braunschweig, Klinkhardt & Biermann, 2. Aufl., vol. i, 1955. 201 illus.

—— 'Neue Beiträge zur Geschichte vom "Werden der Gotik": Untersuchungen zur Baugeschichte der Normandie', *Monatshefte für Kunstwissenschaft*, 1911, vol. iv, Heft 7, pp. 309–23.

GAU, ARCHITECTE, 'De l'emploi du fer comme moyen de consolidation dans les monuments gothiques', *Revue générale de l'architecture et des travaux publics*, 1841, vol. ii, pp. 23–26.

GAUTHEY, H., *Traité de la construction des ponts* (edited by Navier), Paris, Firmin-Didot, 1809–16.

GAUTHIER, J.-L., *Cours de matériaux et éléments de construction: Croquis de stéréotomie* (École Nationale Supérieure des Beaux-Arts), Paris, Éditions Vincent Fréal et Cie, s.d. 60 plates.

GAUTIER, [HUBERT], *Traité des ponts et chaussées*, ..., Paris, André Cailleau, 1716. 131 pp., 28 plates. *Vide* particularly: chap. xiv, pp. 68–71, 'Des Échafaudages'; chap. xv, pp. 71–77, 'Des Cintres, Mortoises, & Poutres armées'; and the nine examples of centering frames on plate xviii.

GÉNERMONT. *See* CHAULIOT and GÉNERMONT.

GENUYS, CHARLES, *Construction maçonnerie* (Bibliothèque populaire des écoles de dessin. Première série: Enseignement technique), 2 vols., Paris, J. Rouam, 1885. Vol. ii: 'Exécution des maçonneries, murs'.

GIBSON, FRANCIS, 'Observations on the Machine called the Lewis', *Archaeologia*, 1792, vol. x, pp. 123–7. 1 plate.

GILMAN, ROGER, 'The Theory of Gothic Architecture and the Effect of Shell-fire at Rheims and Soissons', *American Journal of Archaeology*, 1920, 2nd ser., vol. xxiv, pp. 37–72. 18 illus.

GLÜCK, HEINRICH, *Der Ursprung des römischen und abendländischen Wölbungsbaues*, Wien, Krystall-Verlag, 1933. 287 figs.

GNUSCHKE, H., 'Die Theorie der gewölbten Bögen mit besonderer Rücksicht auf den versteifenden Einfluß der Übermauerung und Überschüttung', *Zeitschrift für Bauwesen*, Berlin, Verlag von Wilhelm Ernst & Sohn, 1892, vol. xlii, pp. 74–106. 38 figs.

GOETHALS, EMILE, *Bogen-Gewelven Koepels*, Uitgaven Kunst van Bouwen, 2 vols. (text 68 pp.; plates 104 pp.), Brussel, n.d. (There is a French language edition of this work, entitled *Arcs, voûtes, coupoles*, 2 vols., Bruxelles, Édition 'Art de Bâtir', 1947.)

GONTARD, FR. GABRIEL, *Les Abbayes de France au moyen âge et en 1947*, Paris, Éditions G. Durassie, 1947.

GOODISON, J. W., *Works of Art in Austria (British Zone of Occupation): Losses and Survivals in the War*, London, H.M. Stationery Office, 1946. 34 photographic illus.

GOODYEAR, WILLIAM H., 'The Leaning Façade of Notre Dame as Compared with that of Pisa', *American Journal of Archaeology*, New York, 1901, 2nd ser., vol. v, pp. 12–14.

—— 'Recent Observations on the "Widening Refinement" in Amiens Cathedral', ibid. 1909, vol. xiii, pp. 55–56.

—— 'Architectural Refinements in Mediaeval French Cathedrals as Related to the Question of Repairs or Restoration in the War Zone', ibid. 1919, vol. xxiii, pp. 71–72.

—— 'Reply to the Criticism of Bilson regarding Architectural Refinements in Amiens', *Journal of the Royal Institute of British Architects*, 1909, 3rd ser., vol. xvi, pp. 715–40.

GOTTGETREU, R[UDOLPH], 'Ein Beitrag zur geschichtlichen Entwickelung der Gewölbe', *Zeitschrift für Bauwesen*, Berlin, Verlag von Ernst & Korn, 1879, vol. xxix, pp. 91–111 (plus plates 12 and 13 in atlas).

GRAEFF, AUGUSTE, *Appareil et construction des ponts biais*, Paris, Dunod, 2ᵉ édition, 1867.

GRIBBLE. See CESCINSKY and GRIBBLE.

GUADET, J[ULIEN], *Éléments et théorie de l'architecture*, 4 vols., Paris, Librairie de la Construction Moderne, [1901–4], [1905], [1910], [1915], édition nouvelle, revue et augmentée, s.d. *Vide* particularly: vol. iii, chap. xi, pp. 305–14, 'Les Églises voûtées: Poussées localisées et résistances extérieures'; and chap. xii, pp. 315–56, 'Les Églises voûtées: Poussées localisées: résistances diverses'.

GUASTAVINO, R[AFAEL], *Essay on the Theory and History of Cohesive Construction Applied Especially to the Timbrel Vault*, Boston, Ticknor & Co., 1892. 149 pp., 62 figs.

—— *Prolegomenos on the Function of Masonry in Modern Architectural Structures*, part i [New York, Record & Guide Press, Printers, 1896].

GÜLDENPFENNIG, HANS, 'Sicherungsarbeiten an den Vierungspfeilern des Kölner Domes', *Die Denkmalpflege*, Berlin und Wien, 1930, pp. 193–201. 11 illus.

GWILT, J[OSEPH], *A Treatise on the Equilibrium of Arches* . . ., 2nd edn., London, Priestley & Weale, 1826.

HAASE, MAX, *Der Gewölbebau: Handbuch für die Praxis des Hochbautechnikers*, Halle, L. Hofstetter, 1900.

HAHNLOSER, [HANS] R[OBERT], *Villard de Honnecourt*, Kritische Gesamtausgabe des Bauhüttenbuches MS. fr. 19093 der Pariser Nationalbibliothek, Wien, Anton Schroll, 1935.

HALL. See SINGER, HOLMYARD, HALL, and WILLIAMS.

HART, JOHN, *A Practical Treatise on the Construction of Oblique Arches*, London, John Weale, [1839], 3rd edn., 1848.

HARVEY, JOHN H., *The Gothic World*, London, Batsford, 1950.

—— *Henry Yevele*, London, Batsford, 1944.

HARVEY, WILLIAM, *Models of Buildings: How to Make and Use Them*, London, The Architectural Press, 1927.

—— *The Preservation of St. Paul's Cathedral and Other Famous Buildings*: A Text Book on the New Science of Conservation, including an Analysis of Movement in Historical Structures Prior to Their Fall, London, The Architectural Press, 1925. 153 pp., 73 illus.

HASAK, E. H. MAX, *Einzelheiten des Kirchenbaues* (Handbuch der Architektur, II Teil: Die Baustile, historische und technische Einrichtung, 4. Band, Heft 4), Leipzig, J. M. Gebhardt's Verlag, 1927.

BIBLIOGRAPHY

HASTINGS, MAURICE, *St. Stephen's Chapel and Its Place in the Development of Perpendicular Style in England*, Cambridge, University Press, 1955.

HECK, JOHN G., *Iconographic Encyclopaedia*, 4 vols. text, 2 vols. plates, New York, Rudolph Garrigue, 1851–2. (Translated from the German *Bilder Atlas zum Conversations Lexicon*, with additions, and edited by Spencer F. Baird.) *Vide*: division x: 'Technology', in plates vol. ii, plates 7, 8; text vol. iv, division x: 'Bridge Building', pp. 36–46; 'Windlasses and Cranes', pp. 57–59. (Pagination is by divisions.)

HEIDELOFF, KARL [ALEXANDER VON], *Die Bauhütte des Mittelalters in Deutschland*, Nürnberg, J. A. Stein, 1844.

HEIDER, GUSTAV [ADOLPH], *Theorie der schiefen Gewölbe und deren praktische Ausführung*, Wien, 1846.

HEINZERLING, JOHANN GEORG ERNST FRIEDRICH, *Constructions-elemente in Holz* (being pp. 94–138 in vol. i of division 3: 'Hochbau-constructionen', in *Handbuch der Architektur*, 24 vols., Darmstadt, 1880–93).

HERPÉ, E., 'La Restauration des tours de Notre-Dame de Paris', *Les Monuments historiques de la France*, oct.–déc. 1955, nouv. sér., vol. i, pp. 155–60. 6 illus.

HESS, FRIEDRICH, *Steinverbande und Gewölbebau aus kunstlichen Steinen* mit einem Anhang von Professor Carl Settler, 'Der Leichgewölbebau', München, Verlag Hermann Rinn, 1948. 300 line drawings plus 30 photographic illus.

HOLMYARD. *See* SINGER, HOLMYARD, HALL, and WILLIAMS.

HOSKING, WILLIAM, *Essay and Treatise on the Architecture and Practice of Bridges*, London, 1842.

—— (Wrote portion on Construction and Building, pp. 1–166, in Ashpitel, *Treatise on Architecture . . .*, q.v.)

HOUVET, ÉTIENNE, *Cathédrale de Chartres: Architecture*, Paris, Académie des Beaux-Arts, s.d. 90 photographic plates.

HOWARD, F. E., 'Fan Vaults', *Archaeological Journal*, London, Royal Archaeological Institute of Great Britain and Ireland, 1911, vol. lxviii (2nd ser. vol. xviii), pp. 1–42. 43 photographic illus. plus 26 drawings.

—— 'On the Construction of Mediaeval Roofs', *Archaeological Journal*, 1914, vol. lxxi (2nd ser. vol. xxi), pp. 293–352. 16 photographic illus. plus 32 figs. of numerous examples.

HUBRECHT. *See* DOYON and HUBRECHT.

HULL, R. B., 'On All Saints' Church, Northampton', *Associated Architectural Societies Reports and Papers*, 1881–2, vol. xvi, pp. 72–87.

HUNTER, L. E., *Underpinning and Strengthening of Structures*, London, Contractors Record and Municipal Engineering, 1952. 162 pp., 110 diagrams.

HUSS, GEORGE MARTIN, *Rational Building*, New York, Macmillan, 1895. (This is the English translation of the entire article 'Construction' in Viollet-le-Duc's *Dictionnaire*.)

HYDE, EDWARD WYLLYS, *Skew Arches: Advantages and Disadvantages of Different Methods of Construction* (Van Nostrand's Science Series no. 15), New York, Van Nostrand, 1875.

INMAN, THOMAS, M.D., 'On a Means Employed for Removing and Erecting Menhirs', *Liverpool Literary and Philosophical Society Proceedings*, vol. xxx, pp. 103–14.

BIBLIOGRAPHY

INNOCENT, C. F., *The Development of English Building Construction* (Cambridge Technical Series), Cambridge, University Press, 1916.

IVES. *See* FRENCH and IVES.

JACKSON, SIR THOMAS GRAHAM, *Byzantine and Romanesque Architecture*, 2 vols., Cambridge, University Press, 1913.

JAGGARD, WALTER R., and DRURY, FRANCIS E., *Architectural Building Construction* (Cambridge Technical Series), Cambridge, University Press, 3 vols. *Vide*: vol. iii, 2nd edn., 1937, chap. xiii, 'Temporary Carpentry', pp. 244–66. 12 illus.

JANNER, FERDINAND, *Die Bauhütten des deutschen Mittelalters*, Leipzig, 1876.

JONES. *See* KNOOP and JONES.

JOUSSE, MATHURIN, *L'Art de la charpenterie* (first published in 1627), Paris, Moette, 1707.

JULLIEN, HENRI, 'Clé de voûte de la chapelle de la Vierge à Caudebec-en-Caux', *Les Monuments historiques de la France*, juill.–sept. 1955, nouv. sér., vol. i, pp. 116–20. 9 illus.

JUTTNER, WERNER, *Ein Beitrag zur Geschichte der Bauhütten und des Bauwesens im Mittelalter*, Köln, Druck: Max Welzel, 1935.

KALINKA, J. E., 'Monolithic Concrete Construction for Hangars', *The Military Engineer*, Jan.–Feb. 1940, vol. xxxii, pp. 54–56.

—— *See* MOLKE and KALINKA.

KING, THOMAS H., *The Study-Book of Mediaeval Architecture and Art*, 4 vols., Edinburgh, John Grant, 1893.

KLETZL, OTTO, *Plan-fragmente aus der deutschen Dombauhütte von Prag in Stuttgart und Ulm*, Stuttgart, Felix Krais Verlag, 1939.

KLYCE, E. W., 'The Z-D System of Shell Roof Construction', *Task* Magazine, New York, Issue no. 4, 1943, pp. 26–29.

KNIGHT, EDWARD HENRY, *Knight's American Mechanical Dictionary*, being a description of tools, instruments, machines, processes, and engineering; history of inventions, general technological vocabulary; and digest of mechanical appliances in science and the arts, 3 vols., New York, J. B. Ford & Co., 1874–6. Illus. with upwards of 5,000 engravings.

KNIGHT, WILLIAM, 'Observations on the Mode of Construction of the Present Old London Bridge as Discovered in the Years 1826 and 1827', *Archaeologia*, 1831, vol. xxiii, pp. 117–19. 3 plates.

KNOOP, D., and JONES, G. P., *The Mediaeval Mason*, Manchester, University Press, [1933], 1949.

KÖMSTEDT, RUDOLPH, *Die Entwicklung des Gewölbebaues in den mittelalterlichen Kirchen Westfalens* (Studien zur Deutschen Kunstgeschichte, 172 Heft), Strassburg, J. H. Ed. Heitz (Heitz & Mündel), 1914. 33 photographic plates, 9 text-figs.

KÖRNER, CARL, *Gewölbte Decken* (being vol. ii, part 3 of division 3: 'Hochbau-constructionen', in *Handbuch der Architektur*, 24 vols., Darmstadt, 1880–93).

KRAFFT, JEAN-CHARLES (same as KRAFFT, JOHANN KARL), *Traité des échafaudages, ou Choix des meilleurs modèles de charpentes exécutés tant en France qu'à l'étranger*. Contenant la description des ouvrages en sous-œuvre, des différentes espèces de cintres, des applications de la charpente aux constructions hydrauliques, &c. Paris, Roret, 1856. 9 pp., 51 plates.

BIBLIOGRAPHY

KRAFFT, JOHANN KARL, *Traité sur l'art de la charpente* mis en ordre et augmenté de 40 planches par Thiollet, 2 vols., 3ᵉ édition, Paris, Bance aîné, 1840.

KUBLER, GEORGE, 'A Late Gothic Computation of Rib Vault Thrusts', *Gazette des Beaux-Arts*, 1944, series 6, vol. xxvi, pp. 135–48. 6 illus.

LACHEZ, THÉODORE, 'Des Échafauds de maçons en usage à Paris', *Revue générale de l'architecture et des travaux publics*, 1842, vol. iii, pp. 145–52 and plate viii, figs. 1–4.

La Construction des ponts et viaducs en bois, en pierre, ponts métalliques, fondations tubulaires. Ouvrage divisé en trois parties, comprenant les nouveaux systèmes de constructions adoptés dans tous les pays, avec la description et planches cotées à l'appui des principaux ouvrages d'art exécutés dans les différentes contrées de l'Europe et des États-Unis d'Amérique. Pt. I: *Ponts en bois, cintres et échafaudages.* Saint-Nicolas, Varangéville, Imprimerie Lacroix: Paris, Librairie E. Lacroix, 1873. 28 pp., 15 plates.

LACROIX, E[MIL], 'Die mittelalterliche Baugerüste', *Deutsche Kunst und Denkmalpflege*, 1934, vol. x, pp. 218–21. 7 illus.

LACROIX, PAUL, *Histoire de la charpenterie*, Paris, Delahays, 1858.

LANGLEY, BATTY, *Ancient Masonry, both in Theory and Practice . . .*, London, 1730. 494 plates.

LASSAULX. See WHEWELL.

LASSAUX, M. DE, 'Description of a Mode of Erecting Light Vaults over Churches and Similar Spaces', *Journal of the Royal Institution of Great Britain*, London, John Murray, 1831, vol. i, pp. 224–40. 11 line drawings.

LASTEYRIE, R[OBERT] DE, *L'Architecture religieuse en France à l'époque gothique*, 2 vols., Paris, Auguste Picard, 1926.

LEFÈVRE-PONTALIS, EUGÈNE, 'Les Voûtes en berceau et d'arêtes sans doubleaux', *Bulletin monumental*, 1921, vol. lxxx, pp. 71–85.

LEIBNITZ, DR. HEINRICH, *Die Organisation der Gewölbe im christlichen Kirchenbau* (Eine kunstgeschichtliche Studie), Leipzig, I. D. Weigel, 1855. 65 pp., 96 figs.

LÉON, PAUL, *La Vie des monuments français: Destruction: Restauration*, Paris, A. et J. Picard, 1951.

LETHABY, W[ILLIAM] R., *Mediaeval Art*, London, Duckworth, 1904.

—— *Architecture: An Introduction to the History and Theory of the Art of Building* (no. 38 in 'Home University of Modern Knowledge' Series), New York, Henry Holt, [1912].

—— *Westminster Abbey and the King's Craftsmen*, London, Duckworth, 1906. (Referred to as *King's Craftsmen.*)

—— *Westminster Abbey Reëxamined*, London, Duckworth, 1925. (Referred to as *Reëxamined.*)

LIANG SSU CH'ENG, 'Open Spandrel Bridges of Ancient China. I: The An-Chi Ch'iao at Chao Chou, Hopei', *Pencil Points*, Jan. 1938, vol. xix, pp. 25–32. 10 illus.

—— 'Open Spandrel Bridges of Ancient China. II: The Yung-T'ung Ch'iao at Chao Chou, Hopei', *Pencil Points*, Mar. 1938, vol. xix, pp. 155–60. 10 illus. (These two articles originally published in Chinese in the *Bulletin of the Society for Research in Chinese Architecture*, vol. v, no. 2 (Dec. 1934, Peiping), and here made available in English for the first time in this translation by Mr. Liang and Wilma C. Fairbank.)

MACKENZIE, FREDERICK, *Observations on the Construction of the Roof of King's College Chapel, Cambridge*, London, John Weale, 1840. 20 pp., 8 text-figs, 4 plates.

MCMASTER, JOHN B., *Bridge and Tunnel Centres*, New York, D. Van Nostrand (Van Nostrand's Science Series no. 20), 1875.

MAGINNIS, OWEN B., *Practical Centring: Treating of the Practice of Centring Arches in Building Construction as Carried on in the United States at the Present Time*, New York, Wm. T. Comstock, 1891. 80 pp., 65 line drawings.

MAILLÉ. *See* AUBERT and MAILLÉ.

MARÉ, ERIC DE, *The Bridges of Britain*, London, Batsford, 1954.

MASSON, H[ENRI], 'Le Rationalisme dans l'architecture du moyen âge', *Bulletin monumental*, 1935, vol. xciv, pp. 29–50. 5 figs.

MAYEUX, ALBERT, 'La ligne de faîte appareillée dans les voûtes en blocage', *Bulletin monumental*, 1912, vol. lxxvi, pp. 562–7.

MAZEROLLE, L., *Le Trait de charpente*, Dourdan, Vial, 1904.

MOLES, ANTOINE, *Histoire des charpentiers*, Paris, Librairie Gründ, 1949.

MOLKE, E., and KALINKA, J. E., 'Principles of Concrete Shell Dome Design', *Journal of the American Concrete Institute*, Detroit, May–June 1938, vol. xxxiv, pp. 649–707.

MONTEL, ALFREDO, *Building Structures in Earthquake Countries*, Translated from the Italian, with additions by the author, London, C. Griffin & Co., 1912. 42 diagrams, 1 folding plate.

MOORE, CHARLES H., *Development and Character of Gothic Architecture*, 2nd edn., New York, Macmillan, 1906.

MOREAU-NÉLATON, ÉTIENNE, *La Cathédrale de Reims*, Paris, Librairie Centrale des Beaux-Arts, 1915.

MOREY, MATHIEU-PROSPER, *Charpente de la cathédrale de Messine, dessinée par M. Morey*, Paris, Imprimerie de Firmin-Didot frères, 1841. 8 plates.

MORTET, VICTOR, 'L'Expertise de la cathédrale de Chartres en 1316', *Congrès archéologique de France*, LXVIIᵉ session tenue à Chartres en 1900, Paris, 1901, vol. lxvii, pp. 308–29.

—— and DESCHAMPS, P[AUL], *Recueil de textes relatifs à l'histoire de l'architecture et à la condition des architectes en France au moyen âge*, 2 vols., Paris, A. Picard. XIᵉ–XIIᵉ siècle, 1911; XIIᵉ–XIIIᵉ siècle, 1929.

MOSELEY, REV. HENRY, *Illustrations of Mechanics*, 2nd edn., revised, London, Longman, Orme, Brown, Green & Longmans, 1841.

—— *The Mechanical Principles of Engineering and Architecture*, 2nd American from 2nd London edn., with additions by Dennis Hart Mahan, New York, J. Wiley & Son, 1869.

MULLER. *See* DENFER and MULLER.

National Geographic Magazine, Washington, D.C., National Geographic Society. Monthly.

NICHOLSON, PETER, *The Guide to Railway Masonry, containing a Complete Treatise on the Oblique Arch*, London, Groombridge & Sons, 3rd edn., 1848.

—— *Encyclopaedia of Architecture*; being a New and Improved Edition of Nicholson's Dictionary of the Science and Practice of Architecture, Building, etc. Edited by Edward

Lomax and Thomas Gunyon, 2 vols., London, The Caxton Press, 1852. *Vide*: Vol. i, pp. 136–40, 'Centre', and p. 407, 'Scaffold'; vol. ii (plates), 'Centering', 4 plates; 'Centering for Groins', 2 plates; 'Carpentry', plates xi, fig. 8, xii, fig. 9, no. 1.

NICHOLSON, W. A., 'Report on the Construction of a Stone Arch between the West Towers of Lincoln Cathedral', *Transactions of the Royal Institute of British Architects*, London, Longman, Brown, Green & Longmans, 1842, vol. i, part ii, pp. 180–3. One plate.

'Nouveau procédé de décintrement pour les voûtes et les arcs de grande portée', *Revue générale de l'architecture et des travaux publics*, 1854, vol. xii, pp. 303–13. 5 illus.

OSLET, GUSTAVE, *Traité de charpente en bois*, Paris, H. Chairgrasse fils, [1890].

PANOFSKY, ERWIN, *Abbot Suger on the Abbey Church of St-Denis and Its Treasures*, Princeton, University Press, 1946.

—— 'Postlogium Sugerianum', *The Art Bulletin*, June 1947, vol. xxix, pp. 119–21.

PAPWORTH, J[OHN] B[UONAROTTI], 'A Suggestion Referring to the Stone Arch at Lincoln Cathedral', *Transactions of the Royal Institute of British Architects*, London, 1842, vol. i, part ii, pp. 184–5.

PAPWORTH, WYATT, 'Notes on the Assumed Use of Chestnut Timber in the Carpentry of Old Buildings', *Papers Read at the R.I.B.A. Session 1857–1858*, London, 1858, pp. 192–9.

—— editor, *The Dictionary of Architecture*, London, The Architectural Publication Society, 8 vols. in 5, 1853–92. (The pagination is separate for each letter.) *Vide* particularly the following articles:

B-122, 'Bow and String Beam'.

C-57, 58, 'Centre of an Arch or Vault'.

D-65, 67, 'Drawing'.

E-50, 51, 'Equilibrium of an Arch'.

F-15, 'Falling or Felling'.

F-74, 'Forfex'.

G-90, 91, 'Groined Vaulting'.

H-14, 15, 'Hammer Beam Roof'.

PAQUET, JEAN-PIERRE, 'La Restauration de Saint-Leu-d'Esserant: Problèmes de stabilité', *Les Monuments historiques de la France*, janv.–mars 1955, nouv. sér., vol. i, pp. 9–19. 11 illus.

—— 'Structures des monuments anciens et leur consolidation', *Les Monuments historiques de la France*, oct.–déc. 1957, nouv. sér., vol. iii, pp. 161–82. 34 illus.

PARSONS, WILLIAM BARCLAY, *Engineers and Engineering in the Renaissance*, Baltimore, Williams & Wilkins, 1939.

PERRAULT-DABOT. *See* BAUDOT and PERRAULT-DABOT.

PERRONET, J[EAN-] R[ODOLPHE], *Mémoire sur le cintrement et le décintrement des ponts, et sur les differens mouvemens que prennent les voûtes pendant leur construction*, lu à l'Assemblée publique de l'Académie royale des sciences, le 21 avril 1773, Paris, Imprimerie royale, 1777. 20 pp., 3 plates.

—— *Mémoire sur une nouvelle manière d'appliquer les chevaux au mouvement des machines en y employant de plus leur poids et celui du conducteur*, 2ᵉ édition, Paris, Bachelier, 1834. 24 pp., 1 plate.

PERRONET, J[EAN-] R[ODOLPHE], *Mémoire sur le recherche des moyens que l'on pourrait employer pour construire de grandes arches de pierre de 200, 300, 400 et jusqu'à 500 pieds d'ouverture qui seraient destinées à franchir de profondes vallées bordées de rochers escarpés* . . ., Paris, Imprimerie nationale exécutive du Louvre, 1793. 44 pp., figs.; 1 plate.

PHLEPS, HERMANN, 'Mittelalterliche Gerüstbauten', *Die Denkmalpflege*, Berlin und Wien, 1930, pp. 111–16. Figs. 121–31.

PLANAT, P[AUL] A[MÉDÉE], *Encyclopédie de l'architecture et de la construction* (Bibliothèque de la Construction Moderne), 6 vols., Paris, Dujardin et Cie, Éditeurs, 1888–93. *Vide* particularly the following articles:
'Levage', vol. v, pp. 369–98 (incl. figs. 46–59 on rolling scaffolding).
'Matériel de Chantier, III: Échafauds', vol. v, pp. 619–33. 31 figs.

PORTER, ARTHUR KINGSLEY, *The Construction of Lombard and Gothic Vaults*, New Haven, Yale University Press, 1911.

—— *Medieval Architecture, Its Origins and Development*, 2 vols., New York, Baker & Taylor, 1909.

POWYS, A[LBERT] R., *Repair of Ancient Buildings*, London, J. M. Dent & Sons, 1929. 41 illus.

—— and WILSON, J. S., 'The Repair of Vaulted Buildings: Two Principles of Repair too often Neglected by Those in Charge of Great Vaulted Churches and Other Buildings', *Journal of the Royal Institute of British Architects*, 12 Oct. 1935, 3rd ser., vol. xlii, pp. 1142–4.

PRENTICE, SARTELL, *The Heritage of the Cathedral*, New York, William Morrow & Co., 1936.

PRENTIS, EDMUND ASTLEY, and WHITE, LAZARUS, *Underpinning: Its Practice and Application*, New York, Columbia University Press, 2nd edn., 1950. 374 pp., 200 figs.

PRICE, FRANCIS, *A Series of . . . Observations . . . upon . . . the Cathedral-Church of Salisbury*, London, Baldwin, 1753.

QUICHERAT, JULES, *Mélanges d'archéologie et d'histoire*, Paris, Alphonse Picard, 1886.

RACKHAM, REV. R[ICHARD] B[ELWARD], 'The Nave of Westminster', *Proceedings of the British Academy 1909–1910*, London, Henry Frowde, Oxford University Press, 1910, pp. 33–96. 6 illus.

RANQUET, HENRI DU, *La Cathédrale de Clermont-Ferrand*, Paris, Henri Laurens, 2ᵉ édition, 1928. 40 illus.; plan in colour.

—— and RANQUET, E. DU, 'Origine française du berceau roman', *Bulletin monumental*, 1931, vol. xc, pp. 35–74. 15 illus.

RAULINE, HENRI, 'The Church of the Sacred Heart at Montmartre: Its Origin and Construction', *The Architectural Record*, New York, The Record and Guide, July–Sept. 1893, vol. iii, pp. 3–28. 20 illus.

REBOLLEDO, D. JOSÉ A., *Traité général de construction*, Paris, Imprimerie de E. Lacroix, [1879]. 1 vol. text; atlas, 35 plates.

REES, ABRAHAM, *The Cyclopaedia; or, Universal Dictionary of Arts, Sciences, and Literature*, Philadelphia, Samuel F. Bradford & Murray, Fairman & Co., 47 vols., including 6 vols. of plates, [1810–24]. 'First American Edition, revised, corrected, enlarged, and adapted to this country.' (The text volumes are totally without pagination. Some of the plates, though identically numbered, are different.)

Reims au lendemain de la guerre: la cathédrale mutilée; la ville devastée, Paris, Éditions Jean Budry et Cie, 1927. 138 plates.

RENNIE, GEORGE, *On the Expansion of Arches* (On the Expansion of Iron under the Atmospheric Variations of Temperature. On the Expansion of Stone Bridges), London, [183–].

REPTON, J. ADEY, 'On the General Size of Stones in Norman Architecture', *British Archaeological Association Journal*, 1848, vol. iii, pp. 105–6.

Rheims and the Battles for Its Possession, Clermont-Ferrand, Michelin et Cie, 1919. ('Illustrated Michelin Guides to the Battle-Fields (1914–1918)'.)

RHEIN, ANDRÉ, 'Étude sur les voûtes des déambulatoires', *Bulletin monumental*, 1923, vol. lxxxii, pp. 255–90. 18 plans plus 2 illus.

RHEINHARD, BAURATH, 'Ueber die Kunst des Wölbens', *Centralblatt der Bauverwaltung*, 1887, vol. vii, pp. 325–7, 339–41, 349–50. 3 figs.

RICKETSON, OLIVER G., Jr., 'American Nail-less Houses in the Maya Bush', *Art and Archaeology*, July–Aug. 1927, vol. xxiv, pp. 27–36. 16 illus.

RIVOIRA, G[IOVANNI] T[ERESIO], *Lombardic Architecture. Its Origin, Development and Derivatives*, 2 vols., Oxford, Clarendon Press, 2nd edn., 1933.

RONDELET, J[EAN], *Traité théorique et pratique de l'art de bâtir*, Paris, L'auteur, 1812–17. 6 vols. text, 2 vols. (of 192 folding) plates.

ROOSVAL. *See* CURMAN and ROOSVAL.

RUPRICH-ROBERT, V[ICTOR MARIE CHARLES], 'Les Voûtes de l'Abbaye-aux-Hommes, à Caen', *Bulletin de la Société des Beaux-Arts de Caen*, Caen, Librairie Hardel, 1861. 16 pp.

SALVADORI, MARIO G., 'Thin Shells', *Architectural Record*, New York, F. W. Dodge, July 1954, vol. cxvi, pp. 173–9. 28 figs.

SALZMAN, L[OUIS] F[RANCIS], *Building in England Down to 1540: A Documentary History*, Oxford, Clarendon Press, 1952.

Samarcande, Les mosquées de. Fascicule I: *Gour-Émir.* (Expédition pour la confection des papiers), St. Petersbourg, Commission Impériale Archéologique, 1905.

SCHMIDT, KARL, *Die Baugerüste*, München, Verlag Hermann Rinn, 1949. 352 pp., 406 photographic illus. and drawings.

SCHULZE, KONRAD WERNER, *Die Gewölbesysteme im spätgotischen Kirchenbau in Schwaben von 1450–1520*, Reutlingen, Gryphius-Verlag, [1940] (Tübinger Forschungen zur Archäologie und Kunstgeschichte, Band XVI). 138 pp., 23 illus., 138 plates.

SCOTT, GEORGE GILBERT, Jr., *An Essay on the History of English Church Architecture*, London, Simpkin Marshall & Co., 1881.

SCOTT, SIR GILBERT, *Lectures on the Rise and Development of Mediaeval Architecture*, 2 vols., London, John Murray, 1879.

—— *Gleanings from Westminster Abbey*, 2nd edn., Oxford and London, John Henry and James Parker, 1863.

SÉJOURNÉ, PAUL, *Grandes voûtes*, 6 tomes in 3 vols., Bourges, Imprimerie Vᵛᵉ Tardy-Pigelet et Fils, 1913–16.

SEVERUD, FRED N., 'Turtles and Walnuts, Morning Glories and Grass', *Architectural Forum*, New York, Sept. 1945, vol. lxxxiii, pp. 149–54, 158, 162. 20 figs.

SEYMOUR, CHARLES, Jr., *Notre-Dame of Noyon in the 12th Century*, &c., New Haven, Yale University Press, 1939.

SHAW, RICHARD NORMAN, *Architectural Sketches from the Continent*, London, Day & Son, 1858.

SIMONIN, [PROF.], *Traité élémentaire de la coupe des pierres, ou art du trait*, Paris, Joubert, 1792. 74 pp., 49 plates.

SIMPSON, F[REDERICK] M[OORE], *A History of Architectural Development*, 3 vols., [1905–11]. Vol. ii: *Mediaeval*, London, Longmans Green & Co., 2nd edn., 1922. Chap. vi, 'Vaulting', pp. 70–102.

SIMSON, OTTO VON, *The Gothic Cathedral*, New York, Bollingen Foundation (Bollingen Series XLVIII), 1956.

SINGER, C., HOLMYARD, E. J., HALL, A. R., WILLIAMS, T. I., *A History of Technology*, vol. ii: *The Mediterranean and the Middle Ages*, c. 700 B.C. to A.D. 1500, Oxford, Clarendon Press, 1956.

SMITH, REV. ALFRED CHARLES, 'On the Method of Moving Colossal Stones, as Practiced by Some of the More Advanced Nations of Antiquity', *Wiltshire Archaeological and Natural History Society*, 1865, vol. x, pp. 52–60.

SMITH, G. E. KIDDER, *Italy Builds: Its Modern Architecture and Native Inheritance*, New York, Reinhold, 1954.

STEFANSSON, VILHJALMUR, *The Friendly Arctic*, New York, Macmillan, 1921.

STOCK, CECIL HADEN, *Treatise on Shoring and Underpinning and generally dealing with Ruinous and Dangerous Structures*, London, Batsford, 1882. 10 plates.

STOKES, MARGARET, *Early Christian Art in Ireland*, Dublin, The Stationery Office, 1932.

STRAUB, HANS, *Die Geschichte der Bauingenieurkunst*, Ein Überblick von der Antike bis in die Neuzeit, Basel, Verlag Birkhäuser, 1949.

STREET, GEORGE EDMUND, *Some Account of Gothic Architecture in Spain*, London, John Murray, 1865.

STRZYGOWSKI, JOSEF, *Early Church Art in Northern Europe*; with special reference to timber construction and decoration, London, Batsford, 1928.

STURGIS, RUSSELL, *European Architecture, A Historical Study*, New York, Macmillan, 1896.

—— and FROTHINGHAM, A. L., *A History of Architecture*, 4 vols., New York, Doubleday Page. Vol. iii, 1915.

TAPPEN, GEORGE, *A Treatise on a New Mode of Building Groined Arches in Brickwork* (plus J. Narrien, *A Theory upon which the Construction of Them is Founded*), London, 1808.

TARN. See TREDGOLD and TARN.

TEAGUE, WALTER DORWIN, *Design This Day*, New York, Harcourt Brace, 1940.

THATCHER, A. G. H., *Scaffolding: A Treatise on the Design and Erection of Scaffolds, Gantries and Stagings*, with an account of the appliances used in connection therewith, London, Batsford, 1904. 146 diagrams, 6 plates.

THIOLLET. See KRAFFT.

THUNNISSEN, IT. H. J. W., *Gewelven hun Constructie en Toepassing in de Historische en Hedendaagse Bouwkunst*, Amsterdam, J. Ahrend & Zoon, 1950.

TREDGOLD, THOMAS, *Elementary Principles of Carpentry* . . . and TARN, E. WYNDHAM, *A Treatise on Joinery* . . ., London, The Technical Press, 14th imp., 1942.

TROUVELOT, JEAN, 'De la restauration des monuments historiques', *Techniques et architecture*, Nov. 1950, 9ᵐᵉ série, nos. 11–12, pp. 38–50. 45 illus.

UNGEWITTER, GEORG GOTTLOB, *Lehrbuch der gotischen Konstruktionem*, 2 vols., Leipzig, Chr. Herm. Tauchnitz, 4. Aufl., 1901–3.

VERHAEGEN, LE BARON, 'Le Voûtement de l'église Saint-Nicolas de Gand', *Revue belge d'archéologie et d'histoire de l'art*, Anvers, janv.–mars 1936, vol. vi, pp. 5–12. 3 photographic illus.

VERNEILH, FÉLIX DE, 'Construction des monuments ogivaux: Épures de la cathédrale de Limoges', *Annales archéologiques*, 1847, vol. vi, pp. 139–44.

VERRIER, JEAN, 'Les Monuments historiques atteints par la guerre', *Bulletin monumental*, 1940, vol. xcix, pp. 239–60. 8 illus.

Villard de Honnecourt, Album de. Architecte du XIIIᵉ siècle, Paris, Catala Frères, 1927. See *Wilars*.

VIOLLET-LE-DUC, E[UGÈNE EMMANUEL], *Dictionnaire raisonné de l'architecture française du XIᵉ au XVIᵉ siècle*, Paris, Librairies-Imprimeries Réunies, 1858–68, 1C vols. *Vide* particularly the following articles:
 'Armature', vol. i, pp. 461–6.
 'Chaînage', vol. ii, pp. 396–404.
 'Charpente', vol. iii, pp. 1–58.
 'Construction', vol. iv, pp. 1–279.
 'Échafaud', vol. v, pp. 103–14.
 'Engin', vol. v, pp. 210–69.
 'Escalier', vol. v, pp. 287–331.
 'Étai', vol. v, pp. 332–45.
 'Galerie', vol. vi, pp. 8–21.
 'Voûte', vol. ix, pp. 464–550.

——— 'De la construction des monuments religieuses en France', *Annales archéologiques*, Paris, Librairie Didron, vol. vi, avr. 1847, chap. v, pp. 194–205. 17 illus.

VOGTS, HANS, 'Das ehemalige Karmeliterkloster in Köln', *Die Denkmalpflege*, Berlin und Wien, 1930, pp. 237–43.

WALDRAM, PERCY J., 'Science and Architecture: Wren and Hooke', *Journal of the Royal Institute of British Architects*, 1935, 3rd ser., vol. xlii, p. 558.

WALTERS, R. C. SKYRING, 'Greek and Roman Engineering Instruments', *Transactions of the Newcomen Society*, London, 1921–2, vol. ii, pp. 45–60.

WARD, CLARENCE, *Mediaeval Church Vaulting* (Princeton Monographs in Art and Archaeology: V), Princeton, University Press, 1915.

WARE, SAMUEL, 'Observations on Vaults', *Archaeologia*, 1814, vol. xvii, pp. 40–84.

——— *Treatise on the Properties of Arches and Their Abutment Piers* . . ., London, 1809. 19 plates.

BIBLIOGRAPHY

WARE, SAMUEL, *Remarks on Theatres; and on Vaulting Them in Brick and Stone: of Domes, and the Vaults of the Free and Accepted Masons*, [Anonymous], London, 1809.
—— *Tracts on Vaults and Bridges*. Containing observations on the various forms of vaults; on the taking down and rebuilding London bridge; and on the principles of arches: illustrated by extensive tables of bridges. Also containing the principles of pendent bridges, with reference to the properties of the catenary, applied to the Menai bridge. And a theoretical investigation of the catenary, [Anonymous], London, printed for T. & W. Boone, 1822.

WARLAND, E[DMUND] G[EORGE], *Modern Practical Masonry*, New York, Dodd Mead, 1929.

WARTH. See BREYMANN.

WATKINS, J. ELFRETH, 'Ancient Engineering', *Cassier's Magazine*, New York. (Quoted in the *Journal of the Royal Institute of British Architects*, 14 Jan. 1899, 3rd ser., vol. vi, p. 136.)

WATSON, THOMAS LENNOX, *The Double Choir of Glasgow Cathedral: A Study of Rib Vaulting*, Glasgow, Hedderwick, 1901.

WAUCHOPE, ROBERT, *Modern Maya Houses: A Study of Their Archaeological Significance*, Washington, D.C., Carnegie Institution of Washington, Publication no. 502, 1938. 53 text-figs., 38 plates.

WEST, GEORGE HERBERT, *Gothic Architecture in England and France*, London, Bell, 1911.

WHEWELL, REV. W[ILLIAM], *Architectural Notes on German Churches, with Notes Written during an Architectural Tour in Picardy and Normandy*. 3rd edn., to which are added 'Notes on the Churches of the Rhine', by M. F. de Lassaulx, Cambridge, J. & J. J. Deighton, and London, John W. Parker, 1842.

WHITE. See PRENTIS and WHITE.

Wilars de Honecort, Facsimile of the Sketch-Book of, . . . with commentaries . . . by J. B. A. Lassus and J. Quicherat. Translated and edited by R. Willis. London, T. H. & J. Parker, 1859. (Also spelled *Vilars.*) See *Villard.*

WILLIAMS, HENRY LIONEL, and WILLIAMS, OTTALIE K., *Old American Houses and How to Restore Them*, Garden City, New York, Doubleday & Co., 1946.

WILLIAMS, SIR OWEN, 'The Philosophy of Masonry Arches', London, The Institution, 1927. 34 pp., 11 diagrams. (*The Institution of Civil Engineers. Selected Engineering Papers*, No. 56.)

WILLIAMS, RICHARD, 'Method of Removing the Centres of Brick or Stone Arches without Risque to the Workmen', *The Repertory of Arts, Manufactures and Agriculture.* . . . Practical and Interesting Papers Selected from the Philosophical Transactions and Scientific Journals of All Nations . . ., London, G. & T. Wilkie, 1817, 2nd ser., vol. xxx, pp. 277–9. 1 plate.

WILLIAMS, T. I. See SINGER, HOLMYARD, HALL, and WILLIAMS.

WILLIS, ROBERT, 'On the Construction of the Vaults of the Middle Ages', *Transactions of the Royal Institute of British Architects*, London, Longman, Brown, Green, and Longmans, 1842, vol. i, pp. 1–69. 22 text-figs., 3 plates (reprinted in 1910). (Referred to as *Vaults.*)
—— *A Description of the Sextry Barn at Ely, Lately Demolished*, Cambridge, University Press, and London, John W. Parker, 1843.

BIBLIOGRAPHY

WILLIS, ROBERT, *The Architectural History of Canterbury Cathedral*, London, Longman / Pickering / Bell, 1845. 53 figs. (Referred to as *Canterbury*.)

—— 'Architectural History of the Cathedral and Monastery at Worcester. Part I: The Cathedral', *Archaeological Journal*, 1863, vol. xx, pp. 83–135. 5 figs.

—— *The Architectural History of York Cathedral*, London, The Architectural Institute, 1848. 6 figs., 5 plans. (Referred to as *York*.)

WILSON, EPIPHANIUS, *Cathedrals of France: Popular Studies of the Most Interesting French Cathedrals*, New York, The Churchman Co., 1900.

WILSON, J. S. *See* POWYS and WILSON.

WITTMANN, W., 'Zur Theorie der Gewölbe', *Zeitschrift für Bauwesen*, Berlin, Verlag von Ernst & Korn, 1879, vol. xxix, pp. 62–74. 28 line drawings and stress diagrams.

WOOLLEY, GEORGE, *The Parish Church of St. Lawrence, Ludlow: A Monograph of the Tower Restoration, 1889–90–91*, Ludlow, George Woolley, 1893.

WRIGHT, THOMAS, 'Anglo-Saxon Architecture, illustrated from Illuminated Manuscripts', *Archaeological Journal*, 1845, vol. i, pp. 24–35. 21 figs.

—— 'Mediaeval Architecture, illustrated from Illuminated Manuscripts: Builders at Work', *British Archaeological Association Journal*, 1844, vol. i, pp. 20–25. 5 illus.

—— 'Notes relating to Architecture and Building, from Mediaeval Manuscripts', *British Archaeological Association Journal*, 1848, vol. iii, pp. 99–101.

ZEMP, J., 'Die Kirche von Romainmôtier', *Zeitschrift für Geschichte der Architektur*, Heidelberg, 1908, vol. i, p. 100.

AUTHOR INDEX

Note: References in bold-faced type signify direct quotations. Choisy and Viollet-le-Duc are cited so often throughout this book that references to them are indexed only when they are quoted directly. Periodicals are cited only when anonymous articles occur, or merely general references to them are made.

Abraham, Pol, **217**, 220, **226 f.**, **256**, **262 f.**
Adams, Henry, 197, **257.**
American Journal of Archaeology, **212.**
Andrews, Francis B., 6, 200, **202**, **203**, **209**, 211, **221**, 223, 237, 247, 280.
Anfray, Marcel, 197.
Architects' Journal, **178.**
Architectural Societies Reports and Papers, 199.
Art and Archaeology, 229, 238.
Aubert, Marcel, **111 f.**, 120, **206**, 211, 216, 217, **219**, 220, **222**, 224, **228**, **256 f.**, 258, 260, **262**, 301.
Aubert and Maillé, 217, 258.

Babcock, Charles, 198.
Baldwin, R., 210.
Bartlett, James, 230, 233, 242.
Baudot and Perrault-Dabot, 219, 249.
Bell, George Joseph, **268 f.**
Bill, Max, 245.
Bilson, John, 215, 257.
Blagrove, G. H., 243.
Blake, Marion Elizabeth, 244.
Bond, Francis, 51, **107**, 197, 213, **215**, 216, 218, 220, 224, 225, 246, **258**, 260, 261, 271, 272.
Brandon, Raphael and J. Arthur, **207**, **229.**
Branner, Robert, 213.
Brayley and Britton, 281, **283 ff.**
Breymann, G. A., 198, 239, 243 f., 246.
Brigham, William T., **231.**
Brodtbeck, Suzanne, **213.**
Brown, G. Baldwin, 197.
Brown, Richard, **275.**
Brunet, Émile, 222, **226**, **228**, 231, 236, **256**, 258.
Buck, George Watson, **268.**
Buckler, John C., **253.**
Bulletin monumental, 199, 246.
Bumpus, T. Francis, 236.

Burnell, George Rowdon, 244.

Caroe, Alben D. R., 199, 220, 226, 231, 245.
Cassier's Magazine, 209.
Cave and Earthwrol, 243.
Centralblatt der Bauverwaltung, 201.
Chauvel, Albert, **178**, **179**, 236, 238, 273.
Choisy, Auguste, 14, **123 f.**, **124**, **211**, **212**, **214**, **221.**
Colombier, Pierre du, 197, 200, 203, 207, 211, 237, 247, 280.
Colson, John Barnes, **274**, **292.**
Conant, Kenneth John, 197, **215**, **219**, **257**, **291.**
Congrès archéologique, 199.
Construction Methods, 245.
Cotton, Vere E., 202, 231, 234.
Creswell, K. A. C., **211.**
Crosby, Sumner McK., **291 f.**
Crossley, Fred H., 272.
Culley, John L., **268.**
Curman and Roosval, 134, 299.
Czarnowsky, Charles, 204, 208.

Deneux, Henri, **207**, 209, **217**, **234.**
Derand, François, 221.
Deutsche Bauzeitung, 199.
Didron, A. N. and E., 200.
Douglas, W. B., 243.

Ecclesiologist, 199.
Engineering News, **207**, **230 f.**, 231, 245.
Enlart, Camille, 197, 204, 205, 211, **215**, 218, **260**, 275.
Eton, William, **175**, 237.

Fitchen, John, 26, 206, 218, 293.
Fletcher, Banister, 221.
Forsyth, George H., Jr., 134, 234, 250, 254 f., 272, 292, 299.
Forsyth, W. A., 276.

Gall, Ernst, **212**, 250.
Gautier, Hubert, 244.
Gervais (Gervase), 5, 199, 290, **304.**
Gilman, Roger, 126, 199, 216, 227, 258.
Glück, Heinrich, 238.
Goethals, Emile, 198.
Goodyear, William H., 226.
Gottgetreu, Rudolph, 199, **215.**
Guadet, Julien, **206, 215.**
Guastavino, Raphael, 66 f., 215.
Güldenpfennig, Hans, 251.

Hacker, 199.
Hart, John, **267** f.
Harvey, John H., 38, 197, 199, **202, 206,** 211.
Harvey, William, 199, **205,** 226, **230,** 302.
Hasak, E. H. Max, 198, 208.
Hastings, Maurice, **281, 283, 286.**
Heck, John G., **225, 235.**
Herland, Hugh, 286, 302.
Hess, Friedrich. 237.
Houvet, Etienne, 202, 222, 226, 239.
Howard, F. E., 219, **222,** 229, 230.
Hull, R. B., **212.**
Hunter, L. E., 242.
Hurst, T. J., 243.
Huss, George M., 205, 206, 218, 219, 222, 223, 224, 226, 227, 256.

Inman, Thomas, 210.
Innocent, C. F., 211, **227, 273** f.

Jackson, Sir T. G., **209.**
Jullien, Henri, **257.**

Kalinka, J. E., 216.
Klyce, E. W., 216.
Knoop and Jones, 197.
Krafft, Jean-Charles, 241.

Lacroix, Emil, **200, 202,** 203, 246.
Lassaux (Lassaulx), 180 ff., **185** f., **214,** 237, 239, **257,** 261, **263.**
Lasteyrie, Robert de, 205, 207, 227, 258, 277, 278.
Laves, 225.
Lefèvre-Pontalis, Eugène, 197, 221.
Léon, Paul, 217, 225, 227, 252, 258.
Lethaby, William, **197, 200, 218, 220,** 228, **275** ff., **282.**
Liang Ssu Ch'eng, 201.

Mackenzie, Frederick, **204, 219** f., **229,** 248, **257.**
Maginnis, Owen B., 244.
Maillart, Robert, 245.
Maré, Eric de, 210.
Masson, Henri, **216.**
McMaster, John B., **210,** 223, **232** f., 234, **235** f., **244, 264, 296** ff.
Moles, Antoine, 197, 202, 207, 210, 211, 228, 230, 233, 236, 247, 252.
Molke, E., 216.
Monuments historiques de la France, 246.
Moore, Charles H., **197, 199, 217, 221** f., **260** f.
Moreau-Nélaton, 250.
Mortet and Deschamps, 200.

National Geographic, 133, 231, **238.**
Nicholson, Peter, **267.**
Nicholson, W. A., 235.

Panofsky, Erwin, 197, 200, **206,** 286, **289**f., **293,** 294.
Papworth, J. B., 235.
Paquet, Jean-Pierre, 225, 234, **238.**
Pasley, C. W., **238.**
Phleps, Hermann, 237, 246, 250.
Porter, Arthur K., **104** ff., 113, 197, 217, 224, 239, 257, 258, **260,** 301.
Powys, Albert R., 199, 245.
Powys and Wilson, 220, 226.
Prentice, Sartell, **258.**
Prentis and White, 242.
Price, Francis, **220, 225, 257,** 276.
Puig i Cadafalch, 197.

Quicherat, Jules, 213.

Rackham, Richard B., **207,** 236, **280** ff., **286** f., **305.**
Ranquet, Henri and E. du, 234, **262.**
Rauline, Henri, 231, **251.**
Rees, Abraham, 210, 211, 213.
Rheinhard, Baurath, 199.
Ricketson, Oliver G., Jr., 231.
Rivoira, G. T., **210,** 301.
Rondelet, Jean, 134, 210, 211, 247.

Sabouret, 84.
Salvadori, Mario G., 215.
Salzman, L. F., 157, 169, 197, 199, 200, 202 f., 207, **211, 212, 221,** 223, 229, **237,** 246, 250, 272, 287.

Schmidt, Karl, 133, 205, 211, 230, 236, 241, 252, 272, 273.
Schulze, Konrad Werner, 198.
Scott, G. G., 198, 277, 280 f.
Scott, G. G., Jr., 218, 228, 248, 275.
Séjourné, Paul, 134, 210, 245, 264 f.
Severud, Fred N., 216.
Seymour, Charles, Jr., 217, 218, 256, 258.
Shaw, Richard Norman, 249.
Simpson, F. M., 220, 236, 256, 258.
Simson, Otto von, 197.
Singer, Holmyard, Hall, and Williams, 208.
Smith, A. C., 210.
Smith, Kidder, 177, 238.
Stefansson, Vilhjalmar, 176, 238.
Stock, C. H., 243.
Stokes, Margaret, 238.
Street, George Edmund, 218.
Strzygowski, Josef, 212.
Sturgis and Frothingham, 198, 225.
Suger, Abbot, 5, 200, 206, 228, 286, 289 ff.

Tappen, George, 213 f.
Teague, Walter D., 241.
Techniques et architecture, 246.
Thatcher, A. G. H., 230, 242, 272, 273.
Thunnissen, H. J. W., 198, 244.
Treadgold and Tarn, 223, 243.

Trouvelot, Jean, 217, 230, 246, 259.

Ungewitter, G. G., 51 f., 198, 209, 213, 246.
Verneilh, Félix de, 234.
Verrier, Jean, 258.
Villard de Honnecourt (Wilars), 6, 7, 33, 38, 123 f., 200, 225, 247, 304.
Viollet-le-Duc, E. E., 15 f., 17 f., 20, 100, 125, 132, 229, 235, 256, 278, 304 f.
Vitruvius, 305.
Vogts, Hans, 207.

Waldram, Percy J., 302.
Ward, Clarence, 197, 222, 224.
Warland, E. G., 218, 231, 243, 266, 267.
Watkins, J. Elfreth, 209 f.
Watson, Thomas Lennox, 198, 202, 204, 206, 216, 219, 222, 303 ff, 306.
Wauchope, Robert, 231.
West, George Herbert, 212, 218.
Whewell, William, 180, 239.
William of Sens, 276, 304.
Williams and Williams, 234.
Willis, Rev. Robert, 123, 198, 199, 200 f., 206, 216, 218, 221, 224, 229, 234, 282.

Zeiss and Dywidag, 67 f.
Zemp, J., 213.

SUBJECT INDEX

Alternate system, 71, 75.
Ambulatory bays, 92 f., 222.
Architect, engineer, and contractor, xi, xiv.

Banded barrel vault, 47, 96, 98.
Barrel vault, 42 ff.
Buildings, exceptional v. average, 37 ff.

Cambering, 99, 184 f., 207, 214, 222.
Catenary curve, 80 f., 219.
Centering, 14, 28 ff., 129, 231.
  Cocket, 210.
  Flying buttress, 26, 126–9, 233.
  Permanent, 208 f.
Centering frames for ribbed vaults:
  Composition of, 159–63, 193, 201.
  Converging, 231, 301 f.
  Crown insert in, 145, 163–5.
  Discontinuous, 135 f.
  Double, 147, 153, 233.
  Not needed for formeret, 188, 208 f.
  Strutting systems used in, 296 ff.
Cerce device, 99, 238 f.
  Perhaps a template, 113, 271.
  Shortcomings of, 99–105, 222.
Church as repository of saints' remains, 204.
Cohesion in vault shells, 68, 215, 216.
Concrete overlay of vault, 83, 220.
Convergence of forces, 73 f., 80.
Corbelling (see also Tas-de-charge), 177, 238.

Decentering systems, 31, 32, 33, 121, 203, 232, 234.
Decentering wedges, 235 f.
  Location of, 166–8, 188.
Discrepancy of courses along the groin, 89–91.
Disengagement of diagonal centering frames, 145.
Domed groin vault, 55 ff., 97.

Eccentricity in loading of piers, 205.
Economy of means, 28, 30, 75, 87, 107, 159, 187 f., 188, 189, 221.

Erection time and rate of progress, 206, 226, 262 ff.
Erection of vaults and domes without formwork, schemes of, 175 ff.

Fissures in the vault, 83, 84, 220.
Flying buttress, 77 f., 123, 124, 126, 128.
Forfex device, 305.
Formwork (see also Lagging):
  Early practices, 30 ff., 66, 238.
  Earth-mounded, 30, 31, 213.
  Of planks or boards, 51 f., 107–9, 112, 115–18, 271 f.
  Supported on rib centerings, 108.

Gantries for high centering frames, 160, 162, 170 ff., 174, 190 f., 194.
Great wheels, 207 f., 223, 281 f., 287, 305 f.
Groin, weaknesses of, 213 f.
Groin ribs, 63 f., 69 ff., 88 ff., 111, 222.
Groin vault, simple, 51 ff., 221.
Guastavino system, 66 f., 215.

Height of vaulting, 169, 228.
Hurdles, 16, 237, 283 f.

Irregularities in vault surfaces (see also Warping and Plowshare twist), 32 f., 181, 186, 239.

Joint along the groin, 109–11, 224.

Keying-in lagging, 141, 143, 148 f., 186 f., 233.
Keystone, function of heavy, 85, 194.
  Pendent, 232.
  Pierced, 228.

Lagging frames, 119 f., 121 f.
  Adjusted for height at either end, 151.
  Allowing masonry to be set from side, 138 ff., 157.
  Doubled, 143.
  Seating at diagonal rib, 147–55.
  Secured to cradles, 155.

SUBJECT INDEX

Lagging frames (*contd.*)
  Set radially, 147 f., 157 f.
  Spacing of, 115, 157.
Lashing, use of, 132 f., 169, 202.
  Deterioration of, 25.
Lifting devices (*see also* Forfex *and* Great Wheels), 27, 28, 33, 51, 190, 207 f., 303 ff.

Manœuvring of centerings, 13, 34 f., 53 f., 163, 193, 195, 239.
  Of gantry falsework, 171 f.
Manuscript drawings, 7, 104, 200, 237, 280.
Medieval mortar, 216, 220, 226, 262 ff.
Metal, non-use of, in falsework, 132, 134–6, 155, 169, 229.
Models of buildings, xi, 5 f., 199, 302.

Organic design, 48, 71.

Passageways, 19–21, 203, 204, 205, 253.
Plastering of vault, 228.
Plowshare twist, 73, 88, 115.
Pointed arch, 78–80.
Pont du Gard construction, 9–13.
Putlogs and putlog holes, 17, 203, 248 ff.

Quadripartite vault, 75, 221.

Ramps, as ancient means of construction, 209 f.
Reconstruction and restoration, 198 f., 233 f.
Rib stems, 69 f., 216.
Ribs, importance of, 14, 87 ff., 222.
  Diagonal *v.* transverse, 88, 89, 95 f., 98.
  Broken in plan, 92 f., 135.
Roman barrel vault construction, 66, 215.
Roof structure, 26 ff., 192, 206, 227, 230, 274.

Salvageability of falsework, 121 f., 159, 165, 273.

Scaffolding, 13, 15 ff., 169 f., 202, 223, 228 f. 236, 271 ff., 281 ff.
  Flying scaffolding, 200, 202, 203.
  Rolling scaffolding, 34, 35, 211, 236.
Separator block or crown cradle, 145, 161 ff.
Sequence of erectional operations, 190–5, 225.
Sexpartite vault, 71 ff., 97, 217.
Shoring, 13, 23 ff., 128 f., 273.
Sills, position of, for centering frames, 127, 167 f., 188 f.
Slope of web courses above tas-de-charge, 73, 115, 225.
  Reverse slope, 224 f.
Stability of superstructure, 98, 126–9, 218 f., 227.
Stiffening action, of transverse ribs, 14, 96, 98, 216 f., 222.
Stiffening action, via doubling members, 130–2, 230.
Stilting, 73, 80, 88.
Stone-weighted rope device, 180 ff., 194.
Structural integration, preliminary, 25 ff.

Tas-de-charge, 75 f., 115, 136 f., 188, 211, 218.
Thin shells, 64–67, 83, 215.
Tie-beams, 26–28, 207, 225, 226, 277 f.
Tie-rods at springing of vault, 124 f., 128, 226, 227 f., 275 ff.
Timber framing, 201, 227, 229, 230, 231, 235.
Trammel device, 176, 183.
Truss, non-use of, 130 ff., 229 f.
  Hammerbeam, 229 f.

Vaulting conoid, fill in, 75, 83, 219.
Vault thicknesses, 220, 256 ff.
Vices (spiral stairs), 21 ff., 204 f.

Warping of vault surfaces, 73, 88, 89, 92, 99, 112, 115.
Weight of web masonry, 147, 222 f.
Working drawings, 234.

ZD system, 67, 216.

INDEX OF PLACES AND BUILDINGS

Abbeville, St-Vulfran, 78, 233, 236, 277.
Acy-en-Multien (Oise), 256.
Ahrweiler, St-Lawrence (Alsace), 181.
Aix-la-Chapelle, Minster, 38.
Alfriston, England (Sussex), 275.
Amiens, Notre-Dame (Cathedral), 77, 78, 82, 124 f., 169, 189, 203, 209, 219, 228, 277, 278.
Amiens, St-Jacques (modern), 228, 236.
Angers, St-Martin, 212, 250, 254 f., 299.
Antwerp Cathedral (Anvers), Belgium, 205.
Arundel, England (Sussex), 275.
Athens, Greece, Parthenon, 9.
Auxerre, St-Étienne (Cathedral), 205, 257.

Bacharach, Wernerkapelle (Alsace), 278.
Barcelona, Spain, 218.
Bassora, Turkey, 175.
Bayeux, Notre-Dame (Cathedral), 205.
Bayonne, Notre-Dame (Cathedral), 78.
Beauvais, St-Étienne, 205.
Beauvais, St-Pierre (Cathedral), 77, 124, 169, 203 f., 219, 227, 228, 249, 275.
Blois, St-Nicolas, 222.
Bohemia, 38.
Bordeaux, St-André (Cathedral), 78.
Boscherville, St-George, 21.
Bourges, St-Étienne (Cathedral), 77, 87, 169, 189, 205, 212, 222, 275.
Braîne, St-Yved, 205.
Bridges:
Baker River, Washington State, U.S.A., 207.
Blackfriars, London, England, 210.
Bulkley River, British Columbia, Canada, 231.
Burma Road, Southeast Asia, 231.
Esk Viaduct, Whitby, England, 201.
King River, Cumberlandshire, England, 269.
Lavaur (Tarn), 264.
Murg River, Black Forest Region, Germany, 201.
Neuilly, near Paris, 202.
Nogent-sur-Marne, 264.

Palmgraben, Austria, 210.
Plauen, Saxony, Germany, 264.
Pont du Gard, near Nîmes, 9 ff., 36, 37, 38, 53, 201.
Bruyères (Aisne), 257.
Burgundy, 20, 51.

Caen, St-Étienne (Abbaye aux Hommes), 21.
Caen, St-Trinité (Abbaye aux Dames), 258.
Cambrai, Notre-Dame, 205.
Cambridge, England, King's College Chapel, 204, 218 f., 219 f., 229, 248, 257, 287.
Canterbury Cathedral, England, 5, 204, 221, 276, 304.
Caudebec-en-Caux (Seine Inférieure), 257.
Chaalis, Abbey (Oise), 258.
Châlons-sur-Marne, Notre-Dame, 205.
Champagne, 20.
Chartres, Notre-Dame (Cathedral), 79, 80, 87, 169, 184, 202, 203, 209, 222, 226, 228, 239, 256, 258.
Chichester Cathedral, England, 220.
Clermont-Ferrand, Notre-Dame de Grâce (Cathedral), 234.
Clermont-Ferrand, Notre-Dame-du-Port, 21, 222.
Cléry, Notre-Dame, 205.
Clochan, Irish, 238.
Cluny, Abbey (Saône-et-Loire), 212, 257, 291.
Cologne, Germany, Carmelite Convent, 207.
Cologne, Germany, Cathedral, 205, 251.
Compiègne, St-Antoine, 78.
Conques, Abbey of St-Foy, 222.
Constantinople (Istanbul), Turkey, S. Sophia, 277.
Cormery, Abbey (Indre-et-Loire), 301.
Coucy, Château (Aisne), 19.
Coutances, Notre-Dame, 204.

Dieppe, St-Jacques, 78.
Dijon, Notre-Dame, 24, 205, 227.

INDEX OF PLACES AND BUILDINGS

Dol-de-Bretagne (Cathedral), 219.
Durham Cathedral, England, 222, 257, 275.

East Pakistani structures, 133.
Ely, England, Sextry Barn, 229.
Épine (L'), Notre-Dame, 205.
Erfurt Cathedral, Germany, 249.
Etain (Meuse), 278.
Étampes, Notre-Dame, 205.
Eu, St-Laurent, 78.
Évreux, Notre-Dame (Cathedral), 205.

Fountaine-Guérard, Abbey of Ste-Marie, 258.
Fountainejean, 258.

Gaillon (Eure), 256.
Gisors, St-Protais et St-Gervais, 258.
Glasgow Cathedral, Scotland, 198, 304.

Igloo, Eskimo, 176.
Île-de-France, 40, 83, 260.
Issoire, St-Paul, 21, 222.

Jersey, Island of, 209 f.
Jerusalem, Palestine, Dome of the Rock, 277.
Jumiège, Abbey (Seine-Inférieur), 21.

Laon, Notre-Dame (Cathedral), 7, 205, 226.
Lärbro, Gotland, 134 f., 147, 161, 299 f.
Lastingham, England (Yorkshire), 215.
Le Mans, St-Julien (Cathedral), 80, 169, 204, 205, 228.
Limoges, St-Étienne (Cathedral), 78, 234.
Lincoln Cathedral, England, 215, 235, 253.
Lisieux, St-Pierre (Cathedral), 205.
Liverpool Cathedral, England, 231, 234.
London, England, St. Paul's, 212.
Longpont, Abbey (Aisne), 217, 224, 227, 258.

Mantes, Notre-Dame, 202.
Mazan (Ardèche), 258.
Meaux, St-Étienne (Cathedral), 205.
Metz, St-Étienne (Cathedral), 205.
Milan Cathedral, Italy, 38.
Montefiascone, Italy, San Flaviano, 210.
Montier-en-Der (Haute-Marne), 21.
Mont-St-Michel, Abbey, 30, 208.
Mouliherne (Maine-et-Loire), 301.
Mycenae, Greece, Treasury of Atreus, 177.

Narbonne, St-Just (Cathedral), 77.
Nevers, St-Cyr (Cathedral), 205.
Nevers, St-Étienne, 21.
Noël-St-Martin (Oise), 257.
Northampton, England, All-Saints, 212.
Noyon, Notre-Dame (Cathedral), 205, 217, 218, 256, 258, 278.
Nuremburg, Germany, St. Sebald's, 249.

Ourscamp, Abbey (Oise), 217, 258.

Paris, Notre-Dame (Cathedral), 77, 120, 169, 184, 205, 207, 212, 228, 250, 256, 257, 258, 261, 288.
Paris, Sacré-Cœur, 251.
Paris, Ste-Chapelle, 77, 205, 209, 278.
Paris, St-Germer, 21.
Paris, St-Julien-le-Pauvre, 277.
Paris, St-Martin, 212.
Picardy, 83.
Poitiers, St-Hilaire-de-la-Celle, 301.
Poitiers, St-Pierre (Cathedral), 97.
Pontoise, St-Maclou (Seine-et-Oise), 205, 221 f.

Reims, Archiepiscopal Chapel, 259.
Reims, Notre-Dame (Cathedral), 6, 7, 26, 27, 29, 77, 123, 124, 125, 127, 139, 169, 205, 209, 217, 227, 228, 229, 234, 250, 256, 258.
Reims, St-Jacques, 259.
Reims, St-Remi, 21, 205, 216, 259.
Rodez, Notre-Dame (Cathedral), 205.
Romainmôtier, Switzerland, 213.
Rome, Italy, Pantheon, 64.
Rouen, Notre-Dame (Cathedral), 80, 169, 178 ff., 217, 236, 238, 246, 259, 273.
Rouen, St-Maclou, 5, 78, 205.
Rouen, St-Ouen, 205.
Rouen, St-Paul, 301.

St. Albans Abbey, England, 286.
St-Denis, Abbey (Seine), 5, 77, 205, 206, 227, 257, 260, 289 ff.
Saintes, St-Eutrope, 212.
St-Leu-d'Esserent, Priory, 224, 225, 234, 250.
St-Nicolas-du-Port (Meurthe-et-Moselle), 205.
St-Quentin (Aisne), 217, 239, 257, 258, 261, 277.
Salisbury Cathedral, England, 220, 225, 257, 275, 276, 277.
Salonika, Greece, S. Demetrius, 277.

Samarcande, Mosque of Gour-Emir, 38, 211.

Sannazzaro Sesia, Italy, 257.

Sassanian Palace drains, 177.

Segesta, Sicily, Greek Temple, 9.

Selby Abbey, Yorkshire, England, 286.

Selles-sur-Cher, Abbey (Loir-et-Cher), 222.

Senlis, Notre-Dame (Cathedral), 205.

Sens, St-Étienne (Cathedral), 205, 224.

Setti Bassi, Italy, 301.

Sisteron, old Cathedral (Basse-Alpes), 301.

Skirlaugh, Yorkshire, England, 275.

Soissons, St-Gervais et St-Protais (Cathedral), 77, 126, 205, 209, 222, 226, 228, 236, 256, 257, 258.

Soissons, St-Jean-de-Vignes, 226.

Soissons, St-Léger, 224.

Strasbourg Cathedral, Germany, 205.

Taverny (Seine-et-Oise), 277.

Tholi (Bee-Hive Tombs), Greece, 177.

Toul, St-Étienne (Cathedral), 205.

Toulouse, St-Étienne (Cathedral), 205.

Toulouse, St-Sernin, 21, 35.

Tournai Cathedral, Belgium, 205.

Tours, St-Gatien (Cathedral), 29, 205.

Tower of Babel, 7, 207, 223.

Triel (Seine-et-Oise), 226.

Troyes, Notre-Dame (Cathedral), 78, 205, 236.

Troyes, St-Urbain, 38, 205, 209.

Truli (Bee-Hive Houses), Southern Italy, 177.

Turin, Italy, Ste Teresa, 178.

Vézelay, Abbey of la Madelaine, 125, 224, 276, 280.

Vienna, Austria, 181, 183.

Vienne, St-Maurice (old Cathedral), 205.

Vincennes, Chapel of the Château, 205, 249.

Westminster Abbey, London, England, 207, 218, 220, 275 ff., 280 ff., 305.

Westminster Hall, London, 286, 302.

Westminster Palace, London, 286.

Westminster, St. Stephen's Chapel, 281, 283 ff., 286.

Winchester Cathedral, England, 234, 274, 275, 292.

Windsor, England, St. George's Chapel, 237.

York Cathedral, England, 206, 286.